RETHINKING THE NUCLEAR WEAPONS DILEMMA IN EUROPE

Also by P. Terrence Hopmann

CUMULATION IN INTERNATIONAL RELATIONS RESEARCH (*co-editor*)
UNITY AND DISINTEGRATION IN INTERNATIONAL ALLIANCES (*co-author*)

Also by Frank Barnaby

THE AUTOMATED BATTLEFIELD
*EMERGING TECHNOLOGIES AND MILITARY DOCTRINE (*co-editor*)
FUTURE WARFARE (*editor*)
MAN AND THE ATOM
NUCLEAR ENERGY

*Also published by Macmillan.

Rethinking the Nuclear Weapons Dilemma in Europe

Edited by
P. Terrence Hopmann
Professor of Political Science
Brown University
and
Frank Barnaby
formerly Director, Stockholm International Peace Research Institute

Foreword by Harlan Cleveland

St. Martin's Press New York

Scholarly & Reference Division,
St. Martin's Press, Inc., 175 Fifth Avenue, New York, NY 10010

First published in the United States of America in 1988

Printed in Hong Kong

ISBN 0-312-67804-5

Library of Congress Cataloging-in-Publication Data
Rethinking the nuclear weapons dilemma in Europe.
Bibliography: p.
Includes index.
1. Europe—Defenses. 2. Nuclear weapons—
Europe. I. Hopmann, P. Terrence. II. Barnaby, Frank.
UA646.R47 1988 355′.0217′094 87-12914
ISBN 0-312-67804-5

Contents

Notes on the Contributors

Frank Barnaby, who holds his Ph.D. in physics, is currently serving as Guest Professor of Peace Studies at the University of Amsterdam. He is the former Director of the Stockholm International Peace Research Institute (SIPRI), and in 1985 he held the Harold Stassen World Peace Chair at the University of Minnesota. His many books include *Arms Uncontrolled* (1975).

Lincoln P. Bloomfield is Professor of Political Science at the Massachusetts Institute of Technology. He has served in the US State Department and the National Security Council, and he was four times visiting professor in Geneva. He is author, among others, of *In Search of American Foreign Policy: The Humane Use of Power* (1974) and *The Foreign Policy Process: A Modern Primer* (1982).

Egbert Boeker is Professor of Theoretical Physics, Free University, Amsterdam. He is the co-author (with Frank Barnaby) of *Defence without Nuclear Weapons* (1982) and author of several papers concerned with non-provocative defence. He was Deputy Chairman of the Advisory Council on Peace and Security, providing advice on defence and security matters to Dutch Ministers of Defence and Foreign Affairs.

Hans Günter Brauch is Lecturer in International Relations in the Institute for Political Science at the University of Stuttgart, West Germany, where he has been informal director of the study Group on Peace Research and European Security Policy. He has published numerous books, including serving as co-editor with Duncan L. Clarke of *Decision-Making for Arms Limitation*, co-editor with Robert Kennedy of *Alternative Defense Postures in the European Theatre*, and editor of *Star Wars and European Defence* (Macmillan, 1987).

Dan Caldwell is currently Professor of Political Science at Pepperdine University, Malibu, California. He is author of *American–Soviet Relations: From 1947 to the Nixon–Kissinger Grand Design* and the editor of *Henry Kissinger: His Personality and Policies* and *Soviet International Behavior and US Policy Options*.

Harlan Cleveland is Dean of the Hubert H. Humphrey Institute of Public Affairs at the University of Minnesota. He has served as US Assistant Secretary of State and was US Ambassador to NATO from 1965 to 1969. His nine books include *NATO: The Transatlantic Bargain* (1970).

Jonathan Dean is currently Arms Control Advisor to the Union of Concerned Scientists. A career US Foreign Service Officer, he served with the US delegation to the negotiations on Mutual and Balanced Force Reductions in Vienna from their inception, including as Ambassador from 1977 through 1981. He is author of *Watershed in Europe: Dismantling the East-West Military Confrontation* (1987).

Jean F. Freymond is Director of the Centre for Applied Studies in International Negotiations in Geneva, Switzerland. He is a Consultant to, among others, some agencies of the United Nations. He is author of *Le Troisième Reich et la réorganisation économique de l'Europe, 1940–1942* (1974) and *Political Integration in the Commonwealth Caribbean, 1967–1974* (1980).

Mike Gapes is a Research Officer in the Policy Directorate of the British Labour Party and the Secretary of the Labour Party's Defence Committee. He is co-author of several books and pamphlets on defence, disarmament, and international issues.

John B. Harris is Assistant Professor of Political Science at Georgia State University in Atlanta, Georgia. He is co-editor of *Nuclear Weapons and the Threat of Nuclear War* (1986).

P. Terrence Hopmann is Professor of Political Science at Brown University, where he is also Director of the International Relations Program and Research Associate of the Center for Foreign Policy Development. He was co-editor of *International Studies Quarterly* (1980–5), and is co-author of *Unity and Disintegration in International Alliances* (1973).

Jan H. Kalicki is Executive Director of the Center for Foreign Policy Development and an Adjunct Professor of Political Science at Brown

University in Providence, Rhode Island. He previously served with the US State Department and the Arms Control and Disarmament Agency, and as chief foreign policy advisor to US Senator Edward Kennedy.

Edward A. Kolodziej, Research Professor of Political Science, is Director of the European Arms Control Project and former Director of the Program in Arms Control, Disarmament, and International Security at the University of Illinois. He has written extensively on international security issues, especially on US–European problems. His books include *Making and Marketing of Arms: The French Experience and Its Implications for the International System* (1987).

John Marshall Lee served for 42 years in the US Navy. After retiring with the rank of Vice Admiral, he has written and spoken widely on nuclear strategy and arms control throughout the United States and Europe.

Eckhard Lübkemeier is a researcher with the Study Group on Security and Disarmament Issues of the Friedrich-Ebert-Stiftung in Bonn, Federal Republic of Germany. He is the author of numerous studies on West German defence and arms control policy.

Dieter Mahncke serves on the staff of the President of the Federal Republic of Germany. He also is Professor at the College of Europe in Bruges, Belgium, concentrating on European security and arms control issues.

Hanspeter Neuhold is Professor at the Institute for International Law and Relations at the University of Vienna. He has served with the Austrian delegation to the UN General Assembly and follow-up meetings of the Conference on Security and Cooperation in Europe. He is co-editor of *The European Neutrals in International Affairs* (1984) and co-editor and co-author of the *Austrian Manual of International Law* (1983–86).

Earl C. Ravenal, a former official in the Office of the US Secretary of Defense, is currently Distinguished Research Professor of International Affairs at the Georgetown University School of Foreign Service and a Senior Fellow of the Cato Institute in Washington, D.C. He is the author of numerous books and articles, including *NATO: The Tides of Discontent* (1985).

Stanley R. Sloan is the specialist in US alliance relations for the US Congressional Research Service in Washington, D.C. He is author of *NATO's Future: Towards a New Transatlantic Bargain* (1985) and *East–West Relations in Europe* (Foreign Policy Association Headline Series 278).

Richard Smoke is Research Director of the Center for Foreign Policy Development at Brown University in Providence, Rhode Island, where he is also Professor of Political Science. His books include *War: Controlling Escalation* (1977) and *National Security and the Nuclear Dilemma* (1987).

David W. Tarr is Professor of Political Science at the University of Wisconsin–Madison. He is the author of numerous works on US national security policy. He is author of *American Strategy in the Nuclear Age* (Macmillan, 1966).

Gregory F. Treverton is Lecturer in Public Policy at the John F. Kennedy School of Government at Harvard University, where he is also Senior Research Associate in the Center for Science and International Affairs. He was formerly Director of Studies at the International Institute of Strategic Studies in London. His most recent book on European–American relations is *Making the Alliance Work* (Macmillan, 1985).

Peter Wallensteen is Dag Hammarskjöld Professor of Peace and Conflict Research at Uppsala University, where he received his Ph.D. in Political Science. Recent books which he has co-authored include *Global Militarization* (1985) and *Dilemmas of Economic Coercion* (1983).

Foreword

There is no more frozen relationship in world politics than the stand-off between the North Atlantic Treaty Organisation (NATO) and the Warsaw Pact of Eastern Europe. It is kept in the freezer by 50 000 nuclear weapons, controlled not by the Europeans but by the United States and the Soviet Union.

The political stability of East–West antagonism has been astonishingly durable for a generation past. But new developments in the late 1980s – changes in the cost-effectiveness of military defence, the growing military irrelevance of 'tactical' nuclear weapons, shifts in public opinion in those countries where public opinion counts, and the 'information revolution' that threatens central planning and control in the others – have sharpened the European nuclear dilemma. Just now the most practical thing to do about the North Atlantic Alliance is to *rethink* its purposes, its policies and its prospects.

With this task in mind the University of Minnesota's Hubert H. Humphrey Institute of Public Affairs invited Dr Frank Barnaby, the British scholar who had for a decade been director of the Stockholm International Peace Research Institute, to become in 1985 the first occupant of a new academic chair in the newly-created Harold E. Stassen Center for World Peace. The Center is named for the former Governor of Minnesota and presidential candidate who is today the only living American, and one of a very few people in the world, who signed the United Nations Charter at San Francisco in 1945).

We teamed our British visitor with political scientist P. Terrence Hopmann, then a professor at the University of Minnesota and also an active member of the Humphrey Institute faculty. While Frank Barnaby was with us in Minneapolis, the two of them organised in the Spring of 1985 a major transatlantic conference on 'The European Nuclear Dilemma', co-sponsored by The Johnson Foundation and held at its conference centre called Wingspread, a spectacular Frank Lloyd Wright house set in the rolling hills and green landscapes of Racine, Wisconsin.

An arms-control community of senior experts on both sides of the Atlantic Ocean has dominated the discussion of mutual deterrence and European security for some three decades. As a sometime member of that community, I think it fair to say that its preoccupation with numbers of weapons and its disinterest in public opinion made most of its assumptions and analyses about 'national security' only a degree or two less frozen than the object of its inquiry. So for this conference we decided to recruit mostly younger scholars, from Europe and North America, leavened with only half a dozen senior specialists.

Nor did we ask those who came to Wingspread to produce conventional research papers, addressed to their peers in the kind of language that produces favourable decisions about academic promotion and tenure but is otherwise opaque to the policy-making public and their puzzled political leaders. We asked them instead to write comparatively short 'policy papers', not just describing the European nuclear dilemma but *rethinking* it. After the conference, in lengthy consultation with the authors, the editors brought together in this volume the best of this rethinking, and added an original essay of their own.

It was my privilege to witness, for almost three days, the stimulating mixture of scholarship and passion that made the Wingspread conference something very special even for a jaded conference-goer.

The notes I made during the meeting (I may as well be candid about it) were mostly not of what other people said but of what occurred to me while they were talking. The editors have asked me to reproduce the 'generalist' comments I made at the final session, but time and the appalling syntax of a transcribed tape recording made that an assignment of dubious utility. What I will do is record, in summary form, the rethinking I was lured into doing as I listened to my junior colleagues rethink the received wisdom about the defence of Europe in the nuclear age. My comments happen to fall into 14 points, which would have pleased Woodrow Wilson.

1. NATO's main disease is the agony of success. It is true that the political lake above the military dam is frozen – on the surface. But it is not time to celebrate this frosty form of peace by taking away the dam. There will be turbulence in the future of the Alliance, but it should not be provided by the Allies' own dynamite.
2. It is useful to remind ourselves, once a month or so, that NATO and the Warsaw Pact are not there just to confront each other but also as an expression of the internal imperatives of both blocs. The

Warsaw Pact was and is important to the Soviet Union as justification for sitting on the heads of the East Europeans. NATO was and is important to all the Allies as a way to make resurgent West German strength respectable and safe.

3. The way conventional forces are deployed in support of NATO has everything to do with history and hardly anything to do with where you would want them if they had to be used for the military defence of Western Europe.

4. The 'theatre nuclear weapons' are certainly theatrical, but their numbers are out of all proportion to how they might be used. Just before taking on my assignment at NATO in 1965, I went over to the Pentagon and reviewed the literature on the basis of which President Eisenhower decided to plant the explosive equivalent of 7000 Hiroshimas in Europe, mostly in West Germany, as 'tactical' weapons. It was a remarkably thin literature. So far as I could then determine, no one tried to explain to the President, at least in writing, what kind of war this dimensional change in explosive power would make possible, even inevitable. The justification had mostly to do with numbers – this kind of howitzer usually needs so many rounds stashed nearby, thus now that we can make nuclear rounds we will obviously need a similar number of nuclear weapons for the dual-capable version of the same weapon. That sort of thing.

5. So they were deployed, and of course the USSR soon followed suit. But insight about the military meaning of theatre-based weapons was even scarcer in the upper reaches of Europe's governments than in the US government. In the mid-1960s, as an antidote to the widespread assumption among political leaders in Europe that tactical nuclears were just superconventional weapons whose use could be localised, we conducted in the NATO Nuclear Planning Group a series of war games. Any way you played the game, most of the people killed turned out to be in West Germany. The result of these war games, as their implications percolated to the political leadership, was a sudden reduction of public arm-waving by German and other politicians about the nuclear hell the Allies were now poised to break loose. For two decades since then, the stockpile of US nuclear weapons in Europe has resembled fish flopping on a dock: they are still alive, but somehow out of their element.

6. Yet there was still – not then or in the two decades since – no fundamental rethinking of the European nuclear dilemma. The declaratory policy of the North Atlantic alliance remains: that the allies (meaning the US) would strike first with nuclear weapons if that

seemed to be necessary to frustrate a conventional attack by the Warsaw Pact (meaning the Soviet Union). But would any US President really and truly use nuclear weapons first? The testimony of former advisers to presidents, including Robert McNamara and Henry Kissinger, dampens NATO's declaratory policy with a heavy blanket of fog. The military historians may record that that policy died in the 1960s, but wasn't buried until the 1980s.

7. It emerged quite clearly from our Wingspread discussions that 'no first use' cannot be a formulation of policy, it has to be a consequence of policy. What counts in world politics (and local politics too) is in the end not what you say but what you do. If our force structure, weapons deployment, military training, and rules of engagement are rethought, unravelled, and put back together again for a credible conventional defence of Western Europe, a NATO 'no first use' declaration would sound as if we meant it. Without the military rethinking, the political talk comes off not even as sounding brass, more like a tinkling cymbal.

8. When advancing technology enabled both sides, first the East and then the West, to deploy intermediate-range missiles, the line between 'tactical' and 'strategic' weapons became irretrievably blurred. Robert McNamara as Secretary of Defence was asked once in a meeting of the NATO Nuclear Planning Group what the difference was. A strategic weapon, he replied, is anything that can hit me. This is still the relevant insight: whatever weapons system you are negotiating about, it is going to look 'strategic' to some of the parties at interest.

9. It began to dawn on citizens and experts alike that by inventing the ultimate weapon modern man might have also invented the ultimately unusable weapon. In more than four decades now, no one has been able to think of a military occasion for which a nuclear explosion was the clearly appropriate technology – that is, where making a bang in the nuclear range would be better strategy and better politics than doing something less dramatic and destructive. For the first time in world history, man may have placed a limit on the scale of violence. In this situation, 'no first use' may not be a viable policy but it is a description of future behaviour with a high probability quotient.

10. If nuclear weapons are militarily dysfunctional yet deterrence of their use continues to be imperative, the deterrent is simply uncertainty – the inability of military advisers or political leaders to plan for the next war because there has never been anything like it. (The historic solution to this problem, which was always to plan for

the last war instead, is not advocated by even the least reflective strategic thinkers of our time.) The Soviets don't know what we would do if . . . because we aren't really sure ourselves. Our uncertainty at least is credible, and that's the deterrent – as long as our capabilities are clear (i.e., aren't secret from the other side).

11. Nuclear weapons are existential. Jean-Paul Sartre might not appreciate this use of his patented word, but it does seem clear that we are going to have to live with nuclear weapons – and with the widespread knowledge of how to make and deliver them. For serious leaders (a string of Soviet General Secretaries and US Presidents including the present incumbents) to say that nuclear weaponry can be totally eliminated is to mislead the policy-making publics in the democracies and the policy-making totalitarian bureaucracies too.

12. We talked a good deal, at Wingspread, about 'coupling'. (The younger members of the arms-control community seem to think that this is a sexual metaphor; they grew up after the age of railroads, and it is to the coupling of railway carriages that the metaphor traces its origin.) The consensus was clear enough: we need to decouple the defence of Europe from nuclear forces, while not decoupling Western Europe from the United States and Canada. But the need for rethinking will clearly be intensified by the next generation of nuclear weapons planned by the French, and by the continued insistence of the Americans (with some scientific and political dissent) that a defence against strategic weapons is possible if enough money and talent is thrown at the problem. A transatlantic dialogue in which French and British nuclear systems and the US Strategic Defence Initiative are defined out of the European dilemma is a dialogue of the deaf, a Mad Hatter's tea-party in Wonderland.

13. All this talk about how we rethink NATO postures and policies leads naturally to the question that kept cropping up at the Wingspread conference: How do we engage the Soviets? No matter how much sense we manage to make of our own strategy, how can we be sure the Soviets will do their rethinking too? My own conclusion, which I won't presume to attribute to the other participants, is deceptively simple: the most important single thing we can do to convince the Soviets to have a sensible and clearly defensive military posture is to have one ourselves. If we *really* don't think nuclear weapons are usable, and act like it; if we *really* mean whatever declaration we eventually make about 'no first use', and act like it; if we have *really* concluded that there is no sense in using nuclear weapons in a localised European war (because it can't be localised),

and therefore get them out of there – then there is a pretty good chance the Soviets will catch on. For four decades they have mirrored, within a few years, most of the twists and turns of US military technology and doctrine (the H-bomb, submarine-borne ballistic missiles, multiple independently targetable re-entry vehicles, cruise missiles, etc.). If we manage to make sense of the European nuclear dilemma, they might bite on that too.

14. In very recent years, in the United States and in Europe as well, a new actor has elbowed his and her way to the table around which the arms control experts have been exchanging their elegant expertise. The new actor is the general public. I don't mean the 'peace movement', though it has played an influential if not dispositive role on some issues for limited periods of time. I mean the policy-making general public, which (in democratic societies) generally perceives before the 'leaders' and their expert advisers do that old policies have died but haven't gone away. (The US Government was the last to learn that the Vietnam war was over.) I think that the general public is gradually becoming convinced – not by expert testimony but (in Daniel Yankelovich's phrase) by 'working through' the problem themselves with plenty, indeed an overload, of information – that (a) nuclear weapons are militarily unusable yet (b) deterrence through uncertainty continues to be imperative, that (c) a conventional Western defence must be possible given the comparative resource bases of West and East, and that (d) detente is desirable but it doesn't have much to do with mutual trust.

I suggested long ago that in Alliance politics 'detente' doesn't translate from the French as 'relaxation', but means something more like 'the continuation of tension by other means'. In what the late Averell Harriman used to call 'competitive coexistence', especially in a world where information is the dominant resource, the West is well placed to make peace. But that requires rethinking some obsolescent but comfortably familiar assumptions. This book is intended as a contribution to that most difficult of human pursuits: rethinking.

HARLAN CLEVELAND

Dean
Hubert H. Humphrey Institute of Public Affairs
University of Minnesota
US Ambassador to NATO, 1965–9

Introduction: Rethinking the Nuclear Weapons Dilemma in Europe

P. Terrence Hopmann and Frank Barnaby

The recent deployment of 572 new US nuclear missiles in Western Europe reawakened a debate about the role for nuclear weapons in the defence of the NATO alliance. Although the missile deployment was intended to reassure America's allies of US commitments to their defence, it has paradoxically often produced the opposite effect: namely a reawakening of a very fundamental debate on both sides of the Atlantic about the dilemma posed by nuclear weapons for the defence of Europe.

The nuclear weapons dilemma in Europe can be simply summarised as follows: The purpose of nuclear weapons in Western Europe is to deter aggression by the Soviet Union and its Warsaw Pact allies against Western Europe. Yet if these weapons are to be used defensively by NATO after an attack has taken place, they almost assuredly will be used on Western European territory, or will lead to Soviet retaliation in Western Europe and perhaps against North America. The terrifying consequences of such usage are so grave that doubts have continued to mount about whether the Europeans would ever want to use these weapons for their own defence, no matter how grave the threat. Similarly fear of retaliation may make the United States reluctant to risk its own territory in defence of its allies. The effect of this dilemma is that the NATO deterrent may no longer be credible since NATO would be 'self-deterred' from using these weapons.

This dependence on a dubious deterrent has also placed tremendous strains on transatlantic relations. Not only do many Europeans fear that the US might not risk nuclear suicide to defend them, but they also fear that American nuclear weapons stationed on their territory might drag them into a nuclear war when their vital interests were not at stake. This paradox of US–West European relations is unavoidable as long as US nuclear weapons remain the cornerstone of NATO's defence policy.

These dilemmas have forced many in Western Europe and the United States to rethink the fundamental role of nuclear weapons in Western defence. To address these dilemmas, the Harold Stassen Project for World Peace in the Hubert H. Humphrey Institute of Public Affairs at the University of Minnesota sponsored a conference at the Wingspread Conference Center in Racine, Wisconsin, in May 1985. This volume contains revised and updated versions of papers originally presented at that conference.

No attempt was made to impose on the authors an artificial consensus. None the less, there is a notable shift in the centre of gravity of thinking about the issues of European security reflected in this book, which differs in some important ways from the main policy emphases currently emanating from Washington and Brussels. There is a widespread feeling that present NATO policy faces some very fundamental problems that cannot be solved by either 'muddling through' or doing more of the same. While there are some differences of emphasis about what should be done to reduce or resolve this fundamental dilemma, there is substantial agreement that some significant changes in direction need to take place soon. Although not all authors represented in these pages would agree with the following observations, there are some important common emphases among a substantial number of the contributions.

First, there is a growing feeling that the only appropriate role of nuclear weapons within NATO is to deter the use of nuclear weapons by others against the alliance. The destructive consequences of the use of nuclear weapons to achieve political or military objectives are far likely to outweigh any benefits that might be achieved. As Vice Admiral John Marshall Lee (US Navy, ret.) observes: 'Nuclear weapons actually fired, are of no military use.' Thus the threat of using these weapons for purposes other than to deter their use by others is not likely to be credible to potential enemies or politically tolerable in any Western society.

This point raises some very serious questions about the current NATO policy of the 'flexible response'. This policy assumes that the Atlantic alliance may be the first to use nuclear weapons in the event that Western Europe is being successfully invaded by a conventional, non-nuclear attack from the East. There is a growing feeling that this strategy is not likely to deter, and that it creates great anxiety for Europeans in that it increases the likelihood that their societies might be destroyed in their own defence, an obvious absurdity. Indeed, the present deployment of battlefield nuclear weapons near the inter-German border might cause any conflict that broke out in Central Europe to escalate rapidly to the nuclear level. According to many European contributors, this creates widespread concern throughout Western Europe, going well beyond activists in the peace movement, about the risks for their survival inherent in current alliance strategy.

Second, there is also a great deal of concern evidenced over the ability to control or limit a nuclear exchange once these weapons were introduced into battle. Many proponents of the flexible response strategy in Europe have also argued for 'escalation dominance', that is a capability to threaten the potential enemy with superior force at the next rung up the ladder of escalation, in order to deter. Yet such a strategy depends fundamentally upon the ability of political leaders to exercise control over the escalation spiral once nuclear weapons have been fired. There are grave doubts expressed by numerous contributors about both the physical and human capabilities to maintain control in an environment of escalating nuclear conflict. To presume in advance that such control is possible, that decision makers will survive and remain calm and rational, that command, communications, and control will survive and will work, and that alliance cohesion will be preserved, is to make some very tenuous assumptions. For this reason, there are serious reservations expressed about controlled escalation of a nuclear war in Europe, and a frequent assertion that, if nuclear weapons ever were used, all effort should be directed at de-escalation and war termination rather than at controlled escalation.

This point is summarised by Lincoln Bloomfield, an MIT political scientist and veteran of the US National Security Council staff: 'Moving toward a nuclear showdown is like falling off a cliff. If you are clinging to a root partway down you do not need lots of options for resuming your fall, or for pulling everyone else over the edge. You need one thing only – a rope to pull you back up. Everything is possible if you get back up. Nothing is possible if you keep falling.'

Third, all of the considerations just outlined led many contributors to this volume to embrace in varying degrees either a policy of 'no first use' of nuclear weapons or in some cases a variant, namely 'no early first use'. There has been a great deal of opposition in official circles in both Europe and the United States to the proposal advanced in *Foreign Affairs* in Spring 1982 by the American 'gang of four' of McGeorge Bundy, George F. Kennan, Robert McNamara, and Gerard Smith supporting serious consideration of moving NATO towards a declared policy opposing the first use of nuclear weapons in a conventional conflict. Yet the authors represented here generally seem to reflect growing support, not only for an eventual NATO declaration of 'no first use', but also for the redeployment of nuclear warheads and the modification of alliance doctrine in order to move towards an effective implementation of such a posture. This point is stressed by Mike Gapes of the Research Staff of the British Labour Party: 'The most important and necessary reform of all must be the removal of nuclear weapons from NATO's forces on the Central front . . . It is a precondition for moving towards an effective, nonsuicidal defence for NATO.' On the other hand, there is little support for totally giving up nuclear deterrence as a response for a nuclear attack on the United States or its Western European allies. Such deterrent forces, however, do not necessarily need to be based in Central Europe, and might most effectively be deployed at sea.

The views expressed herein reveal that there continues to be a great deal of debate about no first use among West Europeans. There are those who argue, like Dieter Mahncke of the President's office in the Federal Republic of Germany, that 'deterrence is more effective a) if damage is threatened also against the home territory of the aggressor rather than against his attacking forces . . . , and b) if an attack implicates the risk of nuclear war'. On the other hand, there is also strong support among European analysts represented here for the 'no-first-use' concept. Eckhard Lübkemeier, an analyst with the Friedrich-Ebert-Stiftung in Bonn, argues that a no-first-use policy would enhance public acceptance of NATO defence policy in Western Europe; that it would enhance crisis stability; that it should improve deterrence, especially against escalation if war did break out; that it would enhance alliance cohesion by reducing dependence on American nuclear forces; and it would improve the prospects for arms control agreements and the reinvigoration of detente, which is of paramount importance to most Germans. Lübkemeier responds to those who argue that a 'no-first-use' policy would remove all dangers for the Soviets of a nuclear conflict, thereby eroding deterrence, by arguing that 'the USSR would be unlikely to rely without any reservations on a no-first use declaration of NATO'. The continued presence of nuclear weapons in the world would always make their introduction into any conflict a real possibility, in spite of pledges to the contrary, and the Soviets could not discount this possibility altogether if they were contemplating military action against the

West. Thus Lübkemeier contends that a 'no-first use policy by the West would in this case not entail a degradation of its deterrence capability'.

Fourth, there is also a general agreement that a move towards lesser reliance on nuclear weapons in NATO's posture would be facilitated by an improvement and stabilisation of the conventional balance of forces in Central Europe. If the nuclear element is to be removed from deterrence of a conventional attack in Europe, then deterrence must be achieved through conventional forces alone. This is essential because there is a widespread consensus among Europeans that a reduction in the likelihood of nuclear war would be of little value if it significantly enhanced the probability of a conventional war. The memories of the Second World War are still very vivid in the public mind, and the knowledge of possible destructiveness of modern conventional weapons has also created an even greater necessity for the prevention of the outbreak of any war in Europe. If war does break out in Europe, of course, most would prefer that it be confined to the conventional realm rather than escalating automatically to the nuclear level. On the other hand, even such a prospect creates such grave concern throughout Europe that deterrence of all war, both conventional and nuclear, remains the paramount objective.

Yet this requirement for stabilising conventional deterrence was accompanied by concern about setting off a conventional arms race in Europe, which might upset any equilibrium that could be achieved. Many contributors feel that the deployment of conventional forces or the adoption of NATO strategic doctrines that might be perceived by the Warsaw Pact as provocative would be most likely to stimulate such an arms race. Thus deployments of weapons to achieve a 'deep strike' capability with precision-guided, medium-range missiles carrying conventional warheads or doctrines such as General Rogers' proposal for a 'Air-Land Battle' concept based on counter-offensive operations against the Warsaw Pact, might all stimulate a conventional arms race. An alternative is summarised by Richard Smoke of Brown University's Center for Foreign Policy Development, who argues that 'the wise course is for NATO to develop a new posture of conventional defence against conventional attack, including secure second-strike nuclear forces, and deliberately excluding any non-nuclear offensive capability that could threaten Soviet security'.

The problem of how to achieve such a credible conventional defensive posture is central. For example, Frank Barnaby and Egbert

Boeker propose the adoption of a non-provocative, non-nuclear defence scheme based on a 50-kilometre deep defensive zone equipped with modern sensors and new, high technology anti-tank, anti-aircraft, and anti-ship missiles with relatively short ranges, and highly mobile forces equipped with the most modern defensive weapons. Hans Günter Brauch of Stuttgart University's Institute for Political Science, argues for a pragmatic or reformist approach that 'calls for a realistic defense posture that takes into account the need to reduce the manpower of the Bundeswehr due to demographic reasons, to reduce the reliance on tactical and theatre nuclear land-based forces and to move gradually to a policy of no-first use in order to regain public support for the future defense posture.' This approach also opposes 'the American plans for deep strike and calls instead for a restructuring of the conventional defense posture'.

Still another approach is suggested by Jonathan Dean, arms control adviser to the Union of Concerned Scientists and the former US Ambassador to the negotiations on Mutual and Balanced Force Reductions (MBFR) in Europe. He proposes a negotiated arrangement for a defensive zone of 50 to 100 kilometres on both sides of the border between West Germany and East Germany/Czechoslovakia. Heavy mobile equipment such as tanks, helicopters, bridging equipment, and all nuclear weapons would be prohibited in this zone. On the other hand, short-range missiles and physical obstacles would be permitted. Indeed, if West German political opposition could be overcome by the multilateral nature of such an agreement, then perhaps a system of defensive barriers might be constructed within this zone on the Western side. He concludes that 'this approach could not have a decisive effect in making conflict in Europe impossible, but it would make it less likely. It would be especially useful in lowering the risk of war through crisis escalation, and it would improve NATO's capability of dealing with conventional Warsaw Pact attack by conventional means'.

Fifth, this volume considers a wide range of arms control measures that also might enhance security and reduce the nuclear weapons dilemma in Europe. There is widespread support for continued efforts to obtain an agreement in Geneva limiting or reducing the deployment of Intermediate-range Nuclear Forces (INF) in Europe. The continued deployment of Soviet SS-20 missiles and US Pershing II and Ground-Launched Cruise Missiles is widely thought to be a step in the wrong direction. While the implementation of the NATO decision to deploy its INF's is generally regarded as a sign of NATO cohesion, there are also reasons to be concerned that, below the surface, it just reinforces Western European dependence upon American nuclear weapons as the cornerstone of NATO strategy, which in the long run is likely to undermine rather than strengthen alliance cohesion. Furthermore, several contributors want to broaden the scope of the negotiations in Europe beyond the issues that have recently been discussed in Geneva, perhaps including serious discussion of a nuclear-free zone in Central Europe along the lines proposed by the Palme Commission or perhaps including the removal of all land-based nuclear weapons from the continent.

But it is also evident that arms control in Europe involves far more than nuclear weapons. Indeed, if dependence on nuclear weapons as a central element of European security is to be reduced, and if budgetary and demographic constraints limit the augmentation of conventional forces, then stability must be achieved at the conventional level at least in part through arms control. Thus conventional arms control can not only stabilise deterrence at the conventional level, it can also reduce the likelihood that conventional wars will lead to escalation to the nuclear level. Escalation to nuclear war is most likely to occur if, early in a conventional struggle, one side seems to be obtaining a decisive advantage, prompting the losing side to resort to nuclear weapons before the tide of battle turns too far against them. Thus the prevention of a surprise attack that might achieve such rapid success is an essential objective not only of defence policy, but also of arms control.

One such measure would be an agreement in the MBFR negotiations in Vienna (or in an enlarged successor forum), that would establish parity of ground and air manpower in a Central European zone. The Vienna negotiations have been largely stalemated since the late 1970s although agreement in principle was reached on manpower parity at 900 000 men on each side, of which no more than 700 000 could be 'ground forces'. A successful agreement could reduce the manpower asymmetry widely perceived as favouring the Warsaw Pact in the Central European area, removing one element that pressures NATO to rely so heavily on nuclear weapons to deter a conventional attack from the East. Yet, as Professor Hanspeter Neuhold of the Institute of International Law and International Relations at the University of Vienna observes, 'the stalemate is not likely to be overcome by more "sophisticated" proposals along the lines on which the two sides have dug in their heels. A breakthrough seems to require an effort at a higher, probably the highest political level.'

In addition, confidence-building measures are presented as an additional set of arms control possibilities for reducing the likelihood of war in Europe. A primary objective of confidence-building measures is for each side to provide assurances that they are not preparing to launch a surprise attack upon the other. One such measure, a voluntary agreement to announce large-scale military manoeuvres and to invite outside observers, was adopted at the Helsinki Conference on Security and Co-operation in Europe in 1975. Measures to broaden and to make these provisions compulsory were adopted by the Conference on Disarmament in Europe in 1986. These include advance notification of all large-scale military movements within a large zone extending from the Atlantic to the Urals, as well as on-site inspection by observation teams from throughout Europe. Such provisions make it difficult to reinforce units now stationed in Europe, either from the US or the USSR, without being observed. An unannounced reinforcement would be likely to communicate hostile intent, and thus provide the justification for a counter mobilisation.

If these CBMs could be combined with other measures such as manpower parity and the establishment of defensive zones in Central Europe, they could reinforce one another to reduce tensions and instabilities. Approximate force parity through a force reduction agreement would make aggression using existing forces extremely unlikely, since neither side would possess sufficient numerical superiority to launch a successful attack against the other without major prior reinforcements. The confidence-building measures could then assure each side that no such reinforcements were being made. This should substantially enhance conventional force stability in Europe. But if a conflict did break out, especially through an incident that got out of control, the more equal balance of existing forces would make a decisive victory by either side quite unlikely. This in turn should reduce the chances that a potential loser in a conventional war might decide to escalate to the nuclear level. It should also enhance the possibility for the diplomatic negotiation process to be engaged before the conventional war had flamed completely out of control or before the forbidding nuclear threshold had been crossed.

A further feature of negotiations like those in the Conference on Disarmament in Europe is that they include not only the two military blocs, but also the European neutral and non-aligned states. Several authors stress that these states have played important roles in promoting agreements between the two blocs, including both initiating their own proposals for improving confidence and serving as mediators between East and West in these negotiations. As Jean Freymond of the Centre for Applied Studies in International Negotiations in Geneva, Switzerland, concludes, 'neutral countries cannot contribute to solving the nuclear dilemma as such. They may, however, help build up confidence and security, so that neither side is tempted to cross the nuclear threshold, and so that, in the final analysis, at no stage does the nuclear option become irresistible.'

One final point, about which the European contributors continually remind their American counterparts, is the significance of a reinvigoration of the process of detente. To Europeans, detente was not just a temporary policy, but rather a fundamental effort to move towards the eventual elimination of conflict and division through the centre of Europe. There is a great deal of concern on the European side of the Atlantic that this objective is of no great significance to their American allies, and that recent US hostility towards the Soviet Union puts that objective very much at risk. Therefore, many Europeans stress the significance of harmonising the objectives of deterrence and defence with those of disarmament and detente, as adopted by NATO in the Harmel report of 1969. Clearly the continued failure of the United States to link these objectives, and indeed to insist that there are some fundamental contradictions among them, will greatly endanger the long-term cohesion of the North Atlantic alliance.

This book does not propose many radical new measures for eliminating those tensions surrounding the role of nuclear weapons in European security and in US–West European relations. Divergent views expressed in the following pages suggest that many obstacles still exist to the attainment of a new consensus about security in Europe. Yet, on balance, most of the chapters in this book point towards a significant change in emphasis which, if reflected in a similar shift among other experts in this field, could lead to a substantial change in direction. That change signals a reduced reliance on nuclear weapons, especially their first use, in NATO strategy. It points towards a new emphasis on a stable conventional defence, which is non-provocative and thus does not stimulate a conventional arms race. Finally, it emphasises a renewed focus on arms control and detente in Europe, especially in the effort to negotiate a linked set of agreements to achieve greater force parity, greater disengagement along the lines of confrontation, and greater confidence and reduced fear of surprise attack.

Whether this shift in emphasis will eventually be reflected significantly in alliance policy is yet to be seen. Several authors note significant signs of discontent in the public in many countries with the status quo, which may have some impact on the willingness of political leaders to undertake significant policy change. Harlan Cleveland, Dean of the Humphrey Institute, and former US Ambassador to NATO, stressed this point in his concluding statement at the Wingspread Conference:

> I believe that the public is gradually becoming convinced, in that messy, inchoate way in which it seems to operate, that nuclear weapons are unusable, that deterrence continues to be imperative, that a conventional defense of Europe must be possible if the experts would just think harder about it, and that detente is desirable . . . So the problem for the leaders is to catch up, because the declaratory NATO strategy with which we have all been living for two decades or more – a strategy that assumes a nuclear riposte to a conventional failure in Europe – is dead.

Hopefully this book may stimulate the process of developing new ideas that leaders can adopt in the years ahead to begin to close the gap between themselves and the mounting concerns so widely evident throughout the general public in all countries of the West.

Editor's Note: The chapters of this book were all completed prior to the signing by President Reagan and General Secretary Gorbachev of a Treaty eliminating all Intermediate-Range and Short-Range Nuclear Forces of the two superpowers at the Washington Summit meeting in December 1987. Obviously this agreement has great significance for the topic treated in this book. Rather than changing any conclusions presented in this book, however, this historic event would seem to reinforce the major trends identified by most of the authors in this collection. Thus, while several specific observations may have been overtaken by these events, in the main the conclusions and recommendations presented in this book would appear to be even more relevant and important after the signing of an INF Treaty than when they were originally written.

Part I

Nuclear Weapons in Europe: Tactical and Intermediate-range Weapons

1 Managing NATO's Nuclear Business: The Lessons of INF

Gregory F. Treverton

This chapter rests on three premises that are sharply different from the assumptions that underlie most of the other chapters in this book. The first is that dramatic resolutions of the nuclear dilemma in Europe will not happen. Those resolutions are, for the foreseeable future, either unwise or impossible, or both. The solutions would be worse than the problem. It is not a case of 'NATO ain't broke, so why fix it?' Rather, the questions are 'how broke?' and 'how fixable?' if fixable means susceptible to bold departures that would resolve the dilemma. My answer to both those questions is 'not very'. My second premise, then, is that the dilemma can only be managed, for better or worse. And the third is that if the dilemma can only be managed, it *can* be managed.

In that spirit, it is worth drawing lessons, even at this range, from the NATO deployments of cruise and Pershing missiles – the Euromissile affair, which, after all, is not yet over. I ask what Washington *presumed* at the time the December 1979 decision was taken, which of those presumptions turned out to be right and which wrong, and why, and what lessons for handling the nuclear dilemma the episode may suggest.

For one thing is certain. NATO will again face a critical nuclear decision. It will probably do so sooner rather than later. The decision may be one about modernising NATO's remaining short-range nuclear systems in Europe; or about deploying new 'mid-range' systems shorter in range than the cruises but longer than battlefield systems; or about a major departure in nuclear arms control policy, perhaps growing out of the Geneva negotiations and the intersection of intermediate nuclear forces (INF) with strategic and defensive systems.

DEBATING THE PREMISES

This is no place for detailed argument about my premises.[1] Yet it is worth spelling them out because they do differ from the assumptions, sometimes implicit, that run through other chapters in this book.

It is useful to trace NATO's nuclear dilemma back to basics. It is rooted in geography: America and its missiles that are the ultimate deterrent are here, while the likely point of Soviet attack or pressure, Europe, is there. Now, and for more than two decades before, there have been essentially four alternatives to something like current NATO arrangements, resting on American nuclear protection 'extended' to Europe: 1. deciding that the weight of Soviet military power adjacent to Europe matters much less than has been commonly held for nearly four decades; 2. moving to some more independent European arrangements, with nuclear weapons to match; 3. adopting 'nuclear' defences that would depend on the threat to use low-yield nuclear weapons immediately in the event of a Warsaw Pact attack; and 4. relying much more on conventional defence in order to rely much less on nuclear weapons.

The third possibility can be quickly dismissed. There is no stomach for defences based on the early use of nuclear weapons on West European soil. European and Alliance politics are strained enough by current nuclear strategies that gave even more pride of place to nuclear weapons.

The second possibility, greater European co-operation, quickly would run into two formidable obstacles. If, in current circumstances, Western Europe finds it hard to come up with the military wherewithal to defend itself *with* the United States, how could it do so *without* America. The second obstacle is the nuclear role of Germany. A European force would hardly be credible without a German finger on the button, but will continue to be politically impossible with it. Half-way measures such as existing NATO 'dual-key' arrangements – Europeans controlling the launchers and Americans the weapons, thus insuring both must agree in order to fire – will not suffice. If Germans doubt the willingness of the United States to use its force in their defence, even with dual keys, they could hardly believe that Britain or France would commit their much smaller forces. Since France, in particular, is on the continent, not an ocean away, its commitment would, other things equal, be more credible than that of the United States. But other things are not equal. Not only is France's nuclear force small by comparison to

America's, it is still – despite some evolution in doctrine discussed elsewhere in this book – pre-eminently a force for last-ditch retaliation, not use earlier in a war.

The first and fourth possibilities merit more consideration. Americans and Europeans, to use crude shorthand, do disagree about the Soviet threat; some of the former fear the latter already have defined away the Soviet threat. That said, however, save for some groups at the fringes of European politics, there is no visible support in Europe for redefining the Soviet menace into insignificance. If the broad mass of Europeans did come to take that view, then NATO's nuclear dilemma would disappear (and so might NATO). The United States would withdraw its ground forces and, no doubt, all but the scantest rhetoric of nuclear 'umbrella', from Europe. Soviet responses and politics among the Western European nations would be left to take their own course.

More likely, though, the future will look a lot like the past. The need to buy some military insurance against Soviet military power in Europe will command broad support on both sides of the Atlantic. Americans and Europeans will disagree over how much insurance and in what form and provided in what measure by whom. Yet they will agree on the need for some insurance and on NATO in something like its current form. When asked a general question like 'do you support NATO?' in poll after poll about three-quarters of Europeans respond affirmatively.[2] NATO-as-insurance seems reasonable. When, however, they are asked to contemplate unpleasant scenarios they had not thought much about – would they like nuclear weapons stationed in their backyard or used on their territory, for example – they react, hardly surprisingly, negatively.

That leaves the fourth possibility, greater reliance on conventional weaponry. The logic is compelling: if deterrence through the threatened resort to nuclear weapons is less and less credible, then raising the nuclear threshold through better conventional defence is preferable.

Unhappily, however, conventional defence will not be a way out of the nuclear dilemma, though NATO can and should try to do better. Part of the reason is that NATO has preached its inferiority in conventional forces for so long it has come to believe it, hence confidence, especially among defence analysts and attentive publics, that NATO can rely less on nuclear weapons will be slow in coming. Moreover, given the uncertainties that surround any reckoning of the balance in central Europe, prudent military planners can hardly avoid making worst-case estimates, and those will never be comforting. Improvements in conventional defence are not only costly, but they also run up against the shortage of personnel which most Western armed forces will experience in the latter part of the 1980s, especially as commitments beyond Europe expand to make more demands on fewer men of age for military service.

Nor will new technologies – like precision-guided weapons for deep interdiction strikes behind the front lines – or new tactics – such as recent enthusiasm for manoeuvre defences – sever the dilemma. They will turn out either not to be cheaper than existing arrangements or to imply changes, such as a NATO posture with more 'offensive' capabilities for counter-attack, that are politically unacceptable. Even if NATO could markedly improve its conventional forces and convince its publics that it had, it would still confront the abiding European horror of a conventional war in Europe: in European eyes, if better conventional defences make a resort to nuclear weapons less likely, the Soviets may in a crisis be *more* tempted to risk such conventional war.

Part of the reason for my last premise – that the dilemma can be managed – is that the dramatic alternatives, including those outlined in this book, will be seen by most Europeans as unappealing. Thus, anti-nuclear protest will wax and wane, and the average heat of the nuclear issue will be higher than it was in the decade before 1977, but the protest will fail for want of something better with which to supplant the status quo.

The nuclear issue can also be managed for reasons that derive from the politics, domestic and alliance, surrounding it, reasons that are paradoxical from the perspective of anti-nuclear protest of the 1980s. Governments will retain control over the nuclear agenda and its connections in domestic politics to a degree they will not for other issues in the Alliance. Even at the peak of nuclear concern in the early 1980s in Europe, the nuclear issue still was not all that salient to the broad mass of citizens. When Germans, for example, were asked what problem was most important to them, they cited economic or domestic issues four-fifths of the time. In these circumstances, NATO government will have considerable room to shape the nuclear issue and to pre-empt opposition. President Reagan did the latter in the INF episode with the 'zero option'; whatever its merits as a serious arms control proposal, it outdid the peace movement. By the same token, what emerged from the American Congress in 1983 were nuclear freeze resolutions that exhorted the President to negotiate bilateral, verifiable freezes with the Soviet Union. With fewer loose words in public about nuclear weapons and with a little more progress in arms control, the Reagan Administration could have pre-empted even those mild freeze resolutions.

To say, however, that the nuclear issue *can* be managed is not to guarantee that it *will* be managed. On that score there is plenty of evidence. So I turn to the Euromissile story. That story has been told often, and well, elsewhere.[3] I need only draw out crucial particulars for the purpose of suggesting lessons about how the Alliance manages its nuclear business.

THE PRESUMPTIONS OF DECEMBER 1979

On Washington's part, the December decision reflected a number of *presumptions* about both the Soviet Union and the allies. I underscore seven, three each about deployments and arms control, and one, critical, about the politics overarching both deployments and arms control:

1. New nuclear missiles, *deployed on land*, were necessary to deal with the concerns of Europeans as expressed by West German Chancellor Helmut Schmidt in his London speech of October 1977 and as echoed by European officials in NATO during two years of INF deliberations. In particular, nuclear systems based at sea would not be visible enough to be reassuring, hence would not do.

2. It would be easier to deploy the Pershing II missiles in the Federal Republic than cruise missiles because a missile called 'Pershing' already was deployed there. This presumption, apparently minor, cast a long shadow over subsequent debates.

3. The question of who owned the new missiles was a technical matter. This detail also seemed minor at the time, but also had a long political tail. All the allies slated to take the new missiles decided not to take them under NATO's so-called 'dual-key' arrangement – the host country owning the launchers and the US controlling the warheads. All, save the Federal Republic, took that decision for reasons of money. But it meant that the new missiles would be paid for and owned by the United States.

4. The Soviet Union would only negotiate seriously over INF if NATO began to deploy new systems of its own, or at least was visibly

prepared to do so. The prospects for INF arms control were not, on their face, promising. Most obviously, Soviet INF missiles, the SS-20s, were numerous and increasing rapidly, while NATO was still years away from its first deployments. NATO was thus in the position of bargaining intentions against missiles in place.

5. SALT II would be ratified, and thus the prospects for INF negotiations would not be entirely bleak. INF negotiations looked most unpromising if pursued *on their own*. If, by contrast, they took place in close relation to the strategic talks, they might be somewhat more tractable.

6. Still, *some* Pershings and cruise missiles would have to be deployed. No negotiation was likely to be so successful as to eliminate the need for new NATO systems. On that score, officials in Washington had no doubts. If European NATO leaders sometimes spoke, hopefully, of negotiations reducing the need for new missiles to zero, Washington assumed that was rhetoric designed for internal political consumption in Europe.

7. Perhaps most critically, European nations would want the new missiles if and when the time came to deploy them. Put differently, European politics would look much the same in 1983 as they did in 1979. This presumption, closely tied to the previous, mostly was implicit. But it was a central element of a larger presumption: that the prospect of deploying new nuclear missiles in Europe, which looked like a plus to NATO's strategy and cohesion, would still seem so four years hence, even if – as Washington assumed – those deployments actually had to take place.

WHAT WENT WRONG?

It seems to me that Washington's presumptions as I have listed them went wrong in five respects:

1. The Soviet Union invaded Afghanistan. Less than a month after NATO took its historic decision on 12 December 1979, Soviet troops began pouring into Afghanistan; by early January they numbered more than 100 000.

2. SALT II was not ratified – one immediate result of the Soviet invasion of Afghanistan. President Carter withdrew the treaty from Senate consideration. Whether SALT II would have been ratified

had the invasion not taken place is one of history's unknowables. With the invasion it was dead. And the basis for INF arms control also was gone, leaving the Alliance with an unpleasant choice: either defer INF negotiations until some strategic talks resumed, or promote INF talks on their own, the latter a dubious proposition.

3. American politics changed. Ronald Reagan was elected President. His major foreign policy commitment was a massive military build-up with a distinctly nuclear emphasis. He pledged himself to try to rid the world of nuclear weapons, but his Administration seemed to many on both sides of the Atlantic to be little interested in arms control.

4. European politics also changed. the British Labour party lost power in 1979, and the German SPD followed it into opposition in 1982. Those changes brought staunch supporters of the INF deployments to power, but they also polarised the European politics of INF. Once freed from the burden of governing, those left-of-center parties moved toward their core of activists. And so in opposition the socialist and social democratic parties of central and northern Europe first split deeply over INF, then wandered (some galloped) away from support for the NATO deployments.

5. Two other presumptions seemed minor, but went wrong in ways that were not: (a) The Pershings were *not* easier to deploy in the Federal Republic than the cruise missiles. Quite the contrary, they became a special object of anti-nuclear protest. (b) The decision not to deploy the missiles under a dual-key increased anti-nuclear protest by playing into the argument that Europe might be drawn into a nuclear war against its will.

WHAT WENT RIGHT?

In the middle of 1981, then, the situation surrounding INF looked bleak. SALT II was dead. The new American Administration, military in emphasis and loss in rhetoric, was being cajoled by Europeans into resuming the INF talks, but little by way of arms control actually was proceeding. Europe's nuclear politics were polarising, and its peace marches were growing. Then living in London, I would have taken an even bet that no NATO missiles ever would be deployed in Europe. Yet I was proven wrong only a little more than two years later. The 'hot autumn' of 1983 was only tepid. What went right for NATO and American policy?

Most important, London, Bonn, Rome and Paris all held firm to the deployments. The changes of government, especially in London and Bonn, had a double effect, fanning nuclear protest just as they made it less likely that the protest would affect official policy.

The Reagan Administration also played its hand better from the autumn of 1981 onward. Its rhetoric changed, and, under European entreaties, it agreed to start INF almost a year before it was ready to hold talks on strategic weapons with Moscow, and later it modified its INF position a number of times. By December 1983 Washington looked, if not exactly eager to negotiate, at least hard to blame as the sole culprit for the failed Geneva negotiations.

The change was evident on 18 November 1981 when President Reagan unveiled the American position for the INF talks, the so-called 'zero option', a political master-stroke even if it was not entirely consistent with the strategic logic of deploying the cruises and Pershings. But, politically, zero was zero. Reagan out-arms controlled the peace movement. The zero option bought the United States and NATO at least a year.

Moscow's heavy-handed propaganda campaign also helped the NATO cause, albeit unwittingly. The core Soviet position – preventing any NATO deployments while protecting as many SS-20s as possible – was plain enough even to European peace movements. Each change of Soviet position – either in the negotiations or for the benefit of West European public opinion – was too little, too late. In 1979, when a moratorium on SS-20 deployments might have turned the tide against NATO's decision, for example, Moscow could only come up with an offer to negotiate. Only in March 1982 did Soviet leader Brezhnev finally announce a 'moratorium on the deployment of medium-range nuclear armaments' – but that applied only to European Russia and would depend on NATO abandoning 'practical preparations' for the deployments. Soviet leaders all but declared their preference for the Social Democrats in the March 1983 German elections, a bit of heavy-handedness Schmidt's successor, Vogel, did not need. Finally, the shooting down of a civilian Korean jetliner by Soviet jets in September 1983 did little for the Soviet Union's image as peace-loving.

In the end, too, the peace movements themselves may not have helped their specific cause. In most countries they brought together coalitions too disparate to be effective, and in many places they were tinged with radical politics that may have turned-off as many would-be opponents of the Euromissiles as they activated.

LESSONS FOR NEXT TIME

What went wrong and what went right in the saga of the Euromissiles hardly provide conclusive lessons for the next time NATO steps up to a major nuclear decision. But it does suggest cautions for the next time around. I offer five, four for Washington and one for American Allies in Europe.

1. 'Don't do it. Don't decide to deploy new nuclear systems on land in Europe no matter what the Europeans say.' This is tempting as the paramount lesson. On balance, I judge that the INF episode has been a plus for NATO's cohesion and sense of purpose, but it was a close-run thing. In retrospect it is easy to see why my bet in the middle of 1981 was a bad one, but at the time several disastrous outcomes for NATO were imaginable. And if NATO had failed the test of INF, the failure would have been self-inflicted. While there were strategic arguments for deploying the new INF systems, elevating that decision into a crucial test of the Alliance was largely a matter of NATO's own doing.

Still, 'don't do it' overstates the point. The real lesson for next time is caution: think and think again before embarking on a decision to deploy new nuclear hardware in Europe, especially on land. Ask if there is any other way. Almost unnoticed in all the fuss over the cruise missiles in Europe, one American administration decided, and its successor implemented and expanded, a decision to deploy hundreds of other nuclear cruise missiles at sea, on attack submarines and surface ships, some of them with a land-attack mission. In retrospect, NATO might have turned the trick with those deployments, somehow connected to European security as visibly as possible, plus arms control initiatives.

Much of the American analysis of INF was strategic, not political. Washington heard the Schmidt speech as a sign of concern. Then it asked itself, as I remember and reconstruct it, *not*: 'do the Europeans really want new hardware on their soil?' Instead, Washingtonians asked: 'if *we* were in their place, would *we* want new hardware?' Once the second question had been answered in the affirmative, the train of decision gathered momentum, and the first question became all but impossible even to pose. And crucial *political* particulars – such as 'would the Pershings become special objects of anti-nuclear protest?' or 'will the lack of dual keys cause problems?' – were lost in the noise.

The 'neutron bomb', or enhanced radiation warhead (ERW), misadventure of 1977–8 probably was decisive in making the Carter Administration, already erratic in the eyes of many Europeans, a believer in new INF hardware. The ERW episode was an accident, but one of those accidents that are predictable in alliance relations. The story has also been told elsewhere.[4] The newly-installed Carter administration was literally unaware of the ERW until a front-page *Washington Post* story labelled it 'the ultimate capitalist weapon, destroying people but leaving buildings intact'. President Carter's senior advisers, on the defensive, then tried to contrive schemes whereby several European countries would accept ERW as a modernisation of NATO's arsenal of short-range nuclear weapons. When, April 1978, Mr Carter said he wanted none of these schemes and decided instead to defer the whole issue, European leaders, especially Schmidt, felt the rug had been pulled from beneath him. Having been perceived as flinching once, the Administration felt it could not be seen to be irresolute again.

2. Try to visualise the state of domestic policies in key NATO members at the time the weaponry will be deployed, *not* just at the time of decision. This is, to be sure, a tall order. It would have meant, for both President Carter and Chancellor Schmidt in 1979, contemplating their own political defeat – hardly a temptation for heads of government or an avocation of their advisers. Washington can, however, ask itself how much the carrying-out of a given decision depends on particular conjunctions of circumstances, politics and politicians in power in Europe. For instance, that INF deployments depended on such an unpromising arms control venture was one cautionary sign. Making the package work required steadfastness in at least Bonn, London and Rome, plus reasonably propitious circumstances for arms control negotiations coupled with tolerable adroitness by the United States in negotiating. All these had to be sustained for four years, perhaps eight – another cautionary sign.

Asking *anyone* to visualise domestic politics in *any* country four years hence probably is asking too much, so two other lessons may serve as partial surrogates:

3. If new nuclear deployments seem imperative, try to shorten the time gap between decision and deployment. If that gap is as long as four or five years, the deployments are bound to become hostage, like the Euromissiles, to calls for negotiating before deploying, with all the attendant pressure in European domestic politics. In 1977, by contrast, ninety additional American F-111s were deployed to

Britain, more than doubling the number of fighter-bombers capable of delivering nuclear weapons. The planes simply arrived, their presence announced only after it was a fact. Similarly, when the Belgian Cabinet decided, in the middle of the night one spring day in 1985, finally to take the cruise missiles allotted to it in 1979, the missiles were loaded and on their way from the United States in a matter of hours. By the time most Belgians heard of their government's decision, the missiles were there, and the terms of the debate were thus changed.

4. If you are a president or prime minister, get a hold on nuclear decisions *early*. Not doing so was Jimmy Carter's failing in the case of the neutron bomb; it was also Helmut Schmidt's mistake in the instance of the Euromissiles. These issues soon disappear into the technical 'yak' of national bureaucracies and their NATO counterparts, surrounded by secrecy. Even presidents and prime ministers, not to mention their political advisers, may be tempted to regard them as technical, not political. Schmidt may have believed he had struck a basic political bargain over INF with Carter at Guadeloupe in January 1979; yet, still, Schmidt's apparent inattention between 1977 and 1979 to how the details of INF deliberations bore on *his* political future is striking.

Moreover, decisions that may look preliminary or tentative will soon become cast in iron by the fact of alliance in NATO. Decisions, once taken, soon become tests of alliance cohesion. To seek to reopen them is to appear a disloyal ally. Once official Washington convinced itself, in the summer and autumn of 1978, that only new nuclear deployments on European soil would suffice, whether Europeans actually *wanted* the new missiles became almost irrelevant. Certainly no German government – and especially no Social Democratic German government – could reopen the issue without seeming to confirm Washington's worst fears about its loyalty.

5. A final lesson for American allies: the American governmental machine is hard to budge, but that also makes it hard to divert once it is in motion on an issue. It will not be easy to adjust if circumstances change, or if Europeans feel Washington heard them wrong in the first place, or if those Europeans change their minds. Put differently, Americans are by nature problem-solvers. So is their government, a feature enhanced by frequent changes of administration, each with its own group of 'in-and-out-ers' on the lookout for problems to 'solve'. Hence, if Europeans do not want a problem solved, they should not ask. Seeming to do so was Schmidt's error in 1977. In the end, that

mistake, among several other factors, cost him the chancellorship.

In conclusion, it is fair to ask what these lessons from the Euromissile affair suggest for the 'next' nuclear issue that actually has arisen to confront the Alliance – strategic defence. This is not an issue the Europeans can be accused of asking for, except in the most indirect way. President Reagan's strategic defence initiative speech of March 1983 came as a surprise to most of his own government, and as a shock to Europeans. If SDI is Mr Reagan's dramatic alternative to NATO's nuclear dilemma, Europeans want nothing of it. They have said, quite explicitly, if SDI is the solution, they do not want the problem solved. In the process, many Europeans, even those who talked of the unacceptability of nuclear deterrence during the INF affair, have been driven back toward nuclear orthodoxy in a way that is suggestive of my premise that there are no dramatic alternatives to the nuclear status quo. The President's vision – making the terror of nuclear deterrence obsolete – matched that of the European peace movement: some of his words could have come from their mouths. Needless to say, however, his means was not theirs.

SDI demonstrated the gap between strategic logic and politics even more starkly than did the Euromissile affair. In strategic logic it has been true since the beginning of the nuclear era, and is true today, that if the United States can achieve a degree of invulnerability from Soviet nuclear attack for its citizens – a big *if* – its nuclear guarantee extended to Europe is more credible. That is so even if Europe remains vulnerable. However, the European reaction to SDI has, to put it gently, been of a different order, intensely political. The reaction has evoked worries over a political decoupling of the United States from Europe's defence, the prospects of an arms race between the superpowers, and a new source of East–West tension.

Two other features of SDI, alas, also pose problems for alliance management that are reminiscent of INF. One is the momentum of the Washington machine. Europeans initially were tempted to hope SDI would simply go away, and the programme was the object of amusement in the American technical community. No longer: by 1985 the US defence science establishment was still sceptical about the grander hopes for SDI, but the challenge of the technological task was appealing. Europeans were thus in the position of seeming to object to something that is 'just' a research programme but knowing in their heart of hearts that momentum beyond research is building.

Much more than for INF, the gap between decisions about weapons and their deployment makes the process hostage to arms control. Any SDI deployments are years, even decades away. In the meantime the Soviet Union will have opportunities aplenty to target arms control proposals where the US and its European allies differ. Pressure for arms control is bound to grow as well in Western Europe. At Reykjavik in 1987 Moscow finally got itself organised to make the kind of proposal that has been set up for several years: it offered deep reductions in strategic and INF systems on the condition that the United States agreed to limit SDI to laboratory research. The Soviet Union had edged toward such a proposal in the past, but always with a nest of qualifications. When Moscow appeared to make it for real, Europeans across the political spectrum regarded it as a good deal, as did many Americans. When an administration committed to strategic defence, like the Reagan Administration, held back, it set off a major row in the Alliance.

By this reading, SDI seems to run parallel to many of the perils to alliance management I noted in the INF affair. It may also provide some confirmation for my presumption against dramatic alternatives. It does not suggest that any lessons have been learned, and it may be a case against my premise that the nuclear dilemma can be managed. Yet I expect the dilemma to survive even SDI. The idea of strategic defence is politically attractive in the United States – it is a typically American answer to the horror of deterrence – and so interest in it is bound to recur.

Yet my bet is that the current round of enthusiasm will wane. With tight defence budgets, Pentagon enthusiasm for it may diminish. The Soviet Union may make an arms control offer that would tempt an American administration to agree to some constraints on defences. More fundamentally, it is likely to turn out that the nuclear defences that are practicable in the near term – point defences of missile silos and other military targets, not the exotica of 'umbrellas' over cities – will prove unappealing to politicians and their publics. Even if such deployments should prove appealing, limited nuclear defences, in particular of missiles, need not be incompatible with deterrence, NATO strategy, or the management of NATO's nuclear dilemma.

Notes

1. I spell out my view in *Making the Alliance Work* London and Ithaca: Macmillan and Cornell University Press, 1985).
2. Ibid. chs 2 and 3 for poll data and supporting argument.
3. This account is pieced together from a number of sources, including my own interviews and experience as staff member for Western Europe on the National Security Council, 1977–8. Brief accounts are in my *Nuclear Weapons in Europe*, Adelphi Paper 168 (London: IISS, 1981); and *The Modernization of NATO's Long Range Theater Nuclear Forces*, Report prepared for the Subcommittee on Europe and the Middle East of the House Committee on Foreign Affairs, 96 Congress, 2 session, (31 December 1980). For fuller discussions that agree on almost all the crucial particulars, see David N. Schwartz, *NATO's Nuclear Dilemma* (Washington: The Brookings Institution, 1983); J. Michael Legge, *Theater Nuclear Weapons and the Nato Strategy of Flexible Response, R-2964-FF* (Santa Monica: The Rand Corporation, April 1983); Paul Buteaux, *The Politics of Nuclear Consultation in NATO* (Cambridge: Cambridge University Press, 1983). See also Raymond L. Garthoff, 'The Nato Decision on Theater Nuclear Forces', *Political Science Quarterly*, 98 (Summer 1983); and David C. Elliott, *Decision at Brussels: The Politics of Nuclear Forces*, California Seminar Discussion Paper 97 (Santa Monica, 1981).
4. The fullest and most readable account of the neutron bomb affair is David Whitman, *The Press and the Neutron Bomb*, available from the Kennedy School of Government, Harvard University. See also Sherri L. Wasserman, *The Neutron Bomb Controversy: A Study in Alliance Politics* (New York: Praeger, 1983).

2 SDI, Alliance Coherence, and East–West Nuclear Stability

Edward A. Kolodziej

The nuclear modernisation programme, offensive and defensive, now being implemented or seriously proposed by the Western nuclear states and the Soviet Union pose critical problems for the stability of the European and global nuclear balance. The Reagan administration's Strategic Defence Initiative (SDI) and the dramatic growth of British and French nuclear capabilities add new strains on the arms race now underway between the superpowers. Current and emerging instabilities must be addressed promptly along a broad political front, within and outside the framework of the Atlantic Alliance, before they further split the alliance and damage efforts – principally those being pursued at Geneva in the superpower arms control talks – to manage the nuclear balance and the conflicts that divide the two blocs in Europe and elsewhere.

The first part of this chapter diagnoses the disturbing elements of the evolving nuclear environment which promotes instability. The second suggests an approach – complex bilateralism – that might be employed to bring these destabilising trends under control to promote the development of more coherent, cohesive, and mutually confident alliance strategic policies than exist today and to enhance East–West stability.

INSTABILITIES WITHIN THE EAST–WEST NUCLEAR ENVIRONMENT AND THEIR IMPLICATIONS FOR THE ATLANTIC ALLIANCE

Requirements of a Stable Western Deterrent Posture

Strategic stability between East and West and the preservation of an effective and credible deterrent posture hinge, from the perspective of the West, on two critical imperatives: coherent and cohesive alliance strategies to meet Soviet and Eastern bloc threats at all levels of potential hostilities, and public support for national and alliance policies. Included within this rubric are (a) agreed policies for the use and threat of nuclear weapons, (b) accord on conventional and nuclear force levels, deployments and C^3I systems, and, finally (c) a common approach to arms control negotiations with the Soviet Union. The second imperative derives from the need to generate domestic approval for national and alliance use, threat, and nuclear arms control policies. These imperatives must be simultaneously met if the Western alliance is to preserve a stable deterrent posture in meeting the Soviet threat, while assuring both the Soviet Union and domestic populations that the East–West conflict will not erupt into a nuclear war.

Maintenance of a stable and effective Western strategic deterrent is challenged by three unfavourable trends. The first stems from the Soviet military build-up of conventional, theatre nuclear, and strategic forces that appear in excess of legitimate security and defensive concerns. Second, there are serious rifts between the US and West European governments, and among the latter, about the proper strategic and arms control response to the Soviet challenge. These rifts have now been extended to the public at large within the Western states, further deepening intergovernmental and bureaucratic misunderstandings and suspicions.

President Reagan's promotion of a Strategic Defence Initiative (SDI) and his reported proposal for the elimination of all strategic nuclear weapons, made at the Reykjavik summit in September 1986,[1] have elicited widespread and conflicting fears from European leaders. On the one hand, an ambitious SDI (especially if viewed against the background of American nuclear offensive systems since the late 1970s) promises to initiate a new and potentially uncontrolled arms race (threatening, incidentally, British and French nuclear forces if the Soviet Union deploys an effective ABM system). On the other hand, a world without ballistic missiles – moving toward the goal advanced by Party Secretary Mikhail Gorbachev on 15 January 1986, of no nuclear weapons by the end of the century –[2] exposes the European states to Soviet superiority in conventional and theatre nuclear forces.[3] It is one thing to advise a controlled and calibrated disarmament of superpower nuclear arsenals to increase East–West stability; it is quite another to abandon nuclear deterrence completely as the framework within which NATO (as well as British and French) security policies have been cast for over a generation.

To these differences now dividing the West should be added the potentially disruptive implications of the modernisation programme of British and French nuclear forces. While global and European strategic stability still primarily depend on US and Soviet behaviour, the West European term of the equation of strategic balance must be accorded more value today as a source of instability than in the past. Unless controlled through Allied consultation and accord, uninhibited pursuit of SDI and European nuclear forces may split the Alliance wider than it is at present, conceivably past the point of management and control.

Soviet Military Build-up

Much of the problem of strategic stability and Western cohesion lies with the Soviet Union. However much American initiatives and US – European differences and misunderstandings may have contributed to current instabilities, the expansion of Soviet theatre and long-range strategic forces (together with the development of impressive air and ballistic missile defence research programmes and conventional force modernisation throughout the 1970s and 1980s) has been responsible for much of Western concern about maintaining deterrence. On these points most of the Western governments appear agreed. British Foreign Secretary Sir Geoffrey Howe in a major policy address of March 1985 – which raised serious questions about SDI – also underscored the Soviet ABM programme as a threat to East–West nuclear stability.[4] French President François Mitterrand has consistently identified the Soviet Union as the principal destabilising force in Europe. German governments similarly oppose Soviet expansion and modernisation of its missile and bomber forces as a threat to the West.[5]

At the European level, Soviet Backfire bombers, tactical aircraft, air defence forces, and theatre nuclear missiles pose a serious threat to NATO forces as well as British and French nuclear systems. Withdrawal of theatre nuclear systems in ranges between 300 and 3,500 miles will reduce but not eliminate the Soviet threat to NATO. At a global level, heavy Soviet rockets, particularly SS-19s and SS-18s – the latter with up to ten 500 kt warheads – threaten American ground-based nuclear systems. These are being complemented by the deployment of SS-24 and SS-25 strategic systems. To this formidable array of nuclear striking power must be added the construction of the phased-radar system at Krasnoyarsk (arguably a violation of SALT

1), an extensive ABM research programme, and a tested ASAT system.[6]

DIVERGENT AMERICAN AND EUROPEAN RESPONSES TO SOVIET NUCLEAR MODERNISATION

Structural Opposition to US Policies

Differing US–European responses to Soviet strategic behaviour also undermine the stability of the Western deterrent posture and the East–West balance. The sources of these differences are fundamentally structural, grounded in divergent geopolitical and strategic perspectives and interests. They serve as a point of departure to an analysis of the contribution of SDI and French and British nuclear programmes to real potential divisions within the Western camps.

First, a significant – if still minority – body of European opinion is (for a variety of reasons) deeply suspicious of most American military and arms control initiatives calculated to match or moderate Soviet strategic moves. If the controversy over long-range theatre nuclear weapons is taken as a crude index, opposition to nuclear modernisation is particularly strong in Britain, West Germany, Belgium, Holland and the Scandinavian countries of NATO. Only the governments of France and (to a lesser degree) Italy escaped heavy domestic pressures opposed to US policies.

The presence of this resistant body of European opinion to American strategic and arms control initiatives at once limits the ability of NATO governments to co-operate with the US on nuclear and conventional arms modernisation and provides the Soviet Union with opportunities to manipulate Western public opinion and governments and to split the Alliance. In anticipation of these domestic forces, and better to manage them, the Europeans insisted on explicit arms control procedures in agreeing to NATO's December 1979 decision to deploy intermediate-range nuclear forces (INF).[7] The Reagan administration's adoption of a zero option negotiating position in INF talks with the Soviet Union in the fall of 1981 was as much aimed at European public opinion to quiet domestic opposition to eventual Pershing II and cruise missile deployments as it was a bargaining chip to persuade the Soviet Union to dismantle its SS-20 forces.[8]

The formula worked. Not only was the Soviet diplomatic offensive to split the Alliance surmounted with the acceptance of either Pershing II or cruise missiles (albeit reluctantly) by five European NATO states but a firm stand also appeared to have contributed – as British Defence Secretary George Younger argued –[9] to the Soviet offer of 28 February 1987 to drop its insistence that the INF question be linked to agreement on strategic offensive and defensive nuclear systems.[10] The Soviet condition to include British and French forces in the INF accord had been abandoned earlier.[11] It may also be plausibly argued that the Gorbachev reform programme required a relaxation of the arms race and political tensions with the West, a view further evidenced by the Soviet proposal of April 1987 to eliminate medium and long-range nuclear systems in Europe.[12]

Structural Constraints on Atlantic Strategic Accord

Second, even in those governmental, bureaucratic and public quarters on both sides of the Atlantic where goodwill and mutual confidence are high, one must continue to expect major differences among the Europeans (and between them and the United States) over security policies. At issue are rival conceptions of nuclear and conventional arms stability. The factors explaining these differences are multiple: differing national strategic needs; geographic and historic circumstances; economic and technological capabilities; dissimilar domestic political environments where parties, elites, and public opinion have different roles and varying impacts in defining national nuclear policies; competing conceptions among Alliance partners of their regional and global roles in promoting security; and contrasting perceptions of the Soviet threat and assessments of the probabilities of achieving reliable and verifiable arms accords with Moscow.

It is against this background that one is able to explain why Europeans generally prefer a posture of nuclear deterrence over American demands for a flexible response defence strategy capable of meeting Soviet aggression over a broad range of conventional, tactical, theatre, and strategic nuclear threats. Germany excepted, the Europeans have successfully resisted American pressures over the past quarter century to increase Europe's conventional forces to a level deemed adequate by Washington to match Soviet non-nuclear modernisation. American threats of pull-out or hedging over the first-use of nuclear weapons have failed to stir the Europeans to increase spending substantially for their non-nuclear forces. The development by Britain and France of their own nuclear forces – aimed primarily at Soviet cities rather than military targets – underlines their primary commitment to nuclear deterrence over conventional and nuclear war-fighting strategies.

Most Europeans also prefer a strategy accenting detente and arms control over a policy of nuclear modernisation striving to match Soviet nuclear capabilities. The INF controversy exposed the deep roots of West Germany's ambivalence toward nuclear modernisation and detente with the Soviet Union. If the Kohl government officially supported Washington on INF, significant elements within the CDU-Free Democratic coalition temporized over Pershing II deployments, while the SPD opposed INF. These splits again resurfaced over the Soviet double-zero proposal. Bonn was torn between the security risks (detailed below) potentially run in acceding to superpower pressures and the damage to détente if it refused. These conflicting concerns translate into a go-slow approach toward a nuclear build-up and to a search for confidence-building measures and stabilising arms control accords.

The British and French positions are (for different reasons) also inclined more toward arms negotiations with the Soviet Union or to diplomatic manoeuvre over political conflicts than Washington. The major exception to this rule is British and French resistance to negotiations with the Soviet Union over their nuclear forces prior to a superpower reduction in their arsenals. Nevertheless, it appears to be no accident that Soviet Party Secretary Mikhail Gorbachev should have made his initial forays in foreign policy (even before his predecessor's death) by visiting Britain and by providing Prime Minister Margaret Thatcher a privileged status in receiving her in Moscow at the end of March 1987 in the wake of his offer to break the deadlock on INF talks.

British Foreign Secretary Sir Geoffrey Howe's speech of March 1985 essentially called for a hard look at SDI before launching a programme for strategic defence that might damage the possibility of reaching some kind of arms stabilisation accord with the Soviet Union. Like his European colleagues in Paris and Bonn, Howe preferred to meet the Soviet ABM threat primarily through arms control negotiations rather than through an accelerated arms race. Two years later, in a major policy address before the International Institute for Strategic Studies, he reaffirmed his previous stance: 'We have to accept that not everything technically possible may be affordable or prudent. The Geneva negotiations aim to prevent an arms race in outer space. Both sides are committed to that objective. The British Government warmly endorses it.'[13]

As the British Conservative Party government of Margaret Thatcher moved toward national elections, it perceived a need to strengthen its record in East–West peacemaking, not unlike previous English governments dating back to Prime Ministers Harold Macmillan and Harold Wilson.[14] The cyclical need of European governments to seek peaceful settlements and to address Soviet demands appear to be permanent features of the European electoral politics, contrasting with the scepticism of Soviet motives and intransigence often characterising American electioneering habits and political attitudes towards the Soviet Union.

French governmental and public opinion has, ironically, been more disposed to American firmness than other European allies in the face of Soviet military expansion. Paris assumes the contradictory stance – more uncomfortable for its allies than for successive French governments of the Right and Left – that the NATO and US nuclear guarantee to Europe must be strengthened, although France remains outside the alliance's military organisation and insists on the independence of its nuclear deterrent. While it would have no part of INF modernisation, Paris urged German deployment of Pershing missiles, partly to reinforce Germany's commitment to NATO and partly to ensure against a neutralist-leaning West Germany whose moorings to the West might progressively weaken and set the centre of Europe adrift. At a strategic nuclear level, Paris of the 1980s prefers deterrence *cum detente* to Bonn's detente *cum deterrence*.

The modernisation of French nuclear forces, discussed below, evidences the determination of the French to maintain an independent nuclear force which can credibly counter the Soviet Union and, as a bonus, solidify French military dominance on the western half of the European continent. This strategic posture bolsters France's privileged status under the Four Power accords governing Berlin and Germany. Its nuclear forces afford Paris – at least in its eyes – the choice of the empty chair in NATO nuclear bargaining or of entering or resisting East–West arms control talks, depending on the terms. Like Washington, Paris arms to parley.

All European states also have a major stake in greater East–West trade, increasing sales of high technology to Eastern Europe, exploitation of investment opportunities, and enhanced access to Soviet raw material reserves. These economic attractions are not only instruments of detente, but important in their own right. The European economies have not enjoyed the same economic resurgence as that of the United States. They rely much more on trade with Eastern Europe than the United States. This dependency makes them more vulnerable to manipulation by Moscow. While they may be counted upon to stand with Washington when a critical issue (like INF) is joined, it strains credibility – as the fiasco of the pipeline episode evidenced – that they will hold ranks when economic advantages are to be had by moderating their diplomatic stances and by relaxing economic restrictions on trade with the Eastern bloc and the Soviet Union. As discussed in more detail below, US–European co-operation in SDI research may hobble European sale or transfer of the technological and economic spin-offs deriving from European contributions to the programme.

SDI: A New Challenge to Atlantic Cohesion

The Strategic Defence Initiative – coming on the heels of the confusion of the Carter years, the concern over the nuclear arms race fuelled by the Reagan administration, and the controversy over INF – threatens to create new and serious cleavages between the United States and Europe. It certainly complicates (and may even preclude) the achievement of a stable and coherent allied response to Soviet nuclear modernisation or exploitation of the possibilities of a new flexibility in Soviet arms control strategy as a consequence of the reformist policies of the Gorbachev regime. Europeans are more ready than Americans to identify a stable nuclear deterrent with low levels of invulnerable offensive nuclear systems on both sides and with arms control accords between the Soviet Union and the United States that confirm a rough nuclear parity between them as long as the American security guarantee to Europe is not weakened. Over the past decade, the American security community has progressively questioned whether the Soviets can be trusted to keep such accords, whether MAD makes sense if deterrence breaks down, and whether nuclear parity (defined in the coinage of throw weight, launchers and warheads) is sufficient to support American diplomacy and bargaining postures *vis-à-vis* the Soviet Union or its surrogates in the developing world.[15] Unlike Europe, the US has never been comfortable with MAD or with the necessarily simpler civilian directed targeting plans of French and British nuclear forces. Even after the McNamara Defense Department's acceptance of MAD was proclaimed, American nuclear planning and targeting remained keyed more to military sites than soft, high value economic and population centers. In a word, the American posture has always been MAD-plus.[16]

Evolving nuclear doctrine and the pursuit of arms control accords with the Soviet Union during the 1970s have been consistent with MAD-plus, not simply MAD. The Schlesinger doctrine and President Carter's Presidential Directive (PD-59) sought simultaneously to provide the American President with a wide menu of nuclear options to fight a controlled, limited nuclear war and to include the Soviet leadership in the calculus of deterrence. PD-59 specifically identified the Soviet power structure as a prime target, despite the difficulties that would inevitably be encountered in attempting to keep a nuclear war limited if the Soviet leadership were annihilated early on in the war.[17] The American security community has always been more concerned than Europeans about damage limitation, controlled escalation, and a war-fighting position at all levels of possible hostilities. US analysts and policy-makers are also preoccupied with intra-war deterrence, with maintaining military superiority in the post-attack environment and with bringing a nuclear conflict to a swift conclusion on terms favourable to the West.

American concern for fighting a nuclear war and for maintaining escalation dominance until a nuclear war can be brought to a favourable close has generated high offensive military requirements, crystallised in the later Carter years and in the first years of the Reagan administration in proposals to modernise US offensive nuclear forces. Justification for these requirements was based on three interlocked and sequential lines of reasoning: a nuclear war-fighting posture matching Soviet capabilities at all nuclear levels – a seamless web, in deterrence jargon; the strengthening of national and extended deterrence through war-fighting, improved nuclear defences, and coupling and commitment strategies embodied in INF; and, following ostensibly on war-fighting and extended deterrence, a position of diplomatic and military strength from which to bargain decisively with the Soviet Union over arms control accords themselves and conflicts in and outside Europe where American and allied interests might be engaged. If the Soviet Union could not be trusted to keep arms control accords, then trust in the Soviet leadership would be rendered irrelevent either by attaining a dominant position in modernising American, NATO and European offensive and defensive nuclear forces – the Soviets would be unable to keep pace in either the technology or the economic race – or by imposing stiff arms control and verification requirements on Moscow, tied to deep cuts in Soviet strategic forces, especially its ground-based systems. Either way, Western superiority and safety would purportedly be assured.

European governmental opinion is at odds with American planners on several key points. These differences revolve around the desirability of lowered offensive nuclear levels, risk-taking with the Soviet Union in negotiating on lower nuclear levels rather than in forcing them on an intransigent Moscow, and appropriate and verifiable restraints on research and development programmes – specifically SDI – that promise a technological breakthrough beyond MAD or MAD-plus. It therefore is not surprising that Sir Geoffrey Howe should have characterised SDI as a fourth option in preserving the West's 'defence into the next century' in contrast to his third and preferred option of maintaining 'sufficient forces to deter any aggression against us and our allies, and to seek at the same time balanced reductions in these forces on both sides.'[18]

Howe's evaluation of SDI essentially summarises most of the concerns of Europeans about the most ambitious claims made for the Reagan proposal. They are worth considering because they identify the major reservations that allied governments like Britain and West Germany, with a long record of co-operation with Washington, have in addressing SDI. What was not said by Howe is equally significant – the threat that an American SDI and its Soviet counterpart poses for the independence and credibility of French and British nuclear forces. This consideration adds to the potential for rift in the Alliance if SDI goes forward in the absence of allied consultations and co-operation.

Improved superpower nuclear defensive systems promise to increase pressures on the British and French governments to increase their offensive nuclear forces to offset presumed Soviet progress in ABM technology.[19] Conversely, superpower accord on INF forces confronts the European nuclear powers with the challenge (already made by Moscow)[20] of cutting back on their forces and of integrating them into a follow-on arms control accord to superpower compromise on INF that might lead to reductions below those desired by Paris and London to support their conceptions of what is required for minimum deterrence, a problem to be addressed in more detail below.

Howe's reservations, varyingly echoed and amplified in other European capitals despite the reported success of the Reagan administration in bringing allies into line, signify a yawning gap in European and American thinking about active defence systems. Discord between the Reagan administration and its European Allies turns on a complex set of arguments and considerations which may be summarised as follows:

1. SDI threatens to narrow political direction of the nuclear modernisation programme since a commitment will be made to an expensive technological programme before its ramifications for strategic stability and mutual confidence-building between allies and the Soviet Union have been fully explored. Politics will be put at the mercy of technology.
2. Highly computerised, electronically controlled systems would reduce human control over reaction time to threats.
3. Limited defence of military installations, if effective, may have the undesired effect of upgrading more vulnerable, civilian targets in Soviet targeting.
4. Countermeasures to SDI are readily at hand, including non-ballistic missile systems such as aircraft, cruise missiles and even covert action for which new and potentially expensive defences will have to be built.
5. Defensive and offensive forces must be viewed as different elements of the East–West strategic balance. Neither can be considered apart from the other. As a result, an expansion of defensive systems is likely to provoke not only a similar Soviet counter-action but an expansion of offensive arms.
6. The costs of building a multi-tiered active defence system would probably be hundreds of billions of dollars.
7. The opportunity costs of SDI, in foregoing other nuclear and conventional systems needed for stability, would be high and potentially destabilising, as NATO would not be able to implement a flexible response strategy.
8. Arms control would be undermined as suspicions grew in Soviet quarters that the US and the West sought nuclear superiority; as the ABM treaty was eroded; as an arms race developed between East and West as both sides increased their offensive nuclear weapons and accelerated their active and passive defence programme; and as opportunities to make real arms control gains – such as limits on ASAT systems – were ignored in the controversy inevitably raised by the new defence programme.

9. Deterrence would be damaged on the long transition process toward implementation of SDI.
10. SDI does little to address the Soviet short-range missile threat to Europe.
11. Doubts would grow in Western capitals whether Allies shared the same sense of the indivisibility of NATO territory and of the equality of risks of nuclear war. As the US reduced damage to its territory through SDI, three trends adverse to US-European cohesions might well develop: (a) US strategic and theatre nuclear forces might well be decoupled; (b) incentives might increase to encourage the United States to reach arms control agreements adverse to European security needs – a temptation foreshadowed in the negotiations over INF and SALT II; or (c) the United States, as a consequence of a superpower arms control condominium, might pursue detente with the Soviet Union at the expense of its West European allies.
12. A partially successful SDI, leakproof against third states but leaky *vis-à-vis* the Superpowers, would threaten British and French nuclear systems and create a *de facto* Superpower condominium.[21]

SDI and Shared Risk-taking

The Europeans appear to be acutely aware of the costs, risks, and potential (if distant) benefits of SDI. As one moves from the speculations projected by strategic analyses to the political positions that governments must assume, the latter are less certain about what policies they should pursue in responding to American initiatives. They share several common tendencies – although with varying intensity, for reasons to be noted below – in formulating their reactions to Washington. First, they are reluctant to encourage or sanction any fundamental changes in the East–West strategic balance. They prefer superpower acceptance of current defence arrangements as well as implicit or explicit arms control accords that would consolidate these understandings and thereby strengthen East–West stability. European governments have based their security policies squarely on NATO and on the US nuclear guarantee. They are sceptical of efforts either significantly to increase superpower offensive or defensive nuclear capabilities or of proposals – like President Reagan's ambitious formulation of SDI or his Reykjavik suggestion to rid the world of ballistic missiles – that appear to depart from nuclear deterrence as the touchstone of European defence.

Second, all want the ABM treaty to be maintained in its present form. Revision, if required, should meet at least three tests: it should be revised only by mutual superpower consent; it should be confined as narrowly as possible to acknowledge the work that is already underway by both sides but short of a line (yet to be defined) whose crossing would catapult the superpowers into an unregulated arms race in space; and, throughout the process of Superpower talks over revision, the Europeans should be informed about the progress of negotiations and their views should be taken into account. The Europeans fear an arms race in which the development of defensive systems will not only be accelerated but also offensive nuclear systems will be multiplied to offset perceived defensive gains. The viability of the French and British deterrents, particularly their ability to penetrate improved and alerted Soviet defences, is directly menaced. All would prefer to deal with the Soviet ABM programme through negotiations, using SDI as a bargaining chip to extract Soviet concessions.

Third, all wish to avoid hard budgetary and political choices at home by slowing down SDI and its Soviet counterpart. Keeping pace with the Superpowers requires more not less resources for nuclear systems, straining already tight defence budgets and diverting funds from other military programmes. There is little support for more defence spending in Europe. The budgetary squeeze also puts pressure on non-nuclear forces whose reduction increases reliance on NATO's nuclear weapons while undermining its flexible response strategy at conventional levels. If these reallocations were undertaken, they would heighten US–European differences over NATO strategy and burden sharing.

Fourth, none of the European states wishes directly to oppose the United States over SDI, although each has its own special reasons alternately for acceding to the SDI programmes and for qualifying its support. Retaining the American nuclear guarantee and gaining access to SDI technology and research and development contracts draw the Europeans to SDI, offsetting the negative features of the programmes outlined earlier. How these conflicting pressures are manifested in Europe's approach to SDI can be understood only by closer examination of the divergent responses of London, Paris, and Bonn to the US proposal. The split European position is itself a symptom of disarray within the Alliance.[22]

In line with traditional British diplomacy which stresses London's special relationship with Washington, the Thatcher government was first to sign an SDI accord, even while raising serious reservations about the strategic and arms control dimensions of the programme. The anticipated scientific, technological, and economic benefits were also too strong a temptation to ignore. In explaining British signature of an SDI accord in December 1985, British Defence Minister Michael Heseltine emphasised to Parliament both the anticipated technological and economic benefits, as well as the political and strategic significance of the British signature. The latter considerations were explicitly defined in terms of a British view of a preceding political understanding reached between the English Prime Minister and the American president in late 1984:

> The Government's policy towards the Strategic Defence Initiative remains firmly based on the four points agreed between the Prime Minister and President Reagan at Camp David in December 1984:
>
> – That the Western aim is not to achieve superiority, but to maintain balance taking account of Soviet developments;
> – That SDI-related deployment would, in view of treaty obligations, have to be a matter for negotiation;
> – That the aim is to enhance, and not to undermine deterrence; and
> – That East–West negotiations should aim to achieve security with reduced levels of offensive systems on both sides.
>
> It was in this context that, at Camp David, the Prime Minister told President Reagan of her firm conviction that the SDI research programme should go ahead as a prudent hedge against Soviet activities in the same field.
>
> The confidential memorandum of understanding reached between the two governments safeguards British interests in relation to the ownership of intellectual property rights and technology transfer, and provides for consultative and review mechanisms in support of the aims of the memorandum.[23]

The economic and technological incentives of SDI should not obscure the larger strategic and political reservations underlying Heseltine's restatement of the British position. The Thatcher government, as suggested earlier, confronts two unpalatable trends in American policy. If SDI goes forward, then it faces the choice of increasing spending to enhance Britain's capacity to penetrate Soviet ABM systems. Having already announced a decrease in defence expenditures, the Thatcher government would have to address domestic opposition (even from within the Conservative party) to spend more on nuclear systems at the expense of non-nuclear forces and possibly to enlarge Britain's deterrent force by increasing the number of warheads on the D-5 missiles of the Trident system which will come into service in the 1990s. It could, of course, abandon Trident, but that would reverse the government's long-established position and destroy the credibility of its defence policies on which it has staked its political future. Such a reversal would also conflict with one set of American expectations that the British Trident go forward as part of NATO's nuclear deterrent and that Britain be firmly locked within NATO and American nuclear planning, including continued US access to British bases for its nuclear submarines and F-111 fighters as well as for its C^3I systems in support of its nuclear operations.[24] At stake would be Britain's special nuclear relationship with the United States.

On the other hand, President Reagan's vision – expressed at the Reykjavik summit in September 1987 – of ridding the East–West struggle of all ballistic missiles and of substituting reliance on defensive systems for offensive striking power threatens from two opposed directions to undermine simultaneously an independent British nuclear deterrent and to weaken NATO's nuclear deterrent strategy to which British forces are officially committed. Selling Britain D-5 missiles for its Trident submarines while dismantling American and Soviet ballistic missiles are not easily reconcilable policies.

Forcing Britain to create and pay for its own independent nuclear programme is also out of the question. In addition, movement toward a defensive-based deterrent favours the strategic interests of the Superpowers because it tends to sanctuarise their homelands. These concerns prompted Prime Minister Thatcher's visit to Washington in November 1986 to repair the Reykjavik damage and to gain presidential backing for her government's conditional support for SDI. Her mission was only partly successful. The joint communiqué was silent about President Reagan's proposal to eliminate ballistic missiles, but it was not confirmed, either. Conversely, American commitments to NATO and to Trident were reaffirmed.[25]

More than other Allied governments, the Thatcher regime has also shown more outward (if still qualified) sympathy for the Reagan administration's insistence on a broad interpretation of the ABM treaty to permit a wider range of testing and development activities than had been initially considered to be allowable under SALT I. While still drawing the line on early deployment of a system,[26] the Thatcher government appears willing to introduce the somewhat vague notion of 'feasibility' into its approach to the treaty interpretation question.[27] It was also more (faintly) sensitive than other European capitals to Reagan administration arguments that SDI components and an SDI system have to be tested to determine their feasibility, and that the ABM treaty be interpreted broadly enough to permit such testing outside the laboratory. The British government has also assumed the position that the revision of the ABM treaty is a matter for superpower resolution since the accord was signed only by them. Since the Congress and the President are deeply divided over the interpretation of the ABM treaty – a split deepened by the lengthy analysis published by Senator Sam Nunn in favour of a narrow interpretation – the British government risks alienating both American branches of government if it is either too forthcoming or too reticent on the issue of the ABM treaty's interpretation.[28]

Paris has been more resolute and vocal in its opposition to an arms race in space and to SDI. It also has more to lose since it is not a member of NATO; possesses no special nuclear relationship with the United States through which to exert its influence; and hinges its security primarily on the preservation of its own independent efforts.[29] The mix of strategic and economic considerations reflected in British tergiversations over SDI animate French responses, although French priorities are different. France is on record against an arms race in space, a position forcefully stated by President Mitterrand in his press conference of November 1985.[30] Former Socialist Defence Minister Paul Quilès crystallised many of France's concerns: pressures to increase spending on space and nuclear programmes at the expense of conventional forces; the decoupling of the American nuclear guarantee to Europe; unequal risk sharing by NATO Allies as the Superpowers improved their home defences; and heightened techno-economic competition, threatening to widen even further the existing gap between Europe and the United States.[31]

Having little leverage over US nuclear policy, France has instead accented the need for European co-operation to meet the Superpower challenge. Its effort to create a united European front runs counter to the approaches of its principal allies (Britain and Germany), who prefer to work from within NATO to influence US policy through internal lobbying rather than to oppose Washington headlong by fashioning a European phalanx – if one could, indeed, be constructed

– at odds with American views. France has called for European participation in joint space projects in missile and satellite development as well as support for Eureka. The latter, an umbrella programme proposed to spur European co-operation on purely civil scientific and technological development, implicitly counters the military thrust of SDI.

France has made little headway in these efforts to staunch SDI progress. First, its own industrialists – like their counterparts in other European Community countries – favour bidding for Pentagon contracts. While the French government opposes a breach of the ABM treaty, it has relaxed its opposition to industrial co-operation on SDI with the United States.[32] Second, Eureka and other joint European ventures are unable to surmount the attractions of bilateral co-operation with US firms over arrangements with European companies since the former appear to be more attractive in terms of profits and technological exchanges. As the British learned in the Westland affair,[33] these tangible gains at the margin offset possible long-term benefits in a distant future under the aegis of pursuing an illusive European unity.

Precluded from having nuclear weapons and totally dependent on the American nuclear deterrent, Bonn is reluctant to contest SDI for many of the reasons underlying British and French thinking. It would prefer to deal with the Soviet ABM programme through arms control, using SDI as bargaining leverage to contain Moscow's ABM programme.

West Germany confronts a dilemma which goes deeper than those besetting its European allies when they address SDI. On the one hand, it is reluctant to oppose Washington on so vital an issue as SDI since its security depends so fundamentally on the United States and (unlike Britain and France) it does not have nuclear weapons. On the other hand, Bonn is distressed that the rapid and unilateral implementation of SDI will dismantle the ABM treaty; will provoke an arms race and undo the gains of strategic stability in Europe and the benefits of detente; and will weaken US resolve in extending its nuclear guarantee to West Germany by the pursuit of a defensive strategy that appears to encourage the decoupling of American and European security interests. An aggressive American nuclear programme, with SDI as its focal point threatens the Kohl government's coalition, which is divided over nuclear policy.

Along a similar line of reasoning, the possibility of a superpower accord on INF that accepts Gorbachev's double-zero option is a source of concern. US withdrawal of medium and long-range nuclear systems is perceived by an important segment of the Kohl coalition as a serious erosion of Bonn's strategic and diplomatic position: aside from the decoupling issue, Germany would be isolated as a nuclear battleground; the risk of nuclear war would be unequally borne by Bonn since, unlike its principal allies, it has no nuclear weapons to deter Moscow; decreased NATO reliance on nuclear weapons would heighten the Warsaw Pact's advantage in conventional and chemical arms, exposing Germany to non-nuclear conflict; and, as a consequence of a degraded strategic posture, Bonn would be susceptible to Soviet diplomatic pressures to accede to its demands.[34]

Bonn has given a European spin to SDI by convincing the Pentagon that Europe give priority to continental security problems rather than to a long-range ballistic missile attack; hence the emphasis on anti-tactical ballistic missiles (ATBMs) to address the problem of the short-range nuclear systems confronting NATO forces. There are, as Pierre Lellouche suggests, several surface advantages to ATBM development: SDI is indirectly supported, and Soviet opposition to European co-operation is less directly challenged; ATBMs adapt SDI to European industrial and military needs; and the ABM treaty is implicitly affirmed since testing and research under ATBM fall outside its strictures.[35]

It is apparent that Europe's influence over US SDI policy is marginal – partly as a consequence of its own divisions – despite assurances to the contrary including the concession that European firms will have proprietary control over discoveries made under SDI contracts.[36] Besides their own modest efforts to kill SDI with kindness, the Europeans can count on several favourable developments that promise to restrain (if not arrest) the SDI programme. First, the success of SDI is hardly certain, not only because of the formidable technological hurdles that it must surmount but also because of Soviet countermeasures, most notably an increase in offensive strike forces to overload an ABM complex.[37] The dual criteria – survivability and cost effectiveness – advanced by Paul Nitze (President Reagan's chief arms control advisor) to justify SDI spending will be difficult to fulfil.[38] In any event, few believe (even among SDI partisans) that President Reagan's vision of going beyond deterrence by providing perfect defence to protect population centres is possible in the foreseeable future. SDI may well go the way of other failed ABM attempts.[39]

Resources are also drying up. Chronic US governmental deficits constrict federal spending. A Congress (and possibly a Presidency) controlled by the Democratic Party promise to lower the priority assigned to SDI to encourage arms control accords with the Soviet Union, to slow the arms race, and to reorient spending to other programmes. Many SDI supporters are also wary of early deployment or hasty development which risk wasting resources, lowering quality standards, and retarding the construction of a solid, broad-based techno-scientific programme to sustain an effective nuclear defensive system.[40] Finally, the prospect of arms agreements with the Soviet Union – signalled by Soviet Premier Mikhail Gorbachev's double adoption of the zero option for European nuclear systems – cautions against uninhibited development of defensive strategic systems before these possibilities are fully explored.

Zero Option: The Challenge of British and French Nuclear Forces

The British and French nuclear modernisation programmes raise two contradictory sets of problems for the Superpowers: the possible loss of control in a crisis and the obstacles that they pose to arms control agreements. The first set of problems arises from the size and sophistication of projected French and British strategic nuclear capabilities in the 1990s.

The French and British nuclear systems, already impressive, will be formidable if current modernisation plans are executed. By the end of the 1990s, France is scheduled to have six nuclear submarines. Each will carry 16 M-4 SLBMs, each armed with six 150 kt MIRVed warheads. Five of France's current force of six submarines will replace their load of 16 M-20 missiles, each topped with a one megaton (mg) warhead, with the M-4 system. A new submarine will replace the first French SLBM which will retain its M-20 missile until its decommission sometime in the 1990s. An advanced M-5 missile is also planned to replace the M-4. In a decade, France is expected to have approximately 576 sea-based warheads with three submarines on station at all times.

To these strategic forces must be added 18 intermediate-range ballistic missiles on the Albion Plateau. Several dozen mobile or fixed IRBMs, yet to be developed, may replace these forces. France will also maintain into the 1990s 15 aging Mirage IVs, equipped with a medium-range air-to-surface missile (ASMP) armed with a 100-300 kt warhead.[41] Tactical nuclear forces – what the French call pre-strategic forces – will be composed of a mix of Mirage 2000 and sea-based super-Etendard aircraft carrying ASMPs as well as the Hadès ground-based system capable of launching 20-60 kt shells over a range of 350 km.[42] The latter will replace Pluton, whose short range threatens West Germany with destruction as much as it may deter Warsaw Pact forces.

The British fleet of 4 Trident submarines, each carrying a currently planned load of 16 D-5 missiles, is scheduled to be deployed in the 1990s. The British D-5 is expected to have up to 8 MIRVed warheads, according to British sources.[43] If one assumes this limit (although the D-5 can deliver up to 14 warheads), the British may dispose approximately 512 sea-based warheads, approximately two and half times the size of its Polaris Chevaline force composed of multiple but not independently targeted warheads. The Tornado aircraft, which will come into full service by the end of the decade, has been assigned to tactical nuclear mission.[44] The attack version of the Tornado is already stationed in Germany.

Combined, the British and French nuclear strategic forces could well dispose over 1000 warheads by the mid-1990s, not counting ground- and sea-launched missiles and warheads, free-falling bombs and depth charges. These forces can no longer be viewed with indifference by either Superpower. Nor can the strategic impact of either force be ignored by French and British policy-makers. From the Soviet perspective, planners will have to take these European systems into account in deciding their offensive and defensive requirements and in targeting increasing absolute portions of Soviet strike forces against these systems.

The British and French systems – officially viewed since the NATO Ottawa declaration as a net addition to the Western deterrent – must themselves be re-examined to determine whether they add or subtract from a stable East–West and West–West nuclear balance. From an American viewpoint, British and French forces pose several acute problems. First, they are autonomous. This is explicitly the case with the French *force de dissuasion*, which has always remained outside of NATO control. It is also implicitly true of British nuclear forces. While they are assigned to NATO as part of the agreement with the United States in supplying Britain with missile and submarine technology, they can be withdrawn in a period of national emergency.

While the decentralisation of nuclear forces in the Alliance may complicate Soviet planning, it should also increase American anxiety about when, where, and under what circumstances nuclear weapons will be threatened or used. The French (and most recently the British) have underscored the notion of a 'second centre of decision-making' which stresses the independent use of nuclear weapons. British targeting practice has been dominated by the so-called 'Moscow criterion', in which minimum deterrence is equated with the capacity of the Polaris system to destroy Moscow. A key justification for the Chevaline warhead was the perceived strengthening of Moscow's ABM defences, permitted by SALT I. The Soviet system generated in British policy circles the requirement for a greater number of warheads and penetration aids. While the Trident system will enlarge Britain's targeting menu, the Moscow criterion has not been abandoned. Similarly, the French will soon have the capacity to be more selective in their nuclear targeting. French strategists now speak of hitting the 'vital works' of the enemy, not just his cities. These new subtleties in the characterisations offered by British and French planners in their targeting aims do not mean that Soviet cities will be spared. In all likelihood they are scheduled to be hit early in any nuclear exchange with the Soviet Union.[45]

Second, European systems (while powerful) are still smaller and potentially more vulnerable than the American system. They may be more easily blinded by a Soviet first strike than their American counterparts. Improvements in ASW or bombardment techniques to create giant waves may render them increasingly susceptible to Soviet suppression. Under crisis conditions, incentives to pre-empt these forces may be overwhelming.

Third, European systems may trigger American nuclear forces – wittingly or not – in their attempt to stop Soviet aggression. French and British nuclear forces have less time and space within which to manoeuvre than those of the United States. Once begun, controlling a nuclear conflict will be increasingly difficult. Both France and Britain essentially follow proportional deterrence strategies in which each threaten the Soviet Union with damage in excess of any possible gain that might arise from an aggressor's attack on their vital interests. Given their smaller systems, the kind of escalation control or calibrated nuclear exchanges envisioned by American planners promise to be nullified as French or British strategies are conceivably forced on the Superpowers in a crisis.

On the other hand, progress in superpower arms control talks may be hindered by British–French refusal to participate in negotiations. Both governments refuse to consider participation unless there are deep cuts in Superpower offensive forces and effective restraints on anti-ballistic missile defences.[46] It is difficult to see how these two conditions might be met. Even if the Superpowers cut their offensive strategic forces by 50 per cent, they would still be ten times greater than British and French forces, whether viewed in combination or on a bilateral basis. Since both Superpowers already have made progress in developing anti-missile systems and will very likely continue to make headway (even if an accord is signed restraining the pace and scope of R & D) London and Paris will have additional cause to resist discussions about cuts in their systems. France has also insisted on the reduction of conventional forces and chemical weapons by the Soviet Union and the Warsaw Pact as a precondition for entertaining proposals for entry into arms control talks with the Superpowers.[47]

The Soviet proposal to dismantle its SS-20 systems in Europe and to eliminate all but 100 of the 1323 warheads of these systems (810 of which are trained on European targets) focus the problems of British–French nuclear modernisation, and the stiff conditions defined by both governments before they will enter into arms talks. The Soviet proposal exempts both systems from consideration in the Superpower phase of the INF talks. Soviet officials insist, however, on bringing the British and French into the process once Moscow and Washington have reached agreement on dismantling and withdrawing their long-range theatre systems.[48]

The initial reaction of Britain and France to the Soviet INF proposal suggests hard bargaining is in the offing.[49] Both are worried about the size of Moscow's conventional forces and chemical warfare capabilities. Bonn has also insisted on retaining its Pershing 72 IA missiles whose warheads are controlled by the United States. Washington thus confronts a dual dilemma in reaching an INF accord with Moscow. If it pressures Bonn to relent, it seems to sacrifice perceived German security interests for an arms control agreement with the Soviet Union. In turn, a Superpower INF treaty exposes British and French nuclear forces to Soviet demands that they be brought within a comprehensive understanding on nuclear weapons. As Soviet pressures mount to bring Britain and France into strategic arms talks, Alliance strains can be expected to grow. US resolve to force cuts in British and French nuclear forces (advised by some American analysts)[50] would heighten already widespread fears in Europe that the American nuclear deterrent would be decoupled from Europe and that the assumed indivisibility of risk binding Alliance partners would be eroded to Europe's disadvantage.

ENCOURAGING WESTERN CO-OPERATION AND EAST–WEST STABILITY

The increasing multilateralisation of nuclear deterrence must now be accepted as a fact of strategic life. The modernisation and expansion of nuclear forces has created a complex set of deterrence relations between adversaries – and, implicitly, between allies – who have an interest in knowing (and in controlling) each other's nuclear behaviour – announced and operational. Several simultaneous mutually dependent bilateral relations can be identified: between the Superpowers; between each of them and the French and British systems; and between the British and French nuclear deterrents. These four interdependent deterrent systems also have an impact on the capacity of other European states (in and out of NATO) in realising their security interests. Most critically, the problem of German perceptions and anxieties over security again arise – and, with them, the adequacy of the policies of the Western nuclear states in reassuring not only each other but also their key non-nuclear allies.

Untangling, analytically, these interdependencies, and identifying those elements that might be influenced to preserve or enhance a stable nuclear balance are not easy tasks. As noted earlier, a Western nuclear deterrent must meet two tests: sufficiency in deterring Soviet aggression through Alliance co-operation and domestic support. The SDI proposal, however much it may address Soviet capabilities, clearly complicates Alliance cohesion; so also does the uninhibited modernisation of independent nuclear systems within the Western bloc threaten Alliance coherence and mutual confidence – and, by extension, the stability of the East–West nuclear balance.

The Western nuclear allies have several options. First, they can ignore the problem – but only at their peril. Second, they can attempt to bring pressure on each other to conform to their preferred strategies, force postures and arms control stances. The record of achievement by going this route is not encouraging.[51] Third, they can begin recognising their shared (if different) problems in dealing with the Soviet Union *and* themselves and begin to develop a systematic consultative *and* negotiating framework between and among themselves to relax (if not resolve) their differences. It is not sufficient for the requirements of strategic stability that only the Superpowers meet at Geneva. The growth of independent nuclear systems – and, now, the possibility of an SDI – points to the need for sustained bilateral talks between the Western nuclear Allies to arrest the erosion of Western confidence and co-operation.

Because of the constraints of national autonomy and the myths of independence entertained by the Western nuclear powers, as well as the record of failure in creating multilateral nuclear decision-making bodies for the Alliance (like the proposal of President Charles de Gaulle for a NATO nuclear directorate or the currently moribund Nuclear Planning Group within NATO), it would seem best that a strategy of complex bilateralism be adopted as a useful way to proceed, but one of larger and encompassing dimensions than the constricted contractual approach of US–European SDI co-operation. Each Western state would approach its nuclear ally as a political equal, aware that its differential strategic needs will have to be bargained about. The aim of these talks would be to achieve some shared notion of Western nuclear stability, including accepted rules and guidelines on modernisation and negotiating postures *vis-à-vis* the Soviet Union. No one set of bilateral accords can ensure stability, but it should be the goal of these institutionalised discussions (as well as associated intergovernmental nuclear and conventional planning sessions) that overall deterrence be enhanced and that the East–West balance be preserved at tolerable levels of shared risk and cost, acceptable to the home populations of the Western states.

The agenda is rich for these bilateral talks. The list itself identifies many of the powerful incentives – positive and negative – that prompt serious consideration of new bargaining and negotiating frameworks within the West. First, the Western nuclear states have a keen interest in each other's targeting priorities, strategies of implementation, nuclear capabilities, and C^3I systems. All have some need to avoid catalytic war (prompted by an ally), redundancy of targeting, uncontrollable nuclear exchanges, and common efforts to bring a nuclear war to a swift conclusion. All of the Western nuclear states have an interest in avoiding accidental, unauthorised, unintended nuclear war as well as slowing or dampening the rate of the current arms race and its mounting costs. While overcoming the many barriers to discussion of these issues is not likely to be possible in the near future, any hope of developing mutual Allied confidence in each other depends on working toward greater understanding in these areas than currently exists today.

These agenda items are linked to the perennial issue of conventional deterrence. Mounting credible conventional warfare strategies implies some control over nuclear expenditures and Allied co-operation in the first stages of battle. The French have been the most reluctant to join in such discussions and planning and (for well-known reasons) will almost certainly continue to resist Allied pressures to agree on joint military plans and to accept a designated Alliance role for their conventional forces. As in the past France will most likely insist on autonomy of decision, most especially in utilising its conventional forces as an instrument of its deterrence manoeuvring. While there is some evidence that the incentives for splendid isolation have slackened in French strategic circles,[52] they cannot be counted upon in the near term to overcome French reservations about any hint of automatic participation in the forward defence of Europe.

The incentives to encourage more bilateral discussions with the French and with the British are logically related to their common interest in American strategic moves and in keeping American forces in Europe as a visible and credible pledge of the American security guarantee, coupled to the American nuclear arsenal. US assistance to decrease the vulnerability of French C^3I systems may be an incentive worth manipulating to bring France to a bilateral French–American bargaining table that might well include co-operation in conventional areas on use-strategies, in sharing strategic responsibilities (tacitly or explicitly) in Europe, and even on joint development and purchase of conventional arms.

SDI is an especially significant area for inner-Allied discussions. The concerns voiced by Sir Geoffrey Howe and others, and the obvious threat posed by active defence systems to British and French nuclear forces, generate incentives for mutual discussions and bargaining over the material terms of Allied deterrence. The two-track process of INF proved too cumbersome and politically awkward to be useful in organising the Western Alliance's management of long-range missile deployments. On so complex an issue as SDI, it is clearly ill-suited as a negotiating framework. On the other hand, the Pentagon's contractual approach is too narrow to encompass the strategic and arms control problems posed by SDI. It is also potentially defective as a response to European concerns about maintaining pace with the United States and Japan in technological development and in the competition for world markets.

Unless adroitly managed, the US offer of contracts to European firms for SDI could boomerang and be a source of conflict rather than co-operation. While European governments are tempted by the prospect that their firms will receive orders, they are also concerned about the implications of the SDI programme for their economies.

Since the Department of Defense will hold patent rights on SDI work, European firms may be denied permission to sell or licence techniques and marketable products that they may have developed through SDI contracts. US permission to transfer technology (especially in sensitive security areas) has been restrictive in the past, evidenced by US–European controversies over the sale of computers and oil pipeline contracts with the Soviet Union as well as the provision of atomic fuels and services. If contracts are won by European firms, they may be contributing their strengths to US firms while receiving little in return. The brain drain of scientists and technicians might be stemmed but at the expense conceivably of distorting European priorities.[53] There may, on the other hand, be much ado about little if European firms fail to compete with their American counterparts for SDI contracts.

CONCLUSIONS

The growing interdependence and multilateralisation of nuclear deterrence are permanent parts of the strategic landscape surrounding the decision-making of the Western nuclear powers and the Soviet Union. To meet the Soviet threat and to ensure a stable nuclear balance between East and West, the Western nuclear powers have an incentive to develop the coherence, cohesion, and mutual confidence required to meet the test of stable deterrence. These needs offset the dubious value of uncertainty created in the minds of Soviet planners by the decentralisation of the Western nuclear systems. The uncertainty generated within the Alliance by the growth of offensive nuclear systems and subsequent doubts about the reliability of nuclear armed Allies when they are most needed do not appear to compensate for the putative benefits of keeping Soviet planners guessing.

The SDI proposal – unless carefully managed and orchestrated in the West – risks straining to a breaking point the structural problems that already mark Allied strategic relations. Given the economic and technological implications of strategic nuclear modernisation, the Geneva talks do not appear wide and deep enough to contain the powerful forces and interests at play within the Atlantic Alliance. Nor does the Reagan administration's contractual approach address these issues. The Western states must address their problems on a scale commensurate with their dimensions. A process of complex bilateralism offers some promise of partially reconciling (if not resolving) continuing assertions of national autonomy with the imperatives of multilateral deterrence and the imperatives of economic and technological interdependence and co-operation. Such an approach adds new dimensions and flexibility to NATO consultations, witnessed by France's decision to join in NATO, conventional arms talks with the Soviet bloc, and is consistent with proposals (emanating from Paris and most recently from London)[54] to revitalise the West European Union as a vehicle for European consultations.

Notes

1. See the analysis of Don Oberdorfer, *International Herald Tribune*, 18 February 1987.
2. Mikhail Gorbachev, *For a Nuclear-Free World: Speeches and Statements by the General Secretary of the CPSU Central Committee on Nuclear Disarmament Problems* (Moscow: Novosti Press, 1987) pp. 7–22.
3. Whether the Warsaw Pact is actually superior in conventional and theatre nuclear weapons or whether that superiority (if real) is sufficient to tempt Soviet planners to attack NATO are hotly disputed propositions; see the essays in this volume on the issue. Also consult an earlier but still relevant theoretical work by John J. Mearsheimer, *Conventional Deterrence* (Ithaca: Cornell University Press, 1983).
4. 'Defence and Security in the Nuclear Age', speech of Sir Geoffrey Howe to the Royal United Services Institute (London) 15 March 1985.
5. See, for example, Ministère de la Défense, *France's Defence Policy*, Information Bulletin 69 (Paris: Service d'Information et de Relations Publiques des Armées, May 1982) *passim*.
6. US Department of Defense, *Soviet Strategic Defense Program* (Washington, DC: Government Printing Office, October 1985).
7. These points are reviewed in Christoph Bertram 'Implications of Theatre Nuclear Weapons in Europe' *Foreign Affairs*, LX, 2 (Winter 1981–2) pp. 305–26.
8. This is one of the implications of Strobe Talbott's analysis of INF in his *Deadly Gambits* (New York: Knopf, 1984).
9. *Hansard, Parliamentary Debates*, CXII, 68, pp. 35–42.
10. *The Times* (London), 2 March 1987.
11. Gorbachev, *For a Nuclear-Free World*, p. 11.
12. This view is suggested by Denis Healey. See *Hansard*, CXII, 68, pp. 47–50.
13. Speech of Sir Geoffrey Howe, 27 January 1987, before the International Institute of Strategic Studies (London) p. 20.
14. J. P. G. Freeman, *Britain's Nuclear Arms Control Policy in the Context of Anglo-American Relations, 1957–68* (London: Macmillan, 1986).

15. The evolution of American strategic thinking is detailed in Lawrence Freedman's *The Evolution of Nuclear Strategy* (London: IISS, 1983).
16. Edward A. Kolodziej, 'Nuclear Weapons in Search of a Role: Evolution of Recent American Strategic Nuclear and Arms Control Policy', in Paul R. Viotti (ed.), *Conflict and Arms Control: An Uncertain Agenda* (Boulder: Westview Press, 1986) pp. 3–23.
17. Jeffrey Richelson, 'PD-59, NSDD-13, and the Reagan Strategic Modernization Program, *The Journal of Strategic Studies*, VI 2 (June 1983) pp. 125 ff. Also relevant is Desmond Ball, *Targeting for Strategic Deterrence*, Adelphi Paper 185 (London: IISS, 1983).
18. Howe, 'Defence and Security', p. 3.
19. For an analysis of British and French thinking, see John Roper and Pierre Lellouche: John Roper, 'Les Implications pour la force de dissuasion britannique du développement des systèmes de défense automissile', in *L'Initiative de défense stratégique et la sécurité de l'Europe* (Paris: Institut Français des Relations Internationales, 1986) pp. 79–92; and Pierre Lellouche, 'La France, l'IDS, et la sécurité de l'Europe', in *Le Couple franco–allemand et la sécurité de l'Europe* (Institut Français des Relations Internationales, 1986) pp. 257–80.
20. *The Times* (London) 3 and 14 March 1987.
21. Howe, 'Defence and Security', pp. 4–11.
22. For a review of US–European policy differences in the 1970s and early 1980s, across a wide spectrum of foreign, security, and socio-economic interests, see David S. Yost, 'European Anxieties about Ballistic Missile Defense', *Washington Quarterly*, VII, 4 (Fall 1984) pp. 7–19; Manfred R. Hamm and W. Bruce Weinrod, 'The Transatlantic Politics of Strategic Defense', *Orbis*, XXIX, 4 (Winter 1986) pp. 709–34; and Edward A. Kolodziej, 'Europe: The Partial Partner', *International Security*, V, 3 (Winter 1980–81) pp. 104–31.
23. *The Times* (London) 10 December 1985.
24. Speech of George Younger, British Secretary of State for Defence, 11 March 1987 at The Royal Institute of International Affairs (London). See also the negative reaction of the Reagan administration to Labour Party proposals to eliminate Britain as a nuclear power and to end US nuclear deployments in Britain, *International Herald Tribune*, 28–29 March 1987.
26. See Howe, speech of 27 January 1987.
27. See Younger, speech of 11 March 1987 pp. 11–12; interviews London, March 1987.
28. Interviews, London, March 1987. See also *International Herald Tribune*, 19 March 1987.
29. Lellouche 'La France', p. 276.
30. *Le Monde*, 23 November 1985. For a review of French reactions in the aftermath of President Reagan's SDI speech of March 1983, see John Fenske, 'France and the Strategic Defence Initiative: Speeding Up or Putting on the Brakes?', *International Affairs* (London) LXII, 2 (Spring 1986) pp. 231–46.
31. Fenske, 'France and the Strategic Defence Initiative', p. 237.
32. Ibid; pp. 243–4. For an informed analysis of Europe's interest in SDI

contracts, see François Heisbourg, 'La dimension technologique et industrielle de l'IDS: un point de vue Européen', in *Initiative de défense stratégique et la sécurité de l'Europe,* pp. 119–32.

33. For an analysis of the problem of choosing between a long-term European solution and apparently immediate tangible economic benefits by co-operating with American firms, see Lawrence Freedman, 'The Case of Westland and the Bias to Europe', *International Affairs* (London), LXIII, 1 (Winter 1986–87) pp. 1–20.
34. Bertram summarises these parallel concerns over SDI and INF in two articles. See n. 7 above and 'Strategic defense and the Western Alliance', in Franklin Long, *et al.* (eds) *Weapons in Space* (New York: W. W. Norton, 1986) pp. 279–96. Also useful for understanding German concerns are Karl Kaiser, 'L'IDS et la politique allemande', in *Le Couple franco–allemand*, pp. 281–96, and Christoph Bluth, 'SDI: The Challenge to West Germany', *International Affairs* (London) LXII, 2 (Spring 1986) pp. 247–64.
35. Lellouche, 'La France', pp. 273–5. He is also sceptical whether these purported benefits will ever materialise.
36. Trevor Taylor reviews these issues from a British perspective reflecting European concerns. Trevor Taylor, 'Britain's response to the Strategic Defence Initiative', *International Affairs* (London) LXII, 2 (Spring 1986) pp. 217–31.
37. See the articles in Long *et al.* (eds) *Weapons in Space*, especially those by Hans Bethe *et al.* pp. 53–72; Donald Hafner, pp. 91–108; and the Appendix by Bethe and Garwin, pp. 313–50.
38. US Department of State, Bureau of Public Affairs, Paul Nitze, *The Promise of SDI*, Current Policy 810.
39. Herbert York, *Strategic Defense, from World War II to the Present* (San Diego: Institute on Global Conflict and Cooperation, 1986).
40. *International Herald Tribune*, 10 March 1987.
41. French strategic forces are sketched in Robbin Laird, 'French Nuclear Forces in the 1980s and 1990s, *Comparative Strategy*, IV, 4 (1984) pp. 387–412; David S. Yost, *France's Deterrent Posture and Security in Europe, Part I: Capabilities and Doctrine*, Adelphi Paper 194 (London: IISS, 1985) pp. 13–28; and the author's *Making and Marketing Arms: The French Experience and Its Implications for the International System* (Princeton: Princeton University Press, 1987) pp. 88–9.
42. See n. 41 above and Eric J. Grove, 'Allied Nuclear Forces Complicate Negotiations', *Bulletin of the Atomic Scientist*, XLII, 6 (June–July 1986) pp. 18–23.
43. See George Younger, Speech of 11 March 1987, pp. 15–19.
44. Grove, 'Allied Nuclear Forces', pp. 18–23.
45. See chapters by Lawrence Freedman and David S. Yost, respectively, on British and French targeting in Desmond Ball and Jeffrey Richelson (eds), *Strategic Nuclear Targeting* (Ithaca: Cornell University Press, 1987) pp. 109–26, 127–58.
46. For a review of British and French reservations, consult Eric J. Grove, *Where and When? The Integration of British and French Nuclear*

Forces with the Arms Control Process, Faraday Discussion Paper 5 (London: Council for Arms Control, 1985). Also the comments of Roy Dean, Director of the Arms Control and Disarmament Research Unit, Foreign and Commonwealth Office in *The World Today*, September 1983, pp. 319–22, and Charles Hernu, 'Equilibre, dissuasion, volonté: la voie étroite de la paix et de la liberté, *Défense Nationale*, December 1983, p. 15.

47. See David S. Yost, *Deterrent Posture and Security in Europe, Part II: Strategic and Arms Control Implications*, Adelphi Paper 195 (London: IISS, 1985).
48. *The Times* (London) 3 March 1987. Moscow has also attacked British plans to build Trident with D-5 missiles: *The Times* (London) 14 March 1987.
49. See *The Times* (London) 2–7 March 1987 and *Le Monde*, 2–5 March 1987. See also the rigid stance assumed by Raymond Barre in resisting the Soviet INF proposal and the exacting conditions that would have to be met before France would participate in disarmament talks on nuclear weapons: Speech delivered at the International Institute for Strategic Studies, 26 March 1987.
50. George M. Seignious II and Jonathan Paul Yates, 'Europe's Nuclear Superpowers', *Foreign Policy*, 55 (Summer 1984) pp. 40–53.
51. In the French case, see the author's *French International Policy under De Gaulle and Pompidou: The Politics of Grandeur* (Ithaca: Cornell University Press, 1974) Chapter 2.
52. Robert S. Rudney, 'Mitterrand's New Atlanticism: Evolving French Attitudes toward NATO', *Orbis*, XXVIII 1 (Spring 1984) pp. 83–101; interviews, London, February–March, 1987.
53. These concerns are discussed by David Greenwood, '*The SDI and Europe*' Aberdeen Studies in Defence Economics (ASIDES) 26, Autumn (1985); Konrad Seitz, 'SDI: The Technological Challenge for Europe', *The World Today*, (August–September 1985) pp. 154–7; and Taylor, 'Britain's response'.
54. *New York Times*, 12 June 1987 and speech of Sir Geoffrey Howe before The Royal Institute of International Relations, 16 March 1987.

3 Coupling and Decoupling: The Prospects for Extended Deterrence

Earl C. Ravenal

Thirty-eight years after the foundation of NATO, the defence of Western Europe still rests on the proposition that an American president will invite the destruction of US cities and the incineration of 100 million of its citizens to repel a Soviet incursion or resist a Soviet ultimatum in Western Europe. On its face, America's war plan – never denied by any president from Truman to Reagan, or by any Secretary of State from George Marshall to George Shultz – is the first use of nuclear weapons, if necessary, to defend Europe. Thus America threatens to turn local defeat into global holocaust. But, under the surface, America's nuclear commitment to Europe is not so sure. The word that encapsulates this problem is 'coupling'. Not the title of an Updike novel or an anthropological treatise by Margaret Mead, coupling is a term of art used by strategic analysts to connote the integrity of the chain of escalation, from conventional war in Europe, to theatre nuclear weapons, to the final use of America's ultimate strategic weapon.

In a larger sense coupling connotes the identity of the fates of the peoples, societies, and political systems on both sides of the Atlantic. The root of the problem is that America, the alliance guarantor, hoping to escape the destruction of nuclear war, will seek to put time between the outbreak of war in Europe and the decision to escalate to nuclear weapons, and will take whatever advantage it can of its distance from Europe. Not that an adversary is likely to test American will with an attack on Europe. Odds of, say, 65 per cent that America will respond with nuclear weapons will restrain a potential aggressor. (Even a whiff of American nuclear retaliation is probably enough to keep the Soviet Union from invading Western Europe.) But those odds will not convince allies of their protection. And the real efficacy of extended deterrence is in keeping allies, not just deterring adversaries. There is a nagging asymmetry about nuclear protection: it takes more credibility to keep an ally than to deter an adversary.

Whether America will fight for Europe, or whether it will in some way use the territorial depth of Europe as a buffer, is not a subject of polite conversation between Americans and Europeans. But decoupling from Europe is America's 'secret' strategy. Not, of course, in the sense that our leaders are keeping it a secret, but rather because strategy (somewhat like 'policy') consists of what a nation – a complex political–social system – will do at the time that strategy must be invoked, not what its leaders profess or prefer, or even what they might have 'planned' to do.

Europeans already suspect this. Virtually every American strategic move – up, down, or sideways – has evoked the spectre of decoupling in one or another of its forms: either the avoidance of a nuclear response altogether or the attempt to confine even a nuclear conflict to the European theatre. This is not something that began suddenly when President Reagan said: 'I could see where you could have the exchange of tactical weapons against troops in the field without it bringing either one of the major powers to pushing the button.'[1] The doubts had been sown long before that, in a series of American moves: the MLF; the emphasis on flexible response and conventional defence by the Kennedy–McNamara administration; the Schlesinger doctrine of 1974, which contemplated the selective use of the American strategic nuclear force; the interest in 'mini-nukes', including such variants as the 'neutron bomb'; and even the introduction of intermediate-range nuclear weapons, such as the Pershing II and the ground-launched cruise missiles. Though these may enhance coupling by perfecting the essential link of theatre nuclear weapons, they may also allow the restriction of nuclear conflict to Europe.

More recently, President Reagan's 'Star Wars', a design to protect American society from Soviet missiles, has stirred European concern that the United States could afford a 'Fortress America' mentality and ignore forward defence in Europe. (Indeed, the course of the strategic bargaining at the Reykjavik Summit in October 1986 confirmed this impression.[2]) And, finally, America's current attempt to endow NATO with 'emerging technology' has had the significance, to some Europeans, of further detaching the United States from its commitment to escalate to nuclear weapons, specifically by promising conventional coverage of some targets that now require nuclear systems.

At issue here is not whether these American strategic moves are well planned or well meant, but whether they have the effect of attenuating the American connection with Europe; whether they provide reasons, or even pretexts, for the United States to make its escalation to strategic nuclear weapons less than prompt and automatic; whether they give the United States additional buffers or 'firebreaks' (a firebreak is any device, strategy, or doctrine that makes escalation to nuclear weapons less than prompt and automatic). Coupling and firebreaks are inversely related. Coupling, across geography and between levels of warfare, is the essence of alliance protection in a nuclear age, but it contradicts the introduction of firebreaks. Firebreaks are an imperative of our security in an era of nuclear parity, but they impair alliance protection. This is more than a simple antithesis; it has the aspect of a paradox, since the enhancement of any level of military recourse can be regarded alternatively as a link to higher levels of escalation and as a self-contained effort. Improved conventional defence can postpone nuclear escalation and widen the firebreak between conventional war and nuclear war. On the other hand, earlier resort to discrete and controlled tactical nuclear weapons invokes the spectre of limiting even a nuclear war to European territory, creating yet another firebreak, this one between theatre and total nuclear war.

Henry Kissinger was clear and prescient about these matters when he addressed a private gathering of American and European strategists in Brussels in September 1979. In a remark that has since gained wide currency, he permitted himself some pessimistic reflections on the validity of the American nuclear guarantee:

> Perhaps even today, but surely in the 1980s, the United States will no longer be in a strategic position to reduce a Soviet counterblow against the United States to tolerable levels. . . . If my analysis is correct, we must face the fact that it is absurd to base the strategy of the West on the credibility of the threat of mutual suicide. . . . And therefore, I would say, which I might not say in office, that European allies should not keep asking us to multiply strategic assurances that we cannot possibly mean or if we do mean, we should not want to execute because if we execute, we risk the destruction of civilization.[3]

Kissinger's remarks should not have been surprising. Fourteen years earlier, he had pointed out that the disabilities of NATO are not peculiar; they afflict all alliances of sovereign nations. Kissinger discovered virtually a law of alliance: the contradiction of military effectiveness and political sovereignty.

> There is an increasing inconsistency between the technical requirements of strategy and political imperatives of the nation-states. . . . The dilemma arises because there is no scheme which can reconcile these objectives perfectly so long as the Atlantic Alliance remains composed of sovereign states.[4]

Nuclear weapons do not resolve this contradiction; they heighten it. Once they have spread beyond the monopoly of one nation, they corrode trust and dissolve the bonds of alliance.

The American guarantee to defend Western Europe carries with it the heightened risk of nuclear war. America's commitment to NATO can scarcely be evaluated without plumbing at least two aspects of nuclear risk: 1. the progressive dominance of counterforce, and 2. various attempts to mitigate the possible nuclear destruction of the United States.

America's drift to a counterforce nuclear strategy is neither perverse nor accidental. Counterforce means the use of some fraction of our strategic nuclear force to attack a portion of the enemy's target system consisting of military installations, logistical complexes, command bunkers, and – to put the most important item last – missiles in their silos. In turn, it entails the acquisition of 'hard target kill capability'. To grasp the rationale of counterforce, it is necessary to understand the logic of extended deterrence. Ultimately, it is adherence to alliance commitments that skews our strategy toward counterforce weapons and targeting and warps our doctrines of response toward the first use of nuclear weapons, prejudicing 'crisis stability' and increasing the danger of escalation to nuclear war.[5] The compelling motive for counterforce is damage limitation – that is, limiting the damage to the United States in a nuclear war. Part of that intent would be to strike Soviet missiles in silos (and, perhaps, also Soviet command bunkers and control and communication facilities). Such a damage-limiting attack, to have its intended effect, must be preemptive. Indeed, counterforce and first nuclear strike are mutually dependent. A first strike implies counterforce targeting, since the only initial attack that makes sense is a damage-limiting strike, the destruction of as much of the enemy's nuclear force as possible. In return, counterforce targeting implies a first strike, a preemptive attack, because a second strike against the enemy's missiles is useless to the extent that one's missiles would hit empty holes.

Any strategic policy will try to protect certain values that are at the core of US national identity and sovereignty. These values include political integrity and autonomy and the safety and domestic property of the American people. These are the proper – and largely feasible – objects of American defence or deterrence. It is when the US attempts to protect more than these objects with its strategic nuclear force that we court the peculiar problems of *extended* deterrence. Then the calculus of credibility that is made with regard to strict central deterrence does not hold. The assumptions of deterrence apply to peripheral areas and less-than-vital interests with much less strength and validity.

As it happens, US protection of Western Europe requires *both* initial conventional defence and credible extended deterrence. One cannot be substituted entirely for the other. Extended deterrence, in turn, requires the practical invulnerability of American *society* to Soviet attack. (This is not to be confused with the invulnerability of its nuclear weapons.) I say 'practical' invulnerability, since absolute invulnerability is beyond America's, or anyone's, reach. Rather, what is required is the ability to limit damage to 'tolerable' levels of casualties and destruction. This is so an American president can persuade others that he would risk an attack on his homeland, or that he could face down a threat to attack that homeland, in the act of spreading America's protective mantle over Western Europe and other parts of the world.

To attain the requisite societal invulnerability, the United States would have to work through both its defensive and its offensive strategic systems. First, we would have to achieve a strategic defence. And this might cost from half a trillion to a trillion dollars, over perhaps, fifteen years, if we were to go about it seriously, not just symbolically.[6] As a second condition of societal invulnerability, we must be able to hold in reserve, after any of the earlier stages of a protracted nuclear exchange, enough destructive power to threaten counter-city strikes. Finally, a significant requisite of societal invulnerability is the acquisition of a nuclear counterforce capability, specifically hard target kill.

Counterforce 'makes sense', then, as an attempt to fulfill some of the requisite conditions of damage limitation or societal invulnerability, and, in turn, of extended deterrence – but, it is fair to say, *only* as such. Thus, US willingness to protect its allies rises and falls generally with its ability to protect its society from nuclear attack, and, more specifically, with the prospective viability of counterforce. If there is any explicit doubt – technical, economic, political – that the US will achieve that invulnerability, or that it should pursue counterforce, then, to that extent, there is implicit doubt that its extensive nuclear commitments, especially to Western Europe, can survive.

What emerges from this analysis is that the attempt to implement extended deterrence – to defend, say, Western Europe efficiently and thoroughly by substituting the threat of nuclear weapons for the conventional defence of the theatre – requires conditions which, if they can be fulfilled at all, are expensive or dangerous or counterproductive.

In order to diminish the risk that stems from US extended deterrence in Europe, arguments have been made against the first use of nuclear weapons. The most notable statement in recent times has been the article by McGeorge Bundy, George F. Kennan, Robert S. McNamara, and Gerard Smith, 'Nuclear Weapons and the Atlantic Alliance'.[7] The latter article is classic, not only in its exposition but also in the problems it incurs in its premises and argument.

Its principal problem is that it insists on maintaining the integrity of the American commitment to the defence of its Western European allies; and yet it seeks to obviate the risk, to the United States, of destruction in a nuclear war. If one is committed, as are Bundy and his fellow authors, both to defend Europe and to avoid the extension of conflict to the American homeland, one must try to reconcile these awkward objectives. Thus, crucial in the Bundy–Kennan–McNamara–Smith proposal is that its apparent renunciation of the first use of nuclear weapons is conditioned on the acquisition of an adequate conventional defence. But those who opt reflexively for conventional defence cannot mean just any conventional effort. They must mean the *high confidence* defence of Europe with conventional arms. And they cannot just exhort or prescribe that the United States and its allies 'must' do more to guarantee the integrity of Western Europe; they have the further burden of *predicting* that this will happen.

In order to determine the feasibility – and hence the predictive probability – of the conventional defence option, we must have a bill of costs. But seldom – nowhere in the Bundy article – is that bill set forth. What would the conventional option in Europe cost the United States? One must look first at what the US is already spending.

In terms of forces, I judge (from an analysis of Secretary of Defence Caspar W. Weinberger's 'Posture Statement' for FY 1987 that the Reagan administration intends the following regional attribution of our total of 21 active ground divisions: NATO/Europe, 11⅔ divisions, East Asia, 3⅔ divisions; Other Regions and the Strategic Reserve, 5⅔ divisions. By applying these fractions to the total cost of US general purpose forces, $240 billion, we can calculate the rough cost of the three regional commitments. By my estimates, Europe accounts for $133 billion, Asia absorbs $42 billion, and the Strategic Reserve, including an expanded requirement for Rapid Deployment Forces, mostly for CENTCOM – that is, the Persian Gulf and Southwest Asia – takes $65 billion. One hastens to point out that the commander-in-chief of a given unified or allied command does not see all those costs. The American forces that he commands are just the tip of the iceberg; most of the costs involve support units and Pentagon overhead. The money is spent in the United States, but it is attributable to the commitment to defend each specified region.[8]

The present American share of the conventional defence of Europe – and this is not even designed to be a self-contained conventional defence – is about $133 billion for FY 1987. This is 42.5 per cent of the $312 billion originally requested for defence by the Reagan administration. Given a reasonable projection of current cost growth, over the next ten years Europe will cost the United States $1.8 trillion. (It may be of some interest to compare this with the fact that, over the 38 prior years of its existence, the cost of NATO to the United States has been roughly $1.6 to 2 trillion. Each year, NATO-related costs have been between 40 and 50 per cent of the US defence budget.) The appropriate question is whether even those resources will be forthcoming, let alone the greater ones required for self-sufficient conventional defence.[9]

Indeed, if the United States were to set for itself, and its allies, the task of providing a confident conventional defence against Soviet arms, principally on the central front of Europe, the costs of this, in terms of American defence spending, would be far higher than most proponents of conventional defence are willing to concede. The exceptional estimate of the entailed costs, in necessarily rough terms, has been given by Leonard Sullivan, Jr: 'Expanding our conventional forces by 20% over the next 10 years to offset the numerically, qualitatively, and geographically expanding threat requires that defense outlays rise . . . to 9½% of the GNP . . . (about ½% more in TOA [Total Obligational Authority]).[10] That 10 per cent, applied to the approximate 1987 GNP of $4.43 trillion, would mean a defence budget authorisation of $443 billion, not the $312 billion requested. The defence of NATO in 1987 would cost $188 billion instead of $133 billion.

Comparing the relative burdens of the United States and its allies is not the point, and so even adjusting these burdens would not be the solution. The question has always been whether the United States is getting its own money's worth out of its forward strategy, and would be getting its money's worth even after some putative redistribution of burdens. Inevitably, we are thrown back on the economy of alliance. There are several ways of formulating this equation, or inequality. It may be that the actual costs of our preparations to support and implement the alliance exceed our gains, including as gains the benefits we derive from the contributions of allies. It may also be that, in the calculus of a possible war, the losses we would sustain through not defending forward are less than those we would incur through defending forward, even if successfully (and the value of both outcomes must be cut by their fractional probability, which is far less than certainty), plus the real costs we would have sustained in preparing to defend in that way. And, in the encompassing calculus of deterrence, the future losses we might sustain by not even deterring attack or coercion against forward countries, reduced by the very low probability that such would occur because we failed to deter, might be less than the cumulative costs of deterrence. If we are assessing bargains, those more comprehensive and more complex calculations are the appropriate ones.

To mitigate the heavy costs of troop deployment, some have proposed the unilateral withdrawal of part of the American forces in Europe.[11] The salient version of this approach was the Mansfield Amendment or Resolution, offered in Congress for eight years until 1975. This proposal, in its various forms, would have reduced American troops in Europe by as much as two-thirds, redeploying them to the United States but not (in all but one year's version) deleting them from the active force structure. But withdrawal of units saves nothing unless they are also deactivated. Nor would the Mansfield proposal have touched the forces kept in the United States *for* European contingencies. (Forces the United States keeps *in* Europe are only about one-third of the forces it maintains for the support of NATO.) Thus it would have made only a small dent in the amount, $133 billion for 1987, that the US spends anually for the defence of Europe. Most significantly, the American commitment to

European defence would remain in full force. This is not a virtue but a flaw; the Mansfield type of initiative represents withdrawal without decommitment, a precarious stance.

Most versions of troop withdrawal are more trivial, some merely symbolic. An example was the amendment sponsored, in the fall of 1982, by Senator Ted Stevens (R-Alaska), Chairman of the Senate Appropriations Subcommittee on Defence, that would have lowered the ceiling on US deployments in Europe in such a way as to return some 23 000 troops to the United States. Of course, as Morton H. Halperin said, in rebuttal,[12] it is cheaper to keep US troops in Europe. But that is not the end of the debate. Cheaper than what? Certainly it is cheaper than keeping the US defensive commitment and just relocating forces to the United States, providing even more prepositioned equipment in Europe and more airlift and sealift to return forces there at the first sign of trouble. But it is not cheaper than absolving the US of the commitment, disbanding most of the forces it devotes to European defence, and also saving the tactical air and surface naval units that go along with it. If the US were to adopt such a non-protective attitude toward Europe, over a decade of progressive disengagement it could save almost 50 per cent of the $1.8 trillion it is now committed to spend on NATO, and, at the end of that decade, it would be spending 70 per cent less than it will if it keeps on the present course.

A thorough and consistent disengagement from Europe would shed the responsibilities as well as the burdens of alliance. The United States would devolve defensive tasks upon the European states, but not insist on the orderly and sufficient substitution of capabilities or harbour illusions of maintaining American political weight in European decision making. The US would establish a measured and deliberate pace of disengagement and would maintain constructive consultation at all stages. Withdrawal from Europe would probably take a decade of preparation, diplomacy, and logistical rearrangement. But those are modalities, however important they may be. They would not alter the objective of scaling down American forces and setting temporal bounds on the US commitment to European defence. The US would progressively reduce Europe's strategic dependence on it, and insulate itself from the consequences of conflict in Europe.

Most NATO loyalists mistake this criticism. One does not have to *urge* the dissolution of NATO, certainly not its instant and formal abrogation. NATO is an alliance that is less dependable year by year, as objective changes in circumstances erode the validity of the essential condition of the alliance: the American guarantee. Conversely, the loyalists should not take as compelling proof of the perpetual durability of the alliance the fact that something called 'NATO' has not been formally repudiated. NATO can dissolve without a scrap of paper being torn up, without a journalist reporting it. NATO need not even perish in acrimony. It can expire in scepticism. The strategic content of the alliance can drain away, measured by the confidence allies repose in the ritual American commitment, and by the hedges they erect against the guarantees the alliance still pretends to offer. NATO need not lose its form, at least until long after it has lost its substance.

Perhaps the situation can be summed up in a metaphor: NATO, after 39 years, is an old unused medicine on the shelf. The bottle is still there and the label remains the same; but, if you ever try it, you find that the contents have long since evaporated or spoiled.

Notes

1. Interview with out-of-town editors at the White House, 1 October 1981. (Bernard Gwertzman, 'President Says U.S. Should Not Waver in Backing Saudis', *The New York Times*, 18 October 1981.)
2. See Earl C. Ravenal, 'The Ironies of Reykjavik', *Viewpoint, The Miami Herald*, 19 October 1986.
3. Quoted in Kenneth A. Myers (ed.), *NATO: The Next Thirty Years* (Boulder, Colo.: Westview Press, 1980).
4. *The Troubled Partnership: A Re-Appraisal of the Atlantic Alliance* (New York: McGraw-Hill, 1965).
5. An extended treatment of counterforce and alliance, their logic, and their relation, is presented in Earl C. Ravenal, 'Counterforce and Alliance: The Ultimate Connection', *International Security*, Spring 1982.
6. Strategic defence alone is not likely to succeed in providing sufficient damage limitation for American society, even at the 'practical' level. It will, therefore, probably have to be accompanied by the second condition (a reserve of offensive missiles) and the third condition (counter-force, a hard target kill capability). Thus, the conditional need for counter-force, with all its liabilities, is not eliminated by the attempt to devise strategic defence. Counter-force will always be thought to be necessary to buttress strategic defence. And, conversely, strategic defence will be thought to make it safer for us to initiate a counter-force attack.
7. *Foreign Affairs*, Spring 1982.

8. A more ample explanatory section appears in Earl C. Ravenal, *Defining Defense: The 1985 Defense Budget* (Washington, D.C.: Cato Institute, 1984).
9. Proposals have been advanced for the relatively inexpensive non-nuclear defence of Europe. The list is quite long. Among them is the proposal of Barnaby and Boeker, in this volume: 'Non-Nuclear Defence for Europe'. Such proposals promise relatively low-cost defence, sometimes through reliance on new technologies, more often through extensive static defence or light mobile anti-tank teams or those measures as a shield for the mobilisation of trained reserves. The problem does not lie in the proposals themselves. Most are intelligent, many promising, but usually only in combination with moves that NATO has already made, or is about to make, or should make, in more 'conventional-conventional' dimensions – such moves as enhancing its ability to counter-attack with heavy armour.

   Thus, the first objection to proposals of 'alternative defence' is that they would not save much, if anything. Second, if taken alone, they would not constitute a sufficiently reliable defensive shield – that is, *for the United States*. And that raises the question that constantly underlies my own exposition: sufficient *for whom*? Barnaby's and Boeker's proposal might be feasible for a Western Europe, or a West Germany, that had to fight alone because the United States was no longer associated with its defence. Indeed, such an alternative defence might be *necessary* for such a Western Europe or West Germany. But it is not robust enough to attract the support of the United States, if it is to remain in the alliance and to remain committed to the forward defence of West Germany.

   Indeed, such a proposal of alternative defence inspires a mini-paradox: if it is not feasible, then why should the United States implicate itself in such an invitation to disaster? But, if it is feasible, then Western Europe – even West Germany by itself – might be able to accomplish its own defence, without the United States.

   In short, proposals for more intelligent conventional defence almost treat the problem of *United States* participation as accidental. On the contrary, I regard the problem as essential to the alliance, and certainly – by tautology – essential to the question of American security. *As long as* the United States is required to provide its guarantee for Europe, it assumes a high degree of risk and a large measure of cost. The risk (mostly the nuclear component) can be, to some extent, traded off against some increment of cost (mostly associated with conventional forces). But 1. not entirely; and 2. even so, not at a cost that would be acceptable to American society; and 3. ironically, precisely if conventional defence were successfully provided, with the ultimate result of *de*coupling the United States from Europe.

   In order to exorcise nuclear risk for the United States, it would be necessary to banish entirely, from American calculations, the consideration of escalation to nuclear war. To do this, we must have *high confidence* – a virtual guarantee – of successful self-sufficient conventional defence against any possible type and weight of Soviet attack. And we must be able to *predict*, not merely prescribe – let alone exhort – that such a degree of conventional defence will be achieved. This is a set of formidable – probably insuperable – conditions.

10. 'The FY84 Defense Debate: Defeat by Default', *Armed Forces Journal International*, May 1983.

11. There are also, of course, proposals that rest on the prospect of *mutual* reductions of arms by NATO and the Warsaw Pact (such proposals as that of Ambassador Dean in this volume). The ongoing effort is Mutual and Balanced Force Reductions (MBFR), a negotiated thinning-out of NATO and Warsaw Pact forces in Central Europe. Through five administrations, since the talks were endorsed by NATO in 1968 and initiated in Vienna in 1973, the prognosis for substantive agreement has remained dim. The approaches of the two sides have been incompatible. Essentially, NATO has insisted on unequal cuts, resulting in balanced opposing forces; the Warsaw Pact has insisted on equal cuts, resulting in unbalanced opposing forces. In June 1978, the Soviets apparently broke with their prior position and offered to set equal ceilings on the residual forces of each side (700 000 on ground forces and 900 000 on ground and air combined). They were also willing to let the United States leave equipment in Europe when withdrawing troops. But the subsequent history of the Vienna talks could engender scepticism, both about the validity of the Soviet concession and about NATO's real intentions. For NATO immediately countered the Soviet offer by discovering or inventing the 'data problem' concerning Warsaw Pact ground forces in the area. The Soviets are unwilling to share intelligence about the starting figure, and Soviet admissions and NATO estimates differ by about 180 000. (The Soviet figure is 805 000; NATO's is between 950 000 and 1 000 000.) The data problem has persisted for nine years, though in March 1984 the United States offered to relax somewhat its method of counting troops and units. It is also not clear whether the Soviets are yielding on their prior insistence on separate national troop ceilings, a device to limit the expansion of the West German army. Moreover, it still appears that mutual force reductions will be defeated by the basic asymmetries of geography – the relative distances over which Soviet and American units would have to be reintroduced – and by the incommensurate types and functions of forces.

    Above all, even the most dedicated proponents of MBFR do not hope for significant cost savings (rather they stress stability and net security). In their view, NATO's considerable drive for arms enhancement and modernisation would have to go forward. The force cuts they envisage are not impressive (see, for example, Jonathan Dean, 'Beyond First Use', *Foreign Policy*, Fall 1982), and even with mutual conventional force reduction, America's commitment to Europe, its forces for Europe, and its annual budgetary costs on account of Europe would remain in their present range.

12. 'Keeping Our Troops in Europe', *The New York Times Magazine*, 17 October 1982.

Part II

'No First Use' of Nuclear Weapons in Europe

4 No First Use of Nuclear Weapons

John Marshall Lee

At present, nuclear weapons are considered legitimate, if terrible, weapons, usable as other weapons are for national purposes. In the West and in the East, strategy, military forces, readiness posture, all are based fundamentally on the threat and, ultimately, the use of nuclear weapons.

In the West this threat is directed not only against a nuclear attack against the US or its allies, but also against conventional, non-nuclear operations beyond our ability to hold. The term for such nuclear deterrence of non-nuclear hostilities is 'extended' deterrence. It has been at the heart of US and NATO policy for a generation.

In the East, the Soviet Union has declared a policy of No First Use of nuclear weapons, a declaration, that is to say, that they would not be the first to use nuclear weapons in any future hostilities, that they would fire them only in retaliation against *nuclear* attack. To make that declaration a sure control over Soviet and Warsaw Pact decisions and actions in crisis, however, and to make it so convincing to others that they can, cautiously, rely on it, the governmental announcement of the No First Use must be supplemented by a host of implementing and indoctrinating measures that are yet to be taken. Nuclear preemption, first use, has not yet by any means been eliminated from Soviet doctrine, force structures and weapons programmes.

Such reliance upon nuclear deterrence of and nuclear firing against conventional operations will result, with high probability, sooner or later, in the unimaginable catastrophe of general nuclear war. We should, therefore, ideally on both sides, give up extended deterrence and nuclear preemption, and depend on conventional forces, reserving nuclear weapons for retaliation against nuclear attack and no other purpose. A policy of No First Use, then, together with the whole range of measures needed to make that policy effective, is our best hope for survival, in East and in West.

Extended deterrence uses the nuclear threat to prevent war of all types, including nuclear. Even conventional war would be terrible, perhaps especially in Europe. The nuclear threat, even if irrational, is a powerful deterrent. What is wrong with using that deterrent power for conventional as well as nuclear peace?

In brief, extended deterrence has these dangerous defects:

- it makes it highly probable that any East–West hostilities would become nuclear;
- it leads to limited nuclear war strategies which would be militarily useless and almost irresistably escalatory;
- by continuously threatening absolute destruction, it perpetuates mortal hostility;
- almost surely, sooner or later, in one crisis or another, it will fail.

In sum, extended deterrence uses the nuclear threat to reduce the risk of conventional war only by accepting substantially increased risk of nuclear war. Preventing the appalling catastrophe of nuclear war must be our primary objective. Conventional deterrence and defence must be provided by conventional means.

What follows expands on these points.

The overriding danger of nuclear deterrence of conventional war is that it raises to near certainty the probability that any East–West war would be, or would quickly become, nuclear. Extended deterrence takes the position that nuclears are legitimate weapons, available for use as other weapons are in case of national need. This concept irresistably nuclearises the armed forces and the security apparatus. In crisis or in hostilities, the nuclear forces will be at instant, hair-trigger readiness, pressing against the control limitations. Both sides will be at the highest pitch of fear that the other is about to strike nuclearly. In case of conventional reverses, there will be immediate demands for nuclear release, and reverses are always expected and feared: every front-line soldier feels his flanks are weak and falling back. General Rogers, SACEUR, is reported to have recently told the NATO Council that he would send them a preliminary release warning – a stand-by – shortly after hostilities started, followed by another alerter a little later, in order to have them instantly ready when his action request arrived. Escalating to the nuclear level thus becomes a normal, doctrinal response in conventional defence. The forces are armed, trained and indoctrinated for it. The pressures to go nuclear, in any difficult situation, would be overwhelming.

Can nuclear weapons be effectively used in defence?

First, virtually everyone agrees that a major, all-out, full-scale nuclear exchange would be an unimaginable catastrophe. This would not merely be conventional war writ large – another step in the long, sad history of human hostilities. There has been a break in continuity; we face a new phenomenon. The levels of death and destruction would be enormously beyond the experience of past wars. The nuclear weapon is too powerful, the fabric of human civilisation too fragile, the global eco-system perhaps too vulnerable, to withstand an all-out exchange. The nuclear winter studies suggest the possibility of the ending of human life. But even without the nuclear winter effect, the dead in a general exchange would be numbered in the hundreds of millions, and the sick and wounded in equally fantastic numbers. The physical destruction would obliterate the fabrics and cultures of the targetted nations. The survivors – probably, as they say, envying the dead – would be reduced to a primitive existence in a poisoned land. It would be an apocalyptic horror, altogether unprecedented in human history.

Here there is little disagreement. All-out, general nuclear war is not defence. But is there hope of successful and survivable nuclear operations in concepts of limited, controlled nuclear war? There are really, here, two questions:

1. Can limited nuclear operations do any military good?
2. Can they be *kept* limited, once started?

Taking them in order, first, can nuclear attacks – under any circumstances whatever – improve the military situation? Would starting the use of nuclears ever make sense, even in the coldest, most ruthless military terms?

What kind of operation is possible?

The most common scenario is a Soviet conventional attack into Central Europe, which breaks through NATO's conventional defences. NATO, as the phrase goes, is 'forced' to use nuclear weapons. To effectively break up that massive attack, NATO will need nuclear weapons certainly in hundreds, probably in thousands – three, four, perhaps five thousand. The Warsaw Pact, of course, responds with nuclear weapons. Presumably, under their existing doctrines as currently understood, they would target at first priority NATO's nuclear resources in the theatre – in Germany, England, the Low Countries, France, Italy – and at second priority the NATO war structures, lines of communications, seaports. There would be dead in millions, wounded and sick in additional millions, enormous material damage, loss of organised control of military forces and governmental agencies – in general: chaos. Chaos in a deep battle theatre on both sides.

It is, then, probably possible to wreck a conventional attack into Central Europe by using nuclear weapons on a large scale, accepting staggering human loss and material destruction. The problem is that wrecking the conventional attack with nuclear weapons simultaneously makes the conventional battle irrelevant. The war becomes a nuclear war, where the issue, the only significant issue, is not victory or defeat but survival. To the extent it is under any control, it will consist only of manipulating the approach of ultimate catastrophe. Our Allies are not defended; they are only destroyed. Most probably, the nuclear war escalates to the horror of an unlimited strategic exchange.

Using nuclears to support a failing conventional defence, then, merely adds a nuclear disaster to conventional reverse, and creates a prohibitively high risk of unlimited escalation and global catastrophe. It does no military good whatever.

There are other limited nuclear uses that have been – indeed are being – considered. These are so-called 'war-fighting' targets, designed to produce military advantage without necessarily inciting an all-out response, for example: counterforce attack on missile silos, strikes on command and control centers, on transportation, power, petroleum systems, 'decapitating' attacks. These plans suffer from the same defect. They would accomplish nothing. After any or all of them had been executed there would be great death and destruction. There would be probably uncontrollable pressure for unlimited escalation. But the essential military reality would be exactly as it had been. Each side would still be able to destroy the other. Neither could force the other into submission. Each side, in other words, would still be dependent on the other for literal survival. No rational end would have been accomplished.

Nuclear weapons, actually fired, are of no military use. None.

Our second question: can nuclear war, once started, be controlled, be limited? Could a nuclear exchange in fact be held to the detonation of tens or hundreds of nuclear weapons, even though each side would have thousands available for use and still be capable of destroying the other?

Almost certainly not. For limited nuclear war to remain limited – to stop, that is, short of complete catastrophe – the two sides would have to work in parallel. They would have to do so with different information, different weapons and controls, different operational concepts and plans and mechanisms, under appalling pressure of event and time, with diametrically opposed objectives, with the continued existence of both nations literally in the balance. Right in the middle of substantial nuclear exchanges and the resulting death, destruction, chaos and loss of control of parts or all of the forces, they would have to work out and put into effect mutually tolerable operational limits – mutually accepted and observed limits, that is, on the kinds of weapons they used and the kinds and locations of targets they fired at. Further, and this is even less conceivable, still in mid-exchange, still under intolerable stress, still with decisive time intervals measured in minutes, they would have to arrive somehow at an agreed outcome, a stopping point short of the ultimate exchange.

It can't be done. Robert McNamara has studied nuclear problems for over three decades. As Secretary of Defense under two presidents, he felt and observed intimately for seven years the pressures and realities of nuclear responsibility. He was driven to this conclusion: 'It is inconceivable to me, as it has been to others who have studied the matter, that "limited" nuclear wars would remain limited – any decision to use nuclear weapons would imply a high probability of the same cataclysmic consequences as a total nuclear exchange.'[1]

Desmond Ball is crisper. Controlled nuclear war, he says, is a 'chimera'.[2]

No one has devised convincing plans for using nuclear weapons which would be to our advantage. No one has devised plans for bringing nuclear exchange, once started, to an end. In short, any firing of nuclear weapons, however limited, is fundamentally futile, and has a prohibitively high probability of producing unimaginable catastrophe for the US, for the Soviet Union, for the allies of both, and for the human race. Launching even a limited attack, from either side, would be mutually suicidal, a monstrous and irrational act.

Of course the key objective is not nuclear victory; it is deterrence – prevention. Is it the existence of these weapons, their readiness, and our asserted willingness to use them that keeps the peace?

It is surely true that our asserted readiness to use nuclear weapons and to use them first, however irrational such action would be in practice, must weigh on Soviet decision-makers. The West, too, is made much more cautious by the Soviet nuclear arsenal.

But consider the time scale of the problem. To avoid catastrophe, we must on both sides refrain from using these weapons not just today and tomorrow, but month after month, year after year, decade after decade. We cannot go wrong, either of us, one single time. And these weapons are under the control of men – human beings – with human failings, subject to stress, anger, frustration, lapses of reasoning, error, desperation. And these men are bound into an antagonistic relationship, driven by clashing objectives, by deep mutual mistrust, and, most powerfully, by the certain knowledge that each side can destroy the other.

On that time scale of the indefinite future, with that dependence on fallible human beings, in that situation of built-in antagonism, it is virtually certain that East and West will have confrontations and crises from time to time.

Sooner or later, in one crisis or another, through some misjudgement or misunderstanding or stupidity, some unlimited dedication to a principle or purpose, or some failure of the staggeringly complex control systems, the day will come when the nuclear threat will not cover the whole range of contingencies, when this all-encompassing deterrence will fail and some sort of hostilities will break out. On that day, we must not be relying on nuclearised forces, armed and indoctrinated to use nuclear weapons when conventional elements get in trouble, at the highest pitch of nuclear readiness, pressing against their nuclear control limitations, and with no stopping point once nuclear use starts.

In brief, extended nuclear deterrence counts on the nuclear weapon – the suicide threat – to deter all East–West hostilities, at any significant level, and to deter them forever. And it promises only unimaginable disaster if that threat fails.

That is a fragile reed to support the fate of the world.

It is worth noting, too, the psychological load involved in maintaining extended deterrence, a load which may in time become powerful enough to drive policy. Extended deterrence requires all our peoples to carry the moral weight of threatening, and ultimately executing, the destruction of civilisation by our own initiative. Growing numbers, at least in the West, by no means only Catholic bishops, are unwilling to support that load. To the opposing side, extended deterrence says that we are willing, ultimately, not merely to defeat them, but to destroy the fabric, the culture and the people of their nation. That assumes an irrevocable hostility, and it perpetuates an irrevocable hostility, on both sides.

Is there not a sounder policy than extended deterrence? Surely there is.

That sounder policy is not to continue on our present track, counting on the threat of mutual suicide to protect us year after year.

It is not to pursue the illusion that more sophisticated science and technology will eradicate the perils that science and technology have created. Star Wars cannot save us.

That sounder policy is No First Use of nuclear weapons, founded solidly on the dominating shared interest of both sides in literal survival, and thus in preventing nuclear war.

To build on that shared interest, we need a redirection of thinking. We must absorb nuclear reality; recognise that, given nuclear arms on both sides, there is no possibility of national advantage from firing nuclear weapons and no circumstances whatever where starting the use of nuclears is rational. Most important, we must understand that we are maintaining a declared policy and a military posture that treats nuclears as legitimate weapons and legitimate deterrent threats against conventional attack or other non-mortal contingency. This puts the forces on both sides on a fundamentally nuclear basis, requires continuous hair-trigger readiness, poses the nuclear alternative – at least for consideration and discussion – in every potential confrontation, and drives the opponent to nuclear readiness. It cannot reasonably be expected to succeed indefinitely. The basic conceptual change needed is to abandon the search for a useful role for nuclear weapons, and to concentrate instead on withdrawing them, as far as possible, from the East–West power equation.

There is one function for nuclear weapons, one role where no substitute exists. That role is to deter the opponent from launching *nuclear* weapons. There is no other known measure of even remotely adequate power and reach to be a convincing counter-threat to, and thus a deterrent of, the use of nuclear weapons. A prerequisite, then, is a reliable nuclear deterrent posture, on both sides, with both sides confident of their own and the other's retaliatory capacity, and both assured, thereby, that firing by either side would bring catastrophe to both. Aside from this mutual nuclear deterrence, anchored in the shared goal of survival, nuclear forces should be given no role whatever, either in threat or in action.

This requires a firm policy of No First Use, a determination that our side will not be the first to fire nuclear weapons in any future hostilities. And, parenthetically, No First Use should include No Snap Response; to avoid the serious risk of going off half-cocked – through misinterpretation, error, over-stress, third-party attack, material failure, insubordinate initiative – we should resolve not to retaliate against an incoming nuclear strike until we have determined the source of the attack, the size of the attack, and the intentions of the attacker. There would be no launch on warning. In a word, we would not retaliate until we knew what we were doing. With a secure retaliatory force, it is not necessary to make a snap response. There is ample retaliation available after taking time for analysis and reflection, and nothing to be gained by haste.

Adopted in the West, such a No First Use policy would eliminate nuclear war started by the US. Further, if No First Use were implemented in a way that made it convincing to the USSR, it would remove its reasons to pre-empt, lower its need for instant readiness, and push it into convincing implementation of their own recent No First Use declaration.

Putting No First Use into effect is a very large undertaking, sure to encounter ardent opposition. Recognising that nuclear weapons are unusable requires a change in a central element of our defence policies, held for over a generation. Changes in such fundamental mind-sets do not come easily. And in addition to the conceptual change, there must be a broad range of military changes – changes in strategy, in plans, in training, in military education, in doctrinal directives, and also in hardware – in the organisation, equipment and weapons of the forces, both conventional and nuclear. There will be hundreds of necessary contributing actions.

Our nuclear forces, in particular, would need to be structured for the purely retaliatory role. The basic need would be the capacity to survive, in ample strength, firmly held under an also-surviving control system. On the other hand, threats to the opponent's retaliatory force should be eliminated: things like anti-missile defences, and silo-killing weapons like MX and SS-18. Numbers of weapons would be sharply reduced, especially tactical and exposed elements.

With No First Use adopted as policy, and the necessary changes and implementing steps in hand, we will have rationally decided, in peace time, that nuclear war is inevitably destructive of our national interest. No First Use will not leave the nuclear decision to a moment of almost intolerable stress in the heat of a deteriorating crisis. We will have made that decision in advance, and built it into our entire military structure. The decision will almost certainly hold during hostilities; from the US standpoint, nuclear weapons except in retaliation would have moved out of the area of legitimate weapons, and into the proscribed area along with poison gas and germ warfare.

How about the Russians? They will be watching our steps toward carrying out these nuclear-avoiding policies. They read our publications, study our defence budgets, listen to our arguments. They will see the impact on military organization, on weapons, on our nuclear posture. As the evidence builds up, they should be won to a cautious belief that they will not be hit by nuclear weapons unless they fire them first, and they know that avoiding that firing is profoundly in their interest as well as ours. They have made a No First Use declaration; it should look better and better to them.

Similarly, we will be watching them, to see what practical effect follows from their recent No First Use declaration. In general, we try to follow their thought through statements by responsible political and military officials, from professional military articles in the press and technical journals, from official doctrinal publications, from observing military manoeuvres and exercises, from their weapon developments and deployments, and from changes in their military posture. If, in the next five or six years, we are able to observe that all these indicators support Soviet adherence to their No First Use declaration, we, too, will be able to operate on the cautious belief, not certainty, that they do not propose to be the first to let go.

The chances should be drastically reduced, then, if not eliminated, of either side firing nuclear weapons preemptively, or on false information, or in panic, or on warning, or, indeed, firing nuclear weapons at all.

We and the Russians must base our strategies and posture on the knowledge that nuclear war would be an unimaginable catastrophe, mutually and perhaps globally suicidal. We must appreciate that each side continues to exist only by the restraint of the other. The other side, then, is an opponent, an antagonist, a competitor, but not, irrevocably, an enemy, much less an inhuman monster. In the end, each side depends on the other for life itself.

Opposing national interests and diversity of goals exist, however. These interests can be defended, on occasion, only with risk of confrontation and even war. In the nuclear age, that risk should be met, not by a great effort to 'win' a nuclear war, not by trying to 'control' nuclear war at some endurable level, but by minimising the nuclear role, by understanding that defence – in any remotely rational sense – can only be conventional defence.

Is conventional defence possible, especially at the most critical inter-German border?

For over a human generation it has been an article of faith in the West that a Soviet conventional attack in Central Europe, not opposed by nuclear fires, could rapidly overcome NATO's forces and penetrate in a short time to the Rhine and beyond. The Warsaw Pact buildup of the last decade has reinforced that belief. Is it valid?

One of the most convincing analysts is Professor W.W. Kaufmann of MIT. His methods, interestingly, are the same as those discussed in Soviet military literature. Thus they assess NATO's performance using means the Soviets also use.

For analytical purposes, we should note, Kaufmann credits the Warsaw Pact with feats of mobilisation, deployment and force performance that no one in the West knows how to duplicate. He gives the Pact full, probably excessive, credit for its capabilities. His analyses are *not* tilted toward NATO success.

What do Kaufmann's calculations tell us?[3] A great many things – here are two of them:

– With current capabilities, NATO would have a staying power of about 15 days of intense combat. It would have more than 90 per cent probability of success, for 15 days, against a 30 division M + 4 attack – the immediate cross-border strike – and an 85 per cent chance, for 15 days, against the better prepared M + 9, 57 division, attack.

– With a set of improvements consisting of barriers, improved lines of communications, co-located operating bases, and 15 days' additional war ammunition and reserves, NATO's lasting power would rise to 30 days. This is probably about the duration of the Pact's ability to sustain intense combat. The price of this entire set of improvements: $36 billion spread over 6 years, for all the NATO nations involved – $6 billion a year. The US share could be paid by killing the MX, a good idea in itself. With these improvements, NATO would have a greater than 90 per cent probability of success for 30 days against the Pact's conceivable 30 to 90 division attacks.

Larger expenditures, on ground and air reserve forces, war reserves, sea lift, and so on, would improve Kaufmann's outcomes. But the present posture offers high probability of success against a sudden attack, and these minor and inexpensive improvements give high percentages against substantially reinforced attacks.

Analysis of this sort, of course, is not, cannot be, and does not pretend to be a precise description of the course of a future war or a sure prediction of its outcome. It is based on a range of estimates, assumptions and approximations. There is no way to predict the level of statesmanship, generalship and military skill that will show up on either side. Also, as George Will wrote, 'War is not chess, or surgery. It is a leap into the realm of chance, desperation and improvisation. Confusion, unintended effects, undesired but unavoidable collateral effects – all these are to be expected.'[4]

Further, there is, of course, a spectrum of views, held by informed people, about where NATO's conventional forces stand and what they most need, and what are the capacities and the limitations of Pact forces. Some contend that the Pact advantage in having the initiative, in numbers, and in the shallowness of NATO terrain are collectively insuperable in Central Europe. Others conclude that NATO could contain a Soviet *blitzkrieg*. There are optimists who argue that the Pact threat is remote, and that NATO as constituted could defeat it if any possible Pact attack were launched. Some analysts want light divisions for NATO, building up NATO's numbers and combat potential and using the terrain to greater advantage. Deep attack advocates lean on technical advances in weapons. There are supporters and detractors of grand manoeuvre tactics. Fresh studies of tactics, organisation, and weaponry are being pursued in Germany, in the US, in SHAPE (Supreme Headquarters of the Allied Powers in Europe) and elsewhere. There is, in brief, a healthy flow of discussion, analysis and development. It is not a field where exact, final prediction is possible.

Nevertheless, Kaufmann and others do establish this much at a minimum. The widely held vision of an enormous Soviet conventional tidal wave ready to break over NATO's conventional forces – forces which are little more than a nuclear tripwire – that vision is simply unrelated to the facts. NATO has within its reach a powerful, credible conventional deterrent.

If we take the minimum, inexpensive, needed measures, no Warsaw Pact leader can have high assurance that a conventional attack against Central Europe would succeed. And if that deterrence were to fail, NATO would have grounds for sober confidence in its conventional defence.

But the driving factor is that we have no alternative – no sane alternative – to conventional defence. There is, in reality, no such thing as nuclear defence. These nuclear devices are not and cannot be weapons, in the sense of tools for accomplishing human purposes. Their effects are too overwhelming to be proportionate to rational ends.

The enemy, the common enemy, of NATO, the Warsaw Pact, and the rest of the world is not one another. It is nuclear war. If we are to survive, that is the enemy that must be defeated.

In brief:

> The common goal is to survive.
> To survive requires nuclear peace.
> Nuclear peace needs No First Use.

Notes

1. Robert S. McNamara, 'The Military Role of Nuclear Weapons: Perceptions and Misperceptions', *Foreign Affairs*, Fall 1983, p. 72.
2. Desmond Ball, 'Can Nuclear War Be Controlled?', Adelphi Paper No. 169, International Institute for Strategic Studies, 1981, p. 38.
3. John D. Steinbruner and Leon V. Sigal (eds), *Alliance Security: NATO and the No-First-Use Question* (Washington, D.C.; Brookings, 1983), Ch. 4 and Appendix.
4. *Newsweek*, 2 August 1982.

5 From Flexible Response to No Early First Use

John B. Harris

There is a growing sense on both sides of the Atlantic that a greater effort must be made to improve the non-nuclear military capabilities of NATO, and raise the threshold to nuclear war. Disagreement has arisen, however, over the extent to which NATO can move in the direction of increased reliance on conventional forces, and away from threatening the first use of nuclear weapons to deter a Warsaw Pact non-nuclear attack on Western Europe. The 'No First Use' of nuclear weapons proposal advanced by McGeorge Bundy, George F. Kennan, Robert S. McNamara, and Gerard Smith in the Spring 1982 issue of *Foreign Affairs*,[1] for example, has received the unqualified support of only a relatively small minority of observers both in the United States and in Western Europe, and is opposed officially by NATO governments on both sides of the Atlantic.

European opposition to an outright no-first-use pledge by NATO, even if it were to be accompanied by substantial improvements in NATO's non-nuclear defence capabilities, has been particularly strong and vocal. This is rooted in a long-standing European and especially German concern that an over-reliance on non-nuclear defences in NATO policy would actually weaken deterrence. Public and outspoken reaffirmation of this traditional European preference for nuclear deterrence, in fact, followed quickly on the heels of the Bundy, *et al.*, *Foreign Affairs* article advocating a NATO no-first-use policy. In a stinging riposte to the American authors published in the following issue of the same journal, four senior members of the West German foreign policy and national security establishment – Karl Kaiser, Georg Leber, Alois Mertes and Franz Joseph Schulze – aired their objections to removing the threat of nuclear escalation as the bedrock of NATO's deterrent to non-nuclear aggression. Among other criticisms, the authors argued that trying to develop a credible non-nuclear deterrent would be so costly as to be beyond NATO's means, and that an explicit no-first-use pledge by NATO would, in effect, send a signal to the Kremlin that a Soviet attack across the inter-German border would no longer carry with it the same risk of nuclear escalation as under present conditions. Abandoning the first-use threat, in their view, might make war more likely in Central Europe by making Western Europe 'safe' for Soviet non-nuclear aggression (i.e., free of the risk of Western escalation to the use of nuclear weapons), without providing the West any guarantee that such aggression could be halted by relying solely on a conventional defence.[2]

The generally cool reception that the No-First-Use proposal has received should not be construed, however, as across-the-board opposition within NATO to any and all attempts to strengthen the alliance's conventional military capabilities. General Bernard Rogers has pushed earnestly for an across-the-board 4 per cent increase in the defence budget of each NATO member, to support improvements in NATO's ability to stymie a large Warsaw Pact armored attack.[3] In general, the Reagan Administration has supported an effort to enhance the readiness and fighting capabilities of US forces dedicated to or deployed for the defence of the West German frontier, and urged similar efforts on its European alliance partners.[4] Moreover, German and other European rejections of the No-First-Use proposal have been accompanied by the recognition that in an era of US–Soviet nuclear parity, the conventional balance in Central Europe has become more salient, and that strengthening the conventional element of NATO's 'TRIAD' will contribute to the overall credibility of NATO's deterrent posture. Based on this judgement that improved conventional warfighting capabilities can enhance both deterrence, as well as the prospects for successful non-nuclear defence if deterrence fails, many European spokespersons have come to support an effort to 'conventionalise' NATO strategy to the point where the Western Alliance would no longer have to rely on the *early* first use of nuclear weapons to deter or defend against a Soviet conventional attack.

The growing European enthusiasm for movement towards a 'no-early-first-use' policy is particularly apparent in Germany,[5] where the call for improved conventional capabilities spans both major political party lines and the German military leadership as well. The goal of achieving a no-early-first-use posture has been endorsed by leading Christian Democratic and Christian Socialist spokespersons (including Defence Minister Manfred Woerner), the recent Social Democratic Party's Report on 'The Further Development of Defence Strategies in West and East', and the General-Inspector of the Bundeswehr, General Wolfgang Altenburg.[6] The four German authors of the afore-mentioned *Foreign Affairs* article, who themselves advocate a shift in NATO's Flexible Response strategy towards a no-early-first-use posture, are testimony to the fact that even the harshest critics of an unqualified NATO no-first-use pledge acknowledge the need for strengthening NATO's non-nuclear forces.[7]

This, in turn, has spilled over into renewed efforts by the alliance to redress the perceived imbalance between the conventional forces of NATO and those of the Warsaw Pact.[8] On balance, however, these endorsements of stronger NATO conventional forces, and related support for the concept of 'no early first use' fall far short of a firm political consensus that NATO can completely abandon the threat of nuclear escalation in trying to deter Warsaw Pact conventional aggression. By and large, both American and European advocates of 'conventionalisation' and 'no early first use', want to enhance NATO's capacity for non-nuclear defence while retaining (and without diminishing) the deterrent effect of nuclear weapons that resides in leaving the first-use option open.

This approach, though, raises a number of questions. Would a NATO 'no early first use' posture, even if coupled to improvements in NATO's non-nuclear military posture, really respond to the liabilities of NATO's current strategy of Flexible Response, and its continuing heavy reliance on nuclear weapons in an era of US–Soviet nuclear parity? More specifically, would it, by preserving a major and continuing role for nuclear escalation in NATO's strategy for deterring conventional aggression, constitute a more effective revision in that strategy than a clear-cut 'no-first-use posture', wherein NATO would foreswear nuclear escalation as a deterrent to such aggression, and rely instead on a robust non-nuclear defence posture to preserve 'conventional crisis stability' in Central Europe? Finally, given that the *express purpose* of 'no early first use', as opposed to that of an unqualified 'no-first-use' policy, is that the credibility of nuclear deterrence of conventional aggression be preserved, what fundamental changes would really be wrought in Flexible Response, whose key prevailing presumption is that inadequate conventional strength can be compensated for by NATO's threat to turn a conventional conflict into a nuclear war?

THE PRESENT DILEMMAS OF FLEXIBLE RESPONSE

NATO's present strategy of Flexible Response rests on the proposition that a Soviet-led Warsaw Pact attack on the Western Alliance can best be deterred by confronting the Pact with uncertainty about the likely character of NATO's response to aggression. In the initial stages of a conflict in which the Pact has initiated hostilities by striking into, for example, West Germany, NATO plans to conduct a forward *direct defence* of NATO territory. In this stage of the conflict, Alliance forces would endeavour to contain the Soviet advance, without using nuclear weapons, as close to the inter-German border as is militarily feasible. Should direct defence fail, then NATO reserves the option to *deliberately escalate* to the 'controlled and limited' use of nuclear weapons. This step is intended less as a tactic for bringing the Pact offensive to a crushing halt through the use of nuclear weapons than it is as a political signal, one in which NATO endeavours to convince the Soviet leadership of the dangers and risks of further aggression, and to bring about an end to the conflict 'on terms favourable to the alliance'. Should the limited use of nuclear weapons fail to accomplish these objectives, however, NATO then intends to threaten a *general nuclear response*, involving large-scale nuclear attacks on Pact forces in the Central European theatre as well as strategic attacks on the Soviet Union itself, in a last-ditch effort to ward off a conventional military defeat.

Whether NATO would in fact carry out such a threat, or even the more limited nuclear response apparently envisioned at the 'deliberate escalation' level, is a question which has become grist for the critics of Flexible Response. The chief difficulty of resting the deterrence of non-nuclear aggression on *any* threat of nuclear escalation, these critics argue, is that the target of these threats – the Soviet Union – possesses a powerful and variegated nuclear arsenal of its own. In the event NATO *was* forced to begin the process of *deliberate escalation*, the most logical thing for the Soviets to do would be simply to respond in kind, and to continue to carry out the successful conventional struggle they are waging on NATO territory, thereby placing the onus for further escalation – to more destructive levels of nuclear conflict – on NATO.[9]

It matters little whether NATO begins such an exchange by launching one or several nuclear artillery shells at Soviet armoured formations in or around the battlefield, or elects, as is apparently the strategy today,[10] to begin by hitting targets behind Pact lines either in

Eastern Europe or the Soviet Union. The Soviets could respond just as readily, and without escalating to a massive retaliatory attack, to the destruction caused by (relatively small numbers of) Pershing II or ground-launched cruise missile warheads impacting in Poland or the Ukraine as they could to a 'limited' number of nuclear artillery shells falling on their troops in West Germany.[11] Further and repeated 'deliberate escalations' by NATO hold little promise for reducing the Kremlin's ability to respond at higher levels of violence, because much of the Soviet's present theatre and strategic arsenal remains impervious to attack.[12] The last resort for NATO in this process, of course, would be a so-called 'general nuclear response'. But once again, since the bulk of Soviet strategic capability remains invulnerable to attack by US strategic forces, NATO can do little more by exercising this 'final option' than to bring down upon the alliance a devastating retaliatory blow from the Soviet Union, one which would consume both the United States and Western Europe.

Alternatively, and particularly if American nuclear weapons had indeed been used against targets on Soviet soil, the Soviets might respond to NATO's 'deliberate escalation' by a massive nuclear response themselves, either within the European theatre or to encompass strategic targets in the United States as well. (This is probably more consistent with the Soviet military's own doctrinal writings on this issue than the assumption that the Soviets would try to wage either a 'limited' theatre or a 'controlled' strategic nuclear war. What they do seem to concede is the possibility of a large-scale nuclear war confined to a specific geographical theatre, like non-Soviet Europe.[13]) But regardless of whether initial and successive Soviet nuclear responses to repeated escalatory challenges from NATO led to a process of ever more destructive attacks and counter-attacks on each side, or the introduction of nuclear weapons into the conflict by NATO is followed swiftly by a massive nuclear escalation by the Kremlin, the end result is the same. NATO ends up destroying itself because it cannot prevent the Soviets from countering each step of NATO's nuclear escalation with retaliation in-kind.

Under current circumstances, of course, there *would* be a way out of this dilemma during such a war. NATO could simply acknowledge its non-nuclear defeat on the ground and sue for peace on 'unfavourable' terms before the process of nuclear escalation is triggered. But accepting defeat as the likely consequence of a non-nuclear Pact attack across the inter-German border would not only destroy the credibility of NATO's deterrent, but the overall credibility and cohesion of the Alliance as a whole. For this obvious reason, the Alliance continues to profess in Flexible Response its intention to accept the risks of escalation in order to deter such aggression in the first place.

Whether this assertion *remains credible* today is a central question in the debate over no first use and conventional deterrence. From a purely logical standpoint, as critics of the nuclear emphasis in Flexible Response have long pointed out, the strategy is flawed. How credible *is* a deterrent, they ask, which rests on NATO's willingness to trigger and then to continue, if necessary, a process of escalation which leads to ultimately suicidal consequences for the alliance?

Supporters of the current concept can and do of course argue, not implausibly, that NATO's first-use threat need not be fully 'rational' to be effective as a deterrent to Warsaw Pact aggression. Given the Soviets' capacity for retaliation at any level of nuclear conflict, logically it *would* be irrational for NATO to escalate to the use of nuclear weapons even if it were suffering a conventional military defeat in Central Europe. But the Soviets can never be certain that NATO *wouldn't* act 'irrationally' by introducing nuclear weapons into the conflict. Since the Soviets can't insure themselves against this risk completely, and since nuclear employment by NATO would carry with it the danger of uncontrolled escalation to the level of general nuclear war, the Soviets, in carrying out aggression against the West, would in effect be accepting the risk that Soviet society would be destroyed as a consequence. The possible destruction of the Soviet Union, argue the critics of conventional deterrence, is a gamble which the Kremlin is not willing to chance: no group of Soviet leaders would be so reckless and foolhardy as to undertake aggression in Central Europe if it meant exposing Soviet society to the risk of general nuclear war. The defenders of present NATO strategy thus argue that despite the seeming 'irrationality' of Flexible Response, the Soviets would be, indeed *are* persuaded that the risks of escalation and uncertainty about NATO's response outweigh the potential benefits of non-nuclear aggression. An over-reliance by NATO on conventional capabilities for territorial defence, they contend, would only diminish the risks of escalation in Soviet eyes. Adoption of an explicit no-first-use of nuclear weapons pledge by NATO would completely remove it, thus eroding the credibility of a deterrent posture which has 'worked' for the past forty years in keeping the peace in Europe, and rendering NATO territory 'safe' for Soviet non-nuclear aggression as well.[14]

Though compelling on the surface, these arguments lose force when examined more closely. A first criticism of this confidence in nuclear deterrence is that we don't know for sure whether in fact nuclear deterrence *has* 'worked for the past forty years' in convincing the Soviets not to attack Western Europe.[15] Though typically asserted by critics of a conventional force posture adequate to deter non-nuclear attacks on the alliance, the evidence adduced to support this claim is simply the fact that there has been no war in Central Europe since the end of the Second World War. This, however, does not constitute proof positive that first the United States' monopoly on nuclear weapons, then American strategic superiority, and now NATO's willingness to manipulate an operationally suicidal threat of nuclear escalation has dissuaded the Soviets from crossing the inter-German border in force over the last two generations. Other factors could have had an equally significant impact, including possibly a general Soviet disinclination to ignite a conflict in the region, whether it be nuclear or non-nuclear.[16] Moreover, even if nuclear deterrence of Soviet conventional aggression *did* work over this period, who is to say that robust non-nuclear NATO capabilities would not have also deterred the Kremlin, by convincing Soviet leaders that such aggression would be met with resistance sufficient to repel such an attack without recourse to nuclear weapons. Barring the unforeseen and highly unlikely release of primary source material from the Soviet Union which would allow us to pass judgement one way or the other on these questions, however, they remain essentially unanswerable. And if no definitive answers to them can be provided, then the self-evident 'truths' offered up by those critics of no first use, who wish not to tamper with the 'good thing' of NATO's nuclear emphasis, remain more in the realm of assertion than they do in the realm of demonstrable claims.

This points us toward a second question: which approach offers a more credible deterrent to Soviet conventional aggression in today's strategic environment, the threat of nuclear escalation, or the capability to conduct a non-nuclear defence of NATO territory? Advocates of no first use, and a strengthened NATO conventional defence, argue that a conventional defence is more credible because NATO would no longer have to rely on the seemingly irrational threat to escalate. Advocates of continuing NATO's present strategy, on the other hand, counter that this would remove the threat of escalation to strategic nuclear attacks on Russian soil, which is the key to deterring any kind of Soviet aggression against the West.

Again, this is a debate which for lack of evidence can never really be proven one way or the other. There are three specific elements of the latter approach, however, which weaken its value as a deterrent.

1. *NATO's strategy, which hinges so heavily on the credibility of the threat of escalation to all-out nuclear war as a consequence of conventional aggression by the Warsaw Pact, nevertheless holds that a nuclear war could be 'controlled' and 'limited' to Europe. This is logically contradictory and diminishes the credibility of Flexible Response. It ignores as well the bargaining advantages which the Pact would enjoy in a major European conflict if it is allowed to maintain its present non-nuclear advantage over NATO.*

As noted above, the efficacy of NATO's threat of nuclear escalation hinges on Soviet perceptions that there is at least a non-zero probability that the West would respond to conventional aggression with the use of nuclear weapons, and most importantly, that such use would trigger a chain of escalation that results ultimately in the nuclear destruction of the Soviet Union. NATO continues to rely on the threat of nuclear escalation in Flexible Response, hoping that the Soviets remain convinced that the West, no matter how dangerous the step would be for NATO itself, might indeed escalate. Soviet uncertainties thus play a key role in the credibility of the western deterrent. The key to maintaining its credibility, therefore, is to prevent these Soviet *uncertainties* about NATO's nuclear response from becoming Kremlin *doubts* about the likelihood of 'deliberate escalation' by its adversaries.

Yet such doubts are bound to be the unavoidable consequence of what senior western policymakers, as well as the coterie of western defence intellectuals who oppose no first use, have projected as the likely consequences of 'deliberate escalation' by NATO. It is most curious, in fact, that while extolling Flexible Response as a strategy which strives to link Soviet non-nuclear aggression to the possibility that Soviet society will be destroyed, these people have simultaneously prophesised that *that nuclear escalation by NATO need not lead ineluctably to general nuclear war*. In fact, just the opposite is argued. American officials like Richard N. Perle, the Reagan Administration's assistant secretary of defence for international security policy, contends that at some point following NATO's initial use of nuclear weapons, 'cooler heads would prevail': the warring parties will manage to negotiate a resolution of the conflict before it spirals out of control and destroys both the Soviet Union and the Warsaw Pact.[17] Indeed, President Reagan himself has opined that he 'could see where you could have the exchange of tactical nuclear weapons against troops in the field without it bringing either one of the major powers to pushing the button.'[18] Nor is such optimism confined to North American supporters of the status quo in alliance strategy. The German *Foreign Affairs* critics of no first use have stated their belief quite clearly that as a consequence of NATO's deliberate escalation 'All indications suggest that both sides would be extremely cautious, in order to avoid precisely the dreaded, possibly uncontrollable escalation which some studies present as a danger, and which the advocates of no-first-use policy present as a certainty.'[19]

The problem with these statements is that at the same time they try to deny the likelihood of unavoidable escalation, they damage the credibility of the threat of escalation, which lies at the heart of Flexible Response's utility as a deterrent to Soviet non-nuclear aggression. The rap against increased reliance on conventional deterrence, after all, is that robust non-nuclear defence capabilities adequate to halt a major Soviet armoured thrust would, as Kaiser and his colleagues put it 'liberate the Soviet Union from the decisive nuclear risk' of attacks on the Soviet homeland.[20] Raising the threshold to *nuclear war*, by insertion of a convincing conventional 'firebreak', in other words, is perceived to have deleterious consequences for NATO's ability to deter *non-nuclear* war. But just as a non-nuclear firebreak can diminish the threat of escalation to general nuclear war, so too can a nuclear firebreak – in this case limited nuclear war in Europe – which implies that 'deliberate escalation' might not lead to highly destructive consequences for the Soviet Union. Indeed, the very essence of Flexible Response, as Earl Ravenal has so cogently observed, is that the direct defence of NATO territory is 'coupled' to the United States' ultimate commitment to use strategic nuclear weapons against the Soviet Union, and that

> By extension, it connotes the integrity of the chain of escalation from conventional war to theater nuclear weapons to the use of America's ultimate strategic weapon . . . [and that] in an era of nuclear parity firebreaks – any device, strategy, or doctrine that makes escalation to strategic nuclear weapons less than prompt and automatic . . . are the very antithesis of coupling.[21]

According to their own logic, therefore, these outspoken opponents of reducing NATO's dependence on nuclear weapons, who argue that first nuclear use may not lead to all-out escalation, may do as much to damage the credibility of NATO's nuclear deterrent as any actual improvements in NATO's non-nuclear capabilities. What they convey to the Soviet leadership is NATO's own (eminently sensible) trepidations about the likely consequence of carrying out their own deterrent threats. In so doing, they place in doubt the continuity of the escalatory chain that is so integral to Flexible Response, sapping the credibility of nuclear escalation as a deterrent to Soviet conventional aggression.[22]

In addition to being logically at odds with the deterrent objectives of Flexible Response, moreover, these assertions about the 'controlability' of nuclear war in Europe appear based on unrealistic predictions about Soviet reactions to NATO nuclear employment. The thesis that escalation control will be achieved after NATO's initial and limited use of nuclear weapons is based on the assumption that Soviet leaders will realise NATO is really 'serious', and will be willing to accept concessions during 'intra-war bargaining' which will make the terms of a negotiated peace 'acceptable to the alliance'. This optimism about the decisive effects of NATO's nuclear escalation on Soviet behaviour ignores, however, the military realities of the East–West power balance in Europe.

Remember the circumstances under which the alliance would be forced to introduce nuclear weapons into a European conflict. NATO would presumably be losing a conventional war on its own soil (otherwise there would be no need to escalate). Although NATO's initial nuclear strike would be intended to have some impact on the Warsaw Pact's ability to carry on their non-nuclear offensive operations, such an attack would be limited in scope. According to General Rogers, it would probably *not* entail the use of short-range battlefield nuclear weapons directly on Soviet armoured formations operating near the forward edge of the battle area, but rather longer range strikes aimed at military targets in Eastern Europe or the Soviet Union itself.[23] Presumably, then, such an attack would not interfere immediately with Soviet fortunes on the non-nuclear battlefield in Western Europe. The Soviets would also possess numerous and survivable means with which to retaliate against NATO targets following NATO's first use. Under these conditions, why would the Soviets readily relinquish the gains they had already made on the ground and sue for peace, simply because the West had launched a nuclear attack against the Warsaw Pact? A much more rational Soviet response would be, as argued earlier, simply to reply in kind, thus placing the burden for either continuing or controlling the process of escalation on the West.

This is a dilemma which under present circumstances is inherent in Flexible Response and one from which NATO cannot escape. Ever more arcane theories of 'controlled nuclear war' and successful war termination on 'terms favourable to the alliance', no matter how elegant or deductively appealing, can not overcome the realities of the East–West military balance in Central Europe: by dint of its non-nuclear advantage and the nuclear parity extant between the United States and the Soviet Union, the Warsaw Pact would hold the high cards in any intra-war bargaining 'competition in nuclear risk-taking'[24] during a NATO/Warsaw conflict in the region.

2. *The Soviet Union has designed and is implementing a strategy for conventional conflict which exploits these tensions in Flexible Response, and which seeks to reduce the risks that NATO would escalate to the use of nuclear weapons in the face of non-nuclear defeat.*

Recent Soviet writings on the prospect of a NATO/Warsaw Pact war in the European theatre have placed great emphasis on defeating NATO in the shortest possible time at minimum risk to the Soviet Union.[25] Soviet military authors have focused in particular on the problem of how to defeat NATO in a conventional war, while at the same time minimising NATO's opportunities for and incentives to engage in 'deliberate escalation' to the use of nuclear weapons as foreseen in Flexible Response.[26] Soviet strategy is in fact predicated on the assumption that NATO will carry out its defence plans in accordance with its official strategy, initially attempting an unsuccessful conventional defence, and followed by escalation to the use of nuclear weapons in a relatively short period of time, perhaps within 4–5 days.[27] To frustrate NATO's plans Soviet planning and strategy have come to concentrate on the tasks of defeating NATO's non-nuclear forces on the ground and in the air over the battlefield, while simultaneously seeking to forestall the use of nuclear weapons by NATO. In order to accomplish these two objectives, the Soviets would have to successfully complete three interrelated phases of a non-nuclear offensive against Western Europe.

First, the Soviets would try to rapidly emasculate NATO's conventional defences, through the massive employment of non-nuclear offensive military capabilities along the inter-German border. The offensive would involve powerful armoured thrusts across several axes of advance into the Federal Republic of Germany, preceded and accompanied by massive artillery barrages, special forces actions and airborne landings behind NATO lines, and efforts to establish air superiority by supporting elements of Soviet frontal (i.e., tactical) aviation. The purpose of these armoured spearheads would be to insert as quickly as possible (within the first one or two days of hostilities) division-sized, mobile, and heavily armed 'operational manoeuvre groups' (OMGs) behind the enemy's front lines, in order to destroy the ability of NATO to recover and establish a coherent defence behind its original defensive positions, and to hasten the overall collapse of NATO's non-nuclear defence.[28]

Secondly, Soviet forces would utilise special forces operating in NATO's rear, preparatory air and non-nuclear tactical ballistic missile attacks, and a portion of its offensive ground forces to diminish NATO's ability to launch a counter-attack using nuclear weapons.[29] British analyst Christopher Donnelly notes the high priority placed in Soviet conventional strategy upon insuring that if NATO *does* make the decision to introduce nuclear weapons into the conflict,

> by that time special-purpose forces, air strikes, OMG raids, sabotage, and the like will, the Soviets hope, have eroded considerably the nuclear stocks and weapons available may also have seriously damaged the command and control system essential to their effective use.[30]

The final link in this strategy would be the attempt to deter NATO from employing its remaining theatre nuclear weapons through a combination of 'mixing' tactics by Soviet armoured elements, the maintenance of extensive and survivable Soviet nuclear retaliatory capabilities in the theatre, and efforts to exploit political divisions within NATO over whether to escalate to the use of nuclear weapons or not. Part of the rationale for achieving early penetration of NATO's forward defence elements early in the conflict is to prevent NATO from establishing clearly drawn battle lines so that Soviet forces can be readily distinguished, for the purpose of target acquisition and discrimination, from NATO's own defenders. If Soviet forces can achieve such 'mixing' with NATO defenders, Donnelly explains, 'it will be extremely difficult for NATO to consider the use of normal nuclear weapons . . . well inside Western Germany against Soviet forces in close combat with NATO troops'.[31]

In addition, the Soviets count on their various capabilities to launch theatre and strategic nuclear attacks, including a relatively recent but growing nuclear artillery capability, to convince NATO of the futility of employing its own (diminished) nuclear assets. It is doubtful that Soviet conventional operations, no matter how effectively and efficiently carried out, could completely paralyse NATO's ability to employ nuclear weapons against either Pact forces operating in Europe or targets on Soviet soil. NATO could probably still 'deliberately escalate', and given the overall invulnerability of American strategic forces, at some point in the conflict inflict great damage on Soviet society. But what NATO will not be able to do is to save itself from a similar fate. Indeed, the apparent Soviet plan for dealing with an imminent NATO nuclear attack is to pre-empt with a theatre-wide nuclear attack of its own, aimed at NATO's remaining combat air forces, targetable nuclear assets, and command and control infrastructure, possibly succeeded by follow-up attacks designed to prevent reconstitution of any surviving NATO nuclear strike capabilities. If pre-emption failed and NATO did succeed in launching a limited nuclear attack, Soviet strategy calls for a retaliatory strike along the lines of that contemplated in a pre-emptive attack. In the meantime, Soviet conventional manoeuvre elements would seek to exploit the damage done by initial and follow-up nuclear attacks.[32] Behind all this would lie the bulk of Soviet strategic forces, threatening a pre-emptive or retaliatory attack. Soviet hopes of bringing the war to a successful conclusion before it spirals out of control thus rest on the not implausible prospect that NATO's decision makers, facing the choice of either acquiescing in defeat or engaging in suicidal nuclear escalation, would be 'self-deterred' from carrying out such escalation, and sue for peace on terms established by the Warsaw Pact.

The desperate choice between suicide or surrender, in turn, may present the Soviets with opportunities to provoke political divisions within NATO, perhaps even precipitate the dissolution of the alliance, and in so doing, prevent NATO from exercising its nuclear option. The likelihood of eliciting western capitulation, before the uncontrolled use of nuclear weapons had begun, might be significantly increased if one or more individual NATO governments could be prevailed upon to unilaterally accept Soviet 'peace feelers'. These might come prior to NATO's decision to use nuclear weapons, in the form of confidential Soviet promises of post-war political autonomy, security from nuclear attack, and the like. The price might be a commitment from the respective NATO member (or members) that it (they) would either withdraw from the alliance completely and immediately, or actively resist within NATO's decision-making councils steps facilitating or ordering the use of nuclear weapons against the Warsaw Pact. Indeed, there appear to be three distinct decision points in the implementation of 'deliberate escalation' where individual NATO governments might fall prey to such Soviet importunings.

The first such wartime juncture would be the question of whether or not to place NATO's nuclear forces on alert and to disperse them into the countryside, away from vulnerable weapons storage sites and base areas. The obvious danger of failing to call an alert and disperse NATO's forces, in the event of a Warsaw Pact attack, would be to leave them sitting ducks for destruction by Soviet special forces, air attacks, or armoured raiding elements. Yet as Paul Bracken has observed, an alert and dispersal would be a politically traumatic step for NATO to take, one in which 'political leaders may be so terrified of the consequences that they will refuse to take even the most precautionary steps in a crisis'.[33] The issue of Soviet countermoves aside, simply the dispersal of NATO's own nuclear forces would in and of itself increase immeasurably the risk of uncontrolled nuclear escalation on the European battlefield. As Bracken has explained:

> Once NATO were to go on alert ... its six thousand warheads would be spread from the North Sea to the plateaux of eastern Turkey. At this point, if fighting were to break out we must assume that operational control of these weapons would devolve to the highly differentiated commands that maintain physical control over them. For example, it is unlikely that centralized control over self-propelled artillery could be achieved, because these forces depend on movement and concealment for their survival. Since NATO's nuclear weapons are integrated into conventional forces, each force would have its own peculiar operating constraints. In an actual battle, even one initially restricted to conventional weapons, the fact that nuclear weapons were deployed with these units would substantially increase the likelihood that some of these thousands of weapons would be fired.[34]

Dispersal of NATO's nuclear arsenal might quickly trigger Soviet pre-emption, adding to the anxiety of NATO's members, particularly those Europeans whose countries would constitute or lie in close proximity to the nuclear battlefield. It could in fact produce such intense bickering that, as Bracken warns, 'The political fighting might lead to outright disruption of the alerting process ...'[35]

The possible authorisation to actually *use* nuclear weapons would undoubtedly provoke even more intense disagreements within the alliance. The question of when and how to actually initiate the use of nuclear weapons should the non-nuclear element of NATO's defences fail is an issue that has stirred controversy among NATO's planners throughout the period of US–Soviet parity. There is no reason to presume that such a decision should be any less contentious under the exigencies of war than it has been in peacetime. It has the potential to divide European alliance members from one another, as well as from the United States. Countries upon or from whose soil NATO's initial nuclear salvo is to be launched may be reluctant to permit such use, despite pressure from other members urging that NATO carry out its deterrent threat of deliberate escalation. What's more, the reluctant party, if the weapon being considered for use is under its national control, would have the physical capacity to deny the alliance the wherewithal to launch the attack. Alternatively, the United States, which retains control over the warheads of all NATO theatre weapons systems except Britain's SLBM force,[36] might refuse to release them to European units which control the delivery systems, in order to forestall possible escalation to strategic nuclear war. Finally, the United States, given the fact that it is the only member that possesses *both* warheads and launcher systems in the theatre, has the capacity to initiate nuclear war unilaterally, without gaining prior concurrence from its allies in the theatre. An American President is bound to consult the West Europeans on this matter only if 'time and circumstances' permit.[37] Who is to say that a failing NATO conventional defence wouldn't propel Washington so rapidly toward the decision to escalate that the European allies could only be informed about the decision shortly before American theatre nuclear weapons actually began hitting their targets, or worse yet, not at all? This risk alone may be enough to push the West Europeans, if and when it becomes clear that NATO's conventional forces are folding in a conflict, to cut the best deal they can with the Kremlin before Washington takes the fate of Western Europe out of their own hands.

Even if these obstacles were surmounted and a unanimous decision to authorise the first use of nuclear weapons could be reached within the alliance, however, these uncertainties and possible political divisions would remain behind to inhibit NATO's capacity to order the follow-on use of nuclear weapons should its first nuclear attack fail to halt Soviet aggression. Having made it through one difficult and fateful decision intact as an alliance is no guarantee that trying to meet the next crisis won't have fissiparous consequences, especially if NATO's original 'deliberate escalation' is followed by Pact retaliation in kind. NATO has in fact not made much headway in planning for the possibly necessary follow-on use of nuclear weapons. Although a consensus was evidently reached in 1975 within NATO's Nuclear Planning Group to the effect that follow-on use should have the same purpose as initial escalation (i.e., to demonstrate NATO's resolve and the dangers of further pact aggression), general guidelines for how this goal would be achieved through the actual use of weapons is apparently still lacking.[38] Thus, the decision to order follow-on use may be just as, if not more, difficult for the alliance to weather intact than the original decision to 'go nuclear' in the first place.

In all three instances – alert and dispersal, initial use, and follow-on use – alliance members would be under enormous strains and pressures, torn between taking a fateful step that carries with it grave risks and immediate physical dangers, and accepting defeat at the hands of the Soviets. Which option appears the least unpalatable to NATO decision makers may be heavily influenced by Soviet diplomacy. To the extent that the Soviets could threaten or promise consequences which persuade individual NATO members that escalation is the least attractive choice, the Kremlin may possess sufficient intra-war bargaining leverage to effect NATO's dissolution precisely at the moment in which alliance cohesion must pass its most demanding test. As Bracket warns, 'Put as starkly as possible, if their choice is to be red or dead, [NATO's political leaders] will invariably choose the former, as it lacks the permanency of the latter.'[39]

3. *Further 'nuclear modernization' by NATO will not reverse the growing incredibility of NATO's nuclear threats of first use and escalation. In fact, certain types of nuclear modernisation may provoke Soviet countermeasures which will increase the risk of rapid escalation to uncontrolled nuclear conflict during a crisis, or out of a non-nuclear war in Europe.*

The ongoing deployment of American Pershing II and ground-launched cruise missiles in Europe is a classic example of this problem. Soviet agitprop and diplomatic rhetoric aside, the combined accuracy and short flight time of Pershing IIs based in the Federal Republic of Germany are likely to stimulate Soviet worries about the survivability of the extensive strategic command and control assets that lie near Moscow, and within range of the new American missiles. Such concerns may prompt the Soviets to place their strategic nuclear forces on a more 'hair-trigger' launch status in a crisis, raising the risk that the Soviets might respond to ambiguous evidence of an American first strike in a crisis by launching a first strike of their own.

Even if American Pershing IIs and GLCMs were actually used against a limited set of military targets in the Soviet Union, in order to demonstrate NATO's resolve to carry on the conflict, the Soviets would possess the option to respond selectively themselves against not just the country from which the missiles were launched (West Germany), but the country which actually launched the weapons as well (the United States). In all probability, the Soviets would do both, in order to deter further escalation by NATO: hit targets in West Germany to demonstrate to Bonn that it can't permit the launch of American nuclear weapons from its soil against the Soviet Union with impunity; and strike targets in the United States to convince Washington that US weapons launched from Europe against Soviet targets will engender a Soviet nuclear response on American soil. This Soviet behaviour would hardly be conducive to escalation control, but cannot realistically be foreclosed.

The only way NATO *could* in fact escape Soviet retaliation, and in doing so, make the nuclear threats in Flexible Response credible, would be by preparing to 'deliberately escalate' in a way designed to incapacitate Soviet command and control, destroy Soviet nuclear forces so as to greatly diminish the destructiveness of retaliation, and to backstop this counterforce capability with homeland defences for both Europe and the United States. As Earl Ravenal has observed, for Flexible Response to be credible, it must be grounded in the 'practical' invulnerability of US society, and that of Western Europe, we might add, to Soviet nuclear retaliation.[40]

Unfortunately, however, the alliance does not presently dispose of such abilities, hence the inherent difficulties with Flexible Response. The only way to generate such a posture is through both offensive and defensive strategic modernisation. Despite the attention paid to and emphasis placed upon counterforce in America, the United States' strategic forces remain far removed from the capacity to eradicate a substantial portion of Soviet retaliatory forces in a counterforce strike.[41] Meanwhile, the West's best hope for homeland defence, President Reagan's Strategic Defence Initiative (SDI), is still in its infancy, and continues to provoke controversy about its technical feasibility, its cost, and its potential vulnerability to Soviet countermeasures.[42]

Even if such a posture could be developed, it may not be desirable, because of its likely impact in raising the risk of nuclear war in a US–Soviet crisis. This force posture would be valuable to Flexible Response primarily by virtue of its capacity to shield the West from Soviet retaliation. In principle, however, counterforce is only useful if it is used before the enemy is allowed to launch his own weapons, because if it is used after the adversary has attacked, the capability is irrelevant to the task of damage limitation.[43] Moreover, as many sceptics of SDI point out, the really only conceivable way in which a space-based shield against nuclear weapons would be effective is if it were to be employed against a 'ragged' Soviet retaliatory blow, one thinned out by an American counterforce attack. If allowed to attack the shield undiminished by attacks on their own strategic forces, the Soviets would simply have a much better chance of penetrating the defences and destroying targets in Western Europe and the United States. The bottom line on strategic defences is that they too are useful only if American offensive forces beat their Soviet counterparts to the punch.[44]

What this in effect means is that the requisites for a credible nuclear threat component in NATO's deterrent to non-nuclear aggression is not simply counterforce and homeland defence, but an overall 'splendid first strike capability' which promises some measure of success in limiting damage to Western Europe and the United States if it has to be used.[45] Yet this same posture, while making NATO's deterrent to non-nuclear war *more* credible, could also increase the risk of nuclear war. If NATO's success in war is contingent on using not only its theatre, but its strategic nuclear weapons first, in order to enhance the prospects for damage limitation, the Soviets may reason that the only way to defeat this strategy is to launch their own weapons first, in order to avoid their loss in an American first strike or to Western strategic defences. Anticipating these thoughts in the Kremlin, American leaders would be encouraged themselves to 'go' as early is possible, to avoid getting caught in a pre-emptive Soviet strategic attack. The overall effect of a synergistic American offensive and defensive damage limitation capability would thus be highly provocative, eroding not only crisis stability in periods of heightened East–West tension when the potential for direct military conflict is high, but the threshold to nuclear war in the event of a European conventional conflict as well. Overall, the impact of such a posture would be to lower the threshold to nuclear war. The more limited, but nevertheless significant counterforce and counter-command and control capabilities of the Pershing IIs and GLCMs can only aggravate this tendency, and are potentially destabilising in their own right. All of this raises a fundamental challenge to those who would reject reliance on conventional forces to deter non-nuclear attacks on the alliance: if preserving Flexible Response means being driven to nuclear modernisation scenarios which, if brought to fruition, could increase the risk of nuclear war, does it make sense to accept those additional and potentially more apocalyptic dangers, all in the name of trying to minimise the likelihood of a *non-nuclear* war in Europe?

FROM FLEXIBLE RESPONSE TO NO EARLY FIRST USE

These, then, are the central dilemmas of deterrence that confound Flexible Response: it holds, in self-contradictory fashion, that nuclear war once unleashed can be controlled and terminated, but that the essence of NATO's deterrent rests on the likelihood of unimpeded escalation; it's self-deterrent qualities appear severely vulnerable to a Soviet strategy intent on exploiting them through conventional aggression, nuclear deterrence, and intra-war diplomacy; and it creates a demand for the deployment of new nuclear weapons systems by the United States, on behalf of its allies, which may significantly increase the risk of nuclear war. I have concentrated primarily on these problems of deterrence, to the neglect of the operational questions of defence under Flexible Response, for the simple reason that aside from their unrealistic hope that the product of initial use of nuclear weapons by NATO will be swiftly followed by remonstrances from Soviet peace suitors, even the most ardent supporters of NATO's present strategy admit that if fully implemented at successively more destructive levels of conflict, Flexible Response will lead to all-out nuclear war. This ought to be implicit, moreover, in the foregoing discussion of the deterrent deficiencies in Flexible Response, for these deficiencies flow directly from the alliance's presumption that it cannot defend itself without resorting to the first use of nuclear weapons. The point is that NATO can't *defend* itself by relying on 'deliberate escalation', either.

The use of battlefield nuclear weapons to alter the fortunes of a crumbling conventional defence has long been recognised within official NATO circles as a futile enterprise. Such short-range weapons would by necessity have to be used on NATO soil, probably in large numbers to have any significant military effect, in some of the most densely populated areas of the world, and offer no prospect of preventing the Soviets from retaliating in kind. All their use would really guarantee is that at a minimum, hundreds of thousands, and more likely millions of citizens in both East and West Germany, would die from the prompt and delayed effects of several hundred tactical nuclear weapons. Battlefield nuclear weapons with 'tailored' effects, such as enhanced radiation weapons or 'neutron bombs', would have at best a marginal impact on preventing widespread collateral damage in such a war, and thus are no real answer to the underlying problem. (The high-speed, highly lethal neutron radiation emitted by such weapons would be as dangerous to German civilians standing in the open or trying to shelter themselves in residential or commercial structures as it would be to Soviet troops in their armoured vehicles.)[46]

As noted above, however, NATO apparently does not intend to initiate the use of nuclear weapons on the battlefield. General Rogers' guidance at present as Supreme Allied Commander in Europe is to begin this process by striking initially at a selected number of military targets in Eastern Europe or the Soviet Union using longer range delivery systems such as manned aircraft or the new American missiles now being deployed in Western Europe. Granted this tactic does shift the initial destruction caused by first use away from NATO territory and onto Pact soil. But it does nothing to prevent Pact retaliation, either in the form of 'horizontal' escalation to the battlefield use of nuclear weapons against targets on NATO soil, strikes with theatre delivery systems of longer range against targets in Western Europe, or even strategic nuclear retaliation against the United States.

Thus, even if NATO succeeded in escalating the conflict, at least initially, in a somewhat deliberate and orderly fashion, all it would really have done is taken a conventional defeat and transformed it into an alliance-wide nuclear disaster. Moreover, it is highly unlikely that NATO could in fact escalate in a deliberate and controlled fashion. Indeed, as Paul Bracken has shown persuasively, exercising any kind of effective command and control over NATO's large and sprawling theatre nuclear arsenal during a conflict, especially after NATO had gone on alert and dispersed its forces, would be almost impossible to achieve.[47] Flexible Response, in its present form, thus reveals serious weaknesses. Its credibility as a deterrent is waning, its utility as a strategy for defence, and the protection in war of NATO's territorial, physical, and human resources remains dubious at best. The central question to be addressed here is whether 'no early first use', as the growing point of contact between North American and West European leaders who would like to see some reduction in NATO's reliance on nuclear weapons, would provide NATO any relief from its present strategic difficulties.

The call for moving to a 'no early first use' posture and strategy appears based on two central concerns about NATO's current mix of nuclear and conventional forces. First, it is believed that NATO's conventional posture is too weak relative to that of the Warsaw Pact to prevent NATO from being forced almost immediately to engage in nuclear escalation if the alliance is attacked. (General Rogers has argued that the conventional weakness of NATO's Northern Army Group (NORTHAG) is so severe that NATO's overall non-nuclear posture in Central Europe today offers nothing more than a 'delayed trip wire' to nuclear escalation.)[48] Secondly, analysts worry that NATO's theatre nuclear arsenal is composed of excessive numbers of short-range systems such as howitzers, which would have to be used relatively early in a conflict to avoid having them overrun by advancing Pact forces. The policy prescriptions which flow from these concerns are twofold: deploy stronger conventional forces, and shift the composition of NATO's nuclear stockpile away from short-range delivery systems.[49]

What 'no early first use' does not prescribe is that NATO strengthen its conventional forces to the point where threatening escalation might become unnecesary. In order to preserve the possibility of nuclear escalation 'no early first use' supporters deliberately advocate a NATO conventional posture which falls short of the requirements for non-nuclear defence against a Soviet conventional attack. The supposed novelty of the approach lies in its attempt to defer the point at which NATO would have to actually escalate, by strengthening NATO's non-nuclear forces somewhat, and altering the bias toward short-range delivery systems in NATO's nuclear stockpile.

But how does this differ from NATO's current deterrent policy? The answer, of course, is not much. In fact, one could logically argue that the alliance's present strategy *is*, in effect, a 'no early first use' policy. After all, the original rationale for shifting in 1967 from Massive Retaliation to Flexible Response in alliance strategy was to insert a graduated series of steps, including both 'direct defence' and 'deliberate escalation' between pre-war deterrence and a general nuclear response by NATO, in order to postpone the point at which NATO would have to escalate from non-nuclear to nuclear war and from theatre to strategic nuclear war.[50] But in shifting from Massive Retaliation to Flexible Response, NATO preserved the centrality of first use as the core deterrent to Pact conventional aggression, and, lacking consensus on the need for an effective non-nuclear defence posture, NATO failed to produce one.[51]

Along similar lines, all 'no early first use' really implies is that NATO should have the luxury, provided by improved conventional forces, of waiting slightly longer before it has to decide whether or not to introduce nuclear weapons into a European conflict. In fact, some official proponents of 'no early first use' perceive its principle value to be the way in which it would enhance the circumstances under which NATO would escalate to the use of nuclear weapons, thereby making the threat to escalate more credible. According to these officials 'no early first use' does not call for conventional forces which, standing alone, could thwart a Soviet armoured attack. What such a policy would require, by contrast, is non-nuclear forces that would provide NATO political leaders more time to determine the appropriate scope, size and nature of an escalatory action if the nuclear threshold had to be crossed. NATO would not then be forced willy-nilly into rapid escalation, as General Rogers has implied might now be the case if Soviet forces poured across the North German Plain and into NORTHAG. Thus, both he and General Altenburg have argued that additional time, afforded by strengthened conventional forces, will provide NATO an intra-alliance crisis decision-making environment more conducive to agreement upon and authorisation of the limited escalation to first-use of nuclear weapons.[52] Deterrence remains firmly rooted in trying to create Soviet uncertainties about NATO's willingness to initiate a suicidal process of nuclear escalation, rather than Kremlin perceptions that NATO's conventional forces would be capable of repulsing a Soviet armoured attack without the use of nuclear weapons. In terms of Alliance deterrence strategy, therefore, 'no early first use' is really nothing new.

Whether in fact the additional decision-making time afforded NATO by a no early first use conventional posture would facilitate more 'rational' procedures for agreeing on and authorising nuclear first-use is a debatable but hardly fundamental issue. The central problem with such a strategy is that it completely ignores the main operational liability of Flexible Response, which is that at every level of nuclear escalation available to NATO, the Soviets can either retaliate in kind or escalate further themselves. As the foregoing section should make clear, NATO's main problem is not *how soon* it would have to initiate the use of nuclear weapons, but that it would have to escalate at all. And because this very marginal revision in NATO's prevailing approach to deterring non-nuclear war does not prescribe conventional forces strong enough for NATO to kick entirely the first-use habit, 'no early first use' fails to come to grips with the central weakness of present strategy. For the same reasons, it is unlikely that a 'no early first use posture', at least when compared to one so robust in conventional forces that NATO felt comfortable in making an unqualified no-first-use pledge, would make a meaningful contribution to NATO's ability to defend itself against a Warsaw Pact conventional attack. It is especially difficult to understand how, if deterrence fails, simply *delaying* (as opposed to removing completely) the need to escalate to the use of nuclear weapons does anything to ameliorate or minimise the potentially disastrous consequences of such an action. 'No early first use' does nothing to address the dangers which Soviet theatre and nuclear retaliatory capabilities have introduced into NATO's strategy for dealing with the failure of deterrence. It would simply delay, by some unspecified period of time, the point at which NATO's leaders would be forced to confront the agonising choices so carefully obscured by the euphemism 'deliberate escalation'. In effect, 'no early first use' does not actually raise the nuclear threshold. It merely shifts it sideways somewhat, providing an illusion of reduced reliance on nuclear weapons where none in fact exists.

The immediate attractiveness of embracing a 'no early first use' orientation in NATO policy, in fact, appears to be political. The concept is based on an imprecisely-defined doctrinal position – a sort of strategic 'middle-ground' which calls for both strengthened conventional forces as well as continued reliance on nuclear escalation. It can at least accommodate, if not wholly reconcile, diverging views within NATO over the proper mix of nuclear deterrent and conventional defence capabilities in alliance strategy. It therefore provides a means by which to preserve the doctrinal compromise between European and American views which facilitated the adoption of Flexible Response as Alliance strategy in 1967.[53] Moreover, as a first step, 'no early first use' could provide a political stepping stone toward at least a de facto, full-fledged 'no-first-use' alliance military posture and strategy. If it became the initial foundation of a political consensus within NATO on the need for strengthened conventional forces, one which would evolve over time and lead ultimately to the kind of 're-conventionalisation' and enhancements of alliance ground forces which John Marshall Lee has advocated in order to implement a 'no-first-use' policy,[54] then 'no early first use' would eventually nourish the strategic, as opposed to solely the political, health of the alliance. The risk of course is that it will become an end in itself, an essentially very narrow revision in prevailing strategy that reaps few strategic benefits at all.

CONCLUSION

We should harbour no illusions, therefore, that emphasising the 'no early first use' of nuclear weapons in alliance strategy will produce any meaningful shift in the character of Flexible Response. It holds a certain appeal from the standpoint of intra-alliance politics, because it would reaffirm the basic cross-Atlantic compromise on strategy which lies at the heart of the present doctrine of Flexible Response. It could, moreover, become the first in a series of evolutionary modifications in Flexible Response toward a de facto 'no-first-use' NATO military posture. But if it becomes a strategic platitude behind which the prevailing core assumptions of Flexible Response are retained, 'no-early-first-use' will simply preserve the existing liabilities of NATO strategy.

Most importantly, it would retain as the primary deterrent to Soviet conventional attack NATO's threat to escalate to the first use of nuclear weapons. This threat may continue to carry serious weight among Soviet leaders, if only because those in the Kremlin remain unsure of what NATO's response would be if the Soviets did attack. But it is being increasingly undermined by its own internal illogic, recent developments in Soviet military strategy, and the demands it creates for new nuclear weapons systems that are at once potentially provocative to the Soviets and highly controversial among NATO publics as well. Relying on nuclear weapons to deter a Soviet conventional attack, moreover, which NATO would continue to do under a 'no- early-first-use' policy, still leaves NATO virtually bereft of options for the defence of Europe that do not at some point require escalating to the use of nuclear weapons.

When measured against NATO's current strategy, therefore, 'no early first use' promises only marginal advantages. When compared to a NATO conventional military posture explicitly configured to avoid the necessity of *any* first nuclear use by NATO, however, one in which nuclear weapons are confined solely to the role of deterring Soviet first use, 'no early first use' suffers from a fundamental liability. Adequate NATO conventional strength, buttressed by survivable theatre and strategic nuclear retaliatory capabilities, promises both credible deterrence as well as the capability for non-nuclear defence if deterrence fails. 'No early first use' offers only a deterrent threat which many consider to have grown incredible, and no real prospect for containing Soviet conventional aggression without escalating to the use of nuclear weapons. As such, it represents no serious 'rethinking' of NATO's nuclear dilemma, and is hardly a viable blueprint for future NATO policies aimed at reducing the risk of both conventional and nuclear war in Europe.

Notes

1. 'Nuclear Weapons and the Atlantic Alliance', *Foreign Affairs*, 60:4 (Summer 1982), pp. 753–68.
2. Karl Kaiser, Georg Leber, Alois Mertes, Franz-Josef Schulze, 'Nuclear Weapons and the Preservation of Peace: A German Response', *Foreign Affairs*, 60:5 (Summer 1982), pp. 1160–2.
3. The so-called 'Rogers Plan' for improving NATO's conventional military capabilities is presented in General Bernard W. Rogers, 'The Atlantic Alliance: Prescriptions for a Difficult Decade', *Foreign Affairs*, 60:5 (Summer 1982), pp. 1145–56; and also his 'Greater Flexibility for NATO's Flexible Response', *The Atlantic Community Quarterly*, 21:3 (Fall 1983), pp. 233–43.
4. See, for example, 'NATO's Conventional Capabilities: A Communication From the President of the United States', US House of Representatives Document No. 98–261, 98th Congress, 2nd Session, 12 September 1984. In coming years, however – particularly if the mandatory budget cuts called for by the Gramm–Rudman–Hollings Act have to be implemented, the Administration plans to distribute budget cuts within the Defence Department so as to protect funding increased for strategic offensive forces and the Strategic Defence Initiative, implying that general purpose force modernisation and readiness may suffer correspondingly. See Bill Keller, 'Missile Shield Program Gets Pentagon's Highest Priority', *The New York Times*, 29 January 1986.
5. Gert Krell, Thomas Risse-Kappen, and Hans-Joachim Schmidt, 'The No-First-Use Question in Germany', in John D. Steinbruner and Leon V. Sigal, editors, *NATO and the No-First-Use Question*, Washington, The Brookings Institution, 1983, p. 167.

6. On Woerner's thoughts on 'conventionalising' NATO strategy, see his discussion of Flexible Response and No First Use in the 1983 White Paper of the Federal German Ministry of Defence, as well as his contribution in Peter-Kurz Wuerzbach, editor, *Die Atomschwelle heben* (Raise the Nuclear Threshold), Koblenz, Bernhard Graefe Verlag, 1983. Altenburg's views are presented in his contribution to the same volume. The SPD document referred to here is 'Fuer eine neue Strategie des Buendnisses: Antrag des SPD-Parteitag in Essen in Mai 1984', Bonn, 1984. See also Krell, *et al.*, op. cit.
7. Kaiser, *et al.*, 'Nuclear Weapons and the Preservation of Peace', pp. 1169–70.
8. At the end of 1984, for example, NATO's Defence Planning Committee approved a $7.8 billion package of proposals aimed specifically at improving the alliance's non-nuclear response capability. William Drozdiak, 'NATO Agrees to $7.8 Billion in Improvements', *The Washington Post*, 5 December 1984, p. 1. NATO also recently approved a plan to co-operate in the development of new conventional weapons systems. See Bernard Gwertzman, 'NATO Will Share Work on Conventional Arms', *The New York Times*, 13 February 1986, p. 6.
9. Phillip A. Peterson and John G. Hines, 'The Conventional Offensive in Soviet Theater Nuclear Strategy', *Orbis*, 27:3 (Fall 1983), p. 725.
10. Note the following testimony given by General Rogers in 1983 before the Armed Services Committee of the US Senate, in which he elucidated NATO's prevailing concept for deliberate escalation:

    > if we are not attacked at the outset by nuclear weapons and only attacked conventionally, then I would anticipate not using the short-range nuclear weapons on our own soil first. And only when we were losing the cohesiveness of our conventional defense, would I request using some kind of nuclear weapons that could reach non-Soviet Warsaw Pact soil and/or Soviet soil. Under these conditions and under my guidance, we would strike only military targets important to us and to the other side in those numbers necessary to let them know that we are prepared, before losing the cohesiveness of our defense, to use any means available to defend ourselves. *That is the guidance under which I function at the present time. Under those conditions, I would not anticipate the early use of the short-range battlefield weapons upon our soil.* (Emphasis added)

    See Senate Armed Services Committee Hearings, *The Department of Defense Authorization for Appropriations for Fiscal Year 1984, Part 5: Strategic and Theater Nuclear Forces*, 15 March 1983, p. 2389. (Hereafter cited as Rogers, 'Senate Armed Services Committee Hearings', 1983. On the evolution of concepts for the initial use of nuclear weapons within NATO's nuclear policy-setting organ, the Nuclear Planning Group, see J. Michael Legge, 'Theater Nuclear Weapons and the NATO Strategy of Flexible Response', (Santa Monica, Ca.: The Rand Corporation, Rand Document #R-2964-FF, April 1983), pp. 17–25.

11. Peterson and Hines, 'The Conventional Offensive in Soviet Strategy', p. 725. Legge, 'Theater Nuclear Weapons and the NATO Strategy of Flexible Response', p. 43.
12. Peterson and Hines, pp. 724–5. NATO's own internal studies have predicted the follow-on use of nuclear weapons would not have decisive effects on the Warsaw Pact's ability to retaliate in kind, even if such use involved the use of hundreds of weapons on NATO's part. Legge, 'Theater Nuclear Weapons and the NATO Strategy of Flexible Response', pp. 27, 43.
13. Christopher N. Donnelly, 'Soviet Operational Concepts in the 1980s', in The European Security Study, *Strengthening Conventional Deterrence in Europe: Proposals for the 1980s* (London: Macmillan, 1983), p. 115. See also Joseph D. Douglass, *The Soviet Theater Nuclear Offensive* (Washington: USGPO, Studies in Communist Affairs, vol. 1, 1976), p. 5.
14. Kaiser, *et al.*, 'Nuclear Weapons and the Preservation of Peace', pp. 1160, 1164.
15. Legge, 'Theater Nuclear Weapons and the NATO Strategy of Flexible Response', p. 41.
16. Such was almost certainly the case in the immediate post-war period. See Matthew A. Evangelista, 'Stalin's Postwar Army Reappraised', *International Security*, 7:3 (Winter 1982/1983), pp. 110–38.
17. Perle's comments to this effect can be found in the Union Of Concerned Scientists film, *No First Use*. See also Edward N. Luttwak, 'How to Think About Nuclear War', *Commentary*, 74:2, (August 1982), p. 26.
18. President Reagan's remark was made in the course of a White House interview with several out-of-town American newspaper editors on 16 October 1981.
19. Kaiser, *et al.*, 'Nuclear Weapons and the Preservation of Peace', p. 1161.
20. Ibid., p. 1160.
21. Earl C. Ravenal, 'Counterforce and the Alliance: The Ultimate Connection', *International Security*, 6:4 (Spring 1982), p. 35–6.
22. Ibid., p. 36.
23. See the quote in note 10.
24. On the notion of 'competition in risk taking' see Thomac C. Schelling, *Arms and Influence* (New Haven: Yale University Press, 1966), p. 94.
25. Peterson and Hines, 'The Conventional Offensive in Soviet Theater Strategy', p. 695.
26. Donnelly, 'Soviet Operational Concepts in the 1980s', pp. 120–1.
27. Peterson and Hines, p. 698; Donnelly, p. 120.
28. Peterson and Hines, p. 729; Donnelly, p. 128.
29. Donnelly, p. 128; Peterson and Hines, p. 708.
30. Donnelly, p. 129. Concern is also growing within NATO that the Soviets might use their new, more accurate 'family' of tactical ballistic missiles – the SS-21, SS-22, and SS-23, armed with conventional waheads, to destroy NATO nuclear weapons storage sites, air bases, etc. in a pre-emptive attack. See Trish Gilmartin, 'Analysts Promote

SDI Technology in Development of ATBM Systems', *Defense News*, 3 February 1986, p. 22; and Friedrich Thielen, 'German Defense Minister Backs Non-Nuclear Defense System for NATO', *Defense News*, 24 February 1986, p. 11.

31. Ibid., pp. 121, 128. In general, Pact armoured elements would operate in such a way as to minimise NATO opportunities for effective employment of battlefield nuclear weapons, running dispersed until just prior to contact with the enemy, then concentrating forces close enough to the enemy's forward lines such that hostile nuclear weapons explosions would also do great damage to the defenders. See Kent F. Wisner, 'Military Aspects of Enhanced Radiation Weapons', *Survival*, 23:6 (November/December 1981), p. 248.
32. Peterson and Hines, p. 730.
33. Paul Bracken, *The Command and Control of Nuclear Forces* (New Haven: Yale University Press, 1983), p. 174.
34. Ibid., pp. 167, 174–5.
35. Ibid., p. 174.
36. Legge, 'Theater Nuclear Weapons and the NATO Strategy of Flexible Response', p. 11.
37. United States Senate, Committee on Foreign Relations, 'Second Interim Report on Nuclear Weapons in Europe', prepared by the North Atlantic Assembly's Special Committee on Nuclear Weapons in Europe, Committee Print, January 1983, p. 8.
38. Ibid., p. 7. Legge, 'Theater Nuclear Weapons and the NATO Strategy of Flexible Response', p. 27.
39. Bracken, *The Command and Control of Nuclear Forces*, pp. 174–5.
40. Earl C. Ravenal, 'No First Use: A View From the United States', *Bulletin of the Atomic Scientists*, 39:4 (April 1983), p. 14. It would be necessary to shield Western Europe as well as the United States from Soviet retaliation in order to prevent the Soviets from using Western Europe as a hostage to deter a US strategic attack.
41. This capacity will grow substantially, barring appropriate Soviet counter-measures (like widespread cruise or mobile missile deployments), once the Pershing II is fully deployed and the very accurate, powerful Trident II (D-5) SLBM is deployed in large numbers. Robert M. Bowman, 'Ballistic Missile Defense: A Strategic Issue', in John B. Harris and Eric Markusen, editors, *Nuclear Weapons and Nuclear War* (San Diego: Harcourt, Brace, Jovanovich, 1986), pp. 472–3.
42. Ibid., pp. 465–75.
43. Ravenal, 'Counterforce and the Alliance: The Ultimate Connection', p. 30; Ravenal, 'No First Use: A View From the United States', p. 14.
44. Bowman, 'Ballistic Missile Defense: A Strategic Issue', pp. 472–5.
45. A classic statement of this view is Colin S. Gray and Keith Payne, 'Victory Is Possible', *Foreign Policy*, 39 (Summer 1980), pp. 14–27.
46. Paul Bracken, 'The NATO Defense Problem', *Orbis*, 27:1 (Spring 1983), pp. 90–3; and Bracken, *The Command and Control of Nuclear Forces*, pp. 160–3.
47. Bracken, *The Command and Control of Nuclear Forces*, pp. 164–9.
48. Rogers, 'Senate Armed Services Committee Hearings', 1983, pp.

2392, 2413. See also Roger's testimony before the House Armed Services Committee, Hearings on *The Department of Defense Authorization for Fiscal Year 1985, Part 1: Authorization and Oversight*, 6 March 1984, p. 897.

49. For a thorough discussion of the liabilities of NATO's present short-range nuclear emphasis, see Leon V. Sigal, 'No First Use and NATO's Nuclear Posture', pp. 110–8, and Johan Jorgen Holst, 'Moving Toward No First Use in Practice', pp. 185–6, in John D. Steinbruner and Leon V. Sigal, editors, *Alliance Security: NATO and the No-First-Use Question* (Washington: The Brookings Institution, 1983).
50. On the shift from Massive Retaliation to Flexible Response in NATO strategy, see David N. Schwartz, 'A Historical Perspective', in Steinbruner and Sigal, *Alliance Security: NATO and the No-First-Use Question*, pp. 11–16.
51. Ibid., p. 16.
52. Rogers, House Armed Services Committee testimony, p. 898; Altenburg in Wuerzbach, editor, *Die Atmoschwelle heben*, pp. 128–9.
53. Schwartz, 'A Historical Perspective', p. 16. See also Steven L. Canby, 'NATO Strategy: Political-Military Problems of Divergent Interests and Operational Concept', *Military Review*, 59:4 (April 1979), pp. 50–52.
54. John Marshall Lee, 'The Use of Nuclear Weapons', monograph presented at the conference on 'Prospects for Peacemaking', Hubert H. Humphrey Institute of Public Affairs, University of Minnesota, November 1984, pp. 30–31. See also the arguments presented in Lee's contribution to the present volume.

6 Current NATO Strategy and No First Use: What Can They Accomplish?

Eckhard Lübkemeier

Spurred by the public controversy about the implementation of the NATO dual-track decision, the Western Alliance is currently in 'the third phase of its strategy debate'.[1] The first phase ended in 1957 with the official adoption of the doctrine of massive retaliation whose centre-piece was NATO's threat to respond to a Soviet attack in Europe by an early and if need be massive use of nuclear weapons.

Soon thereafter this concept was called in question in the US. The critics pointed out that at a time where its vulnerability to Soviet nuclear strikes was growing (the so-called Sputnik shock of 1957 played a special role in this context), it was too risky for the United States to stumble into a nuclear exchange with the USSR over any outbreak of an armed East–West confrontation in Europe. They therefore propounded that the over-reliance of the West's deterrence on nuclear arms be diminished in favour of a stronger conventional deterrent. With the advent of the Kennedy administration in January 1961, this stance became official American policy and was expounded to the European members of the Alliance by then Secretary of Defence McNamara. This second phase of the strategy debate was concluded in 1967 by promulgating the current strategy of Flexible Response.

The strategic concept underlying Flexible Response constitutes a compromise between American and European ideas. Following its own interest to minimise the risk of a European war escalating to strategic nuclear war with the Soviet Union, the US administration was in favour of a conventional defence capability which the USSR would be unable to defeat by conventional means. To the Europeans, and foremost to the then government of the Federal Republic of Germany, this involved the danger of becoming decoupled from the American nuclear umbrella which might invite the Soviet Union to step up its political and military aggressiveness against Western Europe. They therefore did not want to relinquish the explicit threat of nuclear escalation in case of a purely conventional attack by the Warsaw Pact (WP).

These conflicting European–American interests are rooted in an asymmetry of exposure between the US and Europe that is caused by geographical conditions: in contrast to the situation of the US, the threat of a Soviet nuclear attack limited to Europe constitutes a strategic threat to the West Europeans because their very existence would be at stake. As long as Western Europe continues to be dependent on the American military commitment, the Alliance will be faced with the enduring political problem of reconciling the American concern of not being dragged into all-out nuclear war by a conflict in Europe with the European interest in insuring that the Soviet Union cannot preclude that risk of escalation. Since the Atlantic 'ditch' between Europe and America cannot be filled up, no NATO strategy will ever fully satisfy either side. It must therefore be flexible enough so that it can meet both Europe's and America's vital security interests. This need has been met to date by the strategy of Flexible Response.

Flexible Response embodies three types of response: 'Direct Defence', i.e. essentially to defeat conventional attack with conventional capabilities, 'Deliberate Escalation' through a 'politically controlled selective use of nuclear weapons' and 'General Nuclear Response'. Because of the asymmetry of exposure between Europe and America there can be no lasting consensus on the issue of when should be made what response. Moreover, NATO tries to make a virtue of necessity by leaving this question open 'so as to confront an enemy in the eventuality of aggression with a risk he cannot afford to run'.[2]

The reverse of these efforts to leave the Soviets in doubt about what kind of response NATO would make, however, is its inability to agree on definite planning guidelines for NATO's forces. How many and what conventional forces does NATO need to adequately respond to conventional attack by the WP? May it be even so strong conventionally that the Soviet Union will assume that NATO would be no longer bound to resort to nuclear escalation? Would this not diminish the risk of conventional attack for the Soviets and thus increase the danger of war in Europe? And when should which nuclear weapons be employed first against which targets? How would the Soviet Union respond? Would it surrender, respond at the same level or escalate?

This paper is a discussion of these issues which affect the

conceptual basis of NATO's strategy and on which the current third phase of NATO's strategy debate is focusing. My thesis is that NATO neither will nor should give up its basic strategic concept. A deterrence strategy that is to be credible from the point of view of the opponent and that is to be supported by domestic consensus requires the resolve and capability to respond to a range of Soviet military options in such a manner that NATO will not be confronted with the alternative of surrender or provocation by disproportionate counter-measures. In contrast to the current official interpretation of this concept that a capability for flexible military response necessitates the planning and threat of a nuclear first-use, I would argue that NATO will not have a really flexible strategy until it frees itself from nuclear addiction. Because nuclear war cannot be limited[3] – if it could be nuclear deterrence would probably have failed long ago – NATO must no longer stick to plans which include options to cross the nuclear threshold first and extol this even as a virtue of its deterrence policy.

CRITERIA FOR THE ASSESSMENT OF NATO'S MILITARY STRATEGY

In order to discuss the current strategy and its change as proposed in this paper, the following seven criteria will be applied:

1. *Pre-War Deterrence* Does the strategy insure that in the perception of a potential aggressor the cost of military aggression will always be higher than his possible gains and that he will thus be deterred?
2. *Crisis Stability* Does the structure of the military forces put pressure on either the opponent or ourselves to pre-empt in a grave political crisis or even after the outbreak of limited hostilities?
3. *Intra-War Deterrence* How does the strategy meet the goals of quickly terminating the war once hostilities have started, limiting the damage and restoring deterrence on the basis of the status quo *ante bellum*?
4. *Acceptability* Is the strategy, or its essential elements, supported by public consensus?
5. *Alliance Cohesion* Does the strategy provide a common denominator that embraces the interests of all NATO members?
6. *Arms Control Compatibility* Does it promote or obstruct arms control agreements?

7. *Resources* Can the strategy be implemented with current and future financial, material and manpower resources?

PRE-WAR DETERRENCE

NATO asserts that for 40 years its military posture has contributed to securing peace in Europe. Since we do not know whether the Soviets have ever seriously contemplated attack and, if they did, what considerations made them abstain from it, such a claim can neither be proven nor disproven. However, since it is a fact that the Soviets have not attacked and Western defence preparedness has existed throughout this period, those who criticise the current strategy have the burden of the proof: they must be able to show that the changes they are proposing would at least not diminish the West's deterrence capability.

According to conventional wisdom the conflict between East and West, whose geographical divide is in Europe, has not erupted into a military conflict because both sides fear its escalation to a nuclear war of mass destruction. There are two instruments that serve NATO to demonstrate this possibility: first, the US military presence in Western Europe which is to make sure that any military aggression by the USSR in Europe would become immediately an American–Soviet confrontation, and, second, the threat of nuclear first-use which is to make the Soviet Union aware that it cannot start a war and expect to be able to keep it below the self-deterring threshold of nuclear warfare.

The question whether abandoning the second instrument might degrade the West's deterrence will be reviewed under two aspects. First, against the premise made by NATO that the Soviet Union can be reliably deterred only if it does not preclude nuclearisation of a conventional war by the West. Then this premise will be dropped and the question will be asked whether the West's deterrence would be impaired if the USSR were to preclude nuclear escalation by the West.

A no-first-use policy by NATO would be no guarantee against nuclearisation of conventional conflict. Henry Kissinger stated long ago, that 'no war in the nuclear age can ever be completely free of the spectre of nuclear weapons'.[4] Just as NATO cannot bank on the Soviet Union's commitment to never and under no circumstances use nuclear weapons first, the USSR would be unlikely to rely without any reservations on a no-first-use declaration by NATO (if both sides really were to do that they could discard their nuclear arms). A conventional armed conflict between the US and the USSR in Europe would be tantamount to a third world war which would be fought according to rules which would be driven by the then existing interests, judgements and capabilities of the nations involved, but not by any previous declarations. These interests might and probably would cause them to refrain from nuclear escalation (cf. section on 'Intra-War Deterrence'), but neither side can count on that with certainty.

Proponents of the current strategy might respond that on the basis of this argument a no-first-use policy would be the worst of all alternatives: in the last analysis, such a declaration would still not be a watertight safeguard against nuclear war while at the same time an outbreak of war would become more likely because Soviet inhibitions against attacking would be diminished. This argument, however, suffers from an internal contradiction. If the Soviet Union does not preclude nuclear escalation by NATO in spite of the latter's declaration to the contrary, her readiness to commit military aggression would not be increased by it. Thus a no-first-use policy by the West would in this case not entail a degradation of its deterrence capability.

Moreover, such a deterrence loss is unlikely even if the USSR were to assume that she alone could decide when a war would go nuclear but would have to reckon at the same time that she could launch a successful attack against NATO only by using nuclear weapons as well.

> I do not believe that, faced with that prospect, Soviet leaders would start an aggression. I believe they are no more anxious than NATO to cross the nuclear threshold; their uncertainty whether the employment of nuclear short or medium range weapons would not rapidly lead to a strategic nuclear exchange is surely as great as ours. I cannot believe that any leading Soviet politician of the present or any future leadership would want to expose his people to the potential destruction of such an exchange.[5]

But even if the Soviet Union – what is even more unlikely – were to contemplate seriously conventional attack and expected to successfully end or at least stop it before crossing the nuclear threshold, the West's deterrence would not be weakened as long as NATO would have available conventional forces which would frustrate the USSR's prospects of gaining an easy victory. No motive can be identified that could cause the Soviet leaders to attack conventionally if the odds are highly uncertain and if the USSR must fear to lose in the course of such an operation its ability for continued military control over its East European *glacis*.

CRISIS STABILITY

At present NATO has about 6000 nuclear warheads in Europe. This stockpile is to be reduced by about 1400 warheads by the end of this decade, but the balance is to be modernised. In an emergency, these warheads and bombs would have to be deployed from Special Ammunition Storage Sites where they are stored in peacetime to the sites of the launcher systems (aircraft, missiles, artillery). Many of those delivery systems have a dual capability, i.e. they can deliver both nuclear and conventional munitions. In a tense political situation where it would be important to avoid an outbreak of war by provocative military measures but to take precautions in case it did break out, the political leadership would be faced with conflicting pressures fraught with the danger of escalation. If one left the warheads at their storage sites, they might be eliminated by a Soviet attack, but if they were deployed to their delivery systems, the Soviet Union might perceive this move as preparations for their imminent employment and be provoked to counter it by pre-emptive attack (in addition there would be the problem of maintaining political control over the nuclear weapons once they were dispersed to hundreds of launching sites).

In principle, NATO's leadership bodies would be faced with these conflicting goals even if it were only a matter of maintaining one's capability for nuclear retaliation instead of also retaining a first-use option. But the problem would no longer be as acute as under the present circumstances. Currently, the price paid by NATO for a credible threat of nuclear first-use is pressure on the USSR to pre-empt NATO's nuclear first-use with the objective of depriving the West of the surprise of nuclear escalation and/or gaining a military edge. If, however, the Soviet Union were to perceive a nuclear first use by NATO as less likely, she and thus NATO would gain more time to hold back militarily and resolve the conflict by political means.

INTRA-WAR DETERRENCE

After the outbreak of a war NATO would try to 'end the war as quickly as possible under politically acceptable conditions and to restore deterrence'.[6] This goal is to be reached primarily by Direct Defence; but if a conventional Warsaw Pact attack cannot be thwarted with conventional means, 'measures of controlled nuclear escalation in the interest of early termination of the conflict by political means'[7] might be employed.

Such a nuclear first use would be an extremely risky move which probably would fail to reach its goal. Its fundamental problem was addressed briefly when discussing the 'Crisis Stability' criterion: since NATO's primary goal is to prevent war it must wish that the Soviet Union takes its threat of nuclear escalation seriously; but if the USSR would attack conventionally in spite of expecting NATO to honour its first-use threat, it would be doubtful whether she could still be impressed by NATO's resort to nuclear weapons. It should rather be assumed – as noted by the German government itself – that the Soviet leaders, should they 'ever make a political decision in favour of an attack against NATO, would consider that conflict as the final and conclusive conflict between two antagonistic governmental systems and social orders and would conduct that war accordingly'.[8] This, however, means that the Soviet Union would not preclude from the beginning a nuclearisation of such a conflict either by itself or by NATO. In the former case the Soviet Union would cross the nuclear threshold first, and in the latter a nuclear first-use by NATO would most likely be to no avail.

How little NATO can count on a nuclear first use as an instrument of intra-war deterrence and how great on the contrary the danger is that its use might court disastrous destruction at least for Western Europe comes out also in analyses of Soviet strategy. While the USSR seems to have moved away from its earlier position that war in Europe was bound to be conducted with nuclear weapons from the start, Soviet doctrine apparently has it that the only real threshold in war is the one between conventional and nuclear weapons. In other words: if NATO were the first to break the nuclear taboo, a massive nuclear counter-strike from the USSR would have to be expected.[9]

The supreme irony of the first-use option is that NATO should not wish the Soviets to adapt their strategy to its concept of flexible use of nuclear weapons. First, the Soviet expectation that limitation would no longer be possible once the nuclear threshold were crossed contains a strong motive for avoiding any military conflict with NATO because of the danger that it might escalate to uncontrolled nuclear war. Second, if the Soviet Union were to follow NATO's nuclear flexibility, this would mean that both sides no longer precluded limited nuclear wars which in the West European view would not only undermine pre-war deterrence but also its rapid restoration in war.

The dilemmas inherent in any attempt to terminate a war by nuclear first-use are reflected in contradictory requirements in operational planning. To mention but few of them: because of the escalatory risks involved, a first use could not be employed early, but it must come early enough to prevent a collapse of NATO's defence positions; to induce the adversary to end his attack and, if need be, retreat, first-use should be politically and militarily effective without provoking nuclear retaliation from the other side; to preclude as far as possible a nuclear exchange limited to Central Europe, first use should not exclude Soviet territory although this would be contrary to the American interest to spare Soviet territory at least initially.

One might object that once the Soviets had decided to run the immense risk of attacking NATO, it would take a strong antidote in the form of a nuclear first-use to convince them to terminate the hostilities quickly and settle for the status quo *ante bellum*. It can only be hoped that there will never be any evidence to prove or disprove this position. But the attending problems of a nuclear first use analysed here show that it would be an extremely risky venture to pin one's faith on this means to terminate war. Intra-war deterrence would have to be restored by political arrangements with the Soviet Union, and a nuclear first use is more likely to diminish than enhance the chances for such arrangements.

ACCEPTABILITY

Public opinion polls have shown repeatedly that a nuclear first use is rejected by most Germans. While a majority continues to be in favour of membership in NATO and armed defence in case of Soviet attack, only a small minority holds – just as in the US, UK, France and other Western countries – that nuclear first use would be justified.[10] A somewhat similar though not equally strong rejection is found also with people belonging to the security policy élite and with members of the Bundeswehr. According to a study by the Bundeswehr's social science institute, which to date has not been released by the German ministry of defense, less than 20 per cent of the rank and file, only one third of the NCOs and less than half of the officers are reported to be for nuclear defence, if necessary.[11]

In evaluating these results one must avoid falling into the trap of looking for monocausal explanations. NATO's nuclear top-heaviness as reflected in its threat of nuclear first use is only part of the answer. Any citizen will judge a strategy first and above all in terms of its war-prevention capability, i.e. whether and how it will protect him reliably from an outbreak of any kind of war but, in particular, nuclear war. But once the question is asked how war should be really conducted if it did break out, the acceptance of nuclear arms as a means of retaliation diminishes while nuclear first-use is supported even less (in the case of Germany by less than 10 per cent of those polled).

A strategy that relies on such an instrument is bound to encounter problems of acceptance each time the question of what could happen if deterrence failed is discussed by large segments of the public. Nuclear arms are needed and will continue to meet with consensus because and as long as their function is to make the Soviet Union perceive the potentially suicidal consequences of initiating nuclear warfare against NATO. When it comes to deterring the USSR, NATO underscores the cataclysmic dimension of nuclear war; but when it comes to shoring up public support for its current strategy, it has to play down the dangers of Soviet nuclear retaliation to Western nuclear first use and thus the self-destructive nature of nuclearising a war. This obvious contradiction not only strains the acceptability of the current strategy but the potential for consensus on nuclear deterrence as such and should be resolved by relegating nuclear arms to the role of deterring a Soviet nuclear first use.

ALLIANCE COHESION

In view of the geopolitically rooted asymmetry of exposure mentioned above, no NATO strategy will ever fully meet both European and American interests. NATO's security policy is therefore constantly faced with the task of maintaining the viability of the military-strategic compromise between the US and Western Europe by adapting it to a changing political and military environment. By and large, this task has been accomplished hitherto by the strategy of Flexible Response.

But its capability to establish intra-Alliance consensus is diminishing due to two interrelated trends. On the one hand by the 'decreasing acceptance of nuclear weapons in Western societies',[12] which will make it harder to uphold the threat of nuclear first use because it cannot be reconciled with the political function of 'pure' deterrence demanded by the peoples for nuclear arms. At the same time, there is a widespread European perception that the US is refining its capability of limiting nuclear warfare.

With regard to the role of nuclear weapons within Alliance strategy, a divergence of interests between Europe and America does in no way simply consist of a categorical US refusal to cross the nuclear threshold first while Western Europe would press for threatening and implementing early use of nuclear weapons. The conditions and interests on either side are much more complex and contradictory than that.

On the one hand, West European states tend to favour a strategy that maximises pre-war deterrence by making the Soviets believe that war in Europe would inevitably have a catastrophic nuclear dimension; on the other, however, this very notion strains the internal acceptability not just of NATO's nuclear but conventional forces as well. Moreover, in real war, precisely the West Europeans might want to refrain from executing the threat of nuclear escalation because it could trigger massive nuclear retaliation from the USSR against them.

To the Americans, Western Europe constitutes a region of supreme strategic importance though it is not indispensable for their survival. While the US therefore cannot want 'to sacrifice Chicago for Hamburg', it does not want either to let Western Europe fall to the Soviets. In view of this ambivalence of interests it is no wonder then that there are in the US groups that would forgo nuclear first use and the opposite faction that advocates adherence to the current NATO strategy.[13]

Nevertheless, the West Europeans must assume that, if at all, the US would use nuclear weapons first with a minimum escalatory risk.[14] This goal would motivate it to spare Soviet territory in the hope that the USSR, if it were to respond, would limit its retaliation likewise, i.e. strike Western Europe and not the US.[15] The problematic nature of a nuclear first use becomes evident if one considers that in war such an American desire would very likely not even constitute a conflict betwen European and American interests. For it must be assumed that in case of an American first use against her, the Soviet

Union would almost certainly respond in kind at least against Western Europe.

Since nuclear retaliation by the USSR against Western Europe has to be expected, American operational plans for nuclear first use will always give rise to European suspicion that the US is preparing for limited nuclear war on the European battlefield. To remove this strain on the cohesion of the Alliance is, however, primarily a European task. 'Our European Allies should not keep asking us to multiply strategic assurances that we cannot possibly mean or if we do mean, we should not want to execute because if we execute, we risk the destruction of civilization.'[16] In our context, this means that Western Europe should no longer demand a nuclear first-use pledge from the US. If this were accompanied by intensified American efforts for political accommodation with the Soviet Union (especially in the field of arms control), a move to a no-first-use regime could contribute to improving transatlantic relations.

ARMS CONTROL COMPATIBILITY

In discussing this criterion one must take into account that the factors governing the military roles of NATO's current nuclear weapons cannot be neatly differentiated: which and how many nuclear weapons are stockpiled by NATO to maintain its capability for nuclear retaliation and what part of the stockpile is by its characteristics destined for nuclear first-use? There should be hardly any system that could not perform both a retaliatory and an escalatory function.

Hence, advocating a reduction of the West's nuclear arsenal in Western Europe over and above the reduction by 1400 warheads planned by NATO, does not constitute *per se* a demand for a change in strategy. A 'politically controlled selective use of nuclear weapons' could and should be conducted, if need be, with a few weapons to keep the risk of Soviet nuclear retaliation as low as possible. NATO will always have this option as long as it has a capability for nuclear retaliation. Furthermore, even if its current strategy were maintained, NATO could do with much less than 4600 warheads envisaged for the end of this decade. It does not take several thousand weapons in a first- or second-use situation to deter or to rapidly terminate a war with the least amount of damage possible.

An abstract comparison between the current strategy and its reform proposed here, therefore, does not lead to a conclusive judgement with regard to their respective arms control compatibility. Nevertheless, the adoption of a no-first-use policy could act as an important *political* catalyst for purging NATO's nuclear assets. The heated controversy over the INF deployments had already caused NATO to speed up the ongoing review of the need for 6000 nuclear warheads deployed in Western Europe and to agree on the withdrawal of 1400 of them. Since this decision appeared to be taken under domestic pressures and during a limited phase of East–West tensions, NATO governments did not get the credit for it they had expected from internal opposition groups and the Soviet Union. Combined with a new political initiative for detente, however, a reduction of the West's nuclear over-reliance, initiated and conducted by NATO governments on their own and used as an opportunity for even farther-reaching steps in nuclear arms limitation, might give some positive impetus to the prospects of success in West–East arms control negotiations.

RESOURCES

This paper discusses the role of nuclear weapons within NATO's concept of strategic deterrence. Since there is no 'extra need' – as has been shown under the 'arms control compatibility' section – if the nuclear arsenal has to meet an escalatory role in addition to its retaliatory function, a renunciation of the threat of escalation would not lead to cost savings related to the military strategy as such.

In view of an alleged conventional imbalance in favour of the Warsaw Pact, critics of a no-first-use posture assert, however, that NATO would be unable to pay for the required strengthening of its conventional forces. What is right about this argument is that the reform of NATO's strategy propounded here would be doomed if it indeed required a substantial augmentation of conventional capabilities. Except for a dramatic deterioration of East–West relations, massive increases in defence expenditures would not meet with popular consent in Europe and even in the United States.

But such increases should not be necessary. First, realistic assessments of NATO's conventional capabilities by comparison with those of the Warsaw Pact reveal that even today NATO is in better shape than admitted officially. This is not the place to embark upon a discussion of the conventional force ratio; reference to relevant studies must suffice therefore.[17]

Second, NATO has set itself the goal to raise the nuclear threshold by enhancing its conventional defence. To reach this objective, NATO wants to make better use of the financial and manpower resources to be expected in this decade. The avowed purpose of such measures is not so much an improvement of its conventional war-fighting capability as a strengthening of the West's deterrence for in NATO's view the amount of damage caused in a full-scale protracted conventional war comes close to the devastation in limited nuclear war. Although such a comparison belittles the gruesome consequences of nuclear war, one cannot but share NATO's view that any particular policy or measure ultimately has to be judged by its impact on deterrence. Seen in this context the conventional improvements planned anyhow by NATO should be sufficient to maintain a solid conventional defence even if the first-use option were abandoned.

Lastly, arms control negotiations might help to stabilise the conventional force ratio in Europe. How successful such an attempt can be depends less on the subject matter *per se* than on the political will in East and West to reach agreements. But NATO will hardly be able to do without results in arms control negotiations even if it sticks to its current strategy. Considering that the Soviet Union disputes NATO's assertion that the East is conventionally superior and because major increases in defence spending are not in the cards, it becomes plain that without an arms control agreement the Soviet Union probably would foil NATO's aim to raise the nuclear threshold by resorting to conventional counter-measures. Hence, serious Western efforts to reach arms control agreements are needed anyhow, i.e. independent of the issue whether or not NATO's strategy should be reformed.

CONCLUSIONS

The preceding analysis can be summed up as follows: a renunciation of the nuclear first-use policy would at least not diminish pre-war deterrence decisively, would tend to slightly improve crisis stability, make intra-war deterrence less risky, enhance acceptability, strengthen cohesion within the Alliance and facilitate arms control agreements with the Soviet Union without calling for additional resources that would be unaffordable.

But this finding needs two qualifying remarks. First: adopting a no-first-use posture cannot be a panacea for the weaknesses of the current strategy. Because of the geopolitical asymmetry of exposure between Europe and the US and America's role as a globally oriented super-power, European–American security relations will always suffer from recurrent conflicts. To restrain them and keep them manageable will in the last instance be possible only if one seeks persistently to reach an understanding with the potential military adversary and political partner in the East. This insight, embodied in the Harmel Report which NATO in 1967 adopted along with the concept of Flexible Response, must be given a fresh impetus parallel to a change of NATO's military strategy. It is only then that NATO will be able in domestic and foreign policies to fully reap the fruits of such reform. Second, in the age of nuclear parity there will be no deterrence strategy without risks. Deterrence seeks to persuade the other side to refrain from military aggression by threatening unacceptable costs. In this way it contributes to an aggravation of the East–West conflict. Since nuclear weapons cannot be disinvented, however, nuclear deterrence must be so shaped that while it meets its purpose reliably it leaves at the same time room for political co-operation with the adversary.[18]

In view of the Janus face of nuclear deterrence – the price of one's own security is the threat to the other's existence and thus to one's own – there can be no deterrence strategy without running a risk. It must avoid both the Scylla of deterrence through a superior war-fighting capability and the Charybdis of political acquiescence by relinquishing adequate military retaliatory capabilities. Between these two poles a political risk assessment has to be made whose basic problem and goal is to combine political self-assertion with a sufficient military deterrent.

In this paper I have tried to demonstrate that for deterrence purposes NATO could do without the threat of nuclear first use. Until there is evidence to the contrary, i.e until NATO has renounced the first-use threat, this can be proven only by presenting plausible arguments. Even then, however, there would remain a residue of uncertainty because we cannot determine in detail what considerations keep the Soviet Union from launching an attack. It therefore cannot be precluded completely that adopting a no-first-use regime might not lead to a certain loss in deterrence. Provided one could identify this risk at all, it would however very likely be significantly lower than the drawbacks that are associated with the current strategy.

NATO recognises the problematic nature of the first-use option. This is evidenced, among other things, by its efforts to strengthen conventional defence in order to change over to a no-early-first-use policy. But this half-hearted move can only improve things gradually. As long as NATO relies on nuclear first-use – be it earlier or later – the attendant problems as regards crisis stability, intra-war deterrence, acceptability, and Alliance cohesion will in principle continue to exist.

The question whether the pressures caused by these problems will become unbearable and whether at the end of the third phase of the strategy debate NATO will give up its first-use policy will be decided in the political arena. Western Europe would be well advised to be prepared for the day when political forces in the US might prevail which may demand or in fact set about such a change in strategy.[19] Actually the West Europeans should not find it hard to do so for NATO's current nuclear addiction is not in their interest, either. It makes Europe more dependent on the US than it really is and thus impedes a transatlantic 'partnership of equals'.

Notes

1. Remark by the then federal chancellor Helmut Schmidt on 20 September 1982 (cf. *Bulletin of the Press and Information Office of the Federal Government*, Bonn, 24 September 1982, p. 803).
2. The Federal Minister of Defence, *White Paper 1983, The Security of the Federal Republic of Germany* (Bonn 1983), p. 146.
3. Cf., for instance, the following statement made by former SACEUR, General Rogers:

   SENATOR GOLDWATER: Do you honestly believe that the deployment of small tactical nuclear weapons could immediately escalate into strategic weapons?

   GENERAL ROGERS: Yes, sir, I do if those small weapons are employed.

   (US Congress, Senate, Hearings Before the Committee on Armed Services, Department of Defense Authorization for Appropriations for Fiscal Year 1983, Part 7 – *Strategic and Theater Nuclear Forces*, 97th Congress, 2nd Session, Washington, D.C., 1982, p. 4335).
4. Henry A. Kissinger, 'Limited War: Conventional or Nuclear? A Reappraisal', in Donald G. Brennan (ed.), *Arms Control and Disarmament* (London 1961), p. 138.
5. General Bernard W. Rogers, *Greater Flexibility for NATO's Flexible Response*, Strategic Review, vol. XI (Spring 1983), p. 13.
6. The Federal Minister of Defence, *White Paper 1985, The Situation and Development of the Federal Armed Forces* (Bonn 1985), p. 76.
7. Ibid., p. 30
8. Ibid., p. 45

9. For appropriate assessments cf. Stephen M. Meyer, *Soviet Theatre Nuclear Forces, Part I: Development of Doctrine and Objectives*, pp. 21–34, and *Part II: Capabilities and Implications*, pp. 46–53, The International Institute for Strategic Studies, Adelphi Paper No. 187 (Part I) and 188 (Part II), London, Winter 1983/84, as well as Benjamin S. Lambeth, *On Thresholds in Soviet Military Thought*, in The Washington Quarterly, vol. 7, no. 2 (Spring 1984), p. 76.
10. For relevant data cf. Stockholm International Peace Research Institute, *Yearbook 1984*, p. 19, and Bruce Russett/Donald R. Deluca, *Theater Nuclear Forces: Public Opinion in Western Europe*, in Political Science Quarterly, vol. 98, no. 2 (Summer 1983), p. 194.
11. Cf. Peter Schmidt, 'Public Opinion and Security Policy in the Federal Republic of Germany', in *Orbis*, Winter 1985, p. 731, and Süddeutsche Zeitung, 26/27 January 1985, p. 1, and 21 March 1985, p. 12.
12. White Paper 1983 (see note 2), p. 111.
13. Abandoning has been proposed by, among others, McGeorge Bundy/George F. Kennan/Robert S. McNamara/Gerard Smith. Cf. their article 'Nuclear Weapons and the Atlantic Alliance', *Foreign Affairs*, vol. 60, no. 4 (Spring 1982), pp. 753–68. Even the Reagan administration, which defends the current NATO strategy, is in favour of strengthening conventional defence.
14. McNamara reports that as secretary of defense he had recommended to presidents Kennedy and Johnson never to use nuclear arms first. 'I believe they accepted my recommendation.' Robert S. McNamara, 'The Military Role of Nuclear Weapons: Perceptions and Misperceptions', in *Foreign Affairs*, vol. 62, no. 1 (Fall 1983), p. 79.
15. The deployment of Pershing II and cruise missiles, which can reach the USSR from Western Europe, does not contradict this assumption. If the US were prepared to initiate a strategic nuclear exchange with the USSR for the sake of Western Europe it would not need the Pershing IIs to do so but could use its missiles deployed in the US. If it were not prepared to do so, it either would not use the Pershing IIs at all or employ them only against targets in non-Soviet WP countries.
16. Henry A. Kissinger, 'The Future of NATO', in Kenneth A. Myers (ed.), *NATO – The Next Thirty Years* (Boulder and London, 1980), p. 8.
17. For an official evaluation cf. *White Paper 1985* (note 6), pp. 53–65. For analyses arriving at more optimistic results, though in varying degrees, cf. Anthony H. Cordesman, 'The NATO Central Region and the Balance of Uncertainty', in *Armed Forces Journal International*, July 1983; John J. Mearsheimer, 'Why the Soviets Can't Win Quickly in Central Europe', in *International Security*, vol. 7, no. 1 (Summer 1982); Barry R. Posen, 'Measuring the European Conventional Balance', in *International Security*, vol. 9, no. 3 (Winter 1984/85); The International Institute for Strategic Studies, *The Military Balance 1984–5* (London, 1984), p. 151. Christian Krause, 'Worst Case-Denken als Motiv westlicher Sicherheitspolitik', (Worst-Case Thinking as a Motive of Western Security Policy), in Wilhelm Bruns/Christian Krause/Eckhard Lübkemeier, *Sicherheit durch Abrüstung* (Security

Through Arms Control) (Bonn, 1984).

18. This shows the importance of international arms control. A major reason for the stagnation of detente policy since the end of the last decade is the fact that the East–West arms competition, which had not been sufficiently bridled, frustrated all endeavours towards political co-operation.
19. The Strategic Defence Initiative (SDI) as presented by President Reagan in his address of 23 March 1983 ('to render nuclear weapons impotent and obsolete') is tantamount to decoupling Western Europe from the US strategic nuclear umbrella. For if the Soviet Union were to follow suit and build such a defensive shield for herself she could eliminate the danger that a nuclear war in Europe might spread to her own territory. It is this danger that serves NATO to deter the Soviet Union from attacking in Europe. Even in the unlikely event that the US should succeed in building a thoroughly reliable defence against strategic and theater ballistic missiles, Western Europe, that would continue to be threatened by a host of other Soviet nuclear systems (short-range missiles, cruise missiles, nuclear-capable aircraft and artillery), would need to rely on the option of striking Soviet territory with nuclear means.

Part III

Alternatives to Nuclear Deterrence in Europe

7 Non-Nuclear, Non-Provocative Defence for Europe

Frank Barnaby and Egbert Boeker

The conventional wisdom is that if Warsaw Pact forces attacked NATO they would probably win the war in a few weeks unless NATO used battlefield nuclear weapons to stop the advancing Warsaw Pact forces. As General Bernard Rogers, Supreme Allied Commander Europe, put it in a recent (13 January 1983) speech to the Dutch Parliament:

> NATO's current military posture will require us – if attacked conventionally – to escalate fairly quickly to the second response of our strategy, 'deliberate escalation' to nuclear weapons. The plain fact is that we have built ourselves a short war; we simply are unable to sustain ourselves for long with manpower, ammunition and war reserve stocks to replace battlefield losses and expenditures. Therefore, we face the serious risk of having no recourse other than the use of nuclear weapons to defend our soil.

This means, of course, also the risk of having to use nuclear weapons on West German territory; this use would inevitably result in the death of a large number of West German civilians and great damage to property. The cost to NATO in death and collateral damage of using battlefield nuclear weapons would be so high as to make this use incredible.

General Rogers stressed that NATO's need to use nuclear weapons early in a war would occur *even under optimum conditions* in which

> we would have sufficient warning time, in which we would get timely and appropriate decisions from the political authorities to move up that scale of alert measures that are so necessary, that we have our forces in their general defensive position, they have dug themselves in, they have implemented their barrier plan, put their mines out, are ready to blow the bridges in front of them, all of

> those kinds of things, built their fields of fire – and this is all very time consuming – even under the most optimum of conditions, the day will come after a conventional attack when we can no longer sustain ourselves with manpower, with ammunition, and with prepositioned war reserve material to replace losses on the battlefield, such as tanks and howitzers. Therefore, under the guidance under which I function, I must go to the political authorities, before we lose the cohesiveness of our defense and request the release of nuclear weapons to defend.

But would the political leaders give permission to use nuclear weapons? Not if they are rational, many argue.

It is generally believed to be unlikely that a nuclear war could be limited to the use of battlefield nuclear weapons. As General Rogers himself said in the same speech to the Dutch Parliament,

> I do not think that a limited nuclear war in Europe is possible. No, if we have to resort to the use of nuclear weapons under current conditions if attacked or if we reach that conventional capacity I described and the attack is conventional and they resort to the use of nuclear weapons, in my opinion it cannot be limited to Western Europe. I happen to be one who believes there would be fairly quick escalation to the strategic level. We have that strategic umbrella in the United States that is to be used if there are attacks against Western Europe which we cannot handle conventionally and with theatre nuclear weapons. I really think it would escalate and could not be limited.

General Rogers argues that NATO could get out of its dilemma of having to choose, if there were a war in Europe, between nuclear suicide and capitulation by accepting his advice to improve its conventional forces. 'The alternative to the Soviet Union', the General stated, 'if we get a conventional capacity that can frustrate her conventional attack is to withdraw or to escalate. Withdrawal is certainly a more viable alternative to her than capitulation is to us.' The General did not explain why he believes that the USSR is more likely to withdraw (i.e., capitulate) than the West.

General Rogers' plan is based on the use of very powerful conventional warheads, accurately delivered by long-range ballistic missiles on targets far behind the front line, not a non-nuclear one; it essentially aims at delaying NATO's use of nuclear weapons, it is a 'no-early-nuclear-first-use plan'. Medium- and long-range nuclear weapons are still integrated into Roger's Follow-On Forces Attack (FOFA) concept.

This paper will present as an alternative to the FOFA plan, a scheme for the non-nuclear non-provocative defence of Europe, probably achievable within current military budgets and with no reliance on the use of nuclear weapons. The scheme maximises the advantage NATO has over the Warsaw Pact in the electronic order of battle. We believe that the superiority of the West in microelectronics is considerable and the gap will persist to NATO's advantage for the foreseeable future.

In fact, the military technological leads the West has over the East, particularly those based on microelectronics and microprocessors, greatly favour the establishment of a conventional defensive deterrent. This does not mean that we support the continuous effort being made by both sides in military technological developments. On the contrary, we recognise that the struggle by both the USA and the USSR for military pre-eminence is an important cause of the ongoing arms race, nuclear and conventional, between them. The arms race will continue until both sides stop attaching such enormous political importance to gaining and retaining technological superiority.

The defence system we are advocating is based on the principle of *non-provocative defence*: the size, weapons, training, logistics, doctrine, operational manuals, war-games, manoeuvres, text-books used in military academies, etc., of the armed forces are such that they are seen *in their totality* to be capable of a credible defence without any reliance on the use of nuclear weapons, yet incapable of offence. In other words, self defence is permitted (many, in fact, regard the provision of it as the prime duty of governments) and preparations are made for it, but only in a way that neighbouring countries or power blocs cannot reasonably feel threatened by it. The sole purpose of the possession of nuclear weapons would be to deter their first use by the other side. A submarine-based strategic nuclear force would be adequate for this purpose.

The principle of non-provocative defence is not, of course, to be equated with pacifism. It permits a military apparatus, albeit with strong restraints.

It is clear that the implementation of a non-provocative defence would remove one of the factors driving the arms race. If a military posture is demonstrably non-offensive, the 'hawks' in the neighbouring system will find it harder to convince their own establishment that they need new weapon systems for self-protection.

In the non-nuclear non-provocative defence scheme we propose a defence zone, some 50 km deep, to be prepared all along the East–West border (which is about 1000 km in length). This defence zone would be saturated with all kinds of sensors, a vast network of underground fibre-glass cables for communications and numerous positions for troops to take cover. There would be surveillance by, for example, remotely piloted vehicles. Very mobile squads of several nationalities would have trained in the area and become very familiar with it. All would have interchangeable equipment. All details of the area would be fed into computers, so that any hostile troop or tank movements could be located and identified very accurately and destroyed by pre-planned fire. The armed forces would be equipped with a judicious mix of effective anti-tank, anti-aircraft and anti-ship missiles and anti-tank cannons and light anti-aircraft artillery. Command, control, communications and intelligence systems would be mainly computerised but decentralised. Highly mobile squads of troops armed with defensive weapons of high fire power (mainly missiles) would be deployed against any enemy forces which broke through the forward defence zone and troops would be dispersed to deter attack by airborne forces and to defend coastal areas.

The armed forces would not have long-range missiles, main battle tanks, aircraft (except single-role interceptors) or warships (other than fast missile patrol boats for coastal defence and diesel-powered submarines). Nor would they have any long-range air-lift capability. The ranges of missiles would be no more than those required to bombard the defence zone, so that they would be non-provocative. This means that maximum ranges would be roughly 80 km.

A realistic assessment of the performance of defensive weapons leads to a preference for anti-tank, anti-ship, and anti-aircraft missiles using infra-red seekers for terminal guidance, until millimetre-wave and multi-mode seekers become available in a few years' time. Also indicated is a preference for single-role combat aircraft and for small diesel-powered submarines for naval defensive forces. The optimum defensive mix would include, in addition to missiles, such traditional weapons as land mines, light anti-aircraft artillery, anti-tank cannons, and so on. Complex technology would never be used for its own sake but weapons would be chosen for a specific task and operated well within their capabilities.

Last, but not least, the defence would be decentralised. Hostile weapons of mass destruction could, of course, destroy parts of the defending forces, but the rest would be left operational. The only way of occupying Germany would be to destroy it totally, leaving nothing to gain.

From a political point of view, non-provocative defence of the heart of Western Europe would be a part of a renovated 'Ostpolitik' in which good relations between Eastern and Western Europe would be central. It would be the military counterpart of the political reality that a 'liberation' of Eastern Europe is out of the question. The realism of this policy has been shown by NATO non-intervention in Hungary (1956), Czechoslovakia (1968) or Poland (1981).

We do not suggest that NATO is actually planning an offensive into Warsaw Pact countries. We accept NATO statements that all of its war scenarios start with a Warsaw Pact offensive. We believe, however, that as well as holding operations to stop the offence, counter-offensives far into Eastern Europe also figure in NATO's war games. The offensive capabilities required for these troop movements are similar to those required for a first NATO offensive into the East. Non-provocative defence would minimise offensive capabilities to such a low level that a first offensive would be out of the question.

Even now, NATO's conventional capability is, in fact, not high enough for an offensive; according to some it is possibly not even high enough for a successful defence. This is not a matter of money, for NATO Europe spends about \$116 000 million against about \$148 000 million for the Warsaw Pact (including the USSR),[1] which perceives the US and China as enemies as well. The conventional weakness of NATO is, to a large extent, a matter of poor organisation, of competing weapon systems in the different armies, and of protection of the many national weapon industries. These deficiencies cannot be solved by more defence spending, but by more efficient spending.

The slow European movement towards integration may bring about more rational and less wasteful defence spending. But the danger is that it may increase the pressure for a European nuclear force. Even without such a force, Western European military integration as it would evolve would be perceived as a threat by the East.

The best way to increase the chances for peace in Europe is an 'Ostpolitik' supported by a non-provocative military option. Such an option in Germany and the Benelux would lead to the nuclear disarmament of the British and US troops in the region. This would be a dramatic signal of NATO's intention of pursuing peace. It may ease Soviet pressures on the Eastern European buffer states and increase options for liberalisation there.

A CREDIBLE DEFENCE

The defence principle requires a *credible* defence to avoid inviting an attack through obvious weakness. Restricting ourselves once more to West Germany and the Benelux countries, and with the usual hypothesis of an offensive Warsaw Pact, we postulate three kinds of scenarios:

1. An uprising in Eastern Europe leads to Soviet military operation that for some reason crosses the East–West border.
2. Soviet leaders launch a surprise attack to occupy a major part of Germany and the Netherlands, thus establishing a fait accompli. In this scenario the readily-available Soviet troops in Eastern Germany and perhaps Poland and Czechoslovakia would be used.
3. A well-prepared, all-out attack by the Warsaw Pact on NATO, using all resources and requiring considerable mobilisation.

The non-provocative defence would deal adequately with the first two emergencies. The third one would be detected a long time in advance; long enough for NATO or the US to try to stop it by political means. If the Soviet Union then decided to go ahead, it would certainly lead to a global nuclear war. In that situation it would not matter whether there were nuclear weapons in Europe or not.

IF WEST EUROPE GETS RID OF ITS NUCLEAR WEAPONS WILL IT NOT BE VULNERABLE TO SOVIET NUCLEAR BLACKMAIL?

The danger of vulnerability to nuclear blackmail is the most frequent criticism of a non-nuclear, non-provocative defence policy. But the argument that tactical nuclear weapons deployed in Western Europe significantly reduce the threat of nuclear blackmail does not bear examination.[2]

Nuclear blackmail is most likely if the political leaders are reckless and adventurous. Blackmail, nuclear or non-nuclear, is not practised by rational political leaders conducting international affairs in a normal responsible way. If, however, reckless leaders of a nuclear superpower were intent on blackmailing smaller countries, the possession of nuclear weapons would not reduce the probability of being blackmailed. On the contrary, this possession may, in fact, increase it.

Imagine, for example, that some NATO countries were threatened by a Soviet leader and they were convinced that he meant to do what he said, and that if they resisted him he would destroy some West European cities with nuclear weapons. The situation now would be that the blackmailed countries would have a choice of giving in to the nuclear threat or starting a war which would lead to the total nuclear destruction of West Europe. No sane leader in the West would risk nuclear war and would, finally, give in to the threat. The more reckless the leader was known to be the more likely it is that his blackmail would succeed.

If, on the other hand, there were no nuclear weapons in Europe, the USSR would lose much of its standing by making crude nuclear threats against Western Europe countries, certainly internationally but also probably internally as well. Past experience shows that the USSR is sensitive to world opinion; this attitude is not likely to change. World opinion would certainly be extremely critical of a superpower making nuclear threats in peacetime against any country within a nuclear-free zone.

Nuclear blackmail would, in any case, be extremely unlikely in the absence of a military conflict in Europe. Its only objective would be to obtain some political or economic advantage, and it is, to say the least, hard to imagine credible incentives.

Many people worry about a perceived Soviet imperialism. It is argued that the Soviets may start an offensive with conventional weapons to, for example, occupy Western Europe and, if the West successfully repulsed the attack, threaten to use nuclear weapons against one or more Western cities, or against the West's major defence lines to force it to capitulate. NATO, it is said, needs tactical nuclear weapons to deter such a nuclear threat.

There are a number of reasons why we believe this view to be mistaken. To begin with, it is doubtful that the USSR has wanted to occupy Western Europe at any time since the Second World War. The Soviets certainly want a ring of buffer states around the borders of the USSR and are adamant that these states are governed by politicians who co-operate with Soviet wishes in this respect. But the problems of keeping Warsaw Pact countries in line, let alone the problems raised by the multicultural society within the USSR, are already serious enough to prevent the USSR from wanting to compound them by occupying Western European countries.

Another reason why we believe the credibility of a Soviet conventional attack on Western Europe, supported by nuclear blackmail, to be exceedingly low, is that a Soviet move into Western Europe would be totally unacceptable to the US, a fact about which the USSR can have no illusions. The Soviet acquisition of Western Europe would so strengthen the USSR that it would be seen by the US as an unbearable threat to the US economic interests.

The fear of nuclear blackmail is, therefore, misplaced. The withdrawal of nuclear weapons from the European land-mass would not change global parity and would, therefore, not essentially change today's situation. A nuclear threat against European cities would be no more credible after a non-provocative conventional defence had been established than it is now. Quite the contrary. It is just because such a defence would be more credible than the current NATO strategy that a war in Europe would be considerably less likely.

DOES A NON-NUCLEAR NON-PROVOCATIVE DEFENCE MAKE A CONVENTIONAL WAR IN EUROPE SEEM MORE ACCEPTABLE?

It must be emphasised that, assuming rational leaders, it is extremely unlikely that a war will be deliberately started in Europe, whether or not nuclear weapons are deployed here. (Many believe that the main present danger is that a nuclear war will occur through accident, miscalculation or madness.)

The choice for Europe is not between nuclear war and conventional war but between war and no war; this will remain the case for the foreseeable future. A non-nuclear non-provocative defence in Europe would greatly decrease the probability of *any* war in Europe. And this is vitally important because any war in Europe is likely to escalate to a strategic nuclear war between the superpowers. But the unlikelihood that a nuclear war will be deliberately started in Europe will be seriously undermined by the deployment of significant numbers of nuclear-war fighting weapons in Europe. If these weapons are deployed, they will become integrated in military tactics. The perception will then quickly grow that a nuclear war is 'fightable and winnable' and the probability of a nuclear war will be considerably increased.

Moreover, some conventional offensive weapons (like fuel air explosives, area denial munitions, etc.), have now become so destructive that a full-scale conventional war in Europe would cause unimaginable damage, even though no nuclear weapons were used. The smallest nuclear weapon now deployed in Europe is an atomic demolition munition, a man-portable weapon with an explosive power equivalent to that of about 10 tons of TNT. A fuel air explosive (in which an aerosol cloud of an explosive mixture is ignited when the cloud is at its maximum size) can be made to explode with an explosive power equivalent to that of several tons of TNT.

The gap between conventional and nuclear weapons has, therefore, been eroded. The absence of a 'firebreak' between conventional and nuclear weapons would increase the chance that tactical nuclear weapons would be used because military commanders would urge the use of these weapons in response to an attack against their positions with very powerful conventional weapons. As we have argued above, once any nuclear weapons were used, a war would almost certainly escalate to a strategic nuclear war in which most, if not all, of the nuclear weapons in the superpower arsenals were used.

Modern offensive conventional weapons should, therefore, not be regarded as a useful alternative to tactical nuclear weapons in, for example, schemes involving the withdrawal of battlefield nuclear weapons from central Europe.

IS A CONVENTIONAL DEFENSIVE DETERRENT A 'TECHNOLOGICAL FIX'?

Another frequent objection to a non-nuclear non-provocative defence is that it is simply a 'technological fix to a political and strategic problem'. Modern weaponry, it is said, is always going wrong, is expensive to repair, and is enormously demanding in terms of maintenance time, simply because it is so sophisticated.

We agree that this is true for almost all offensive weapons and for highly centralised command, control, and communications systems. (As Franklin C. Spinney has demonstrated, increasing technological complexity in these areas is, in fact, seriously reducing combat readiness.) But we do not believe it to be true for many defensive weapons and their supporting technologies, provided that they are operated well within their design characteristics. If this is done, and realistic values are used for their lethality, weapons can be chosen to provide a strong defensive deterrent. The key is the selection of an appropriate mix of weapons of the right quality in suitable numbers.

There is no doubt that highly exaggerated claims are made about the performance of nuclear weapons and some offensive conventional weapons. This is usually done in an attempt to make more credible requests for funding the next generation of weapons. Because of this, it is often wrongly assumed that all statements by military technologists about the performance of all weapons are exaggerated.

Weapons are, of course, not the only, or even the most important factor in defence policy. The tactics, operational skills and motivation of the troops are perhaps more important. Morale inevitably plays a critical role. The success of a military policy will be determined by whether or not the armed forces understand their function and are convinced of its usefulness. Current NATO strategies are so incredible that NATO forces cannot be expected to be motivated by them. Moreover, the reliance on the threat to use nuclear weapons soon after a war begins in Europe, involves preparing NATO troops for actions civilised societies regard as unacceptable morally and of doubtful legality. On the other hand, a conventional non-provocative defensive deterrent is totally consistent with the universally recognised right of self-defence and is, therefore, morally acceptable and unambiguously legal. And it is militarily credible. For these reasons, the armed forces should have no difficulty in identifying with it.

WHY DO YOU CONCLUDE THAT NON-NUCLEAR NON-PROVOCATIVE DEFENCE IS BETTER THAN OTHER NON-NUCLEAR DEFENCE STRATEGIES?

The other main alternatives suggested to defence policies which rely on nuclear weapons are: non-resistance (pacifism); passive resistance (as adopted, for example, by the Czechs when the USSR invaded their country); territorial defence (the involvement of the whole society in defence, as practised by Sweden, Switzerland, and other countries); and the replacement of battlefield nuclear weapons with conventional offensive weapons. We believe that there are serious snags with each of these alternatives.

Non-resistance and passive resistance are, in our opinion, not credible policies for the vast majority of the population. This we believe to be regrettable but the political reality.

Territorial defence leads to a level of militarisation of society that would probably be unacceptable to many NATO countries.

The replacement of battlefield nuclear weapons with conventional weapons of more or less comparable destructive power is, in our opinion, no solution because it would not reduce significantly the probability of nuclear war (it may even increase it) nor would it be seen by the other side as less aggressive than current NATO policy. It would not, therefore, help stop the arms race but would increase crisis instability and make more difficult arms control negotiations.

The only defence policy for NATO which would reduce the increasing danger of a nuclear war in Europe; would be cost-effective; would be as cheap as or cheaper than the current policy and, therefore, affordable; would be acceptable to most people and satisfy their demand for security; would help stop the ever spiralling East–West arms race; would be morally acceptable; would be unambiguously legal; and which would have the support of much of the military, seems to be non-provocative defence.

Notes

1. 'Military expenditure in 1982 (in 1980 dollars)', in SIPRI, *World Armaments and Disarmament, SIPRI Yearbook 1983* (London: Taylor & Francis, 1982).
2. Barnaby, Frank, and Boeker, Egbert, 'Defence without Offence: Non-Nuclear Defence for Europe', *Peace Studies Papers*, no. 8, (London: Bradford School of Peace Studies, and Housmans, 1982). An extended version was published in Dutch: *Defensie zonder Kernwapens* (Amsterdam: Meulenhoff Informatief, 1982).

8 West German Alternatives for Reducing Reliance on Nuclear Weapons

Hans Günter Brauch

Nuclear deterrence in general and the US doctrinal concept of mutual assured destruction as well as the common strategic understanding of mutual vulnerability, codified by the SALT process, and the nuclear first use option of NATO's flexible response strategy (MC14/3) have come under attack,[1] both from official[2] and unofficial circles,[3] in the United States and Europe likewise. In spite of the general agreement, that the time may have come to search for alternatives, to move from MAD to MAS (mutual assured security), as President Reagan indicated in a New York Times interview[4] or for a 'Common Security' posture, as called for by the Palme Commission,[5] nevertheless major disagreements and contradictions exist as to how European security could be enhanced with a defensive posture beyond deterrence.

Two groups of alternatives are being distinguished in this chapter: *official efforts* in the United States and in Europe, to use the anti-nuclear sentiment, to legitimate changes in the operative doctrine of the US and of NATO forces and to obtain funds both for a comprehensive buildup and modernisation of conventional forces in Europe and for a Strategic (SDI) and probably soon also for a European Defence Initiative (EDI) or an extended air defence, and *unofficial proposals* by American,[6] European[7] and West German[8] experts for a non-provocative,[9] inoffensive defence[10] or for a gradual defensivity[11] consisting of static and mobile components.

THE DOMESTIC AND THE ALLIANCE CONTEXT FOR THE SECURITY POLICY OF THE FEDERAL REPUBLIC OF GERMANY IN THE 1980s AND 1990s

Three Fundamental Domestic Challenges: Consensus, Manpower and Defence Budget

West German security policy will be confronted with three fundamental challenges in the 1980s that have to be considered in any discussion on alternatives:[12]

- a persistent *crisis of acceptance* of nuclear weapons in general and of the first use option of NATO's flexible response strategy in particular;[13]
- severe *manpower* and *recruitment problems* for the Bundeswehr;[14]
- and an *approaching fiscal crisis* of procurement policy as a consequence of cost overruns, an increasing emphasis on sophisticated equipment and high maintenance costs.[15]

All three domestic challenges are interrelated. In a period of severe manpower shortages the personnel costs for substituting draftees by conscripts may rise by a factor of five or more per soldier. The costs may even be higher the more severe the competition between the military and the private economy will be for young men and the lower the support for the armed forces will become. A mere continuation of the present trends may lead to a major crisis of legitimacy for West Germany's security policy in the 1990s.

'Whether a strategic doctrine is acceptable to the people for whom it has been developed is as important in an alliance of democratic societies as the doctrine's ability to impress the enemy,'[16] Lawrence Freedman correctly stated. The best military equipment, the most consistent doctrine and the toughest political rhetoric may not impress an opponent, if the security policy lacks the support of the people that is to be protected by the military establishment. The call for higher defence expenditure at the cost of additional cuts in the social budget in a period of the highest unemployment rate since 1945 will neither overcome the decreasing support for NATO's defence posture especially among the well-educated 'successor generation' nor will it contribute to the thorough re-examination of the conditions for consensus, Kurt Biedenkopf, a former deputy chairman of the CDU, called for in September 1982 in an address to the IISS conference.[17]

According to the Report of the Commission for Longterm

Planning of the Armed Forces of June 1982 from 1984 onwards, there will be a gradual decrease of the number of young men eligible for military service. By 1995 according to this official West German Defence Department report some 104 000 conscripts will be missing and if no decisions are taken soon the manpower of the Bundeswehr may be reduced from 495 000 men to 297 000 men by 1998.[18]

Much more severe, in the short run, will be the shortage of funds to fulfill past and future commitments. Irrespective of previous and present statements,[19] the West German Defence Minister will not be able to increase the West German defence budget by 3 per cent, agreed upon by NATO, or by an additional 4 per cent, as was called for by General Rogers to fund FOFA, and to shift from a 'fiscal orientation' to a 'threat orientation' of defence spending.[20] What impact would a real increase of 3 or 4 per cent have on the federal budget of the FRG in the 1980s and 1990s?

Hartmut Bebermeyer[21] and the research firm SALSS have published economic projections about the development of social and military spending in West Germany for the 1980s and 1990s. SALSS[22] based its budget projections for West Germany from 1985–97 on an average growth rate of 2.3 per cent and an average inflation rate of 3 per cent. SALSS argues that a nominal increase of defence expenditure of 3.5 per cent would still be tolerable. However, based on present official assumptions the manpower costs would have to increase by 5 per cent, and military procurement including R & D would have to rise by 9 per cent in nominal terms (see Figure 8.1[23]). This projection does not include a potential German contribution for the Strategic Defence Initiative or for a European Defence Initiative or an extended air defence for the late 1980s and early 1990s.[24]

If the present plans of the German Minister of Defence should be realised the portion of defence in the federal budget would increase from 20 per cent at present to 26 per cent by 1997. Given a slight increase of social expenditure from 31 to 34 per cent by 1997, only 40 instead of 50 per cent would remain for all additional functions of the Federal Government. If the West German government would comply with the NATO demand for an annual real increase of 3 per cent and for an additional 4 per cent to realise the Rogers-Plan or the FOFA concept (Follow On Forces Attack), only 21 per cent would remain for all additional tasks of the West German government[25] (see Figure 8.2[26]).

No German government, be it right or left of centre, may be expected to act according to the unrealistic defence demands of some

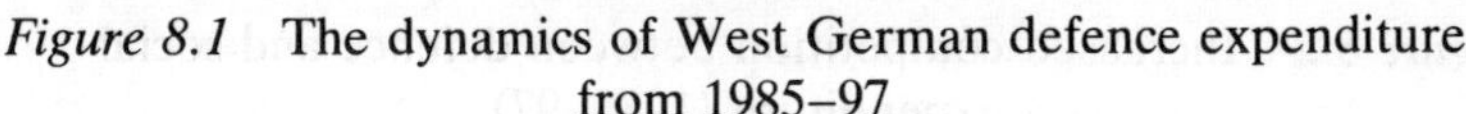

Figure 8.1 The dynamics of West German defence expenditure from 1985–97

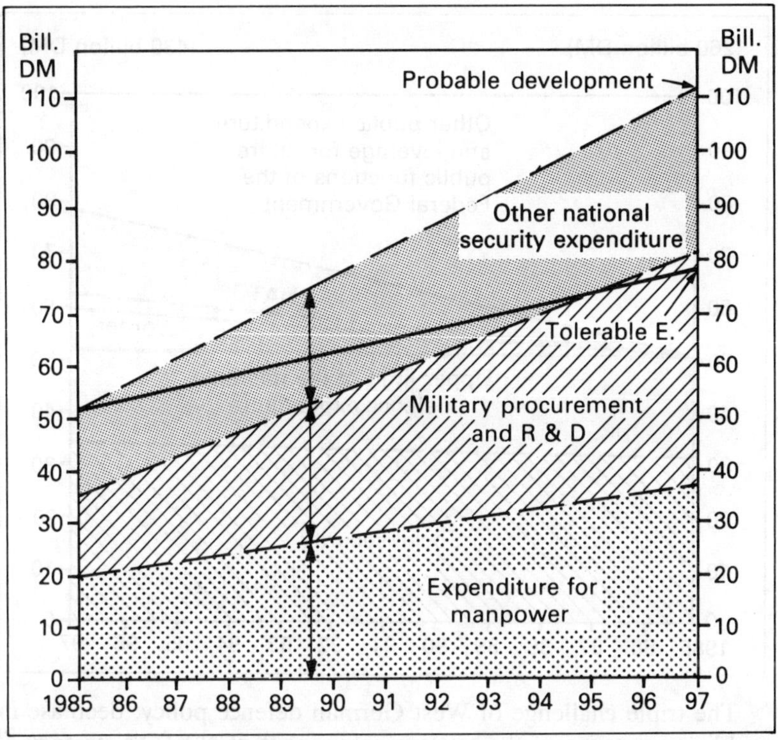

defence planners. Even the application of shock therapy, as has been repeatedly suggested by certain defence officials,[27] will not be able to change these economic constraints. It may further undermine the public support for NATO's common defence.[28]

Neither a higher reliance on nuclear weapons nor additional defence expenditures would solve the defence dilemma of West Germany and of many other West European countries. If a major increase in the defence burden could only be implemented by even deeper cuts in the social budget, especially in unemployment compensation, in the support of the pension fund from the federal budget and in the support of large families and the poor, a drastic shift in the electoral behaviour towards the left, an increase in social unrest and a decrease in domestic stability may be a direct consequence.

Figure 8.2 Increased competition between defence and social expenditure (1985–97)

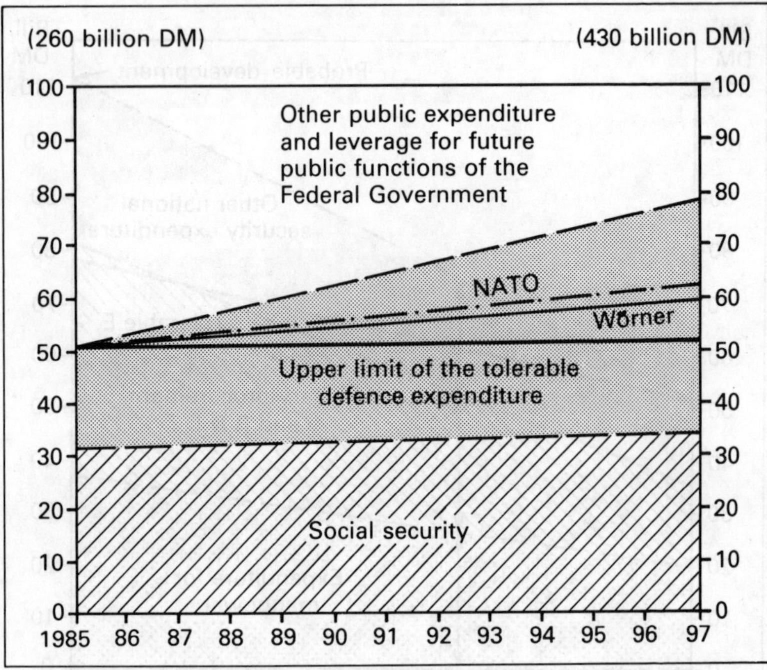

The triple challenge of West German defence policy: decrease in public acceptance of the nuclear component of NATO's strategy,[29] severe manpower shortages and budget deficits cannot be solved by a policy of incremental adaptations or of muddling through.

The manpower crisis can only be overcome and financed if a broadly-based defence consensus can be achieved in the near future. No public relations programme will be able to overcome the deep scepticism especially among the highly educated 'successor generation' relating to NATO's defence posture and strategy.

Not 'how much is enough?' will most likely dominate a realistic defence planning for the 1980s and 1990s, but 'how much can we afford' and 'how much is our population ready to accept.'

In order to regain a new domestic consensus a thorough reassessment of the nuclear and conventional foundations of NATO's defence posture will be needed combined with major political efforts and initiatives to return to a policy of relaxation of tensions and co-operation in Europe.

The Disintegration of Public Moods and of the Threat Perceptions – a Major Factor Behind the Structural Crisis within NATO

The transatlantic political squabbles on 'how much is enough' have to be seen against the background of different experiences during the 1970s. In the early 1980s the basic components of Western security policy as contained in the Harmel Report of 1967: 'defence and detente' have been questioned from two opposing angles: While the need for a sufficient defence effort and the continued reliance on nuclear weapons and on the first-use option has been questioned by the peace movement in Western Europe and by the freeze movement in the United States, the second element of 'detente' has been declared dead by the US government after the Soviet intervention in Afghanistan and by Soviet leaders after the deployment of Pershing II and Cruise Missiles in Western Europe.

While the West European NATO members in general and West Germany in particular have been admonished repeatedly by US government officials and members of the US Congress for not spending enough for their own defence, even Secretary of Defence Caspar Weinberger had to admit in his Defence Posture Statement for Fiscal Year 1983:

> An examination of long-range historical trends in a number of major burden-sharing indicators e.g., total defense spending, total defense spending as a share of GDP, total military and civilian manpower, indicates that several of our NATO allies in the aggregate, steadily assumed more of the burden over the past decade. For example, U.S. real defense spending during the 1971–79 period declined by an average of around two per cent per year, as compared to a two per cent per year increase for the non- U.S. NATO allies.[30]

Secretary Weinberger acknowledged further that traditional comparisons of the defence burden ignore the political costs of conscription:

> Germany and the other European Allies which rely heavily on conscripts feel traditional comparisons of total defense spending understate their efforts and ignore the political cost of conscription that we in the United States have chosen not to impose on our youth.
>
> National commitments cannot be measured in terms of defense

> outlays and resource commitments alone. Since Western Europe is the potential battlefield in a NATO/Warsaw Pact confrontation, our allies contribute the entirety of their civil infrastructure to the potential war effort. . . . In Germany . . . land allocation is a burden of some concern. The estimated current fair market value of all German land devoted to military use is over $80 billion compared with less than $30 billion for all U.S. real estate allocated to military purposes.[31]

Obviously it is not the lack of the defence effort on behalf of the West Europeans to defend themselves that is behind the transatlantic dispute on the defence burden but rather the disintegration of public moods within NATO based on different evaluations of the political achievements and benefits after a decade of moderate relaxation of tensions.

By many Americans, especially in the Reagan Administration, the 1970s were perceived as a period of *decline* in US military power and in global military, economic and political influence; of *humiliation* and domestic upheaval as a consequence of Vietnam, Watergate and the Iranian hostage crisis; of a declining *US defence effort* and of a steadily *increasing Soviet military buildup* and as a decade that coincided with an *economic shift* of power towards Western Europe and Japan combined with an *increased assertiveness* of its allies. As a consequence many Americans felt that the Europeans and especially the Germans have become ungrateful for the contribution the American taxpayer makes to the common Western defence effort.

The experience of the West Europeans and especially of the young generation in West Germany has been somewhat different: after the Moscow and Warsaw Treaties of 1970, the Quadripartite Berlin agreement of 1971 and the Inter-German Treaty of 1972, the 'German question' as a cause of East–West tension and anxiety has been removed from the top political agenda at the same time contributing to a multilateral detente process in the context of the CSCE. The results of Ostpolitik have been accepted by the large majority of the West German population as rather positive both on the humanitarian, the economic and on the policial level. Though detente could not solve or overcome the East–West conflict at least it initiated a process of bridge-building between the smaller European countries and it opened up many new channels of communication among West and East Europeans. This rather positive experience had an impact on the perception of Soviet intentions and of Soviet military power in West Germany. The US perception of the aggressive nature of the Soviet Union and its interpretation of the military balance in Europe has not been shared by many well-informed West German defence experts, some of them former generals, like Lt. Gen. Count von Baudissin or Brig. Gen. Christian Krause,[32] a former Parliamentary State Secretary in the Defence Department: Andreas von Bülow[33] and the Study Group for Alternative Security Policy (SAS).[34]

With the change of Government from Helmut Schmidt to Helmut Kohl in October 1982 no major change in the level of defence expenditure occurred in real terms. A tougher rhetoric and a more conservative threat analysis[35] have been combined with a fiscal conservative attitude as far as overall government spending and defence spending are concerned. Therefore, the transatlantic squabbles on the defence burden are back on the political agenda. The structural features of the bilateral German–American resource dispute are likely to stay during the late 1980s and 1990s.

Both the domestic challenges (consensus, manpower, fiscal resources) in West Germany and the different perceptions of the Soviet threat and of the future East–West relations in the US government and in the West European publics provide major constraints for the development of alternatives to nuclear deterrence. Irrespective of differences, all major West German parties of both the old and the new coalition government have repeatedly stressed their support for NATO's double strategy of defence readiness and detente as it has been developed in NATO's Harmel Report of December 1967 on 'future tasks of the alliance':

> Military security and a policy of détente are not contradictory but complementary. Collective defense is a stabilising factor in world politics. It is a necessary condition for effective policies directed towards a greater relaxation of tensions. The way to peace and stability in Europe rests in particular on the use of the Alliance constructively in the interest of détente . . . The allies are resolved to direct their energies to this purpose by realistic measures designed to further détente in East–West relations. The relaxation of tensions is not the final goal but is part of a long-term process to promote better relations and to foster a European settlement. The ultimate political purpose of the Alliance is to achieve a just and lasting peaceful order in Europe accompanied by appropriate security guarantees.[36]

Four levels of Alternatives to Nuclear Deterrence and to the Present Security Policy of NATO in General and of West Germany in Particular[37]

Four levels of alternative concepts of security policy may be distinguished:

- the *foreign policy framework* (e.g. Atlanticism, Trilateralism, Europeanisation, non-aligned Europe, a neutral confederated Germany);
- the *philosophy of security policy* (e.g. policy of strength, balance of military forces, policy of common security, a deliberate policy of inferiority);
- the *strategic concepts* (e.g. the maintenance of NATO's deterrence strategy by upgrading either the nuclear or the conventional warfighting capabilities, or the overcoming of deterrence by a gradual restructuring of the armed forces and by a gradual de-nuclearisation of Europe or even unilateral disarmament);
- the *force structure concepts* (e.g. within the present force structure of both NATO and the Bundeswehr, or slight or major modifications of the force structure with or without changes in the strategic concepts).

In this chapter I shall focus on both official and unofficial alternatives for alternative strategic concepts and force structures. Will these concepts provide an alternative to nuclear deterrence in general or to the present US nuclear doctrine of mutual assured destruction and to NATO's option of first use of nuclear weapons?

OFFICIAL ALTERNATIVES TO ENHANCE THE EUROPEAN SECURITY

Four official alternatives will be discussed briefly:

1. The *official position of the West German government*, as articulated in the German Defence White Paper 1985, that there is at present no alternative to NATO's strategy of flexible response including the nuclear first use.
2. The *announced NATO policy* to *reduce the number of battlefield nuclear weapons* in Europe as an effort to raise the nuclear threshold.
3. The *new operative doctrine* of the *US Army* (AirLand Battle, AirLand Battle 2000, Army 21) as well as other deep strike

concepts (Counterair '90, Focus 21) and *NATO's long-term defence guidance* to deal with second and third echelon forces (Follow-on-Forces-Attack).
4. The *Strategic Defence Initiative* of the American Administration and the call for a European SDI (EDI) or for an extended air defence.

The Official Position of the West German Government

The German Defence White Paper of 1985[38] states that at present no alternative is foreseeable to nuclear deterrence and to NATO's flexible defence doctrine. In the official German view no alternative exists in the future to nuclear means as long as no better way of war prevention may be achieved. Both limited nuclear weapons free zones and a no-first-use posture are being rejected. The official German view supports FOFA and SDI research and AirLand Battle as long as it is in agreement with the principles of NATO defence. The limitations of both the financial and the manpower resources are being stressed and the expectation for a greater balance in the transatlantic armament co-operation is being expressed.

The German Defence White Paper 1985 rejects all unofficial proposals for area defence, an inoffensive defence as well as the renunciation of nuclear weapons. While admitting the domestic challenges for West Germany's defence policy in the 1990s, the White Paper does not present a persuasive answer as to how those fundamental challenges could be met within the framework of the present doctrine given the severe manpower and fiscal constraints. However, the official German Defence White Paper avoids both a detailed analysis of the defensive conventional alternatives and a discussion of the implications of all three domestic challenges in order to prevent a major crisis of legitimacy of West Germany's defence policy in the 1990s.

Reduction and Modernisation of NATO's Tactical Nuclear Forces

NATO's Nuclear Planning Group (NPG) at its 34th meeting in Montebello announced on 27 October 1983 that 1400 nuclear warheads were to be withdrawn from Europe in addition to the 1000 warheads that have already been withdrawn since December 1979. However, both in the 'Decision of Montebello' and in the Final Communiqué of NATO's 37th NPG-meeting in Luxembourg on 26 and 27 March 1985, NATO agreed on several measures to modernise the remaining nuclear battlefield systems in Europe. While the NPG communiqués do not mention the specific nuclear modernisations, Secretary of Defence Weinberger, in his Defence Posture Statement for Fiscal Year 1986, described the Short-Range Nuclear Force Modernisation in detail admitting: 'Due to the greater effectiveness of the new rounds (the W79 and the W82 warheads for 203 and 155mm nuclear shells) the older ones can be replaced on less than a one-for-one basis.'[39]

If the projected nuclear warhead production plans of the US Department of Energy[40] should be realised, the following short-range theatre nuclear forces (SRINF) may be added to the US arsenals within the next decade and they may also be projected for later deployment in Western Europe: a new Advanced Atomic Demolition Munition (ADM); up to 500 Enhanced Radiation Warheads (W-70-3) for the Lance; neutron warheads (W-79-1) for the 203mm artillery shell; up to 1000 W82 warheads and possibly also nuclear warheads for the Army Tactical Missile System (ATACMs) and Patriot-ATM.

Given Secretary Weinberger's Posture Statement and the proposed nuclear warhead production schedule it appears unlikely that the role of the nuclear weapons in the defence of Europe will be downgraded. More likely may be a shift from short-range nuclear systems to medium-range systems.[41] However, these modernisations will be constrained by the Extended Zero Option on long-range INF and on short-range INF (with ranges between 500 and 1000 kilometres) that is expected to be signed in late 1987.

Deep Strike Concepts for US and NATO Forces

With the adoption of Field Manual 100-5 Operations of the US Army on 20 August 1982,[42] a shift in the operative doctrine from frontal defence ('Vorneverteidigung') towards forward defence ('Vorwärtsverteidigung') took place within the US Armed Forces. While FM 100-5 is, according to its preface 'consistent with NATO doctrine and strategy', the West German Defence Department denied its applicability for Europe initially and in 1985 it considered its applicability to Europe only as long as it will be consistent with NATO's defence principles.[43] The Defence White Paper 1985, while supporting NATO's long-term defence guideline to fight against follow-on forces (FOFA-concept), categorically excludes a forward defence ('Vorwärtsverteidigung').

However, with the increasing emphasis in the US on *deep strike concepts* that stress both the offensive, Blitzkrieg scenarios to achieve victory in a future battle (e.g. AirLand Battle 2000, Army 21, Focus 21, Counterair '90)[44] and on *emergent technologies* (ET's)[45] that call for near real time intelligence and near-zero CEP, the crisis stability is likely to decrease with increasing potentials that have to be used early in the battle in order not to be destroyed by the other side.

However, with the increasing possibility of either side to launch surprise attack options without strategic warning and without prior mobilisation, political efforts to inhibit surprise attack options by confidence- and security-building measures (CSBMs) in the context of the results of the Stockholm Conference[46] become increasingly irrelevant. Deep strike concepts and the emergent technologies called for their efficient implementation may be in conflict with the second goal of NATO's Harmel Report: detente.

On 9 November 1984 the Defence Planning Committee adopted the FOFA-Concept or the so-called Rogers-Plan as a Long Term Planning Guideline.[47] However, it appears highly doubtful whether the Rogers-Plan (FOFA) will be able to solve the structural problems of NATO and to raise the nuclear threshold as claimed. Given the dual-capability of many of its launchers they may further worst case assumptions of an opponent and undermine the verifiability of its ballistic and cruise missiles in an arms control context. FOFA-deep strike systems may lower crisis stability and increase the probability of an escalation in war. Given the pressures for pre-emption FOFA may also further a process of delegation of authority from the political to the military level already at an early stage in a conflict. The call for deep strike stand off forces that will target the GDR, Czechoslovakia and Poland may and has already provoked counter-measures on behalf of the WTO countries that undermine the security of Western Europe. The call for an annual increase of an additional 4 per cent over a ten-year period to finance the Rogers-plan (FOFA) is completely unrealistic. FOFA does neither solve the manpower problem nor the problem of acceptance. FOFA may undercut both the Stockholm and the Vienna negotiations and their successors and may violate the spirit of the 1967 Harmel Report.[48]

SDI and Extended Air Defence – Realistic Alternatives to Nuclear Deterrence

Both the High Frontier Group and President Reagan offered a space-based ballistic missile defence system as an alternative to the present nuclear doctrine of mutual assured destruction based on mutual vulnerability and as a strategic vision to overcome nuclear deterrence.[49] Will a Strategic or a European Defence Initiative or an extended air defence be able to provide an absolute area protection against Soviet nuclear weapons? Or will these concepts initiate an intensification of the offensive nuclear and the defensive arms race?

Since President Reagan's so-called 'star wars' speech, the expectations for a comprehensive and absolute area defence system that could protect the US population and its allies have been toned down by spokesmen of the SDI Organisation.[50] In the context of an even more ambitious plan: Strategic Defence Architecture for the year 2000 (SDA-2000),[51] the US Defence Department called for efforts not only against ballistic missiles (SDI), but against air-borne weapons as well: against aircraft (Air Defence Initiative (ADI)) and against cruise missiles. Given the inability of SDI to protect Western Europe against Soviet SRINF (SS-21, SS-22, and SS-23) both American and European politicians have called for a second SDI (TDI or EDI) for Europe.[52] However, neither anti-tactical missiles (ATMs)[53] nor deep strike weapons (like the US-Army TACMS) that have been mentioned as potential systems for a European Defence Initiative or for an extended air defence will be able to provide an area protection for Western Europe.[54] A requirement of up to 1000 Patriot-ATMs has been suggested to protect the Patriot air defence missiles, Pershing II missiles, air bases and special ammunition sites against Soviet SS-21, SS-22 and SS-23 attacks.[55] ATMs could only provide a limited point defence for the most vulnerable military targets. The second alternative that is being favoured by some Pentagon experts suggests to destroy the Soviet SRINF before they are being launched. However, the potential use of the Army TACMs for pre-boost phase destruction – an integral part of some deep strike concepts (AirLand Battle or FOFA) may increase preemptive pressures and may therefore decrease crisis stability.[56] If the Soviet Union should react to SDI, EDI, or an extended air defence with a greater emphasis on forward deployed short-range ballistic and cruise missiles, it will become more likely that Western Europe will become the first battlefield of a nuclear war. If both, the US and the USSR, should deploy a space based BMD, escalation dominance loses its credibility for both the Soviet Union and for the American allies in Western Europe.

None of the four official alternatives includes a 'no-first-use posture' for nuclear weapons, and none calls for a stop of the modernisation of new battlefield nuclear systems in Western Europe. It appears doubtful whether any of the alternatives can overcome the problem of acceptance of nuclear weapons for the defence of Europe. No cost projections have been published for both the implementation of FOFA and for a Tactical Defence Initiative and an improved air defence within the next 10 or 15 years. The costs of either programmes have not been included in the long-term plans of the Bundeswehr till the end of the 1990s.[57]

Though the continuation of the present defence posture and a limited modernisation of the battlefield nuclear systems in Europe will have no relevant effects on the prospects of arms control and detente it is to be expected that both FOFA, SDI, and an extended air defence will stimulate the arms competition in Europe. Neither FOFA nor an extended air defence provide an alternative to nuclear deterrence as a basis for European security.[58]

Any alternative to nuclear deterrence as a basis for European security should be in agreement with the double strategy of the Harmel-Report:

- to maintain a credible conventional defence posture,
- to pursue a policy of relaxation of tensions in Europe.

A twofold alternative strategy may be preferable to the official alternatives:

- a policy of *restructuring of the conventional forces* in such a way as to disable them for offensive operations (non-provocative defence, inoffensive defence, gradual defensivity, etc.) and
- a *policy of confidence and security building measures* that contain the most likely causes of war in Europe: an unintentional nuclear war as a consequence of increased crisis instability in Europe.[59]

This chapter will deal only with the restructuring of the conventional forces and with those proposals that have been published by West German experts.

NON-PROVOCATIVE AND INOFFENSIVE DEFENCE POSTURES FOR CENTRAL EUROPE: A SURVEY OF PROPOSALS IN THE WEST GERMAN DEBATE[60]

Instead of efforts to counter the perceived Soviet and WTO forces with similar means and a similar force structure by optimising present force structures, by increasing defence expenditures and by incorporating high technology components many defence experts both in the United States and Europe have suggested to put more emphasis on force economy through structural change. 'Structural change should', in the words of Lutz Unterseher, 'lead to functional differentiation' with forces consisting of:

- a static area defence system which employs reactive tactics,
- mechanised troops forming the active element,
- and a 'rearguard', or object-oriented system.[61]

The present German debate on structural changes of the Armed Forces was influenced by a criticism of NATO's flexible response strategy by Carl Friedrich von Weizsäcker and Horst Afheldt,[62] by a reception of both the writing of the French officer Brossolet and by the Austrian model[63] and to some extent by previous proposals by Col. Bogislaw von Bonin and Ferdinand Otto Miksche who had suggested highly mobile infantry forces as the best anti-tank force[64] in the early 1950s taking into account the previous proposals by John Frederick Charles Fuller for an 'archipelago defence' and by Liddell Hart.[65]

The present German debate on 'alternative defensive force structures has been influenced by at least three contrasting "pure" structural designs:

- the model of '*Area Defence*' (Raumverteidigung) proposed by Horst Afheldt;[66]
- the '*Area Covering Defense*' (raumdeckende Verteidigung) suggested by Jochen Löser;[67] and
- the '*fire barrier*' (Grenznahe Feuersperre) by Norbert Hannig.[68]

Other authors have modified or combined these pure designs with elements of the present structure (Uhle-Wettler,[69] Canby,[70] E. Afheldt,[71] Gerber[72] and Study Group on Alternative Security Policy (SAS)).[73]

Profiles of Competing Pure Structural Designs[74]

The *area defence* model by *Horst Afheldt*[75] would set up a network of techno-commandos all across the Federal Republic of Germany – excluding only the highly populated urban areas. He calls for a static light infantry of several thousands of autonomous units made up of 20 to 30 men each who are very familiar with a territory of 10 to 15 square kilometres which they are supposed to defend. In the forward area these forces are active permanently in order to provide a protection against surprise. Further back the reserve component to be recruited locally will increase. The equipment is based on means for blocking the aggressor (e.g. mines) and an AGTW for direct fire. The infantry component of the defensive network will neither be able to attack nor to mass forces. Any possible effort of the aggressor to concentrate his mechanised divisions will be countered by precise fire of artillery rockets directed at invading forces while (not before) they try to cross the demarcation line. These rockets (ranging between 20 and 80 kilometres) are based deep in the defender's hinterland. Just like the camouflaged positions of the techno-commandos, their launchers are randomly distributed – in order to avoid easy detection.

Major General *Jochen Löser* (Army, Ret.)[76] suggests, in the context of his *area covering defence model*, doubling the number of brigades of the Bundeswehr by relying more heavily on reservists (cadre-type organisation): the further away from FLOT (forward-line of troops) the higher the reserve proportion would be. Löser proposes that during an early phase of a longer period of transarmament, 'shield' forces consisting of light infantry should co-operate with traditional – allied and German – units functioning as 'sword' forces. In the process of trans-armament the covering elements should become preponderant and even the remaining 'sword' forces should approach the organisational pattern of light and small units. Löser maintains that the best troops would be those that could use the terrain by specialising in mine warfare, erecting field fortifications, fighting with light and easy-to-handle weapons like mortars, machine-cannons, and ATGW, having developed a high degree of fluidity (being motorised with simple vehicles of civilian make).

The concept of a forward *fire barrier* or more recently of a defence wall has been developed by the retired Air Force Lt. Col. *Norbert Hannig*[77]. He suggests that a strip along the demarcation line, four kilometres deep, should be controlled permanently with electronic sensors, and, in case of conflict, it should become impossible to cross that barrier anywhere as a consequence of concentrated fire from the rear. The essential components of fire (ATGW, partly on elevated fighting platforms, mortars with terminally-guided projectiles, artillery rockets of different calibre for transporting scatterable mines and armour piercing submunitions) are deployed in several echelons according to their range – primarily on lightly armoured vehicles in a mobile mode. In addition, according to Hannig, anti-tank helicopters would be needed. The fire power would be controlled by highly specialised units of about company size which receive their orders from a relatively centralised command structure.

Against the still valid doctrine of the Bundeswehr several military experts have argued, among them General Uhle-Wettler,[78] until July 1987 Commandant of the NATO-Defence College in Rome, that only the North German Plains and probably parts of Lower Bavaria may be defended in a cost-effective way with the present force structure – not the wooded, hilly and mountain terrain that is typical for wide areas west of the demarcation line.

More fundamental is the criticisms that the present doctrine – at least for the Bundeswehr – maintaining that the Federal Republic has to be defended with a phalanx-type-deployment of mechanised units, is a contradiction in itself. Our armoured units need space for manoeuvre. In order to develop their true talents they should be able to move freely across wide areas – both forward and backward.

Besides these common sense considerations, operation research studies conducted at the University of the Armed Forces in Munich[79] have indicated that multipurpose forces representing our current posture would to a lesser extent be able to stop or to slow down a locally superior mechanised aggressor than several reactive defence options with light, motorised infantry. But taking the case of Löser's proposal that did relatively well in the early simulations[80] it has not yet been simulated and it is doubtful whether motorised forces would be able to survive under the conditions of heavy fire.

Not only the nuclear component of our defence offers risks of destabilising political crises but also the very structure of our conventional forces raises various problems:

- The concentration of heavy equipment and large bodies of troops in stores and barracks as well as on the march in areas close to the frontier tends to be an invitation for enemy fire.
- If our mechanised forces, which could be used both for defence and (counter) attack have to be filled up with reserves, the opponent may perceive a threatening increase in the offensive potential that should be countered as early as possible.

A static defence would avoid this problem: it cannot be overcome by area covering artillery fire. Calculations have concluded that more than 100 000 rounds (155 mm howitzer) would be needed in order to destroy only one of several thousands of techno-commandos.

Hannig's concept may demonstrate a high degree of stopping power provided that the sensors are not fooled, the munitions supply for the firing units cannot be interrupted and the centralised co-ordination and command remain intact.

For all three alternatives future technological problems have to be solved. While the armed forces of today do employ various principles of tank breaking (kinetic energy and HEAT (high-explosive anti-tank) warheads, innovations in the field of armour technology provide major challenges for this very principle. The argumentation that the development potential of HEAT has not been fully exploited and that a vehicle could not be protected effectively from threat aimed at the bottom, the top, or the rear side, however, is not fully persuasive in the advent of so-called 'active armour'.

Probably the other side cannot afford to wait as a potential consequence of a crisis within its alliance that might weaken its incentive for coming first with bold strokes, and – if conventional means are insufficient to do the job – may favour the early use of nuclear weapons.

If a military exchange occurs on the battlefield probably the warning of many experts will become true: armoured and mobile units are not suitable to hold a line. If our side opts for manoeuvre warfare instead, even without the use of means of mass destruction, living in such an extended battle zone would be practically impossible for the inhabitants of Central Europe (e.g. Air Land Battle).

By adding the option of deep conventional strikes with precision guided munitions (e.g. FOFA) the destabilising tendency will be further enhanced. During a crisis, presupposing a sudden stroke ('Blitz') by the other side and if one's own means of interdiction are only effective before an opponent can develop his forces, the rationale for pre-emption becomes even more obvious.

If one uses weapons that could carry chemical or nuclear warheads as well, the opponent has no way to differentiate what is going to hit him next: escalation will become a plausible reaction.

The alternative models would like to provide as few targets as possible. To combine this concept with a *structural inability to attack*, hereby minimising the perception of threat, would remove the very reasons for pre-emptive strikes. The introduction of territorial reserves into a defensive organisation does not increase the ability to defend ourselves but does not provoke the adversary.

So far as this common philosophy is concerned, Afheldt's proposal seems to come closest to the ideal – namely 'no targets' and absence of offensive potential. Speaking about Löser's concept, there is the objection that 'everything is moving'. There is only a verbal but no structural guarantee that those light infantry units will not infiltrate the opponent's territory. Hannig's original concept, at least at present, somewhat resembles a fence, which may lead to the assumption that one could break through with concentrated fire. For this very reason (and not only as a measure against airborne assaults) both Afheldt and Löser provide an area protection. Finally, the concentration of fire in Hannig's model may be objectionable. Will not command posts (even if there are several of them) be rather inviting targets, e.g. for electronic counter-measures?

As far as the protection of the civilian population is concerned, the reviewed alternatives seem to provide a better guarantee for a limitation of the battle zone and for a prevention of the use of nuclear weapons than the existing NATO posture.

Hannig calculated that his proposal for trans-armament (vehicles, weapons and munitions) would require 18 to 20 billion dollars. Over a ten-years' time span this could be financed if *most* of the resources planned for traditional weapons systems were to be reallocated. However, are the cost estimates of the defence industry (used by Hannig) reliable for weaponry and equipment that at present are not yet ready for mass production?

He may also run into problems with the increasingly limited manpower resources. The 'military work' inherent in his concept would be so demanding that a considerable proportion of functions could not be performed by reservists.

The somewhat simpler tasks in Afheldt's structural proposal may facilitate the integration of the reserve component. Moreover, his concept – in contrast with the other two alternatives and with the existing force structure – would be advantageous because it would not require maintenance costs for mobile, possibly even armoured, carriers of defensive fire.

However, static defence too has its cost problem: one might be surprised at the prices industry will demand for adequately precise and efficient artillery rockets (the 'trouble shooters' of the area defence network). As far as the resources needed for the alternative military concepts are concerned, it should be concluded that more detailed studies will be required. It appears to be plausible that savings will be possible not so much in technical trans-armament but more so in the area of maintenance costs and by the substitution of active soldiers by reservists.

The Interactive Frontal Zone Model of the Study Group on Alternative Security Policy (SAS)[81]

The 'integrated concept' of SAS combines suggestions by Guy Brossolet, by Eckhart Afheldt, Richard Simpkin and Lutz Unterseher.[82] It tries to incorporate the following suggestions in an as cost-effective alternative as possible:

–no manned aircraft, cruise and ballistic missiles for deep strike against second and third echelon forces that could be misunderstood as a provocation;
–lack of major targets for nuclear, chemical and conventional strokes;
–frontal defence by a combination of static and mobile elements;
–predominance of static forces that are incapable for the offensive in relation to the mobile components.

The alternative defence model of SAS consists of three major elements:[83]

–a static area defence system ('Fangnetz') which employs reactive tactics;
–mechanised troops ('Feuerwehr' or 'Kavallerie') consisting of relatively compact elements including armour, cavalry and mechanised infantry forming the active element;
–and a 'rearguard' ('Rückendeckung') or object-oriented system.

According to Lutz Unterseher, the conceptual thinker of SAS:

> Close interaction between static and mobile elements could prove advantageous under many aspects: the area covering system would wear down the aggressor's strength, canalize his movements, and serve as a source of intelligence as well as cover for own counter offensives; as a result, quantity and unit size of our heavy counterattacking forces might be reduced.
>
> The mechanized force may not only be trouble shooter at the weak spots of the area defense system, there are also tasks like boosting morale of isolated outposts as well as evacuating them in case of imminent danger. There are indications that a combination of mobile and static elements could stop an invader east of the Weser-Lech-line.[84]

The static area defence system of the SAS-model calls to exploit the artificial obstacles while leaving cities undefended. In peacetime the static element would require about 150 000 soldiers to be more than doubled by reservists from the region in times of crises of which up to 80 per cent would be combat personnel. According to Unterseher: 'Mobilizing reserves for a *static* defense system could not be perceived as threatening by the adversary. The closer to the border, the higher the percentage of active personnel with the area defense: this is what safety from a surprise attack requires. Mechanized elements should consist entirely of active personnel (no buildup in times of crisis!).'[85] This static infantry force, Unterseher argues, could be well protected from concentrated artillery fire 'if the following inexpensive measures are taken: small installations (2–3 men per position only), hard cover (pre-fabricated concrete elements), 3–5 positions per crew, camouflage/plenty of decoys, dislocation in depth, and random distribution. Basic assets of static warfare are mines, other cheap engineer-made obstacles, short range, mass produced ATGMs, and simple anti-personnel-rocket launchers.'[86]

The mobile element in order to reduce the costs for the trans-armament could integrate about 70 modern fighting battalions of the Bundeswehr and 80 to 90 similar ones of the allies. The German component would comprise between 75 and 80 000 soldiers not all of them consisting of tank forces. According to Unterseher:

> The mechanized part itself could undergo functional differentiation: besides a heavily armored force, it might consist of cavalry and mobile infantry mounted on light armored vehicles: tanks are not the only currency to pay with. In order to draw advantage from Western high technology, the mobile element of a future defense should include advanced anti-tank helicopters and rocket launchers for indirect fire.[87]

The 'rearguard' (Rückendeckung) would provide the protection of objects and of the rear area. The rearguard would be highly cadred and it could – to varying degrees be manned with regional reserves. In times of crisis it could comprise about 120 000 soldiers, about 90 per cent of them being reservists.

As far as the costs of the SAS-alternative defence structure are concerned it is not assumed that PGMs and other equipment required would be cheaper. Most of the funds would be saved from active personnel (the requirements could be decreased from 495 000 down to 330 000) and from maintenance because only one third of the present mechanized vehicles would be required.

In the context of the domestic challenges that will confront West German defence policy in the 1990s the SAS-model in comparison with the official alternatives would have the following advantages:

–It would reduce those components that might beg the adversary to pre-empt; therefore it would increase crisis stability and it would provide additional time for political crisis management.
–If deterrence would fail the pressure to escalate from a conventional to a nuclear war would be reduced.
–The social system could still be financed without major shifts from the social to the defence budget which could lead to social instability.
–The future soldiers of the Bundeswehr would not be confronted with a major increase of the period of their service from presently 15 up to 24 months or more.

In comparison to the pure alternative models, the combined SAS-model could be more easily implemented in the present NATO context. Nevertheless Unterseher assumes major obstacles against the implementation of the SAS-model: bureaucratic sabotage against structural changes and by the guardians of the official threat and enemy image. As most components of the alternative model could be produced in Europe a fundamental opposition on behalf of the German and European armament industry could be avoided. Given the severe economic problems of the Soviet Union and the WTO countries it could be expected that at some stage the East might have to reconsider its own military posture due to the immense costs.[88]

EVALUATION OF THE OFFICIAL AND UNOFFICIAL ALTERNATIVE DEFENCE POSTURES

Given the domestic constraints of a decreasing manpower supply, increasing demands on the defence budget, and persistent criticisms against nuclear weapons and NATO's 'first use option', which of the official and unofficial alternative defence postures may more likely offer an affordable defence, acceptable to the people concerned, and being both credible but not intimidating for the assumed adversary?

Before moving towards a military and a political evaluation of these alternatives, a synoptic survey of basic elements of structural alternatives for defensive purposes may be appropriate.

A Synoptic Survey of Alternative Defence Postures According to Unterseher

Lutz Unterseher, the chairman of the Study Group on Alternative Defence (SAS), isolated in a synoptic comparison both from pure concepts and from the mixed concepts basic elements for which military and technological characteristics may be offered.[89] Based on these basic elements, Unterseher argued, that a combination of units both of the traditional force structure and the alternative defensive concepts may be developed (Table 8.1[90]).

This approach will broaden the public and the scientific debate which has focused in the FRG nearly exclusively on the proponents of pure alternatives: Afheldt and Löser. Most of the semi-official critiques have concentrated on the aspect of military efficiency, the alliance context and they were often based on best case assumptions about the present defence and on worst case assumptions about the area and other alternative reactive defence options.[91]

As an example for the traditional viewpoint in the West German security debate, Dieter Mahncke focused his criticisms only on two of the pure alternatives (Afheldt and Löser) excluding Hannig and the proponents of mixed or integrated concepts. Several of his criticisms against the reliance on new technologies and the weakening of the escalation ladder may apply more specifically for the Strategic Defence Initiative. For Mahncke 'only a completely effective system on both sides would lead to potential destabilization by creating precisely that situation – the elimination of nuclear weapons – which many of the alternatives seek to achieve'.[92]

A Military Evaluation Based on Operations Research Techniques

Hans W. Hoffmann, Reiner K. Huber and Karl Steiger included in their 'comparative systems analysis of alternatives for the initial defence against the first strategic echelon of the Warsaw Pact in Central Europe' on 'Reactive Defence Options' four *active defence options* consisting of structural variants within the present German Army Structure 4 (A-D); *four static area reactive defence options* including Afheldt and the SAS infantry forces but also the Swiss Territorial Defence system and the Austrian Area Defence (E.H); *three dynamic area reactive defences* including Löser's area defence concept, the SAS-battalion size cavalry regiment and the antitank teams of Füreder's[93] Cellular Defence Concept (I-L), two *continuous*

Table 8.1 Basic Elements of Structual Alternatives for Defensive Purposes: Technological, Military and Political Implications According to Unterseher

Category	*Static*			*Dynamic*		
Designation	*A* Technocommando	*B* Archipelago Defence	*C* Fire Barrier	*D* Techno-Guerilla	*E* Motorised Infantry	*F* Mechanised barriers
Short description	attrition fire, static decentralised dispersed positions, area defence mines	mutually supporting strong points based on terrain features (e.g. villages, urban sprawl)	fixed, limited firing zone, mobile (light armoured) carriers of fire arranged in depth	fluid units in covered terrain acting according to principle of hit & run; no organic vehicles, very light weapons	motorised infantry using reinforced fighting terrain zones according to the principles: block, fire, evade in mobile battle	mobile mechanised infantry operationally fighting from field fortifications of limited depth
Typical proponents	Horst Afheldt (Guy Brossollet)	P. Bracken, Fuller Garrett	Hannig	Channon/Paxon/Wise Weiner/Uhle-Wettler	Buchhorn/Löser/ Füreder	Gerber/Hofman
Emphasis on high technology	medium-strong	medium-strong	strong	medium	medium	medium
Integration of indirect fire	important	important	very important	important	less important	less important
Munitions requirements	high	high	high	low	medium	medium
Logistical requirements in battle	low	medium	high	low	high	high
Communication: hierarchical lateral	important less important	less important very important	very important less important	important less important	important important	important important
Valuable targets for adversary	low	high	medium	low	medium	medium
Battle in the rear of aggressor	yes	largely excluded	excluded	yes (infiltration)	largely excluded	largely excluded
Active/ reactive	reactive	reactive	reactive	reactive/active	reactive/active	reactive/active

fire barrier reactive defences (CFB) including Gerber's[94] ATK-Sam belt and Hannig's fire barrier (M-N) and their own light infantry battalion (P).

The comparison of the relative investment cost requirements for these 14 basic forward defence options relative to 'alternative defence options' by Hoffman *et al.* indicates (Table 8.2) that most of the alternative ('reactive') defence options are obviously more cost-effective.

Systematic OR tests and field exercises of the different defence options are extremely rare both in the United States[95] and even more so in the Federal Republic of Germany.[96] The official rejection of alternative options by arm-chair strategists like Farwick[97] contrasts with the findings of a combat simulation of 14 alternatives by Hoffmann/Huber and Steiger in 1984 that concluded:

> Overall, the results of our experiments suggest that the incorporation of properly designed reactive defense into NATO's existing force structure could indeed contribute to a significant improvement of NATO's forward defense at acceptable cost and without having to rely on 'emerging technologies', the operational performance of which tends to be overestimated, especially with regard to enemy adaptability and the demands of a battlefield environment.[98]

Unterseher pointed out that there will be no alternative to OR tests of alternative options. Nevertheless, he referred to both methodological and other weaknesses of the past tests, e.g. their limited focus on fire and attrition and their exclusion of the domestic challenges (consensus, personnel and costs) and their impact on crisis stability.

A Systematic Political Evaluation of Twenty-five Alternative Security Concepts

In my own systematic armchair evaluation I grouped 25 alternative security policy concepts in four broad categories: *foreign policy outlook* (1–5), *philosophy of security policy* (6–9), *strategic concepts* (10–14), and *force structure concepts* (15–25). I then tried to evaluate these alternatives in the framework of the following five criteria (Table 8.2):

1. They have to be in *conformity* with both the *constitutional* and the *international law*, especially with articles 24, 25 and 26 of the Basic

Law and with the charter of the United Nations and with the principles of the Final Act of Helsinki.

2. They have to be in conformity with both the *NATO* and the *WEU-treaty* and with the *goals of the Harmel Report*.
3. They have to be *acceptable for the population* concerned.
4. They must be achievable with the foreseeable *manpower*. Any suggestion that calls for an increase of the manpower of the Bundeswehr is unrealistic.
5. they must be in conjunction with the available *financial resources*. Any alternative that calls for major increases, e.g. of more than 3 per cent in real terms is unrealistic.

In the next step I distinguished among three over-all political approaches consisting of different elements of the 25 alternatives in Tables 8.2 a *conservative* or *traditionalist* approach, a *pacifist* approach and a *pragmatic reformist* approach.

The *conservative* or *traditionalist* approach to security policy in the West-German debate consists of the following components: close transatlantic ties with the goal of German reunification in the NATO-context. As far as the philosophy of security is concerned it vacillated between a policy of strength and a policy emphasising an overall balance of power. It called for an improvement both of the nuclear and of the conventional war fighting and deterrence forces. It supported the deployment of theatre nuclear forces and the modernisation of the short range nuclear systems, for tactical reasons (public acceptance) it preferred to be silent on the issue of binary weapons. While it stressed differences with the American Air-Land Battle concept it supported without restrictions the Rogers-Plan (FOFA-Concept). It is highly doubtful how the present manpower size can be maintained and the old and new commitments as well as the future plans for an extended air defence can be financed. Both the continued emphasis on NATO's deterrence posture and the support for SDI and extended air defence may intensify the problems of legitimacy of West German security policy in the 1980s and 1990s. The *traditionalist* approach is supported by the CDU/CSU and with certain reservations also by the liberal party (FDP). In the words of Unterseher:

> Nowadays, the Christian Democrats, perpetually ruling out the possibility of defensively oriented structural change – are trying to put together four elements of policy – the combination of which is inconsistent, beyond West Germany's resources, and dangerous:

Table 8.2 Evaluation of 25 Alternative Security

Criteria for the evaluation of alternative security policy options	Foreign policy context: within the NATO-framework			outside the NATO-framework		Philosophy of security policy			
	Atlanticism	Europeanisation	Reunification in the NATO-framework	Two neutral German states	Nonaligned Europe	Policy by strength	Policy of the balance of power	Policy of common security (Palme Commission)	Policy of calculated inferiority
Options	1	2	3	4	5	6	7	8	9
Compatibility with constitutional and international law	x 1	xx 2	x −− −1	x 1	x 1	? 0	x 1	xx 2	? 0
Compatibility with NATO	x 1	xx 2	x −− −1	− −− −3	x −− −1	? 0	x 1	xx 2	−− −2
Acceptance for the population	x 1	xx 2	xx 2	xx 2	x 1	−− −2	x 1	xx 2	−− −2
Manpower realisability	x 1	x 1	xx 2	x 1	x 1	−− −2	x 1	xx 2	? 0
Budgetary realisability	x 1	x 1	xx 2	x 1	xx 2	−− −2	x 1	xx 2	xx 2
Summary evaluation	5	8	4	2	4	−6	5	10	−2

Note:
Criteria for evaluation: (x) = compatible (+1), (−) not compatible (−1),

Policy Concepts According to Five Criteria

Strategic concepts					Alternative defence and force structure concepts										
thin the deterrence posture			beyond		in the framework of 'flexible response'					concepts of transarmament					
warfighting capability	Improved convent. warf. capability	'Disarmament by transarmament'	'Disarmament by denuclearisation'	Unilateral disarmament	Maintenance of frontal defence	Deployment of theatre nuclear forces	Nuclear & chemical weapons modernisation	'Rogers-plan Fofa-concept'	'AirLand Battle & AirLand Battle 2000'	Area defence model (Horst Afheldt)	Covering defence (Jochen Löser)	Fire barrier (Norbert Hannig)	Area defence + mechan. res. (E. Afheldt)	Interactive frontal zone defence (SAS)	Civil resistance
	11	12	13	14	15	16	17	18	19	20	21	22	23	24	25
	x	xx	xx	? / ––	x	?	? / ––	?	–	x	x	x	xx	xx	x–
	1	2	2	−2	1	0	−2	0	−1	1	1	1	2	2	−1
	x	xx	x	––	x	x	x	x	? / ––	x / ––	x	x	xx	xx	––
	1	2	1	−2	1	1	1	1	−2	−1	1	1	2	2	−2
	x	xx	xx	––	?	–	––	?	–	?	x	x	xx	xx	–
	1	2	2	−2	0	−1	−2	0	−1	0	1	1	2	2	−1
	––	xx	x	x / ––	x	x	x	?	?	xx	?	x	xx	xx	xx
	−2	2	1	−1	1	1	1	0	0	2	0	1	2	2	2
	x	xx	xx	xx	x	x	?	?	––	x	?	?	xx	xx	xx
	1	2	2	2	1	1	0	0	−2	1	0	0	2	2	2
	2	10	8	−5	4	2	−2	1	−6	3	3	4	10	10	0

(xx) = advantageous (+2), (– –) hardly realisable (−2), (?) = uncertain

> Beefing up the *mechanized forces*, investing in a moderate form of conventional *deep strike*, but nevertheless insisting upon a *first-use* doctrine of nuclear deterrence based on adequate assets, while at the same time trying to get on Reagan's *SDI-ticket*.[99]

The *pacifist approach* calls for a withdrawal of both German states from their respective military alliance aiming at a non-aligned Europe. The pacifist approach supports a policy of calculated inferiority beyond deterrence based on steps of unilateral disarmament.[100] The proponents of this approach[101] call for a policy of defence by non-military means (civil resistance[102]). This approach is being supported by a majority within the Greens and parts of the peace movement. A minority within the Greens pleads for a non-provocative defence for a transitional period.

The *pragmatic or reformist approach* calls for a realistic defence posture that takes into account the need to reduce the *manpower* of the Bundeswehr due to demographic reasons, to reduce the reliance on tactical and theatre nuclear land-based forces and to move gradually to a policy of non-first use in order to *regain public support* for the future defence posture. Given the budgetary constraints for West German defence policy in the 1980s and 1990s the pragmatic approach opposes both the perspective of SDI and EDI and the American plans for deep strike and calls instead for a restructuring of the conventional defence posture. The reformist approach interprets the *saving of the Welfare State* as a necessary condition to maintain domestic stability and to strengthen the motivation to defend one's own territory without committing suicide.[103]

The Social Democrats, once again in opposition, gradually shifted away from their *traditionalist* approach to a pragmatic and reformist approach in the defence area. At the Party Congress in Essen in May 1984 the SPD adopted a formula that stressed a policy of Europeanisation within NATO (two-pillar concept), of gradual denuclearisation, of security partnership with the East and a shift towards an unambiguous defensivity which remains rather vague. However, Unterseher correctly criticises the lack of conceptual clarity both in the resolution adopted at Essen and in the work of the new security commission:

> The proposal of replacing nuclear rockets like Pershing I and Lance by conventional precision guided missiles for deep strike purposes makes it obvious that neither the concept of security partnership nor the principle of defensivity has been understood

properly.... The subject of an alternative defence is currently treated in a somewhat dilatory manner – the perceived impact of the peace movement fading away and the lieutenants of Schmidt having regained their self-confidence.[104]

Nevertheless, the SPD is still the only party that has been discussing the possibility of gradually moving towards a 'defensive defence' posture since the early 1980s.

The *pragmatic* or *reformist* approach towards the defence of Central Europe may have an opportunity to initiate reforms in the security area if the Social Democrats should return to power in 1990. and if the Democrats should form the next American administration. A shift in the US–Soviet relationship and a similar outlook of a new American and a new German government could provide favourable conditions for an agonising reappraisal of the present defence posture of NATO. In the foreign policy context such a parallel conceptual innovation took place in the late 1960s and early 1970s in the era of 'detente' and 'Ostpolitik'.

Notes

I would like to thank the research and consulting firm SALSS GmbH, Riemannstr. 31, D-5300 Bonn 1, West Germany for permission to use figures 8.1 and 8.2 and the Study Group on Alternative Security (SAS), Von Guericke-Alle 1, D-5300 Bonn 1 for permission to use Table 8.1. I am especially grateful to Lutz Unterseher for permission to quote from his SAS-Working papers.

1. Horst Afheldt, *Verteidigung und Frieden* (München: Hanser 1976); K.-Peter Stratmann, *NATO-Strategie in der Krise?- Militärische Optionen von NATO und Warschauer Pakt in Mitteleuropa* (Baden-Baden: Nomos, 1981).
2. President Reagan's speech, in: *Weekly Compilation of Presidential Documents*, 28 March 1983, 19, 12, pp. 423–66; Fred Charles Iklé 'Nuclear Strategy: Can there be a happy ending', *Foreign Affairs*, Spring 1985, pp. 810–26.
3. Daniel Graham, *High Frontier, A Strategy for National Survival* (New York: Tom Doherty Associates, 1983); National Conference of Catholic Bishops, 'The Challenge of Peace: God's Promise and Our Response', *A Pastoral Letter on War and Peace*, 3 May 1983, (Washington, 1983); Edward M. Kennedy and Mark O. Hatfield, *Freeze! How you can help prevent nuclear war* (Toronto, New York, London, Sydney: Bantam, 1982) p. 169–70.
4. 'Transcript of Reagan Interview on a Range of Foreign Issues', *New York Times*, 12 Feb. 1985, p. 10.

5. *Common Security. A Programme for Disarmament, the Report of the Independent Commission on Disarmament and Security Issues* (London: Pan Books, 1982).
6. R. Levine, T. T. Connors, M. G. Weiner, R. A. Wise, 'A Survey of NATO-Defense Concepts', RAND Note N-1871-AF, June 1982; Steven Canby, 'The Alliance and Europe: Part IV: Military Doctrine and Technology', *Adelphi Paper* 109 (London: IISS, 1975); Steven Canby, 'Light Infantry Perspective', Paper presented to Infantry Commander's Conference, Ft Benning', Ga., 6 March 1984; J. J. Mearsheimer, 'Why the Soviets Can't Win Quickly in Central Europe', *International Security*, Summer 1982, pp. 5–39; J. J. Mearsheimer, 'Nuclear Weapons and Deterrence in Europe'. *International Security*, Winter 1984–85, pp. 19–76; Dietrich Fischer, *Preventing War in the Nuclear Age* (London and Canberra: Croom Helm, 1984).
7. Frank Barnaby and Egbert Boeker, 'Non-Provocative, Non-Nuclear Defense of Western Europe', Paper for the conference on Non-Nuclear War in Europe, Groningen, 28–30 November 1984; Adam Roberts, 'The Possible Role of Territorial Defense in NATO Strategy', in Hylke Tromp (ed.), *Non-Nuclear War in Europe – Alternatives for Nuclear Defence* (Groningen: Groningen University Press, 1986) pp. 139–78.
8. Hans Günter Brauch and Lutz Unterseher, 'Review Essay: Getting Rid of Nuclear Weapons: A Review of a Few Proposals for a Conventional Defence of Europe', *Journal of Peace Research* 21, 2, 1984.
9. See Frank Barnaby and Egbert Boeker, 'Defence without Offense: non-nuclear defence for Europe', *Peace Studies Papers*, 8, London, 1982.
10. Studiengruppe Alternative Sicherheitspolitik (Ed.), *Strukturwandel der Verteidigung. Entwürfe für eine konsequente Defensive*, (Opladen: Westdeutscher Verlag, 1984).
11. Hans W. Hoffmann, Reiner K. Huber and Karl Steiger, 'On Reactive Defense Options', in R. K. Huber (ed.), *Modelling and Analysis of Conventional Defence in Europe: Assessment of Improvement Options* (London & New York: Plenum 1985).
12. Hans Günter Brauch, 'Rejoinder', in Netherlands Institute of International Relations, Clingendael (ed.), *Conventional Balance in Europe: Problems, Strategies and Technologies*, (Zoetermeer, the Netherlands, 11–13 May 1984, pp. 43–49; see Hans Günter Brauch (ed.), *Sicherheitspolitik am Ende? Eine Bestandsaufnahme, Perspektiven und neue Ansätze*, (Gerlingen: Bleicher: 1984).
13. Wolfgang R. Vogt, 'The Acceptance Question and the Legitimacy of NATO's Nuclear Defense Posture in the FRG', (working title) in Hans Günter Brauch and Robert Kennedy (eds), *Alternative Conventional Defense Postures in the European Theater. The Future of the Military Balance and Domestic Constraints* (forthcoming in 1988).
14. Bernd Grass, 'The Manpower Shortage of the Bundeswehr till the Year 2000', in Brauch and Kennedy, *Alternative Conventional*

Defense Postures.

15. Hartmut Bebermeyer, 'The Fiscal Crisis of the Bundeswehr', in Brauch and Kennedy, *Alternative Conventional Defense Postures*.
16. Lawrence Freedman, 'NATO Myths', in *Foreign Policy*, 45, Winter 1981–2, p. 48.
17. Kurt Biedenkopf, 'Domestic Consensus, Security, and the Western Alliance', *Adelphi Paper* 182 (London: IISS, 1983) pp. 6–13.
18. 'Kommission für die Langzeitplanung der Bundeswehr', Report, Bonn 20 June 1982.
19. Bundesminister der Verteidigung, *Weißbuch 1983. Zur Sicherheit der Bundesrepublik Deutschland* (Bonn: Der Bundesminister der Verteidigung) and *Weißbuch 1985* (Bonn: Der Bunderminister der Verteidigung, June 1985).
20. Brauch Rejoinder.
21. Hartmut Bebermeyer and Bernd Grass, 'Unsere Streitkräfte auf dem Wege in die Ressourcenkrise', in Hans Günter Brauch (ed.), *Sicherheitspolitik am Ende*? (Gerlingen: Bleicher, 1984), p. 176–89.
22. Forschungsgruppe SALSS, *Die Verteidigung der Bundesrepublik Deutschland: Krisententendenzen und Strukturalternativen*, (Bonn: SALSS, 1985).
23. Forschungsgruppe SALSS, p. 36.
24. Hans Günter Brauch, 'Elements of a Tectical Defense Architecture', in Brauch (ed.), *Star Wars and European Defence, Implications for Europe – Perceptions and Assessments* (London: Macmillan, 1987).
25. Forschungsgruppe SALSS pp. 29–43.
26. Forschungsgruppe SALSS, p. 40.
27. Jeffrey Record and Robert J. Hanks, *US Strategy at the Crossroads: Two Views* (Cambridge Institute for Foreign Policy Analysis, 1982).
28. SALSS, *Sicherheitspolitische Grundorientierungen und 'defensive Verteidigung': Sekundäranalyse und gruppendynamische Exploration* (Bonn: SALSS, May 1985); see Vogt (note 13).
29. SALSS, *Sicherheitspolitische Grundorientierungen* and Vogt 'The Acceptance Question'.
30. Caspar W. Weinberger, Annual Report to the Congress, Fiscal Year 1983, (Washington: U.S. Department of Defense, 8 February 1982), p. 111–12f.
31. Weinberger, 8 February 1982.
32. Wilhelm Bruns, Horst Ehmke, Christian Krause (eds), *Bedrohungsanalysen. Eine Sachverständign–Anhörung* (Berlin, Bonn: Dietz, 1985).
33. Andreas von Bülow, *Die eingebildete Unterlegenheit. Das Kräfteverältnis West–Ost, wie es wirklich ist* (München: Beck, 1985).
34. SALSS and SAS, *Konventionelle Landstreitkräfte für Mitteleuropa: Eine militärische Bedrohungsanalyse* (Starnberg: Forschunginstitut für Friedenspolitik, 1984).
35. Der Bundesminister der Verteidigung, *Weißbuch 1985. Zur Lage und Entwicklung der Bundeswehr*, (Bonn: Bundesminister der Verteidigung, June 1985).
36. 'Future Tasks of the Alliance, Report of the Council (The Harmel

Report – December 1967)', in *NATO-Handbook* (Brussels, May 1979) pp. 75–7.

37. Hans Günter Brauch, 'Sicherheitspolitik im Umbruch? Außenpolitische Rahmenbedingungen und Entwicklungschaneen sicherheitspolitischer Alternativen', in Wolfgang R. Vogt (ed.), *Streitfall Frieden. Positionen und Analysen zur Sicherheitspolitik und Friedensbewegung* (Heidelberg: C. F. Müller Juristischer Verlag, 1984), pp. 145–59.
38. *Weißbuch* 1985, Bonn 1985 on alternative defence, pp. 80–1, on AirLand Battle, p. 30, on SDI, pp. 31–3.
39. Caspar W. Weinberger, Annual Report to Congress Fiscal Year 1986, 4 February 1985, (Washington: U.S. Department of Defense, 1985), p. 221.
40. William M. Arkin, Thomas B. Cochran and Milton Hoenig, 'Resource Paper on the U.S. Nuclear arsenal', in *The Bulletin of the Atomic Scientists*, Aug./Sep. 1984. pp. 12s–14s.
41. The official study of the NATO Nuclear Planning Group is generally being referred to as 'shift study'.
42. Huba Wass de Czege, L. D. Holder, 'The New FM 100-5', in *Military Review*, vol. LXII, no. 7, July 1982, p. 53–70.
43. *Weißbuch 1985*, (Bonn: 1985) p. 30.
44. Franz Borkenhagen, 'FOFA – "Konventionalisierung" und Auswitung des Gefechtsfeldes – Der "Rogers-Plan" im Rahmen der NATO-Strategie "Flexible Response"', Manuscript, 1985.
45. James P. Wade, Jr, 'New strategies and technologies', in *Netherlands Institute of International Relations*, Clingendael (ed.), *Conventional Balance in Europe: Problems, Strategies and Technologies*, (Zoetermeer, the Netherlands, 11–13 May 1984) pp. 21–9.
46. Hans Günter Brauch (ed.), *Vertrauensbildende Maßnahmen und Europäische Abrüstungskonferenz, Zehn Jahre KSZE – Analysen, Dokumente und Vorschläge* (Gerlingeu: Bleicher, 1987).
47. Bernard W. Rogers, 'Die langfristige Planungsrichtlinie FOFA: Behauptungen und Tatsachen', in *NATO-Brief*, Nr. 6/1984, p. 3–11.
48. ISFH (Institute for Security Policy and Peace Research at the University of Hamburg) 'Angriff in die Tiefe. Ein Diskussionsbeitrag zum Rogers-Plan', in *S + F*, 1/85, pp. 53–8.
49. See R. Reagan (note 2) and D. Graham (note 3) for a vision beyond deterrence.
50. See reference to a statement by Gerald Yonas, SDI chief scientist, quoted in *The Arms Control Reporter 1985*, 575.B.48 for 27 May, 1985.
51. Edgar Ulsamer, 'The Battle for SDI', in *Air Force Magazine*, February 1985, pp. 45–53.
52. Konrad Seitz, 'SDI – die technologische Herausforderung für Europa', in *Europa-Archiv*, 13/1985, 10 July 1985, pp. 381–90; see my critical assessment in: 'Oberlegungen zur Militarisierung des Weltraums und zur Betroffenehit der Bundesrepublik Deutschland', in *Die Friedenswarte*, Fall 1985.
53. Hans Günter Brauch, 'Antitactical Missile Defense – Will the European Version of SDI Undermine the ABM-Treaty?', AFES-

Papier no. 1, AG Friedensforschung und Europäische Sicherheitspolitik, Institute für Politikwissenschaft, Universität Stuttgart, (July 1985).

54. Hans Günter Brauch, 'Elements of a Tactical Defense Architecture', in Hans Günter Brauch (ed.), *Star Wars and European Defence Implications for Europe – Perceptions and Assessments*, (London: Macmillan, 1987).
55. Fred S. Hoffman, 'The "Star Wars" Debate: The Western Alliance and Strategic Defense: Part II', in *Adelphi-Papers*, no. 199, The International Institute for Strategic Studies, London 1985, pp. 25–33; Joseph Fitchett, 'First Part of U.S. "Star Wars" Defense Advocated by Mid-90's', in *International Herald Tribune*, 27 September 1984.
56. Hans Günter Brauch, *Militärische Komponenten einer Europäischen Verteidigungs initiative (EVI.). Amerikanische militärische Planungun Zur Abwehr Sowjetischer Pallistischer Raketen in Europe* (Stuttgart: Ab Friedensforschung und Europäische Sicherheitspolitik, June 1986) AFES-Papier No. 3.
57. See the speech by K. H. Schnell presented to a meeting with German defence industrialists in Bad Godesberg on 2 April 1985: 'Grundgedanken zur Beschaffungsplanung der Bundeswehr und ihre Auswirkungen auf die Industrie'. For a critical assessment of the costs of the NATO Infrastructure Plan see Hajo Hoffmann, MdB: '6,5 Milliarden DM im Handstreich für NATO-Infrastrukturausgaben (1985–90) beschlossen', 16 November 1984; John Pike, *The Strategic Defense Initiative – Budget and Program – A Staff Study* (Washington: Federation of American Scientists, 10 February 1985).
58. Hans Günter Brauch, *Angriff aus dem All – Der Rustungswettlauf im Weltraum* (Berlin, Bonn: Dietz, 1984).
59. Hans Guñter Brauch, 'Vertrauensbildung and Vertrauens-und Sicherheitsbildende Maßnahmen zwischen Rüstungsdynamik und Rüstungskontrolle – Überlegungen zur Weiterentwicklung des V(S)BM-Konzepts', in Brauch (ed.), *Vertrauensbildende Maßnahmen,* op.cit., ch. 18.
60. Lutz Unterseher (SAS), 'Towards a Feasible Defense of Central Europe – A German Perspective – empirical and normative theses', Paper presented at a German–American workshop conference: "Improving NATO Conventional Capabilities," Strategic Studies Institute, US Army War College, Carlisle Barracks, 15–16 April 1983.
61. Lutz Unterseher, 'Konventionelle Verteidigung Mitteleuropas: Etablierte Struktur und Alternativen im Test', in Hans Günter Brauch (ed.), *Sicherheitspolitik am Ende*? (Gerlingen; Bleicher, 1984). pp. 214–22.
62. Carl Friedrich von Weizsäcker (ed.), *Kriegsfolgen und Kriegsverhütung* (München: Hanser, 1972). Horst Afheldt, *Verteidigung und Frieden* (München: Hanser, 1976); Afheldt, *Defensive Verteidigung*, (Reinbek: Rowohlt, 1983); Afheldt, *Atomkrieg. Das Verhängnis einer Politik mit militärischen Mitteln* (München: Hanser, 1984).
63. Guy Brossollet, *Essai sur la non-bataille*, (Paris, 1975); Alain Carton,

Discussion infranucleaire – l'école allemand de techno-guerrilla, (Paris: CIRPES, 1984).

64. Bogislaw von Bonin, *Opposition gegen Adenauers Sicherheitspolitik. Eine Dokumentation, zusammengestellt von Heinz Brill* (Hamburg: Verlag Neue Politik, 1976); F. O. Miksche, 'Präzisionswaffen verändern das Kriegsbild', in *Wehrtechnik* 5/1977, p. 17–23.
65. J. F. C. Fuller, 'Armor and Counter-Armor, Part 3: Defense Against Armored Attack', in *Infantry Journal*, 1944, p. 39–43; B. H. Liddell Hart, *Geschichte des Zweiten Weltkrieges* (Wiesbaden: Fourier, 1970), pp. 611ff.
66. Afheldt, *Verteidigung und Frieden*.
67. Jochen Löser, *Weder rot noch tot. Überleben ohne Atomkrieg – Eine sicherheitspolitische Alternative*. (München: Günter Olzog Verlag, 1981).
68. Norbert Hannig, *Abschreckung durch konventionelle Waffen. Das David-Goliath Prinzip* (Berlin: Berlin Verlag Arno Spitz, 1984).
69. F. Uhle-Wettler, *Gefechtsfeld Mitteleuropa – Gefahr der Übertechnisierung von Streitkräften* (München: Bernard Graefe, 1980).
70. Canby, 'The Alliance and Europe'.
71. E. Afheldt, 'Verteidigung ohne Selbstmord: Vorschlag für den Einsatz einer leichten Infanterie', in Horst Afheldt, *Defensive Verteidigung* (Reinbek: Rowohlt, 1983).
72. Johannes Gerber, *Bundeswehr im Atlantischen Bündnis*, sec. 10: 'Analytischer Rückblick und prognostischer Ausblick' (Regensburg: Walhalla & Praetoria, 1984); Gerber, 'Fordert die Wirtschaftlichkeit eine neue Struktur des Heeres?' in *Heere International, vol. 3, Herford 1984*.
73. Studiengruppe Alternative Sicherheitspolitik (ed.).
74. Brauch und Unterseher 'Review Essay' (note 8).
75. Afheldt, *Verteidigung und Frieden*; Horst Afheldt, 'Tactical Nuclear Weapons and European security', in SPIRI, ed. *Tactical Nuclear Weapons: European Perspectives* (London; Taylor and Francis, 1978), pp. 262–95; Horst Afheldt, 'The necessity, preconditions and consequences of a no-first-use policy', in Frank Blackaby, Jozef Goldblat and Sverre Lodgaard (eds), *No-First-Use* (London and Philadelphia: Taylor and Francis, 1984), pp. 57–66; Horst Afheldt, 'Flexible Response and the Consequences for the Defense of Central Europe', in Hans Günter Brauch and Robert Kennedy (eds), *Alternative Conventional Defense Posture in the European Theater* (forthcoming in 1988).
76. Löser, *Weder rot noch tot*.
77. Hannig, *Abschreckung durch Konventionelle Waffen*. Norbert Hannig, 'Can Western Europe be defended by conventional means', in *International Defense Review*, no. 1, 1979, pp. 27–34; Norbert Hannig, *Verteidigen ohne zu bedrohen – Die DEWA-konzeption als Ersatz für NATO-FOFA*, AFES Papier No. 5 (Stuttgart: AFES, 1986).
78. Uhle-Wettler, *Gefechtsfeld Mitteleuropa*.
79. See note 11.

80. R. K. Huber, K. Steiger and B. Wobith, 'Ober ein analytisches Modell zur Untersuchung der Gefechtswirksamkeit von Heeresstrukturen', in *Wehrwissenschaftliche rundschau* 1/1981, pp. 1–10; R. K. Huber, 'The Systems Approach to European Defense – A Challenge for Operational Research Gaming', *Phalanx*, vol. 15, no. 3, September 1982.
81. See Studiengruppe Alternative Sicherheitspolitik; Lutz Unterseher, 'Friedenssicherung durch Vermeidung von Provokation? Ein pragmatischer Vorschlag für eine alternative Landesverteidigung', in Wolfgang R. Vogt (ed.), *Streitfall Frieden*, pp. 95–103.
82. R. E. Simpkin, *Mechanized Infantry* (Oxford: Brassey's Publishers, 1980), Lutz Unterseher, 'Für eine tragfähige Verteidigung der Bundesrepublik: Grundgedanken und Orientierungen', in Studiengruppe Alternative Sicherheitspolitik, *op. cit.*, pp. 108–130 and the SAS-papers in the Appendix.
83. 'Arbeiten der Studiengruppe Alternative Sicherheitspolitik (SAS): Landstreitkräfte zur Verteidigung der Bundesrepublik Deutschland, Anmerkungen eines Logistikers, Das Personal alternativer Landstreitkräfte, Über Luftstreitkräfte einer defensiven Verteidigung', in Studiengruppe Alternative Sicherheitspolitik (ed.), *Strukturwandel der Verteidigung. Entwürfe für eine konsequente Defensive* (Opladen: Westdeutscher Verlag, 1984)
84. Lutz Unterseher, 'Towards a Feasible Defense', p. 7.
85. 'Towards a Feasible Defense', p. 9.
86. 'Towards a Feasible Defense', p.19
87. 'Towards a Feasible Defense', p.8
88. Unterseher, in Vogt, *Streitfall, Frieden*.
89. SALSS and SAS, *Spezialisierung auf die Defensive. Einführung und Quellensammlung Ein Übersichtsgutachten* (Bonn: SALSS, August 1984).
90. SALSS and SAS, *Spezialisierung auf die Defensive*, p. 24.
91. K. H. Lather, H. Loquai, 'Alternative Konzeptionen der Verteidigung I', in *Truppenpraxis* 9/1982, pp. 623–7; H. Loquai, part 2, in *Truppenpraxis* 10/1982, pp. 703–12; K. H. Lather, part 3, in *Truppenpraxis*, 10/1982, pp. 703–12; H. E. Freiherr von Steinaecker, 'Zur "Raumverteidigung"', in *Wehrwissenschaftliche Rundschau*, 31/1, p. 1–10.
92. See the chapter by Dieter Mahncke in this volume.
93. G. Füreder, 'Non-Nuclear Defense of Europe: Example Germany, Part I and II, Working Paper 1983.
94. Gerber *Bundeswehr im Atlantischen Bündrus*.
95. Levine *et al*. 'A Survey of NATO-Defence Concepts'.
96. R. K. Huber, K. Steiger and B. Wobith, 'On an Analytical Quick Game to Investigate the Battle Effectiveness of Forward Defence Concepts', in *Journal of the Korean Operations Research Society*, 6, 1, April 1981, pp. 33–55.
97. D. Farwick, 'Flexible Reaktion und alternative Strategien. Eine vergleichende Betrachtung', in *Soldat und Technik*, 4/1984, pp. 163–9.

98. Hoffmann *et al.* 'On Reactive Defense Options'.
99. Egbert Boeker and Lutz Unterseher, 'Emphasising Defence', in Frank Barnaby and Marliester Bora, eds., *Emerging Technologies and Military Doctrine. A Political Assessment* (Basingstoke - London: Macmillan, 1986) pp. 89–109.
100. See Brauch, in Vogt, *Streitfall Frieden*, p. 155.
101. Komitee Grundrechte und Demokratie (ed.), *Frieden mit anderen Waffen* (Reinbek: Rowohlt, 1981).
102. Theodor Ebert, *Soziale Verteidigung*, 2 vols (Waldkirch: Waldkircher Verlagsgesellschaft, 1987).
103. Eckardt Afheldt, 'Verteidigung ohne Selbstmord. Vorschlag für den Einsatz einer leichten Infanterie', in Carl Friedrich von Weizsäcker, ed. *Die Praxis der defensiven Verteidigung* (Hameln: Sponholtz, 1984), pp. 41–88. A shortened English version will be published in Hans Günter Brauch and Robert Kennedy (eds), *Alternative Conventional Defense Posture in the European Theater – The Future of the Military Balance and Domestic Constraints*, Lada: Macmillan).

9 Are we Talking About the Right Issue?

Dieter Mahncke

THE NUCLEAR WEAPONS DILEMMA IN EUROPE

The so-called nuclear weapons dilemma in Europe consists, in fact, of three elements: (a) the actual defence dilemma (b) the issue of American nuclear support and (c) the problems of nuclear defence in general.

The defence dilemma rests on the fact that a defence of Western Europe against military aggression seems practically impossible without involving widespread, if not complete destruction of precisely that which is to be defended: Western Europe, its territory, its population and its society. This is obviously true in case of a nuclear conflict, but it applies almost equally to an extended conventional war. The reasons for this are the destructive capacity of modern weapons, the high density of population, particularly on the central front, and the lack of territorial depth.

The only way to avoid this defence dilemma has been to place primary emphasis on the avoidance of war. Since the threat of war is seen primarily in the possibility of Soviet aggression,[1] avoidance is first and foremost the result of effective deterrence.

NATO's deterrent posture, however, has constantly suffered from an inferior conventional force posture. Hence, from a relatively early stage onward, NATO began to emphasise nuclear weapons as a fall-back position: NATO then was superior in this field, nuclear firepower seemed less expensive than conventional manpower and, in addition, the use of nuclear weapons implied the threat of United States nuclear retaliation. This latter threat, indeed, was considered the ultimate underpinning of deterrence.

But with the development of Soviet nuclear capacity and the advent of United States' nuclear vulnerability the second main problem of European defence arose: would Americans risk their cities for the defence of Western Europe? The first half of the 1960s saw an intensive debate on this issue from MLF (Multilateral Force) to NPG (Nuclear Planning Group). At times, indeed, it seemed that

European doubts were the more difficult problem rather than the question of whether the Russians believed in the American guarantee.

Short of an independent nuclear force (the Gaullist answer) there is no final resolution to this problem. As long as the Europeans are dependent on the American nuclear umbrella they will have to rely on American assurances. This seems acceptable, however, from the European standpoint firstly, because American interest in the defence of Western Europe is evident, secondly, because American forward-based conventional and nuclear forces would immediately be involved in case of a Soviet attack, and thirdly, because the European allies are closely involved in the nuclear planning process in the Alliance, thus influencing American thinking and bringing their own interest to bear. In addition, Europeans are aware that they render a contribution to the American commitment by their own reliability and defence contribution in the Alliance.

European–American and, in particular, German–American relations have gone through alternating phases with regard to the American nuclear commitment: in the 1950s there was concern that the United States might draw the European allies into a nuclear war, in the early 1960s Europeans feared that the Americans might not stand by their commitment. At present we seem to be experiencing a phase with elements of both: whereas some see cause to fear an easy and rapid American resort to nuclear weapons, others emphasise signs of American withdrawal and decoupling and thus a weakening of deterrence.

This brings to the fore the third main problem of West European defence: the enormous destructive capacity of nuclear weapons. Although it is this destructive capacity which is an essential element of their deterrent capacity on which Europeans have relied and which they have stressed in earlier phases, uneasiness has grown not only among the peace movement. Can these weapons perform any sensible function? If they are defined as 'political weapons' only, can deterrence be credible with a doctrine that cannot guarantee its success but has no answer in case of failure? And even if deterrent logic remains superior, must not the horrible outlook in case of failure lead to an almost frantic search for alternatives?

SOME MOTIVES OF THE SEARCH FOR ALTERNATIVES

Uneasiness and concern, then, would be an appropriate heading for the varied motives behind the search for alternatives to the present system of NATO defence. For one could hardly claim that the current defence set-up has failed; it is the fear that the system *might* fail that spurs the hunt. Two factors are important here: the elapse of time and the decline of American superiority. Indeed, the long period of peace we have experienced in Europe – 40 years – seems to be more a cause for concern than for comfort, for the longer the period lasts the more doubts grow as to whether it can last much longer. Is this not historically completely unprecedented? What justification is there in a world in which human beings have morally and psychologically failed so often and changed so little to put our confidence in the deterrent system? How long can massive armaments programmes be continued without leading to eruption? And, while it is true that the enormity of destruction to be expected in case of a nuclear war is an essential factor in deterrence, is not the very elapse of time likely to reduce this factor – as European, American and Russian memories of the Second World War fade and as we get used to these weapons?

Paradoxically, however, it is the younger generation in Europe and America – those born into the age of nuclear deterrence and without memories of the Second World War – that seems particularly concerned. Yet psychologically this is quite understandable: it is the young that are asking whether a deterrent system, which is marked by constantly increasing destructive capacities, can last and guarantee their own futures – however well it may have functioned in the past.

But not only have ever-increasing armaments given rise to questions. There is much to be said for the thesis that the relative decline of American superiority and the enormous increase of Soviet military force have had an influence, perhaps even the spurring influence, in creating and increasing 'Angst' and doubts about the reliability of the system.

Perhaps this is also the background for new doubts about American reliability. Those who lack confidence in the viability of deterrence and foresee a likely use of nuclear weapons find a – presumed – American desire to withdraw from its commitment, to decouple and to limit any outbreak of nuclear violence to Europe easily understandable. Hence, they conclude, Europe must rely more on itself; moreover, and more importantly, it must seek alternatives to the present defence system.

CATEGORIES OF ALTERNATIVES

It is somewhat difficult to categorise the alternative proposals because they sometimes belong in different categories depending on what particular aspect is emphasised. But despite these overlaps a very rough division according to aims and means into three broad categories seems possible: defence without force, mobile 'backward' defence, and advance forward defence.

Proposals of the *first category* are the only ones which attempt to find a complete, a revolutionary alternative to the present system of defence and deterrence. An example is the concept of 'social defence', a concept of a 'defence without the use of force', of passive resistance and civil disobedience, as proposed in Germany, for example, by Theodor Ebert.[2]

The basic idea is that in case of an attack the victim would not offer any military resistance at all. Instead, after occupation, the occupied population would offer passive resistance by refusing to co-operate in any way with the occupiers, thus making it exceedingly difficult, if not impossible, for the occupier to 'run the country'. Terror and violence by the occupier would be endured much as danger to life and limb is borne during a war. At the same time the occupied population would seek a dialogue with the occupying soldiers, the aim being to disconcert and in the long run subvert them. In short, the occupied society must turn out to be 'indigestible' for the occupier.

Moreover, this prospect is to be made clear to any potential aggressor before aggression with the purpose of deterring aggression in the first place. Such deterrence would be enhanced by extensive preparations and even formal exercises in 'social defense' in order to make the determination of the defender clear. This means that the concept of deterrence is not sacrificed, rather a method is chosen that would be considerably less destructive should deterrence fail.

Prerequisite to such a system would be a highly cohesive and mobilised society. Preparations would have to be extensive and detailed; means to reduce the possibility of collaboration would have to be found. Citizens would have to be trained not only to endure personal terror but to endure witnessing terror and torture also against their families.

Here, obviously, lies the major difficulty: this concept would require a rather different human being and society than we now have, and it is questionable whether such a society and its individual citizens would be more humane. In other words, it is not only doubtful whether these aims are achievable, it is also doubtful whether they are desirable.

The distinguishing criterion of this concept is non-violence by the defender; by contrast all other alternatives foresee some form of military resistance.

Among these the *second category* is the largest. The proposals in this category differ in many ways, but generally they have in common the motives, the basic concept – and the weaknesses. The motives are dominated by four considerations: a defence stance is sought that would appear 'less provocative' and hence reduce the likelihood of war, that would limit damage in case of conflict, that would decrease reliance on nuclear weapons, and that promises to be more effective in case of actual conflict.

For most the basic approach involves (a) the restructuring and rearming of forces, usually to create small anti-tank units, light infantry, etc., and (b) to differing degrees the sacrifice of territory in order to allow the enemy to move in and to wear himself out as he is attacked by these highly mobile, small anti-tank units. In addition, in many proposals there would be armoured conventional forces to the rear, as a reserve, but also to regain territory once the enemy comes to a standstill. Last, but not least, the role of nuclear weapons would be reduced.

The most far-reaching example in this category is the proposal by the Afheldt cousins, who base their ideas on the Austrian Emil Spannocchi and the Frenchman Guy Brossollet.[3]

The concept consists of three elements: the withdrawal of nuclear weapons from land in Europe, the creation of a first zone of defence in which only numerous small and independent units of anti-tank forces would be operating, and a second zone to the rear in which conventional mechanised and armoured divisions would be assembled: as a reserve in case defence in the first zone fails to stop the attacker and as a force with which to liberate zone one after the attacker has been weakened.

It is believed that this concept is non-provocative ('defensive Verteidigung' = defensive defence), would limit damage in case of an attack (the defenders would defend only conventionally and outside of population centres), and would give the defender time to mobilise his conventional forces in the second zone in case the attacker does not stop his attack after suffering increasing losses in zone one. The defending conventional armoured forces would then be used to strike back against the weakened aggressor and to regain lost territory. Nuclear forces would be sea-based, but earmarked as a 'political weapon of last resort'.

Of course, the assessment of this concept is to a large extent a military assessment as to its likely effectiveness. The more effective it is considered to be, the higher its deterrent value is likely to be. It is clear that this is the decisive factor, because obviously this concept entails that the risk for the aggressor within at least the first zone of defence is considerably more calculable, quite apart from the fact that, should the first zone of defence fail to stop him, the defender would be confronted with a conventional war deep in his own territory.

To avoid this dilemma some (e.g., Carl-Friedrich von Weizsäcker, Johan Galtung) propose supplementing the system with elements of guerilla warfare and 'social defense'.[4]

It may be unjustified to seriously call the other proposals in this category alternatives in a strict sense because they are rather a further development, at most a modification of the present deterrent system. Nevertheless, they ought to be discussed here.

They have in common with the Afheldt-proposal the motives of reducing reliance on nuclear weapons and of making conventional defence more effective; more importantly, they are concepts of 'in-depth defense' ('backward defense'), i.e. concepts which foresee the sacrifice of some territory in order to create more room for successful defence. While the motive of making NATO's conventional defence more effective is completely in line with NATO history – practically from the date of its founding the Alliance has had to deal with the issue of conventional sufficiency – the idea of in-depth defence contrasts to the fundamental principle of NATO's forward defence concept.

There is a wide spectrum of proposals here that can basically be divided into concepts resting more on a rearrangement of forces[5] and concepts concentrating on a type of mobile area defence.[6] The former all feel that in view of NATO's persistent conventional inferiority it would be unwise to try to stop advancing Soviet tank armies with the same type of, but numerically inferior force. Similar to Afheldt, but considerably less radical, they propose the creation of specialised anti-tank units, usually light infantry equipped with modern precision-guided weaponry and adapted to the specific territory in which they would be operating. The issue here, as in the case of Afheldt, is to what extent such a strategy could be expected to be successful and how much territory would be sacrificed.

Sacrifice of territory is also the main issue for the latter group of proposals involving a mobile area defence: although such a mobile in-depth defence may indeed promise greater success, how much territory does NATO, does the Federal Republic of Germany have for this type of defence?

All of these proposals involve military and technical aspects which cannot be assessed here.[7] All of them, however, seem to take for granted that in case of aggression the battle would take place on Western territory, more or less – usually less – close to the demarcation line. The difficulties – physically and psychologically – that this involves are obvious. None the less, battle on NATO territory is accepted almost as a matter of course. This, in fact, is true also for the present doctrine of forward defence, although, of course, according to this doctrine the avoidance of loss of territory is a prime aim: practically no territory is to be sacrificed. An obvious reason for the presumption of battle on NATO territory is that NATO would be the victim; the only conceivable war in NATO planning would start by Warsaw Pact forces crossing the demarcation line into NATO territory. But more important are two other reasons. Firstly, NATO under no circumstances wants to appear offensive: some years ago even the expression 'Vorwärtsverteidigung' (forward defence) was changed to 'Vorneverteidigung' (in-front, front-line defence) in Germany. Secondly, every counter-attack would also cut first into German – East German – territory. At least in public there was thus a tendency to ignore these difficulties and to concentrate on the aim of avoidance of war in the first place.

Of course, NATO military doctrine has always included the possibility, indeed the likelihood of air interdiction in Warsaw Pact territory in case of a Warsaw Pact aggression. Nevertheless, under the general heading of 'deep strike'[8] this issue has been newly discussed recently, and a number of proposals have been made. Again, they are generally a further development of current NATO strategy rather than really an alternative, but still they should be mentioned here as a *third category*, particularly since the chances of realisation for some of these proposals – or aspects thereof – are probably higher than for most of the others.

There are two basic lines of thought here: one includes extensive interdiction attacks with the aid of new conventional technologies against the second and third echelons of Warsaw Pact forces (the first echelon being held by existing NATO forces), the other comprises an immediate counter-attack into Warsaw Pact territory.

The former idea is not really new: NATO strategy has always foreseen interdiction attacks, indeed, it is simple military logic once an aggression has occurred. What is new is a clearer emphasis and also some enthusiasm about the possibilities of new technologies. Hence, the arguments against this concept – high cost, limited effectiveness, Soviet response (attack without large reinforcement requirements, attacks in numerous phalanxes and echelons)[9] – really refer to over-reliance on interdiction (will it – alone – stop the advance?) and excessive expectations with regard to the new technologies; they do not, however, invalidate the entire idea of interdiction in case of a Warsaw Pact attack.

Clearly more far-reaching is the concept of 'conventional retaliation', i.e. an immediate or early conventional counter-attack into Warsaw Pact territory (e.g. from Bavaria into Czechoslovakia and the GDR) irrespective of the stability of the forward defence line and ongoing interdiction strikes against Warsaw Pact follow-on forces.[10]

If this proposal is seen not as a replacement, but as a supplement to current forward defence doctrine (in other words, the forward defence line should not be neglected or sacrificed), its strategic advantages are obvious: battle would not automatically be concentrated only on NATO territory, more importantly, in case of a Soviet attack an immediate and serious threat would be posed to the Soviet Eastern European empire. As long as battle takes place on Western territory, the Eastern Europeans would have little choice but to remain alongside the Soviet Union, but once Western troops moved successfully into Eastern Europe the reliability of her Eastern European vassals, always a thorny question for the Soviet Union, would become doubtful – for it is rather likely that Western troops would be greeted not as invaders but as liberators.[11]

Thus it is doubtful whether the major disadvantage which some attribute to this strategy – an estrangement from Eastern Europe – would really be effective. If such estrangement was not to be expected, however, the second disadvantage, viz. the complete unacceptability of this strategy to the Western European NATO allies,[12] would at least lose its objective basis (although even without objective reasons it might still be unacceptable considering how extremely concerned many Western Europeans – and many Americans, too – are about appearing 'provocative'[13]).

If deterrence is the primary goal of Western strategy, the main advantage of this concept would be the expected enhancement of deterrence – because what would immediately be threatened after a Soviet attack would be Warsaw Pact territory and, more importantly, the reliability of Soviet allies and indeed the very stability of the Soviet empire in Eastern Europe.

But paradoxically this gain might also lead to the most significant disadvantage of conventional retaliation, viz. a possible redeployment and, in particular, strengthening of Soviet forces in Eastern Europe. This, rather than the 'threat' from Western forces would disturb Eastern Europeans and, in addition, it could create new problems for NATO's forward defence.

In conclusion, a few general points on the efforts to improve conventional defence may be noted.

Firstly, one of the primary motives derives from the expected effects of nuclear weapons; concentration on these effects is at the expense of their deterrent value.

A large-scale conventional war in central Europe would be disastrous, but, with regard to long-run effects, less disastrous than a nuclear war. In this sense, there is some potential damage-limiting effect of a conventional strategy. But if, on the other hand, a primarily conventional strategy should decrease deterrence[14] and, indeed, lead to war, then, of course, comparatively damage would be much greater.

To an extent, at least, deterrence and damage limitation contradict each other, for deterrence may decrease as expected damage decreases and as the risk becomes more limited and calculable. Hence, improvement of and increased emphasis on the conventional component in Europe is in this sense always a double-edged issue – particularly from the European standpoint.

It is double-edged also in a second sense. For significant improvement of the conventional component may always imply a degree of decoupling of the United States. From the American point of view it is understandable and logical that the United States would want to avoid a quasi-automatic nuclear involvement in Europe in case of a conflict.[15] And it is true, of course, that the nuclear commitment of the United States to European defence rests more assuredly on the assessment of American interest in the effective protection of Western Europe than on any automatic process of involvement. But a European conventional defence capability equalling or considered adequate in comparison to that of the Soviet Union could lead to a reassessment of escalation and this, at least, could lead to misunderstandings as to the reliability of the ultimate

American nuclear commitment which in turn would be bound to weaken deterrence.

SOME CRITERIA FOR THE ASSESSMENT OF ALTERNATIVES

In judging the feasibility and acceptability of alternative concepts a set of criteria may be useful.

1. Does the alternative concept contribute to the major aim of Western security policy, i.e. the prevention of war by deterrence?

All of the proposed alternatives recognise the validity of deterrence, none wants to replace it by something else. In other words, all of the alternatives seek to maintain an effective deterrent function, although for many of them damage limitation rather than improved deterrence is the primary motive.

If deterrence is accepted as a valid aim, however, then alternative proposals must be questioned as to their contribution to deterrence. The proposals consider two different 'deterrent values': one is to deter by reducing the proposed gain, the other is to deter by threatening punishment.

Clearly belonging to the former type is the concept of 'social defence'. According to this concept the conquered country is expected to be 'indigestible' for the conqueror, hence he is expected to refrain from the effort to conquer in the first place.

Basically, too, all the proposals with the primary aim of thwarting an attack by forms of 'in-depth' or 'backward defence' belong in the first category. Their primary aim is to deny gain rather than to threaten punishment. If seen purely in terms of conventional defence even the present concept of forward defence falls essentially into this category. Only the proposal of conventional retaliation would then clearly be of the second type.

But, of course, most of the forms of 'in-depth' defence and, clearly, forward defence involve the possibility of nuclear escalation, thus threatening severe punishment. In this sense, then, they would belong in the second category.

Two elements can thus be distinguished here: (a) how early and to what extent is punishment threatened on enemy territory, and (b) what is the role of nuclear weapons?

Nuclear weapons have differing functions in the various proposals.

Their role can be limited to deter only against the use of nuclear weapons by the potential aggressor, they can be maintained as a means of last resort in case of impending defeat or they can be attributed a relatively large role by giving them a deterrent function against all forms of aggression through the threat and risk of escalation.

Theoretically, deterrence is more effective (a) if damage is threatened also against the home territory of the aggressor rather than against his attacking forces ('expeditionary corps') only and (b) if an attack implicates the risk of nuclear war. Deterrence would decrease if the aggressor would at most run the risk of losing a limited conventional war in central Europe.

2. Does the alternative proposal take into consideration the (deterrent) value of NATO integration, i.e. the risk an aggressor faces of immediately being confronted by all NATO member-states and the entire Alliance force in case of an attack?

None of the proposals advocate a withdrawal from the Western Alliance (although 'social defence' is very near such advocacy), but some proposals might create problems for present forms of military integration and the system of mixed deployment ('layer-cake') along the front line.

3. Does the alternative proposal conform to the requirement of forward defence, i.e. sacrifice of as little territory as possible, ending of military operations as early as possible and damage limitation? All of these are political demands at present valid.

Obviously, many of the proposals do not fulfill the demand of forward defence of trying to sacrifice practically no territory at all. Indeed, it is the essential element of most of the proposals that territory should be sacrificed in favour of (a) a more effective and hence presumably credible defence and (b) damage limitation. Whereas the proponents of forward defence argue that it is psychologically and politically unacceptable to base a defence concept on the sacrifice of territory, the advocates of 'in-depth' defence would probably claim that sacrifice of territory would become psychologically acceptable because it would go together with limitation of damage. Present strategy, by contrast, is considered unacceptable because of the likely destruction that would go along with it. In addition, the advocates of the alternatives consider their proposals to be more effective and hence more deterring, which is, after all, the best method of damage limitation.

Of course, the extent to which damage could be limited would depend on the extent to which the aggressor abides by the rules of the alternative strategy – and if he abided by them while moving forward would he also abide by them when he is forced back? Naturally, the proponents of alternatives may be little impressed by this reference because in their opinion damage would be less in any case (not least because of the higher chance of avoiding nuclear war). One might conclude that reasonable deterrence by conventional capability plus damage limitation should deterrence fail appears a more sound concept to many proponents of alternative concepts than emphasis on nuclear weapons and nuclear deterrence.

According to current doctrine, damage would be limited by keeping the enemy away from home territory and by ending hostilities as soon as possible by the threat of escalation and massive destruction. The proponents of some of the alternatives have twofold doubts about this threat: *will* it be used in view of the terrifying prospects it entails and *can* it be used in a controlled manner once war has proceeded to that stage? Of course, these doubts apply equally to all of those alternative proposals that see nuclear weapons as a last resort.

4. Is the alternative realisable in terms of technology, money and manpower?

Some of the alternative proposals tend to rely very heavily on modern technology, possibly overestimating new capabilities, e.g. in anti-tank warfare, underestimating counter-measures and falling into a recurrent misapprehension of many NATO strategists, viz. the assumption of abiding Western technological superiority.

In addition, all alternatives emphasising increased conventional capabilities have to cope with the questions of decreased manpower resources and increased costs in the next ten to twenty years. But it should be pointed out that current doctrine is expensive and depends on modern technology and sufficient manpower. A reallocation of resources is always theoretically conceivable.

5. Does the alternative concept solve the nuclear weapons issue satisfactorily, the issue being (a) the existence and threat of nuclear weapons and (b) the credibility of a possible counter-threat?

Of course, no alternative concept can make nuclear weapons vanish from the international political scene nor would proponents argue that their proposals give assured protection against irrationality. But – and indeed this is one of the central elements of much of alternative thinking – they would argue that the incentive to use nuclear weapons would be greatly decreased (a) by removing nuclear weapons from certain areas, preferably all of Western Europe, thus offering no nuclear targets and (b) by thinning out rather than massing forward defence forces.

If forces are indeed thinned out the latter expectation would seem reasonable; if, however, massed strike forces are assembled further back (as, for example, in the Afheldt concept) an incentive for a nuclear strike might again be given.

The target argument seems plausible, although there may be other attractive targets, for example major population centres which could be struck in an effort to demoralise the defenders, and this incentive might increase the more effective and difficult it is to cope with the in-depth anti-tank and guerilla tactics. In addition, there is no reason why nuclear targets should be struck at with nuclear weapons: there may be considerable reason to prefer to overrun them with conventional forces or to eliminate them by conventional air strikes. The disincentive to use nuclear weapons rests on the threat of retaliation rather than on the lack of targets.

But is the threat of retaliation credible? This is perhaps the more important question, and it is certainly one of the inherent dilemmas of NATO strategy, indeed of all nuclear strategy.

NATO tries to solve this dilemma by combining conventional defence with forward stationing of some nuclear weapons and the threat of nuclear escalation. The idea of forward stationing is to make it difficult for an aggressor to avoid coming upon NATO's nuclear forces: the aim being deterrence, because these forces implicate the entire American nuclear retaliatory capacity. At least this means uncertainty and hence risk. At the same time the concept of escalation tries to split up the credibility problem – will this enormous retaliatory force be used? – into, as it were, digestible portions: if there may be doubt about the use of American strategic forces, there is bound to be less doubt about the use of a forward-based, limited (in range and capacity) nuclear weapon, and once such a weapon has been used doubt about further escalation is likely to decrease. In other words, the greater credibility of the limited, forward-based weapon is expected to reflect upward along the escalation ladder.

The proponents of alternatives, however, fear this escalation ladder: those, who do not eliminate nuclear weapons from their concepts altogether – and most of them don't – argue that it is necessary to withdraw nuclear weapons from this quasi-automatic process and to give them a sole last resort function. This comes close to NATO's former 'massive retaliation' concept with its well-known weaknesses, particularly with regard to credibility. If, for example, nuclear weapons were to be withdrawn from Western Europe and were to be sea-based, at what stage of a European war would they be employed, how extensively and against which targets? After a prolonged, but failing conventional defence of Western Europe it might be expected that the United States, having had time to mobilise, would think more about conventional reinforcements than about unleashing a nuclear war.

The prime purpose of nuclear weapons is deterrence: would deterrence be increased if the possibility of a prolonged conventional conflict became part of NATO strategy? Would the American nuclear commitment become more credible?

6. Is the alternative acceptable to the public? Many proponents of alternatives to forward defence and deterrent strategy start their argument from the premise of an inevitable erosion of public support for NATO's present doctrine.[16]

There is some reason to doubt the validity of this assumption. It is possibly based in part on an overestimation of the various 'peace movements' and their effect on or reflection of public opinion. But even where public opinion polls can be cited in support of the erosion thesis, other opinion polls lead to quite different conclusions,[17] rather confirming the questionable value of many opinion polls. Whatever such polls may indicate, governments have been elected and re-elected on clear and firm platforms supporting current doctrine – also at the height of the debate on the dual-track decision.

Furthermore, even if such an erosion were taking place – and to some extent it probably is taking place – the question arises whether the best or only way of coping with the issue is a change of doctrine (until something more acceptable is found, which would be something like finding a 'strategy by plebiscite'). Certainly an alternative approach would be to improve understanding of the present doctrine by education of the public.[18] Public acceptability is not really the first criterion for selecting a military strategy, but rather a necessary derivative of other elements such as feasibility, credibility and, most importantly, effectiveness in the light of given political aims, i.e. maintenance of peace (through deterrence) and ability to effectively defend in case of conflict.

The acceptability of the various alternatives is usually taken for granted; it has not been tested. Of course, the simple proposition of reduced reliance on nuclear weapons and improved damage limitation could be expected to increase the acceptability of any doctrine.

The same would be true for enhanced effectiveness. Indeed, these are common denominators for all of Western strategic thinking.

On the other hand, the idea of a 'non-provocative' defence would seem less important for public acceptance. The Western public – rightly so – does not consider present Western forces or doctrine as being provocative, nor is there much evidence that the Soviet Union considers them to be provocative. More serious is the problem of misunderstanding or accident: these criteria are considered important also for present doctrine.

Perhaps the most serious disadvantage of the alternatives proposing 'in-depth' defence is the sacrifice of and the conduct of battle on home territory. It is at least dubious whether this could be outweighed by an – equally uncertain – promise of damage limitation. In addition, while reduced reliance on nuclear weapons would be attractive, the possibility of reduced deterrence because of this would not be. Any strategy that increases the risk of war or that raises any doubts about this at all would be on losing ground as far as public acceptability is concerned.

But even if the advantages of alternative proposals outweigh the disadvantages they cannot be postulated only: both military and political leaders have to be convinced of their validity. Here, perhaps, lies one of the decisive deficiencies of all of the alternative proposals.

THESES FOR DISCUSSION: ARE WE TALKING ABOUT THE RIGHT ISSUE?

1. Even the most convincing set of arguments in favour of the present doctrine of deterrence and military strategy of forward defence could not deny a series of difficulties and disadvantages that accompany these concepts.[19] Even if they have been successful – or have, at least, not failed – it does not follow that ever more of a good thing is also necessarily better. Present doctrine does not give complete reassurance – yet neither do any of the alternatives. In other words, the advantages and disadvantages of alternative proposals have to be weighed against the advantages and disadvantages of current doctrine.

In this sense alternative proposals perform a valuable function in a constant process of rethinking and reassessment, even if the alternatives are not accepted in the end. Change is a constant factor, and it is most likely to come about as a result of technological advance.

But such change alone will not overcome either the concept of deterrence (which is as old as man, and which none of the alternatives discussed replace) or the need to deter. To achieve this other factors have to be taken into consideration, and the question posed here is whether a concentration on strategy is not really narrowing the field of investigation unduly – at least for political if not for military thinking. A more fundamental look at the underlying causes and reasons for deterrence and present military strategy may be useful and indeed necessary.

2. Internationally, we are confronted by a Hobbesian world. Despite all existing and growing interdependencies this world is marked by sovereign states recognising no authority above themselves. There is no monopoly of power and, much more important, there is a lack of consensus on a basic, common value system. At the same time the system is marked by various conflicts between states: conflicts of interest, of power, of misunderstanding.

In this world, states choose to rely on military force as an arbiter in conflict, at least as a means of last resort, as an *ultima ratio*.

Indeed, outside the European–Atlantic area arms have a much more obvious (although not more significant) role. The philosophical doubts about the value of arms and, more so, the moral rejection of force, is a specifically European–American development.

No doubt, this development was fostered by the experience of two world wars and, perhaps even more so, by the development of the nuclear bomb. At the same time, the memory of war and the possibility of nuclear disaster have brought the European–Atlantic area an historically unprecedentedly long period of peace. Thus, the possibility of disaster is the basis of deterrence, but as time has proceeded discomfort has grown about the tenability of this 'uneasy peace'. Improvements and indeed alternatives are being sought – but less to the Hobbesian world than to the deterrent system within this world.

3. The basic problem in the East–West conflict in its present form is the Soviet Union.

The Soviet Union builds on a long Russian tradition of dictatorship and imperialism. Both the dictatorial and the imperialist element have found a modern continuation in communism.

Communist ideology, however, has led to an economically incompetent and domestically insecure society. This insecurity is experienced particularly acutely in the Soviet Eastern European empire.

Tradition and insecurity both lead towards an expansionist and militarist policy. The military is the only field in which the Soviet Union is competitive with the West. Internationally Soviet power and prestige is based almost entirely on its military potential. At the same time military capacity has not only police functions in Eastern Europe, but is the only area in which 'superiority of socialism' can be demonstrated, by which the expectation of a long-run Soviet victory can be fostered and – not least – the people of Western Europe can be intimidated and led to accommodation, for the freedom and prosperity of Western Europe is, by its very existence, a constant element of destabilisation in Eastern Europe.

The insecurity of the Soviet system and the high Soviet reliance on military power are important explanations for the relative lack of success in arms control and why the Soviet Union continues to be seen as a threat to Western Europe.

4. Apart from improvements to the present deterrent system no convincingly superior and realisable alternative has been presented thus far to cope with the threat that is felt to be posed by the Soviet Union.

The alternative proposals all operate within the existing international system. While this appears realistic, it obviously makes it difficult to unhinge a deterrent system which is based on several decades of intellectual effort.[20]

There are a number of common weaknesses of the alternative proposals, all related to motivation and aim rather than to specific details.

The strongest motivation for alternative proposals is the fear of war – but the fear of war is at the same time the basis of deterrence. It is difficult to conceive of a deterrent within the present international system that would not be based on fear. An alternative that raised less fear would at the same time encompass the possibility of increasing the likelihood of war.

In a subconscious manner many of the alternative proposals have already accepted the failure of deterrence, hence their enormous concentration not on deterrence, but on the elimination or reduction of the role of nuclear weapons and on damage limitation. For many the working hypothesis is: 'A war is likely to occur, hence let us find a means of surviving it'.[21] As to the proposal of 'social defence' it seems that the decision 'better red than dead' has practically already been made.

5. Within the existing system of international politics there is no solution to the dilemmas of nuclear weapons or deterrence in Europe. These dilemmas are threefold: that defence means destruction, that there is no ultimate certainty as to the American nuclear guarantee for Europe and that there is no absolute certainty that the fabric of the deterrent system will hold.

We have to live with these dilemmas. What can and is being done, however, is to reduce their sharpness, in other words to stabilise the deterrent system so as to reduce the chance of actually being confronted with the choices these dilemmas pose. Such efforts include a wide range of measures, e.g.

– measures to improve conventional defence in order to avoid an early first use of nuclear weapons,

– improvement of command and control systems in order to be able to control escalation and to make possible the use of escalation to re-establish deterrence and end hostilities,

– close co-ordination and integration of American and European nuclear planning,

– efforts to stabilise the deterrent system, prevention of accidental war, arms control, but also political efforts under the headings of crisis management and detente.

In this context the United States Strategic Defence Initiative (SDI) ought to be mentioned, although at this early stage it is far from realisation.

Several points can be made. Firstly, it is, of course, not new in principle. The Soviet Union has been pursuing research in the field of ballistic missile defence for many years. NATO may thus be confronted by a missile defence system whether the United States and Western Europe pursue the SDI concept or not.

Secondly, if only the United States were to achieve a complete or near-complete ballistic missile defence system this would bring NATO back to the situation of the fifties: the United States would be less vulnerable, and under these circumstances the nuclear guarantee for Europe would gain in credibility.

Thirdly, if both sides were to achieve a completely effective system – which is highly unlikely – the conventional balance in Europe would become much more important. Escalation would lose its deterrent value for Western Europe. Theatre nuclear weapons would be maintained only as a counter to a potential use of such weapons by the other side. Strong efforts would have to be made to secure deterrence by a clearly adequate conventional defence posture.

Fourthly, if both sides achieved a near-complete ballistic missile defence system the potential threat to the deterrent system would be greatest if either side thought it might be an advantage to attempt a first strike. This does not seem very likely, however, because a defensive system would tend to decrease the motivation for a first strike. Thus the situation would be completely different from previous situations in which a first strike could be expected to lead to an extensive destruction of the enemy's land-based missiles, in which case there may have been hope of destroying his incoming, second-strike (mainly sea-based) missiles by an effective ballistic missile defence system (this argumentation formed the background to the ABM-Treaty). If, however, a near-complete ballistic missile defence existed, a first strike would mean an extensive elimination of the attacking missiles, rather than those of the attacked.

In any case, there would be uncertainty about how many missiles would be destroyed and which would survive.

Thus, only a completely effective system on both sides would lead to potential destabilisation by creating precisely that situation – the elimination of nuclear weapons – which many of the alternatives seek to achieve.

6. In the long run the risk of war will be significantly reduced only by changes and alternatives outside the deterrent system, i.e. rather than concentrating on changing the deterrent structure within the existing system of international relations more effort should be invested in changes and improvements of the latter. Both arms and the deterrent system are not a cause, but a reflection of the international political system.

Proposals that have been made can be divided into short-run and long-run suggestions. Among the former belong all measures to decrease tensions, to foster co-operation in various fields, to stabilise the deterrent system, to increase information and openness. Detente, arms control, crisis management and confidence-building measures should be considered in this category.

These measures may go hand in hand with a policy aimed at reducing the extrinsic and intrinsic factors conducive to an expansionist and militaristic Soviet outlook. There is not much in terms of active policy that the West can do to change Soviet society, but it can frustrate Soviet expansionism, and it can constantly point out that there are better ways than suppression to achieve internal security in the hope that Soviet leadership may eventually, in the long run, change.

A fundamental change in the Soviet Union will not alter the system of international politics, but it could eliminate one of the most fundamental problems of the present system – an expansionist Soviet Union basing its power primarily on military force – and it could contribute to creating prerequisites for a long-run change of the system.

There are two basic requirements for such change, requirements which in themselves involve fundamental change: firstly an expanding agreement on basic values – e.g. respect for life, freedom from force, freedom of opinion – that would still allow for different domestic political systems, but would at the same time make – secondly – the gradual, but significant development of peaceful methods of conflict resolution possible. Peaceful conflict resolution rests on confidence, confidence on at least a degree of shared values. One of the more important problems of the present international system is not the existence of conflict, but rather the non-existence of functioning and pervasive methods of peaceful, non-military conflict resolution.

Long-run changes of this nature are the only hope for a real solution to the nuclear dilemmas of the present international system.

Notes

1. Of course, the possibilities of accidental war or escalation of a crisis, e.g. in Eastern Europe or elsewhere, of war by tension or extension are not ignored, and both unilateral as well as bi- and multilateral measures to curb the danger of accidental war as well as methods of crisis management have been developed.
2. See Theodor Ebert, 'Von aggressiver Drohung zu defensiver Warnung. Das Konzept der Sozialen Verteidigung, in Dieter Senghaas (ed.), *Friedensforschung und Gesellschaftskritik* (München, 1970), pp. 179–211. I refer here also to the extensive hearings on 'Alternative Strategies' by the Defence Committee of the German Bundestag from 28 November 1983, to 6 February 1984, during which Ebert was also heard, see Bundestag, *Stenographische Berichte*, p. 15/158 ff.
3. See Horst Afheldt, *Verteidigung und Frieden. Politik mit militärischen Mitteln* (München/Wien, 1977); Horst Afheldt, *Atomkrieg. Das Verhängnis einer Politik mit militärischen Mitteln* (München, 1984); Emil Spannocchi, 'Verteidigung ohne Selbstzerstörung', in *Verteidigung ohne Schlacht* (München/Wien, 1976), and Guy Brossollet, 'Das Ende der Schlacht. Versuch über die 'Nicht-Schlacht', ibid. See also H. Afheldt in *Bundestag, Stenographische Berichte*, p. 19/65 ff., and E. Afheldt, ibid., p. 19/166 ff.

4. See Weizsäcker, *Bundestag, Stenographische Berichte*, p. 15/37 ff., Galtung, ibid., p. 19/210 ff.
5. E.g. Franz Uhle-Wettler proposes the creation of a new force of light infantry, see Gefechtsfeld Mitteleuropa. *Gefahr der Übertechnisierung von Streitkräften* (Munich, 1980). More radical are the proposals of Hans-Joachim Löser, who would completely do away with heavy tanks and large fighting units, see 'Vorneverteidigung in der Bundesrepublik Deutschland', in *Österreichische Militärzeitschrift* 2/1980, p. 116 ff. F. Birnstiel, 'Die Vorneverteidigung. Kern der konventionellen NATO-Abwehr', in *Europäische Wehrkunde* 5/1980, p. 213 ff., proposes an initial 'Sperrsystem' along the demarcation line with a mobile and mechanised defence behind that.
6. See Steven Canby, 'Military Reform and the Art of War', in *Survival*, May/June 1983, p. 120 ff., William S. Lind, 'Military Doctrine, Force Structure, and the Defence Decision-Making Process', in *Air University Review*, May/June 1979, and Edward N. Luttwak, 'The Operational Level of War', in *International Security*, Winter 1980/81, p. 61 ff.
7. For a broad assessment of these as well as the following proposals, however, see Josef Joffe, 'Das Unbehagen an der Stabilität: Kann Europa sich konventionell verteidigen?' in *Europa-Archiv* 18/1984, p. 549 ff. A critique of the suggestions of Birnstiel, Löser and Uhle-Wettler can be found in Karl-Heinz Lather and Heinz Loquai, 'Alternative Konzeptionen der Verteidigung', in *Truppenpraxis* 9/1982, pp. 623–7, 10/1982, pp. 703–12, 11/1982, pp. 787–94.
8. Also Follow-on-Forces Attack (FOFA) or 'Rogers Plan', see Bernard W. Rogers, 'Das Atlantische Bündnis: Rezepte für ein schwieriges Jahrzehnt', in: *Europa-Archiv* 12/1982, p. 369 ff.
9. See Joffe, op. cit., p. 553 f.
10. See Samuel Huntington, 'The Renewal of Strategy', in Huntington (ed.), *The Strategic Imperative* (Cambridge, Mass. 1982), also Huntington, 'Conventional Deterrence and Conventional Retaliation in Europe', in *International Security*, Winter 1983/84, p. 32 ff.
11. I disagree with Joffe here, who sees as the major disadvantage of this idea the supposed aggressiveness which it would signal to the Eastern Europeans, see Joffe, op. cit., p. 556.
12. Ibid.
13. See H. Afheldt, Galtung and others in *Bundestag, Stenographische Berichte*, op. cit. At the same time it should be remembered that Warsaw Pact manoeuvres usually assume attack and occupation of Western territory: Warsaw Pact forces 'play' that they are moving e.g. from Hannover into the Ruhr area as frequent observation of their telecommunications show, see report in: *Frankfurter Allgemeine*, 24 October 1984.
14. John J. Mearsheimer, *Conventional Deterrence* (Ithaca, 1983), points out that from 1938 to 1973 conventional deterrence failed in 10 out of 12 cases.
15. This has been a strong motive in many American proposals, beginning with then Defence Secretary Robert S. McNamara in 1960 to McNamara, McGeorge Bundy, George F. Kennan and Gerard Smith

in 1982 ('Nuclear Weapons and the Atlantic Alliance', in *Foreign Affairs*, Spring 1982, pp.753–68) and to Fred Iklé in 1985, see *Nuclear Strategy: Can There by a Happy Ending?* ibid., Spring 1985, pp. 810–26.

16. Cf., for example, the contributions by Lübkemeier, Brauch and Smoke in this volume.
17. See, for example, the Sinus-study 'Sicherheitspolitik, Bündnispolitik, Friedenspolitik' of autumn 1983 (thus at the height of the dual track decision debate) according to which 43 per cent of those questioned in the Federal Republic of Germany thought that *nuclear deterrence* had prevented the Soviet Union from attacking the West in the past 30 years, 37 per cent disagreed and 19 per cent were undecided. Of course, this does not say anything definite about confidence in deterrence in the future. A lot depends on how and when the question is posed. For example in the fall of 1983 28 per cent of those questioned thought that the stationing of Pershing II enhanced the possibility of a Soviet attack, 40 per cent thought that it enhanced our security, and 28 per cent thought that it had no influence. A year later those who thought security was enhanced had risen to 48 per cent, those who thought it made an attack more imminent had declined to 22 per cent and those who thought it had no influence remained stable at 28 per cent. (EMNID *Repräsentativerhebungen zur Sicherheitspolitik*.)
18. This is one of the aims of a revitalised Western European Union as decided upon at the Rome meeting of WEU foreign and defence ministers, 26–27 October 1984.
19. For some of them see the first and second sections of this essay.
20. The article by Iklé, op. cit., criticising this previous effort, is clearly unfair and incorrect in this respect.
21. See, for example, C.F. von Weizsäcker, op. cit.

10 For a NATO Defensive Deterrent

Richard Smoke

This essay proposes that NATO should adopt, in a gradual and orderly fashion, a grand strategy and accompanying posture distinctly different from its present one. The strategy I recommend has variously been termed 'non-provocative defence', 'defence-only defence', or 'defensive deterrence', I shall employ the latter term here. By it I mean a militarily sound strategy relying solely on conventional weapons so long as the enemy uses only conventional weapons, and a posture that is unambiguously capable only of defence. Secure, second-strike nuclear forces would be retained for deterrence of any nuclear use by the opponent. This goal is consistent with the goal stated in Frank Barnaby's companion paper in this volume; here however I shall lay the emphasis on political and politico-military rationales for a defensive deterrent. The paper begins with two brief arguments why a shift in NATO strategy is needed, advances some distinctions among the possible alternatives, and then presents some seven rationales for its recommended policy.

Two points should be mentioned at the outset to avoid possible misunderstandings, although the points will be developed later. First, there are a number of sound military and political reasons why the shift I recommend must be accomplished over some significant span of time. Nothing in this paper is meant to imply that the change should be sudden; some fifteen years might be a minimum for a sound transition.

Second, I do not doubt that NATO has been perceived for at least two deades by informed Soviet leaders as militarily almost incapable of a successful, sustained offence against the Warsaw Pact, at least under nearly all plausible conditions. In that sense NATO is already, in an important sense, in a defence-only deterrent posture. But that Soviet perception may be beginning to change, as I shall discuss.

FOR A SHIFT IN STRATEGY

The first argument I advance why a shift in NATO strategy is needed is that the political support undergirding the present strategy is eroding. In my judgement that erosion is more likely to continue than to halt or reverse itself. Indeed to me it seems open to question whether sufficient support to sustain the current policy will last out the century.

That there is less of a political consensus sustaining NATO's policy now than there was ten years or more ago is widely recognised, and discussed in many of the papers in this volume; it need not be dwelt upon here. The revival of interest in the 1980s in No First Use, or at least in movement in that direction, is only one element in what is now, especially in Europe, lively requestioning of basic NATO strategy.

In the United States, a large proportion of the public does not understand what NATO policy is, and when offered that policy as a hypothetical possibility, rejects it firmly. Probably the best-known recent evidence of this is a 1984 survey by the Public Agenda Foundation. No less than 81 per cent of the respondents thought it is current US policy to respond with nuclear weapons only in the event of a Soviet attack with nuclear weapons. Offered the policy option of employing nuclear weapons 'if the Soviets invade Europe or Japan with soldiers and tanks, even if they don't use nuclear weapons', 69 per cent rejected this option; only 22 per cent supported it, 9 per cent being unsure. [1]

Similar percentages of the public in the major NATO countries of Europe (with the significant exception of France) also reject nuclear first use, when it is presented as an option. In the Federal Republic and in Great Britain the percentages rejecting it are significantly higher. [2]

There are several reasons for believing that the political sustainability of NATO's nuclear first-use policy is more likely than not to continue to erode. One is that that policy dates from a time when NATO enjoyed definite superiority in theatre and tactical nuclear weapons, and hence could credibly threaten to initiate their use expecting the enemy to back down rather than counter-escalate. But that time is now long past, and political awareness must inevitably catch up with that fact.

Another reason is that it always is politically difficult for NATO and its member governments entirely to disconnect the first use policy from the tangled and provocative problems of the deployment of NATO nuclear weapons, especially Intermediate Nuclear Forces (INF), on European soil. Future deployment issues, especially contentious ones, are more likely to subtract than add to support for the first use policy.

But the most fundamental reason for anticipating continued erosion in this support is that democratic societies that feel relatively secure cannot forever base their strategy on what amounts to a threat of global suicide. Political leaders and the public alike tend to assume that the use of nuclear weapons in Europe is very likely to lead to nuclear warfare in Europe on a large scale. (That is, theorists' models of controlled use of small numbers of nuclear weapons are disbelieved – a judgement shared, incidentally, by many professional military officers.) Large scale nuclear warfare in Europe, in turn, is very likely to lead to global nuclear war; to accomplish exactly that is the entire purpose of 'coupling' European-based and US nuclear forces, which is a central NATO objective. Today much of the NATO public understands that a likely consequence of global nuclear war is the extinction of human civilisation.

It is politically important, in this context, that the European allies feel *relatively* secure from imminent attack. Democratic societies that feel highly insecure might sustain politically a first-use threat. This is one of the reasons why such a posture was easily accepted by NATO in the 1950s. But the current preservation and continuation of a significant degree of detente in Europe, even in a period of chilly superpower relations, both symbolizes and results from a sense of comparative security. The USSR is not seen in most European quarters as posing a severe imminent military threat.

If this sense is sustained, it will become steadily more difficult, in my judgement, for the NATO democracies to sustain what amounts to a threat of the extinction of civilisation, as a consequence of anything other than their own nuclear extinction. (Political support for nuclear *retaliation* following an enemy nuclear attack is likely to continue; that is, a second-strike posture will remain politically sustainable.)

A second argument I put forward for a shift in basic NATO strategy is closely related. I do not believe an ethical strategist or policymaker can consider it moral to threaten the extinction of civilisation as a consequence of conventional invasion, *particularly if any possible alternative is available*. Possible alternatives are available.

This statement is not meant as a condemnation of NATO. When NATO first adopted nuclear first use as its basic deterrent posture, not only were there good reasons for doubting that the opponent would be able to counter-escalate, but in addition, the extinction of civilisation was not the likely consequence of carrying out the threat. Now it is. My argument is merely that it is time for NATO policy to catch up with the practical and moral realities.

Some strategists reject moral considerations as extraneous to sound strategising. Others would argue that morality must be one of the starting-points of sound strategy. Be this as it may, the *political leadership* of democratic nations, and an alliance of them, cannot exclude the moral dimension; national leaders must consider more than 'strategy' in its narrow sense. (Furthermore, as a practical political matter they will have to, for if they seek to exclude that dimension they will eventually find it coming back upon them, in forms they will experience as political pressure.) From the viewpoint of NATO leadership, then, the question of what threat can morally be sustained, to deter conventional invasion, is indeed relevant, whether it be so from the professional strategist's viewpoint or not.

From the analysis to this point, I conclude that both morality and our fundamental commitment to democracy demand that, over an appropriate period of time, we change our NATO policy better to reflect the judgement of our citizens, presuming a feasible alternative can be found. Conversely, I believe and assume that a feasible alternative, publicly understood, could become the basis for a new and durable political consensus that could preserve NATO and its purposes on a sustainable basis.

ALTERNATIVES TO FIRST USE

If NATO is to shift from a nuclear first use strategy to an alternative, that alternative can only be, for the foreseeable future, some kind of conventional force posture. The NATO publics would certainly – and in my judgement, correctly – not support a conclusion that no military threat exists at all; and of course not a decision to base NATO defences on something unconventional like chemical or biological weapons. I concur with the observation made in Frank Barnaby's paper in this volume that purely territorial defences, non-violent resistance, and non-resistance are not viable options, at least for some time (although the first two might well be worth re-examination under different, future conditions.) We are left, then, with some form of conventional force posture as the only reasonable alternative to reliance on a nuclear first use threat.

The question is: what form?

I believe there is a moderately clear distinction between offensively-oriented and defensively-oriented conventional postures for NATO. The distinction has not been central in NATO thinking heretofore, because NATO's conventional forces by themselves have been obviously too weak to consider offence, and more importantly because the conventional and nuclear forces have been so intermingled, both in tactical planning and in deployment, that little need for the distinction has arisen. It is obvious that nuclear deterrence requires offensive *nuclear* forces. But to confine these forces to a second-use-only role automatically means one is contemplating the possibility of a strictly conventional war in Europe. On that premise, the question of offence versus defence arises at once.

That the No-First-Use issue forces the offence/defence distinction to the very centre of our attention, and that NATO otherwise has not needed to cope with it in its fundamental form, are important implications of the issue which are sometimes overlooked. For decades, hardly anyone has imagined that a nuclear battle in Europe might be fought on one side (either side) of the inter-German frontier only. To visualise a nuclear battle is to visualise a battle with strong offensive components. But to visualise a conventional battle brings the question of offensive or defensive policies to centre stage and compels, for reasons this paper will raise, a rethinking of what, fundamentally, NATO seeks to achieve and why.

In the current debate, one can readily distinguish offensively and defensively oriented proposals, with a number of intermediate positions possible as well. The US Army's AirLand Battle 2000 strategy is highly offensive in orientation, and incorporates nuclear as well as conventional 'deep strike' options. General Roger's FOFA (Follow-On Forces Attack) involves conventional forces only, and in its more limited range is somewhat less offensive than AirLand Battle 2000. Toward the other pole, strategies can be devised that, if not purely or absolutely defensive, are so unambiguously so that they cannot credibly be portrayed or misunderstood as other than defensive. Frank Barnaby describes one such in his paper in this volume. Many others have also been brought forward in recent years.

Almost all these alternatives, offensive and defensive, rely on some combination of advanced or 'emerging' technologies (E.T.) Which combination of which technologies can vary considerably.

THE NATO SHIFT OF THE 1980s

A shift is beginning to occur in NATO strategy in the 1980s from anything that has been accepted within NATO since its origins; that is the shift toward offensive-oriented theorising, and to some extent, an offensively-oriented posture. The AirLand Battle 2000 doctrine, and the acceptance of FOFA, are creating a climate within NATO in which NATO plans and programmes are being geared to some extent for offensive warfare. How far this shift toward the offensive will go in practice is debatable; that the movement is in this direction is undeniable.

Of the many important implications of this shift, especially if it is carried very far, two are important for my argument. One is that it alters the context in which debate is joined over the defensive alternative. For example, many NATO officers who are sceptical of defensive postures argue, in essence, that the posture of the last couple of decades clearly has succeeded in its basic purpose of deterring war; hence the best course is to continue to make moderate, incremental improvements in the existing strategy. But that is not the actual context today. NATO grand strategy is now shifting in an offensive direction from what it has been for decades, and may shift further in that direction. That movement, not just the merits of the traditional posture, is part of the actual context of a debate over defensive alternatives.

The second implication of that movement is its consequences for Soviet perceptions. As I remarked at the outset, there is little doubt that informed Soviet leaders have traditionally viewed NATO as essentially incapable of a sustained, successful attack on the Warsaw Pact. Whatever Soviet propaganda may claim, Soviet leaders know from their excellent intelligence that in fact NATO has lacked both the planning base and the forces adequate for such an attack. This perception has no doubt been fundamental in all Soviet policy making in European affairs.

This perception may now be changing, or may change soon if the NATO shift toward the offence proceeds very far. The possible consequences deserve some sober thought. (I will address just one of them later in this paper.) Although it would be alarmist to draw too quickly the conclusion that the Soviets are about to change fundamentally their perception of the potential dangers NATO may pose to them, it would also be shortsighted not to begin considering the consequences in the Kremlin of NATO's offensive shift, if it goes very far.

FOR A DEFENSIVE DETERRENT

In considering the offensive-defensive spectrum, I believe there are reasons – powerful now and likely to become even more so – why the most preferable strategy by far is one that is unambiguously defensive only, excepting solely for its second-strike nuclear capability. By this I mean a posture, employing conventional technologies only, adequate to give all parties high confidence that a Soviet/Warsaw Pact *conventional* attack on Western Europe cannot achieve victory, and which is designed such that NATO is *unable* to conduct offensive operations of any magnitude beyond NATO territory. A predictably successful defence will serve as an adequate deterrent to Soviet attack. Secure second-strike nuclear forces should be retained, in non-forward areas, as a deterrent against any Soviet first use of nuclear weapons. These forces should be sufficiently flexible to be able to halt operation after only a few nuclear weapons have been detonated by both sides, and sufficiently secure and powerful to be able to ensure that the Soviets cannot meaningfully 'prevail' in any theatre nuclear war.

Clearly, this posture is recommended for NATO as an alliance, not for the United States. American forces deployed in Europe would be structured in this posture, but not American forces elsewhere. (In what follows I shall omit the complication represented by the US Sixth Fleet; it does not change the arguments in their essentials.)

Defensive deterrence is a concept capable of many variations. Unlike some of its advocates, I do not suggest that NATO should be incapable of any military operations east of the inter-German border. Considerable NATO attack capabilities within some reasonable zone such as 100 miles of the border will ease NATO's task and will not resemble an offensive posture to the Soviets. Eastward from that zone, NATO military capabilities should be severely limited but not necessarily nonexistent. Certain specialised capabilities may enhance Western security without significantly threatening Soviet security. An example may be a limited number of missiles carrying advanced conventional 'runway-busting' warheads that can disable Warsaw Pact military airfields but cannot do widespread damage. (Here and elsewhere NATO could take advantage of the fact that the Soviets will accurately know the quantities of NATO's various forces.)

Thus defensive deterrence should not be defined by mechanical or strictly military criteria, but by a politico-military criterion. A defensive deterrent posture as I conceive it is one that, taken as a whole, assures NATO security while not significantly threatening the security of the Soviet Union or of Soviet control of Eastern Europe (assuming that NATO's second-strike nuclear forces are not called into play by Soviet first use.)

In presenting my rationales for this view, I will not dwell on the military/technical arguments why such a posture is feasible, nor on the economic arguments why its cost can be held to roughly the current NATO expenditure level. Substantial work has been and is being done on these points by various specialists and groups. I am persuaded that the expenditures saved by NATO denying itself many strike aircraft, much armour, and other major offensive capabilities would be sufficient to pay for an ample defensive capability taking full advantage of advanced technologies. Exotic or 'gold-plated' high-tech items should be eschewed in favour of effective, relatively cheap, and extensive anti-air and anti-armour capabilities especially. The considerable variety of detailed postures and tactics that have been conceived for this kind of strategy emphasise such capabilities; a final choice among these postures and tactics, by NATO or any group, would be premature at this time.

Only one military/technical point of general significance will be mentioned here. In making the military argument for a defensive conventional posture, it is not necessary to demonstrate that emerging technologies require or even favour such a posture. It is only necessary to demonstrate that they (or some subset or combination of them) *can sustain* such a posture adequately.

If, as currently seems likely, the predictable technologies can support some *range* of strategic options, then a choice of options within that range can be guided by non-technical considerations. This remains true even if it could be shown that some of the new technologies would be even more advantageously employed (from a strictly operational-effectiveness viewpoint) in offensive modes. So long as they can sustain a defensive posture adequately, then the military/technical case is made, and if that posture is preferable at the level of grand strategy, one can and should choose it.

I now turn, therefore, to the level of grand strategy, where political and politico-military considerations always dominate, within the domain of the feasible.

THE CASE AGAINST

Before discussing the arguments for my recommended strategy, let me mention briefly what I regard as the strongest argument against it, together with what I believe is an adequate rebuttal.

The strongest case against a strictly conventional NATO posture, in my judgement, is that it makes an intentional Soviet attack somewhat less unlikely. That is commonly said and it is true – to a degree. Conversely, the strongest case for the current NATO policy of nuclear first use is that it makes an intentional Soviet attack unlikely in the extreme, because the predictable consequence might well be global catastrophe.

I believe, however, that under the kind of NATO posture I recommend this consequence remains non-negligible, in the literal meaning of the term: Soviet planners could not neglect it. NATO retention of secure second-strike nuclear forces, in non-forward areas, would remain a consensus position in NATO. Cautious planners (and Soviet planners are nothing if not cautious) would assess the nuclear danger as too high. Under conditions of powerful nuclear forces existing on both sides, the 'fog of war' that historically has defeated so many of the best-laid battle plans could lead to nuclear use by some commander somewhere, on one side or another. Once that occurs, it becomes more likely than not that overburdened, degraded C^3I systems will register that the war has 'gone nuclear', and the inexorable, uncontrollable escalation will proceed. All this can readily be anticipated ahead of time in Moscow.

There are other nuclear dangers. Can Soviet planners contemplating an invasion of Western Europe be positive that ample US sea-based or strategic nuclear forces will never be brought into play? Can Soviet planners imagine that they can invade French territory without the French resorting at least to tactical/theatre, and possibly Eurostrategic, nuclear weapons? (Or – the only possible alternative – are they to leave France uninvaded, wherepon France becomes an ideal staging ground for the inevitable American counter-attack?)

In short, 'residual nuclear deterrence', or as McGeorge Bundy calls it, 'existential deterrence', would remain. That is, much of the deterrent effect of a first-use posture would still remain in a second-use posture. No prudent planner is going to *deliberately* run even a very small risk of general nuclear war. Hence the probability of an intentional Soviet attack in Europe will remain extremely small.

Another argument occasionally heard is that if NATO did not have a first-use posture, the Soviets might calculate they could *win* a theatre nuclear war in Europe, and hence initiate it themselves. This argument evidently makes the unwarranted assumption that NATO's continuing second-strike nuclear forces would be inadequate. Nothing of the sort is recommended here. As noted, NATO's second-strike forces must be sufficiently secure and powerful to be able to deny the Soviets any nuclear victory. This might actually be easier rather than harder under the proposed posture. Almost all variants of the defensive deterrent concept call for highly decentralised NATO forces. Hence Soviet nuclear forces might find little that was profitable to shoot at, and could not deliver any military victory (short of virtually obliterating Western Europe, scarcely a meaningful military objective.)

SKETCH OF SEVEN ARGUMENTS FOR A CONVENTIONAL DEFENSIVE POSTURE

Let me now turn to the major arguments for a defensive deterrent posture, which appear to be mutually reinforcing. Due to space limitations I shall have to state them succinctly.

1. Under this posture the probability of an *unintended* war would be vastly reduced. In common with many analysts, I believe that in the existing situation there is a far greater likelihood of war erupting by misperception, miscalculation and misunderstanding in the midst of some severe crisis than by preplanned major attack. Or as it is sometimes put, we are in something much more resembling a 'pre-1914' than a 'pre-1939' situation. (I will not review here the arguments why.)

In a defensive conventional posture NATO would be able to reduce substantially the danger of such an unintended outbreak, and reduce greatly its consequences should it occur. Such a posture, even if not reciprocated by the Pact, would be considerably less likely to facilitate crisis miscalculation, for various, mostly familiar, technical reasons. (Analysis of these is outside the present scope.) Probably more important, if the crisis miscalculation nevertheless occurred and a Pact attack begun, it would be far less difficult to get the war stopped than it would be under anything resembling the current NATO posture.

2. Related to crisis miscalculation is the danger posed by the Soviet doctrine of *pre-emption*. A defensive-deterrent posture for NATO would reduce enormously, perhaps almost completely, the Soviet incentive deliberately to pre-empt, in the event of some future crisis

in Europe (where the Soviets were motivated primarily by security concerns, not aggressive designs).

Either the current NATO first use posture or any strongly offensive conventional posture severely threatens the USSR itself and/or the Soviet position in Eastern Europe. That threat greatly strengthens the Soviet incentive to pre-empt, indeed is one of the sources of their doctrine of pre-emption. Conversely, a NATO defensive-deterrent posture would almost entirely remove, in a crisis, the Soviet sense of a security threat. An unambiguously defensive posture would reassure Moscow that NATO was not about to strike – because it could not – and hence that there was no security need for Soviet pre-emption.

In Europe or indeed anywhere else, by far the greatest *crisis stability* is achieved when the Soviets know two things with high confidence: that it is very risky to attack, *and* that it is very safe *not* to attack. The current NATO posture, or any offensive conventional one, establishes the first condition but not the second. A defensive deterrent posture establishes both.

These two, related problems – crisis miscalculation and the danger of pre-emption – represent, in my judgement, by far the greatest dangers of any war actually occurring in Europe. Substantially reducing the dangers that are the greatest dangers is virtually a decisive reason all by itself for adopting the proposed posture, so long as doing so does not materially increase other dangers.

3. A defensive deterrent posture, properly presented to the publics of the NATO democracies is likely to command much greater political support. This is the obverse of the theme struck near the outset of this paper, that the current posture does *not* command public support. Neither would markedly offensive conventional postures, for an alliance that is explicitly defensive in its fundamental purpose. A posture that was only defensive and conventional (except of course for the necessary second-strike nuclear capability) could command sustained public acceptance and support, which is essential to NATO's future. This presupposes, as this entire paper does, that the proposed posture *would* permit high confidence that a Soviet conventional attack could be defeated, and could be credibly so presented to the public.

In addition to the basic good sense of a defensive alliance having a defensive strategy, all the arguments being presented in this paper would reinforce the political acceptability of a defensive deterrent strategy. That acceptability would be further enhanced by the fact that a defensive strategy would be far more *comprehensible* to the public than the current, complicated one that is based on such sophisticated notions as 'incalculability', deliberate ambiguity, and the conscious creation of a 'threat that leaves something to chance'.

4. There is a reason, sometimes overlooked, why almost any NATO conventional posture with a strong offensive component could be significantly more dangerous than a continuation of the policy status quo of nuclear first use. This brings us back to the question of Soviet perceptions of that kind of NATO posture.

Western strategists, being so completely convinced themselves of unlikelihood that the West would ever *begin* a war, persistently underestimate the extent to which Western behaviour really can look threatening as seen from Moscow. This general principle applies in the following way here. Moscow is well aware of the longstanding American belief that there is such a thing as controllable escalation – and in particular, that the 'firebreak' between conventional and nuclear weapons can be held.

In a context, such as exists now, of a NATO doctrine of first *nuclear* use, that firebreak has only modest significance. But a NATO offensive conventional posture might well be interpreted in Moscow as signifying that the Americans, at least, had decided that they could hold the firebreak in a European war, which could mean that the Americans had decided that it would be all right to fight a European war.

In other words, as long as NATO relies heavily on nuclear weapons, Moscow can conclude that the West will surely not launch a war. But conventional reliance, combined with an offensive doctrine, could be interpreted as implying that under some circumstances the West just might do so. If Moscow's perceived probability of war goes up, the consequences could be serious, and most serious of all in any intense crisis.

None of these considerations apply to an unambiguously defensive posture relying on conventional technology.

5. Any offensively-oriented NATO posture – the current nuclear one or any offensive conventional one – provides an important measure of justification for the continuing Soviet buildup of European theatre capabilities. It provides justification to the East Europeans, to the Soviet people, and probably most important, to those within the Moscow bureaucracies who might otherwise use pressing economic needs to accomplish a reduction in Soviet military spending. All offensive NATO postures unwittingly play into the

perpetual Soviet fear of invasion from the West (a fear that remains keen in part because of Moscow's assiduously keeping alive the memory of the Second World War).

Conversely, NATO's shift to a defensive posture could seriously undermine the justification and reduce the fear. For maximum effect on both the willingness and the ability of Soviet policy makers to sustain their European theatre buildup in the face of a NATO defensive posture, that posture must be sustained over time; be consistently carried out; and be well and continuingly publicised to East European and Soviet audiences.

6. A defensive deterrent posture favours arms control and arms reductions. For a variety of reasons, it would be more difficult to achieve meaningful European arms reductions, or even confidence- and security-building measures, in a situation of offensive force buildups and doctrines on both sides, than in one of a defensive NATO posture. Playing out the detailed arms control implications of various offensive postures is beyond the scope of this paper; that they make arms control more difficult, probably much more difficult, should be almost self-evident. Facilitation of real European arms control is one of the significant arguments for a defensive deterrent.

However, this argument should not be overdrawn, to the point where arms control appears to be the main reason for a defensive NATO posture. Moving toward such a posture for that reason might tend to give the Soviets a 'veto' over NATO maintaining the posture for the long term – something that is in fact highly desirable for other reasons, and independent of Soviet behaviour.

7. A NATO defensive deterrent posture could enormously assist the long-term evolution of European security and politico-military affairs, indeed might turn out to be almost a pre-requisite to achieving a favourable long-term transition out of the division of Europe that has been so frozen for so long. At this point in my argument I shall deliberately be both provocative and somewhat speculative.

The West is constantly handicapped, in world affairs, by its difficulty in articulating a long-term vision for itself or the world that can command consensus support even among its own population, to say nothing of others. *What is our positive vision of the future?* Important segments of the public on both sides of the Atlantic, and perhaps especially in Europe, have become disenchanted with the continual perpetuation of the status quo. The lack of a vision that is clear, feasible and attractive weakens the West's political foundations, in ways that are subtle, but important over the long run.

I believe some sense of a possible future for 'Europe' is emerging among Europeans on both sides of the Iron Curtain. Still rather inchoate, it visualises a Europe that develops a gradually growing identity of its own, independent of both the US and the USSR. Perhaps the division created by Yalta can be slowly loosened, and at least in some respects, overcome.

While the tendency in this direction could pose an obvious danger for the West, it also could present an enormous opportunity. A 'finlandisation' of Eastern Europe, in which the Soviets allow (or are obliged to allow) a loosening of political and cultural controls over their satellites, while retaining, perhaps improving, their own military security in Europe, could be the best outcome the West could reasonably hope for in the foreseeable future.

This is not the place to explore such a possibility. But one point is important in this context. Reaching toward this kind of vision almost compels a shift by the two military blocs – eventually both of them – toward defensive postures.

It would be much harder for the two halves of Europe gradually to evolve some sense of common identity if they simultaneously were threatening each other with highly offensive military postures. Conversely, the *great reduction in threat* that defensive postures would mean could hasten this evolution. In the case of Eastern Europe particularly, it is hard to imagine the Soviets permitting significant loosening of controls, unless they feel their security remains at least as great, and preferably greater, under the developing conditions.

The West does not, of course, control Soviet decisions regarding strategy. But it does control NATO strategy, and the perceptions throughout Europe of the political meaning of each side's decisions could become increasingly important.

Consider two cases. If NATO strategy is perceived as favouring the developing European identity, and only the Soviets as attempting to block it, the political result throughout Europe would be advantageous for NATO and the West. In the long run, these perceptions might unleash greater pressures on Moscow to go along with *mutual* threat-reduction and a developing European identity than Moscow could easily withstand.

Conversely, if *NATO* is the one that is perceived as impeding this development, because of an insistence on offensive postures and strategies, NATO's political base even among its own peoples is more likely to shrink than to expand. In that unhappy future, NATO's prospects as a politically viable entity might increasingly be in doubt.

It is worth noticing that this argument is the opposite of the one commonly advanced about the political perceptions and implications of a strictly defensive conventional posture for NATO. The usual argument, heard especially in the Federal Republic, is that such a posture would be perceived as deepening the *division*, not the unity, of Europe. This presupposes that a strictly defensive conventional posture requires a highly visible fortified border – a wide no-man's-land, extensive tank traps, fixed fortifications, etc., all of which would emphasise a frontier that most Germans and many Europeans would like to see de-emphasised. But those tactics and methods are only one possible approach. Many military specialists in defensive deterrence are more interested in highly decentralised tactics. While some form of 'barrier' at the frontier is highly desirable even using such tactics, it need *not* be visible. Under defensive deterrence, the frontier need not look any more like a permanent border than it does now.

Meanwhile, the well-publicised, credible abolition of any offensive threat to Eastern Europe or the USSR, as a sustained policy, would cumulatively have a positive effect. It would render increasingly non-credible the Soviet effort to sustain the division of Europe on grounds of military necessity. It would free the Eastern Europeans from any need to give credence at all to the idea of a security threat from the West. It would allow the Soviets themselves to feel more genuinely secure on their Western marches. And these things, in turn, could largely remove what presently may be some of the largest elements blocking the development, in Eastern as well as Western Europe, of a sense of *European* identity.

CONCLUSION

I conclude that, for many reasons, the wise course is for NATO to develop a new posture that will be sounder and stronger than the current doubtfully-credible threat of first use, and the even more questionable threat of taking to the offensive. That posture would be one of conventional defence against conventional attack, including secure second-strike nuclear forces, and deliberately excluding any non-nuclear offensive capability that could threaten Soviet security.

There are many good reasons why a transition to this posture should not be attempted quickly. The reasons are both military and political. The NATO military planning horizon is five years. Any significant change must be contemplated for further ahead than that, and for various reasons the larger the shift the more time would be required for a sound, stable transition. (National militaries may have a longer planning horizon; in the Federal Republic it is 12 years.)

Furthermore, a substantial analytic and planning task must be accomplished before a major shift in posture can even be brought before political leaders. So far, NATO has not gone beyond a (justified) critique of theorists' early, first-generation ideas – many of which are impractical by themselves – to deploy its vast analytic and planning resources toward designing a credible defensive posture. Most of the ingredients, including selective use of emerging technologies, have been brought to light; their integration into a sound posture remains to be completed.

After this is done, the political task to be accomplished will require some time. It will also require an unusual degree of political leadership. Political figures would be required in major NATO countries who grasp both the politics internal to NATO and the larger issues involved for the future of Europe. However a large political payoff awaits the leaders who recognise the simplicity, comprehensibility, and wide appeal of the new posture compared to the existing one, and can seize the emerging opportunity of refashioning the political consensus that undergirds NATO.

A militarily and politically sound transition probably locates implementation of the new posture slightly beyond the year 2000 even if clear movement becomes visible soon. The goal in view is a new and sound posture for a new century.

Notes

1. Public Agenda Foundation, *Voter Options on Nuclear Arms Policy* (New York, 1984).
2. Flynn, Gregory and Hans Rattinger, *The Public and Atlantic Defense* (London: Rowman & Allanheld and Croom Helm Ltd, 1985). See in particular pages 26–7, 78–86, 124–6, 191–3, 232–5, 299–300. Also Schmidt, Peter, 'Public Opinion and Security Policy in the Federal Republic of Germany', *Orbis* vol. 28, no. 14 (Winter 1985).

11 NATO Strategy: Can Conventional Forces Deter a Conventional Attack?

David W. Tarr

Nuclear weapons are for NATO both the primary instrument for deterring a nuclear attack and the fall-back option if, in the event of a conventional assault, NATO's non-nuclear defence forces cannot hold. The dilemma of depending upon potentially self-destructive nuclear responses if deterrence fails and defence falters has always haunted NATO strategy, but after the Soviets achieved nuclear parity with the United States, this dilemma became more intensely perceived. Now the credibility, viability, acceptability, sensibility and morality of nuclear weapons for deterrence and defence are increasingly at issue. As a result, an increasing variety of non-nuclear ('conventional') alternatives are being advanced to replace or supplement nuclear deterrence for the Alliance.

The thrust of my remarks is to attempt to apply the definitions, requirements, and other key conceptual distinctions of nuclear deterrence found in the body of western strategic literature to three categories of non-nuclear alternatives currently in vogue: 1. strengthened conventional forces; 2. deployment of new, high-technology non-nuclear weapons; and 3. adoption of an offensive manoeuvre strategy. Let me, therefore, begin by listing the basic definitions, concepts and apparent requirements of deterrence which the 'deterrence theory' literature offers.

General and immediate deterrence.[1] First, by 'deterrence' we mean either those *policies* designed to prevent a hostile state from attacking or the existing *condition* of deterrence itself. Flexible response is the current policy of the Alliance. A condition of 'general deterrence' exists when an otherwise hostile state is not inclined to attack due to its perception of the unfavourable balance of forces and threats to retaliate arrayed against it. A condition of general deterrence exists between the United States and the Soviet Union and between the

Warsaw Pact and NATO. There is no sense of alarm, but there is a state of readiness. Deterrence policies of military preparation and statements of intent to retaliate are usually employed to sustain such a condition. 'Immediate deterrence' on the other hand, is a condition of extreme crisis in which attack appears to be imminent. The forces and policies appropriate to general deterrence – military preparedness and a doctrine of retaliation – are not always sufficient to meet the conditions of an impending attack, for in the latter case the right combination of military capabilities must be reinforced by credible resolve to use them, effectively communicated by the defender, and clearly perceived by the prospective attacker, if deterrence is to be successful.

Denial, punishment and retaliation. Deterrence is thought to work by means of threats to retaliate (deterrence by retaliation and punishment) – which usually means the threat to impose unacceptably high costs on the attacker – and by the capacity to defend (deterrence by denial) – that is, having the strength necessary to frustrate the attacker's attempt at gains, often conceived in terms of the ability to fend off the aggressor by effective territorial defence.[2] Thus an adversary sufficiently imbued with concern over prized assets threatened by retaliation and either convinced that the defender cannot be defeated, or that victory would come at too high a cost, should be 'deterred'. The combination of these two factors, the sword of retaliation and the shield of defence, should thus convince one's opponent that the outcome of armed conflict would be unacceptable to him. NATO forces have presumably deterred attacks both by deploying forces to defend territory and by invoking threats to retaliate and punish. Nuclear weapons have played a key role in both conceptions of deterrence but have never functioned as the exclusive instruments of deterrence. Instead, the Alliance has attempted to establish and retain a 'seamless webb' of armed forces and weapons capable of deterring aggression, as well as by defending and defeating prospective attacks, employing both conventional and nuclear weapons for these tasks.

Primary and extended deterrence. Nuclear deterrence is also usefully divided into 'primary' deterrence (deterring attacks on one's homeland) and 'extended' deterrence (deterring attacks on others). For the United States, on the one hand, and its NATO partners on the other, the significance of the distinction can hardly be overstressed, especially when taking into account the issue of credibility. Since the United States is the nuclear guarantor for NATO security, a major problem, in terms of credibility of the nuclear threat, is to convince ally and adversary alike that the American commitment to use nuclear weapons (i.e., extended deterrence) would in fact be carried out on behalf of the Alliance, despite the risk that nuclear escalation entails – which could ultimately endanger the survival of the United States itself.

Credibility. The 'credibility' of one's threat, which most analysts have regarded as the quintessential requirement of deterrence, has always been problematical when applied to *nuclear* deterrence.[3] One needs the capability to carry out the threat and the will to do so. The threat to use nuclear weapons, especially 'first-use', which has been an essential element of NATO's strategy of flexible response, carries with it the burden of accepting the consequences of executing the threat, which when posed against another nuclear adversary raises considerable doubts, given the potential for disaster. If one is doing this on behalf of one's allies (extended deterrence), the credibility is clearly less convincing than if one is threatening to impose the nuclear sanction in response to an attack upon one's own territory. Apologists for French nuclear strategy make this point very clearly. Indeed, most analysts today argue that the credibility of NATO's nuclear threat has been in decline, both because the Soviet Union has gained nuclear parity with the United States, thus offsetting the American promise to respond on behalf of its allies, and because the use of nuclear weapons in Europe (first-use or any use) entails unacceptable risks to the allies themselves.

Presence and possession. The credibility of nuclear deterrence in Europe has been shored up by special applications: the very 'presence' of forces in being, which are placed in harm's way, especially American armed forces (which carry with them the 'whiff of nuclear retaliation', to borrow the interesting phrase of our colleague, Earl Ravenal)[4] enhance the credibility of nuclear deterrence. NATO's forward deployed[5] armed forces are hostages to an attack. They will be engaged because they are there. Thus, they function as 'trip-wires' to military response. They are the 'threat that leaves something to chance',[6] This 'deterrence by presence' or location is further enhanced by 'deterrence by possession': these forces have nuclear capability; possession may well lead to use once the combat forces are engaged in battle. In this way the credibility of the nuclear threat is presumably bolstered. Credibility need not be perfect; it need only to be to some degree probable, but to what degree remains a matter of serious controversy.

Uncertainty. Deterrence theory makes much of the value of uncertainty: deterrence is presumably enhanced if the prospective attacker is unable to conclude with certainty whether, when and what kind of responses the defender will undertake. It is likely that the Soviets are deterred by their perception of a low probability, say a 10 per cent chance nuclear weapons might be used, whereas America's European partners seem perturbed if the probability is perceived to have declined below 90 per cent (the difference between deterrence of an adversary and assurance of an ally). Furthermore, nuclear weapons impose incalculable risks, as compared to the more calculable consequences of conventional responses (although the latter calculus is perhaps too confidently made – witness the wide disparity of conclusions concerning the current conventional 'balance' between the two alliances). There is no experience to draw upon in assessing the costs and risks of nuclear war. The probability of uncontrolled escalation is a clear and present danger to any military planner no matter how effective one's own controls are believed to be. Furthermore, uncertainty in the face of NATO nuclear capabilities requires the Pact forces to deploy *as if* a nuclear response is anticipated, because not to do so (e.g., massing forces) invites nuclear first-use. Thus, most of the uncertainties associated with attempting to anticipate responses and calculate outcomes is thought to work in favour of the deterrer and against the aggressor.

Targeting options. We now come to one of the most troubling and troublesome distinctions in the nuclear literature: 'counter-force' versus 'counter-value' targeting. Nuclear weapons can, of course, be used against any imaginable targets, although with how much discrimination remains at issue. Deterrence by defence and by retaliation can be fostered by threatening both categories of targets. However, the strategic literature on deterrence by *punishment*, usually associated with the concept of 'unacceptable' punishment or with threatening 'highly valued' assets, most often addresses counter-value targets such as industrial/population centres, while counter-force targets are selected for war-fighting and damage limitation. NATO's 'tactical' or 'battlefield' nuclear weapons have always had counter-force roles although their prospective use has just as consistently raised fears of collateral damage to adjacent military and civilian facilities and personnel. However, NATO's longer range nuclear weapons (including those of France) have the capacity to punish, both in carrying the war to the Soviet and Eastern European homelands and in attacking either military or civilian targets. It is in this sense that they are 'Euro-strategic', having the same controversial target policy options as those of the American strategic triad. Thus, NATO's nuclear arms, whatever the credibility of their use, give the Alliance the capacity to inflict unacceptable costs upon the WTO, in the immediate battlefield and beyond.

The nuclear threshold. Another key concept is that of 'threshold' – the point at which one moves from conventional to nuclear options. Where that point lies depends upon the interrelationship between one's conventional and nuclear capabilities and one's tactics and strategy. Thus, the threshold can be 'raised' by enhancing conventional capabilities and/or deliberately choosing not to acquire certain types of nuclear weapons, such as neutron bombs that might have temptingly useful tactical roles, or by choosing not to deploy such weapons in forward locations; or 'lowered' by adopting a strategy of heavy dependence on nuclear weapons and integrating the deployment, for example, of very low yield, accurately delivered and thus 'useable' nuclear weapons into the structure of the defending forces.

The nuclear firebreak. Similarly, the distinction between nuclear and non-nuclear weapons can be enhanced or minimised by the types of munitions deployed and/or strategies and doctrines adopted. Low yield nuclear weapons arguably facilitate the decision to escalate from conventional to nuclear weapons. The attempt in NATO to 'couple' nuclear weapons 'across geography and between levels of warfare', as Earl C. Ravenal points out,[7] runs contrary to establishing clear firebreaks. One line of argument maintains that lowering the threshold and minimising firebreaks enhance the credibility of the nuclear threat and therefore of deterrence, while another view points with alarm at the danger of doing so.

Non-military factors. Before moving on to consider how several alternative conventional enhancement proposals might affect deterrence, there is one final set of factors to take into account that influences both nuclear and non-nuclear options: the political, psychological, moral and economic components of costs and gains. The calculus undertaken by policy makers contemplating the use of force surely includes anticipated domestic political, economic, psychological and moral costs, estimates of the political cohesion of one's allies, and perceptions of the determination and morale of the populations of one's opponents. Some have argued that the policy of first use of nuclear weapons, even in a failing defensive effort, may have higher domestic costs than any other course of action. Indeed, the paradox of depending upon the nuclear option for NATO security is that the dangers it entails tends to undermine the psychological sense of security of its people. On the other hand, resistance to higher defence expenditures and conscription rates have been a factor in the assigned role of nuclear weapons in the Alliance.

Conventional alternatives to nuclear deterrence. In 'rethinking the nuclear weapons dilemma in Europe' (the theme of this conference) a number of military reforms have been suggested to reduce, change or minimise dependence on nuclear weapons for deterrence of a conventional assault on NATO. The reformist impulse in many of us is motivated by a widely shared belief that, as Samuel P. Huntington put it recently, 'nuclear deterrence of a Soviet conventional attack... suffers from a lack of credibility, [while] NATO conventional deterrence ... suffers from a lack of capability'.[8] Let us review, therefore, several possible reforms in the context of the concepts discussed above. As I indicated at the outset, I propose to address the following categories of reform:[9] 1. improved conventional defence capabilities; 2. enhancement of conventional forces by means of emerging high technology weaponry; and 3. shifting from a defensive to an offensive manoeuvre strategy.

IMPROVING THE CONVENTIONAL BALANCE OF FORCES

Putting aside for the moment that argument that the present balance of conventional capabilities does not seriously disadvantage NATO, one cluster of options favours adding conventional forces to counterbalance the Pact conventional threat. The 1978 Long-Term Defence Plan called for a 3 per cent increase in defence expenditures; more recent proposals call for a 4 per cent increase. How might this adjustment affect deterrence?

Clearly this option attempts to rectify deficiencies in deterrence by denial (improved conventional defence capabilities), to manage but not resolve the nuclear dilemma by raising the nuclear threshold a bit, and to engender stronger public support by some de-emphasis of nuclear weapons. It is not a change in deterrence strategy so much as it is simply an increase in numbers. Forward strategy, flexible response, and first use remain in place. With stronger conventional defences NATO might be able to hold off the decision to go nuclear longer, assuming the attack remains conventional, or force the Soviets to confront the moral burden and high risk of going nuclear first because they may not be able by any other means to achieve a breakthrough. Deterrence ought to be improved, by this method, because the most credible use of force – conventional defence – is enhanced, while the least credible option, nuclear first use, is either delayed or (preferably) transferred from the defender to the attacker.

Non-military factors that relate to deterrence, especially the psychological perturbations and moral opposition to nuclear dependence and first use, are addressed by these reforms to the degree that domestic opposition might be allayed by the new emphasis on conventional capabilities. However, the economic burdens, already a factor that has frustrated achieving the 3 per cent goal, will likely be even more pronounced. Moreover, as Mearsheimer argues,[10] larger manpower commitments may not be feasible. The demographic factors in Germany make even retaining present levels of military manpower difficult over the next decade. Increases may not be politically acceptable. The situation among the other NATO members, including the United States, is not much better. The most obvious pressure is in the other direction: to decrease force levels and expenditures, not to increase them.

The fundamental problem from the American perspective is to assess how the enhancement of conventional defences will affect the credibility of *extended* deterrence. Even if greater conventional strength were politically feasible, such enhancement might, in fact, further erode the credibility of the American nuclear guarantee because it suggests a greater than ever American reluctance to go nuclear combined with an improved capacity to avoid the nuclear option. The delicate balance of conventional and nuclear options appears to require, from our intercontinental perspective, 'enough' conventional defence in Europe to deny the Soviets quick territorial gain at low cost, but not enough to provide a sustained defence, lest the American nuclear threat lose its credibility altogether.[11]

But then there are many voices that argue that nuclear deterrence of a conventional Soviet attack is, in fact, nearly or completely incredible now: Huntington succinctly states the range of views:

> what causes the problem now is the very high probability – some would say virtual certainty, and I would agree with Secretary McNamara on this – that no American President will authorize the use of nuclear weapons in response to a Soviet conventional attack on Europe. Our policy will in fact be the 'cosmic bluff' that George Ball has called it.[12]

TECHNICAL SOLUTIONS

If deterrence of conventional aggression by the Soviets cannot be obtained by additional conventional strength because of domestic resistance to increased expenditures and extended conscription, one must find credible substitutes for the nuclear threat or effective alternatives to increased manpower. Two interesting approaches currently under discussion are: the 'high-tech' option, and the defensive technologies, non-provocative defence option.

If nuclear weapons are too dangerous to ourselves to provide a sufficiently credible threat, perhaps high-technology/non-nuclear weapons – the so-called 'emerging technologies' (ETs) – will provide a more believable and effective answer. The Report of the European Security Study,[13] (under the auspices of the American Academy of Arts and Sciences) is perhaps the most notable example of this genre of deterrence enhancement. It argues for the rapid development and deployment of advanced conventional weapons technologies, to include precision guided munitions, ballistic missiles, cruise missiles – a host of 'smart' weapons with non-nuclear armaments, for medium and deep interdiction and choke point missions, plus large numbers of close-in battlefield weapons with terminally-guided warheads. Three common themes of conventional technical fixes of this sort are: enhanced firepower, radically improved accuracy, and deep strikes. Presumably a Soviet conventional assault of the central front would employ blitzkrieg tactics, with second and third echelon reinforcements pushing ahead to flow through and exploit the break in NATO defences. Deep strikes could according to some proponents disrupt these reinforcements while smart battlefield weapons (which enthusiasts claim will give the defence a significant advantage over the offence) counter superior numbers.

These claims are hard to assess because they are for the most part conceptual schemes rather than actual weapons systems. While there are some precision-guided munitions in our weapons inventory, these proposals largely speak of emerging technologies. The European Security Study, for example, calls for large numbers of weapons that do not yet exist. Moreover, the question is *which* problem is the technology to fix, the unfavourable conventional balance (denial), or the need for nuclear weapons (retaliation/punishment)? If a technical fix can improve the balance of conventional capabilities, it still suffers the same deficiencies in deterrence that obtain in the category discussed above (strengthening conventional defences). If they are to be substitutes for nuclear weapons, on the other hand, can they really do the trick without being employed deliberately against countervalue targets to maximise the harm they can do? Moreover, if conventional munitions are to be used for deep strike missions, how will the Soviet know whether these are nuclear or conventional weapons when they assess the forces they confront?

Conceptually, then, how would the exploitation of 'emerging technologies' enhance deterrence of a conventional attack? What they seem to add, were they to operate as advertised, are two rungs to the ladder of flexible response: more intense and lethal defences (denial); and accurate non-nuclear deep strike interdiction. Willingness to use such weapons in these roles would be more credible but the latter mission would not exact punishment to the degree that nuclear weapons could, although it would bring the war to the enemy (retaliation).

Basically, ETs are a new category of expensive weapons to be used because, like other conventional forces, they provide an additional cushion between conventional defences and the nuclear option. Thus they raise the conventional threshold instead of lowering the nuclear one.

Some authorities, Albert Wohlstetter, for example,[14] see a long-term trend of weapons accuracy that will lead to the gradual replacement of nuclear munitions with more accurate conventional ones, dramatically raising the nuclear threshold. NATO will thus be able to slug it out with the Soviets, holding on to its forward line of defence, while wreaking havoc on military bases, forces and weapons in the rear. Other authorities are more sceptical. Freeman Dyson, for example, warns of the illusory attractiveness of complex weapons technologies as solutions to military problems – 'technical follies', he calls them.[15]

Attractive as technological enhancement might be as compared to the awful risks of nuclear first use, the problem remains that unless nuclear weapons are not retained, ET's simply push the nuclear option up higher on the ladder. The high cost of development and deployment (estimated at 10–20 billion additional dollars by the Academy Study) will not ameliorate NATO's dilemmas. High profile investment in such technology will make the American President's alleged 'cosmic bluff' more apparent than ever, yet dependence on the new technology, which the Soviets certainly would try to offset with their own weapons, strategy and tactics, is unlikely to improve the overall efficacy of conventional deterrence. Why? The cost of preparation for war may rise, but the cost of aggression may decline. Moreover, the contribution of such weapons in crises (immediate deterrence) could be negative. The deep strike ETs would be counter-force-capable first-strike weapons (possibly containing nuclear munitions from the Soviets point of view), encouraging pre-emptive incentives. Deployment of such systems would make arms control arrangements that verify their non-nuclear status, for example, urgent but probably impossible unless a contrived method for total separation of nuclear and conventional missiles is adopted – most likely by the removal of long range theatre nuclear weapons from Western Europe, something the Soviets would certainly encourage us to do. Thus, the credibility of NATO's nuclear deterrent would likely decline and with it some margin of the efficacy of deterring conventional attack.

A second type of technical fix proposal, one of a very different character, is represented in this conference in the paper by Barnaby and Boeker, 'Non Nuclear Defense for Europe'.[16] Instead of deep interdiction conventional weapons to supplement nuclear deterrence, this latter proposal would forgo deep strikes, both nuclear and non-nuclear, altogether. It advocates instead a nuclear-free zone ('the nuclear disarmament of the British and US troops in the region'), protected by unambiguously defensive (i.e., short-ranged), high-technology conventional weapons – mainly anti-tank, anti-aircraft and anti-ship missiles and artillery of the highest precision, exploiting the military technological lead of the West, especially 'those [systems] based on microelectronics and microprocessors'. The underlying conceptual principle of this proposal consists of non-provocation – an exclusively defensive system that by the very character of its weapons and the location, training and structure of its armed forces, is capable of defence while at the same time being incapable of offence. It conceives of a nuclear-free Western Europe (it is silent about France) defended entirely by conventional means, the central front defined by a 'defensive zone' some 50 kilometres deep within which highly automated sensors and prepositioned and/or pretargeted exclusively defensive weaponry stand at the ready.

Would a non-nuclear, non-provocative defence enhance deterrence? Can deterrence of a conventional attack be sufficiently effective if it is based solely on denial? If retaliation by manoeuvre, counter-attack and deep strikes, even by conventional means is foresworn, the defences in place must endow the defenders with extremely high confidence of success and discourage aggression by the assessed improbability of surmounting the defence. Defence obtained primarily by means of intensive, extremely accurate, computer-aided firepower will not induce fear of retaliation on the Soviet side; therefore it must induce discouragement – a sense that an attack would be futile. The Soviet bloc forces are to be deterred not by fear of punishment or of escalation, therefore, but by the conclusion that they could not achieve significant gains by force of conventional arms. The idea is to convince the Soviets that the expected benefits from aggression are low and that the political costs of trying are high.

This proposal combines unusual faith and confidence in new, yet to be developed, non-nuclear defensive technologies with an equally optimistic assessment of the political consequences that would ensue in adopting a self-inhibiting, non-nuclear, 'non-provocative' posture: it is designed to promote detente and 'Ostpolitik'; it would presumably engender the support of 'world public opinion' against superpower nuclear threats; and in any case, Barnaby and Boeker assure us of two things: the Soviets were never inclined to invade Western Europe; but even if they became so inclined, the US would regard that territorial acquisition 'as an unbearable threat to the US economic interests'. Hence, Barnaby and Boeker's non-provocative defence posture depends upon the least credible form of extended *nuclear* deterrence by the USA: the notion that the Soviet would perceive that United States would not tolerate a Soviet invasion ('a fact about which the USSR can have no illusions') should deter the Soviets from that undertaking! In making this assertion the authors are silent on the matter of how the American nuclear guarantee – extended nuclear deterrence – might be so credible, especially as they advocate a nuclear-free zone for Western Europe. To assert that 'the withdrawal of nuclear weapons from the European land-mass would not change global parity and would, therefore, not essentially change today's situation', is to overlook implicitly the significance of the distinction made between primary and extended deterrence, to fail to confront the claim by proponents of nuclear deterrence of the deterrent value of placing nuclear weapons in harms way (deterrence by location and possession), and to disregard the presumed advantage uncertainty plays by means of the integration of nuclear weapons in NATO's defence posture.

Barnaby and Boeker assert that 'the present danger is that nuclear war will occur through accident, miscalculation or madness', and not by deliberate action by rational leaders. That, and not the Soviet threat, constitutes the 'real' danger in Europe. In other words, the main purpose of this proposal is to diminish the perceived danger of nuclear war, not to enhance deterrence *per se*. It is hard to understand why their claim that 'a non-nuclear, non-provocative defence in Europe would greatly decrease the probability of *any* war in Europe', is any more valid than the opposite assertion – that a strategy of flexible response best deters any kind of war.

Indeed, the whole thrust of the Barnaby/Boeker proposal is to address issues which tend to discount the importance of deterrence – the danger of: nuclear war posed by the possession of nuclear weapons; of Soviet misperceptions posed by NATO's offensive capabilities; of a militarised society posed by territorial defence shemes; of wasted resources posed by increased defence expenditures. That each of these are legitimate concerns is obvious; that deterrence would be enhanced by such alternative measures as they propose, is not.

STRATEGIC REFORM

A final cluster of alternatives addressed to NATO's nuclear dilemma involve rectifying NATO strategy. I have in mind, in particular, Huntington's strategy of 'conventional retaliation', and the US Army's new Airland Battle doctrine of manoeuvre and counterattack.[17] For sake of brevity I will focus on Huntington's proposal which conveniently addresses the requirements of deterrence directly and explicitly. He argues that in the shift toward conventional deterrence one ends up with a strategy that defends (deterrence by denial) but does not threaten punishment (deterrence by retaliation). Deterrence by denial, he asserts, is much weaker than that obtained by threatening retaliation. None the less, nuclear retaliation in response to a Soviet conventional attack is, in Huntington's view, virtually incredible as it now stands. Therefore, NATO strategy must be altered to provide a credible conventional threat to place at risk 'highly valued assets' of the Soviet Union. His answer: 'a conventional retaliatory offensive directed at the Soviet's empire in Eastern Europe' in which NATO's conventional forces would drive into East Germany, for example, instead of counterattacking at the point of the Soviet offensive.

Huntington's strategic reform stands the tests of deterrence theory better than the first two categories of conventional alternatives because he addresses the key weakness of conventional deterrence – reliance on denial without substantial enhancement of punishment. Yet his manoeuvre strategy substitutes an allegedly 'incredible' nuclear option for a conventional one that may be politically unfeasible. He abandons the high risks of nuclear engagement for the gravely uncertain alternative of swapping territorial advances – of counter-envelopment. But these conceptions require public support for offensive options that are widely regarded as too provocative and too problematical. They may heighten tensions by adopting explicitly offensive postures instead of emphasising a 'defence-oriented' strategy. This approach risks convincing the Soviets that their paranoia with respect to imperialist intensions is well placed.

Both the manoeuvre strategy reform and the 'high tech' option tend to favour barrier defences and fortifications (to complement PGM deployments, on the one hand, and on the other so that units can be released from forward defence positions in order to function as reserves for flanking manoeuvres into Eastern Europe). Prepared barriers and fortifications along the inter-German border strike a most sensitive nerve (the permanent division of Germany), while preparations for offensive manoeuvres might be equally unappreciated on both sides of the border. The deficiency in Huntington's deterrence theory (quite apart from the question of how militarily sound such manoeuvre strategies actually might be) lies in the non-military factors of psychological, moral and therefore political support. The 'unprovocative' defence concept would doubtless garner more public support than would the manoeuvre strategy. Neither would be regarded by Europeans as resolving the nuclear dilemma because removing the nuclear option is widely understood to be destabilising, regardless of the unpopularity of nuclear weapons, *per se*. There is no reason *not* to be schizophrenic about nuclear weapons: they are good for deterrence, but bad as defences.

Concluding remarks. Is the threat of a conventional assault on NATO on the rise? Is there growing evidence that the Soviets have a tangible interest in military conquest of Western Europe? General deterrence seems healthy indeed. The existence and readiness of dual-capable NATO armed forces has served deterrence well. The characterisation of nuclear deterrence as an American 'cosmic bluff' is a cliché, not a criticism. (Ball, McNamara and Huntington are wrong.) The 'whiff of retaliation' is sufficient (Earl Ravenal is right, at least in that respect).

But is nuclear deterrence too dangerous even if war is so remote? It is not the case that we (NATO) have more to lose than to gain in *threatening* a nuclear response and being prepared to use it; but it is clear that we would and should be most reluctant to carry out that threat, unless forced by events to do so, because then we might very well feel we have more to lose. That is the dilemma. Nuclear weapons support the condition of general deterrence effectively. But analyses of potential crises scenarios leads analysts to focus on the risks such dependence on nuclear weapons entails under circumstances in which general deterrence deteriorates toward immediate deterrence, and thence to the failure of deterrence altogether, followed by war-fighting scenarios in which nuclear weapons are introduced – whether first use, delayed first use or second use – and in which any and all uses flirt with disasters distinguished only by their various magnitudes of horror.

However, the risks involved with nuclear weapons work both ways: we are reluctant to resort to nuclear weapons, but so are the Soviets. In my judgement that danger promotes deterrence, not aggression. It may bother us that the threat that leaves something to chance seems to operate here, even though deterrence is enhanced. Moreover, it should concern us that there are both undeterrable events and unexpected (surprising) happenings. That is why confidence-building measures and other methods of reducing tension and alarm are vital to European military stability. Nevertheless, from the perspective of the requirements of deterrence, conventional alternatives to nuclear options come at a price: the cost of aggression declines the more remote the nuclear option becomes.

The three types of proposals reviewed here suffer in terms of their efforts to balance the political need to reassure public apprehensions concerning the danger of nuclear war against the military requirements for making deterrence stable and defence viable. In doing so, they suggest another kind of nuclear dilemma: that which makes military sense is sometimes not politically acceptable; that which is acceptable sometimes does not make military sense.

Notes

1. See Patrick M. Morgan, *Deterrence: A Conceptual Analysis*, 2nd edn, (Beverly Hills: Sage Publications, 1983) for an elaboration of this distinction.
2. Glenn H. Snyder's conceptual distinction between punishment and denial is now classic, *Deterrence and Defense* (Princeton, 1961), pp. 14–16).

3. The classic exposition is still that of William W. Kaufmann, 'The Requirements of Deterrence', in William W. Kaufmann, *et al.*, *Military Policy and National Security* (Princeton: Princeton University Press, 1956) ch. 1.
4. 'Counterforce and Alliance: The Ultimate Connection', *International Security*, vol. 6, no. 4 (Spring 1982), p. 36.
5. Dieter Mahncke reminds us in his contribution, 'Alternatives to Nuclear Deterrence as a Basis for European Security', that the German term is now 'front-line defence'.
6. Thomas C. Schelling, *The Strategy of Conflict* (New York: Oxford University Press, 1963), ch. 8.
7. See his contribution to this conference, titled 'Coupling and Decoupling: The Prospects for Extended Deterrence'.
8. Samuel P. Huntington, 'Conventional Deterrence and Conventional Retaliation in Europe', *International Security*, vol. 8, no. 3, Winter 1983/84, p. 35.
9. *International Security*, vol. 9, no. 3, Winter 1984–85, contains two articles addressing military reforms in which similar categories are addressed: John J. Mearsheimer, 'Nuclear Weapons and Deterrence in Europe', pp. 19–46; and Barry R. Posen, 'Measuring the European Conventional Balance: Coping with Complexity in Threat Assessment', pp. 47–88.
10. Mearshiemer, pp. 33–5.
11. The American nuclear threat is composed of two elements: US strategic forces; and theatre nuclear forces. Almost every proposed modification of the deployment and employment policies related to these forces has, in Earl C. Ravenal's words, '... evoked the specter of decoupling in one or another of its forms: either the avoidance of a nuclear response altogether or the attempt to confine even a nuclear conflict to the European theater'. (Quote from the conference draft of 'Coupling and Decoupling: The prospects for Extended Deterrence'.
12. Samuel P. Huntington, 'Correspondence', *International Security*, vol. 9, no. 1, Summer 1984, p. 212.
13. *Strengthening Conventional Deterrence in Europe: Proposals for the 1980s* (New York: St. Martin's Press, 1983).
14. See his 'Bishops, Statesmen, and Other Strategists on the Bombing of Innocents', *Commentary*, June 1983, especially p. 30.
15. *Weapons and Hope* (New York: Harper & Row, 1984), ch. 5.
16. All references made here are to the paper by this title by Frank Barnaby and Egbert Boeker presented at the Wingspread conference, and presented in this volume in a revised version.
17. See Samuel P. Huntington, 'Conventional Deterrence and Conventional Retaliation', cited; and US Army, *Operations: FM 100–5* (Washington, USGPO, 1982).

Part IV

Crisis Management and War Avoidance in Europe

12 Conventional Wisdom and Unconventional Possibilities

Lincoln P. Bloomfield

Discussions of European security tend to deal with abstractions such as grand strategies and long-term relationships. Alternatively, they centre on detailed tactical scenarios featuring clashing armies and air forces. The focus here is the linkage between military planning and the processes of crisis management in the event such abstractions ever become realities. The question this analysis seeks to answer is: *'What is likely to happen when the European security system is subjected to maximum real-life strain?'*

Theoretical debates about 'the threat' which stress strategies, tactics, and alliance diplomacy fail to supply adequate answers to that question. To examine what might be called the micromanagement of nuclear crises in Europe, one must ask a second, more problematic question: 'What would probably happen at 2 or 3 a.m. in the White House Situation Room or in the heart of the Kremlin if national leaders, called suddenly from their beds to confront ambiguous but highly worrisome intelligence, feel impelled to place their armed forces on high alert status and take other precautionary measures against worst-case contingencies, measures that in the nature of things will invariably be parallelled or reciprocated by the other superpower?'

In considering such potential real-life circumstances, a crucial ingredient is the human-psychological factor of individual and group behaviour in crisis. This element is surely as important as the relative military balance, but tends to be ignored or at a minimum dangerously underrated in policy debates about crisis in the European Theatre. It is impossible to do justice here to this vital issue, and instead the reader is referred to a documentation of malfunctions of individuals, groups and complex systems in high-intensity crisis situations.[1]

This caveat is particularly *à propos* when one considers the changes now taking place in weapons accuracies, deployments and targeting doctrines. Such changes will make future crises far less stable than they have been in the past. The effects will include: raising the perceived cost of waiting for more solid information when confronted with ambiguous indicators; placing a higher premium on pre-emption and pre-programmed computerised responses; and encouraging the historically-dubious custom of assessing intentions primarily on the basis of capabilities.

The changing military technology that produces such pernicious effects is well-known, above all highly accurate warheads on MIRVd Soviet SS-18s and future SS-24s, and on US MX ICBMs and soon-to-be-deployed Trident IIs. A strategic world dominated by such weapons systems will emphasise time-urgent targets and counterforce strategies, along with increased pressures to 'use them or lose them'. At the theatre level, NATO Pershing-II intermediate-range missiles and Soviet offshore deployment of Yankee-class submarines will cut potential warning time for key targets from a theoretical 30 to a possible 5–10 minutes. So-called Decapitation Doctrines put at risk the very political and other command centres so crucial for regulating the employment of nuclear forces, reinforcing tendencies toward automated launch-on-warning procedures. The ultimate consequence will be to breach the essential firebreak between nuclear and conventional forces that maintains the possibility of keeping a NATO-Warsaw Pact clash non-nuclear.

In recognition of this self-created dilemma the US and, one hopes, the Soviet Union are taking important steps to enhance command, control and communications capabilities – so-called C^3 (C^3I if one adds Intelligence). One laudable purpose is to maintain central control over any release of nuclear weapons. A second benign purpose is to be able to terminate unwanted hostilities as quickly as possible after their outbreak. But a third and malign purpose, to which we will return, is to wage a 'protracted nuclear war' under a delusionary fantasy of victory amid the radioactive rubble. (Some have argued that C^3I upgrading might also perversely enhance dangers already inherent in the system of 'crisis-unstable' weapons and strategies.[2]) To get to the root of this hazardous trend will require not just secondary remedies through C^3I, important as that is, but fundamental alterations in policy concerning weapons systems, deployments and targeting doctrines.

The discussion so far has focused on broad strategic trends and dilemmas. All have particular relevance to European security.

Few believe that the Soviet Union will deliberately launch a blitzkrieg across the classic invasion routes – North German plain, Göttinger Corridor and Fulda Gap – an attack against which NATO defensive strategy traditionally forfends. Conventional wisdom holds that the most likely source of future superpower nuclear crises will be 'third areas' outside of Europe. A favourite candidate for possible escalation is the Middle East, where indeed the Hotline has been used the most, and which saw US forces placed on a world-wide Defcon 3 alert in 1973 when Moscow threatened to send Soviet airborne troops to Suez. Nor should one exclude the Caribbean, where the US went on a Defcon 2 alert in the 1962 Cuban Missile Crisis. Southern Africa is coming up fast as a potential *place de crise*. 'Client state' conflicts which draw in superpower patrons will inevitably alert the superpower forces drawn up in permanent proximity in Europe, and can bring the troops out of their European casernes almost as readily as a new Berlin Blockade.

But it is also worth re-examining assumptions commonly made regarding presumed stability *within* Europe. The chances may be growing for a German–German move that one day could give reality to the familiar wargaming scenario in which a nuclear-armed Warsaw Pact battalion appears on FRG territory or vice versa and where it is unclear if it is acting independently, or represents a probe or even an indicator of attack. The chances are also non-trivial for future uprisings in Poland or elsewhere in Eastern Europe, accompanied by Soviet military moves that, as before, automatically send NATO forces on higher levels of alert.

Such false alarms are a constant. In June 1950, when the North Koreans invaded the South, the US State Department looked immediately to Berlin as the likely real target. In 1968 the Yugoslav authorities took the Soviet invasion of Czechoslovakia as a signal that the Red Army was about to march through Romania, and called a censorship-shrouded alert, to the extent of emplacing AA guns around Surchin airport. In 1981, when Warsaw Pact forces manoeuvred in strength around Poland, a Washington that had been burned by guessing wrong about Afghanistan incorrectly assumed a probable invasion. In these and other false or ambiguous alarms, whether in the Middle East or Europe, intelligence reports usually flood in of overflights, submarine sightings, and satellite-observed movements, most of which later turn out not to have happened at all, or in any event to have been innocent.

Alternatively, they may turn out to have been *precautionary*, which is the crucial point. Whether such instances represent accidents, misinformation, or calibrated probes, the natural response on the other side is a heightened state of readiness that may entail aircraft dispersals, cancellation of military leaves, and troop movements. Washington became understandably nervous when Moscow began signing up volunteers during the 1956 and 1967 Middle East wars. The US 86th Airborne Division was put on a highly visible alert during the 1973 war when Soviet troop carriers were believed to be loading troops. The process is obviously reciprocal, and will happen again and again in crises, whether created by the superpowers or by others. It does not really matter, then, if the first cause of an escalating superpower crisis is an indigenous Middle East or African or Caribbean conflict, or a Soviet probe, or a gross misunderstanding of ambiguous evidence. The fuse is likely to burn its way to Europe – the one place where the nuclear-armed superpower forces stand in permanent confrontation.

When it comes to policy within the Western Alliance itself, conventional wisdom supports expectations that rest on increasingly questionable assumptions. The most obvious illustration is the set of premises embedded in the 'Flexible Response' doctrine enshrined in the NATO Guidelines of 1967 and 1969. Former West German Chancellor Helmut Schmidt in recent speeches has pronounced an obituary over flexible response, implying that there may actually be rather a de facto 'no first use' policy, even if not publicly acknowledged. If conventional force buildups and the western Deep Attack strategies deter and, in a worst case, actually work, perhaps one can abstract the nuclear component from the real-life crisis equation.

But some analysts not only assume flexible response but also flexible manipulation of nuclear war in the form of a kind of preferentially controlled escalation that has come to be labelled 'escalation dominance'. Even apart from its morally noxious implication of controlled genocide, this concept seems patently absurd on the face of it. The mechanics of planned nuclear war micromanagement should boggle the imagination of anyone whose telephone lines have been down in a thunderstorm.

Common sense dictates that nuclear weaponry in reality has one purpose and one purpose alone: to deter war. But one also has to ask at what point in an intense crisis managed by fallible human decision makers the nuclear option in Europe might seem irresistible, however intolerable the probable consequences. It is sobering to speculate about the decisions that might have been made if a contingent nuclear option had been available in 1916 to Britain, France or Germany while they watched one million of their youth slaughtered in the sanguinary stalemate at Verdun, or in 1940 at Dunkirque.

A second piece of arguable conventional wisdom about European security is the assumption that in a grave crisis the NATO allies will be united and in good mutual communication. Under current doctrines a US President carefully retains release authority until he is ready to delegate it to US commanders including CINCEUR and, in a parallel fashion, through allied governments to the NATO command.[3] But in this sense, as in so many others, people who correctly assume a fog of battle incomprehensibly assume a clarity of multinational decision making by politicians under unprecedented personal stress, working with ambiguous signals, and possibly cut off from reliable communication with their own nuclear forces.

A third element of the conventional wisdom may also not hold up under real-life crisis conditions. It is popular today to cite the unplanned cascade of events leading to the First World War to illustrate how alliances can inadvertently be mobilised and activated.[4] But if a European war *really* threatened, with one or more nuclear weapons actually going off in anger (or error), the reverse might actually take place. Instead of a chain of alliance-implementing mobilisations, there might instead ensue a cascade of alliance-*unravelling* defections on both sides. The already problematic plans for crisis communication and of command and control would become even more of a nightmare.

Several conclusions follow logically from this brief analysis.

1. The same axioms of common sense that ought to guide overall stratgegic policy should, *a fortiori*, guide alliance policy in Europe. All these rest on the premise that in real life there is no intelligible subject entitled 'protracted nuclear war' and no meaningful topic called 'nuclear victory': both are intellectual oxymorons. Moving toward a nuclear showdown is like falling off a cliff. If you are clinging to a ledge partway down you do not need lots of options for resuming your fall, or for pulling everyone else over the edge. You need one thing only – a rope to pull you back up. Everything is possible if you get back up. Nothing is possible if you keep falling.

2. The de-escalation and war termination option is thus the only rational one if nuclear war actually threatens, and represents the best argument for massively upgraded C^3I. This in turn argues for a restated 'Definition of the Threat'. Since an all-out surprise attack

remains highly deterred but future crises are predictable, the chief danger to everyone's security would be to respond too fast or too hysterically to what is most likely to be a false alarm, reciprocal precautionary alert, or paranoid misreading of intentions. The consequences of such a sequence could, at worst, be the same as if a Soviet attack had in fact occurred.

3. According to the same logic, the central requirement for crisis stability is the ability to wait out a crisis in which information is ambiguous and the consequences of mistakes fateful. Logically the focus should be on clarifying intentions rather than making fateful judgements on the basis of capabilities. Just as capabilities deter, intentions either threaten or reassure. Specifically, this means three things.

4. First it means a clear priority, both in force posturing and in arms control, for weapons systems that buy maximum decision time in a crisis, and against systems that shorten such breathing room. This axiom applies both to first-strike-capable systems that are themselves vulnerable to a first strike, and to quick reaction theatre forces in Europe or forces deployed close to superpower borders elsewhere. For Europe, as for everywhere else, the logic of intentions-clarification argues against fixed offensive strategies, launch-on-warning doctrines, plans for 'horizontal escalation', decapitation targeting, and competitive anti-satellite warfare capabilities. It also argues against 'strategic defence initiatives' that are asymetrically pursued (though not against *mutual* defences that discourage first strikes).

5. Second, it means moving toward greater transparency in deployments and other military activity. The favoured instrument for achieving this today is CBMs – confidence-building measures. Indeed, since the Rapacki and Eden plans of the 1950s it has been recognised at least by some that a maximally-clear reading of intentions is essential for stability in Europe. The Helsinki Final Act accepts the norm of greater openness in its modest provisions for advance notification and observation of major manoeuvres.

Some military sceptics dismiss CBMs. But if the most probable dangers will come from inadvertence or miscalculation, accident, third-party mischief or escalation of crises elsewhere, reassurance becomes paramount. CBMs correctly focus on the *frame of mind* of those trying to manage crises under desperate conditions. But they are so far much too modest. Various constructive proposals have been made that could help move CBMs to an operationally useful stage, including fact-finding for reassurance through multiple channels, mutual or neutral crisis-control centres, agreements on accidental ground intrusions similar to the Incidents at Sea agreement, a European Security Commission possessing redundant communication links, a larger role for neutrals, and the like.[5]

Nuclear crisis management in the European setting is a subset of the general issue of nuclear crisis management. In the special case as in the general case, the potentially fatal flaw in contemporary strategic reasoning lies in implicit expectations about the capacity of humans in the White House and Kremlin to make rational judgements about use or non-use of genocidal force under shrinking time constraints and intolerable conditions of stress.

It cannot be repeated too often that the crucial capability for the nuclear superpowers in the nuclear age is to have time to check things out and de-escalate crises without being stampeded into making lethal decisions. Without significant policy changes that capacity will dwindle in perilous ways.

Notes

1. See Lincoln P. Bloomfield, 'Nuclear Crisis and Human Frailty', in Harlan Cleveland and Lincoln P. Bloomfield (eds), *Prospects for Peacemaking: A Citizen's Guide to Safer Nuclear Strategy* (Cambridge, Mass.: MIT Press, 1987).
2. See, *inter alia*, Desmond Ball, 'Can Nuclear War Be Controlled?' Adelphi Paper 169 (London: International Institute for Strategic Studies, 1981), pp. 35–6, and Paul Bracken, *The Command and Control of Nuclear Forces* (New Haven: Yale Univ. Press, 1983), pp. 41–4.
3. On Presidential nuclear release authority see Congressional Research Service, 'Authority to Order the Use of Nuclear Weapons' (Washington, G.P.O., 1977); Department of Defense Directive No. 5100.30 dated 2 Dec. 1971 as amended, pp. 1–4; Adm. Gerald E. Miller, 'Existing Systems of Command and Control', in Franklyn Griffiths and John C. Polyani (eds), *The Dangers of Nuclear War* (Toronto, Univ. of Toronto, 1979), p. 56; Scott Sagan, 'Nuclear Alerts and Crisis Management', *International Security*, Spring 1985; and Paul Bracken, op. cit.
4. See symposium on the First World War in *International Security*, Summer, 1984, pp. 3–4, particularly Stephen van Evera, 'The Cult of the Offensive . . .'; also, *mea culpa*, L.P. Bloomfield, op. cit.
5. See various proposals by Senators Jackson, Nunn and Warner, Press Conference, Washington, DC, 15 April 1982 and Report of Nunn/Warner Working Group on Nuclear Risk Reduction, Nov. 1983, reprinted in *Survival*, May/June, 1984, pp. 133–5; also William L. Ury, *Beyond the Hotline*, (Boston, Houghton-Mifflin, 1985).

13 Confidence and Security Building Measures and the European Neutrals

Jean F. Freymond*

Confidence and Security Building Measures (CSBMs), to use the Stockholm Conference terminology, are instruments which aim at reducing the possibilities of armed conflicts resulting from accident, misunderstanding, miscalculation or failure of communication as well as at strengthening confidence among states. In other words, they constitute means to change the perception and nature of the threat and to lessen tensions. An agreement on a set of mutually complementary CSBMs which would alter the threat significantly within the forseeable future, if enforced, could certainly help modify the nuclear dilemma as it now stands.

In this perspective, the possible contribution of the European Neutrals (Austria, Finland, Sweden and Switzerland) and perhaps of the European Non-aligned countries (Cyprus, Malta, Yugoslavia) is worth examining. The role of the Neutrals is often overlooked and not well-known. However marginal it might be, it should be taken into consideration.

The Neutrals and Yugoslavia are one of the dimensions of European overall balance and security. They occupy strategic locations on the European map. They are committed to defend their sovereignty and their territory by conventional means and do not constitute military vacuums. Their military forces are, however, of a defensive nature. Thus they do not represent a threat to any of their neighbours. The European Neutrals often devote ample resources to their defence, more sometimes than do some members of the North Atlantic Treaty Organisation (NATO). Their capacity to resist an invasion is indeed not unlimited. In the case of Sweden and Switzerland at least, and probably Yugoslavia, the strength of their defence, however, is such that the cost of any invasion would likely be substantially higher than its possible 'benefit'.[1] This in itself is a contribution to the security and the stability of the continent.

National defence is only one of the dimensions of the European

Neutrals' security policy, whose main objective is to preserve their independence. Their foreign policy also constitutes an element of such security policy. This foreign policy is very much rooted in – and therefore influenced by – the state of neutrality which, strictly speaking, implies no intervention in conflicts between other states. Each of the Neutrals interprets differently the requirements of neutrality in times of peace, when no international legal rules apply. This explains some of the differences in the manner they conduct their foreign policy. However, all the Neutrals, in their own way, tend to adopt a predictable policy – characterised by constancy and continuity – whose purpose is to show their determination not to take sides in any armed conflict which may arise: in other words a policy which is confidence-building. The European Neutrals have an immediate interest – for the sake of their own security – in a stable and secure European environment. This partly explains why each pursues a more or less active policy aimed at contributing to such increased European security and stability through such means as good offices, and the active search for acceptable solutions to some of the problems undermining security.

In this context, one of the features of today's all-European scene is the role which (jointly and often together with the Non-aligned countries) the European Neutrals have been playing for the last ten years in the context of the Conference on Security and Co-operation in Europe (CSCE). For the first time since the Second World War, all the Neutrals and Non-aligned countries (N + N) were invited to participate fully in a major conference of a political nature involving all European states. For the first time, they have been allowed to negotiate as 'equal' partners next to the Superpowers and their Allies in a forum where decisions are taken by consensus and not through majority vote, thus with no risk of being overruled. This has represented an opportunity for the Neutrals to have a say – however modest – in the regular discussions on the future of the continent in general and on its security in particular. The Neutrals were given the possibility of defending their overall interest, their concept of security and their ideas on how increased security can best be achieved.

In addition, they have been (and are) acting as host to many of the meetings of the CSCE process. They have been (and are) engaged in the search for solutions acceptable to both NATO and the Warsaw Pact. They are also requested, sometimes, to act as go-betweens.

As a consequence of this involvement in the CSCE process, the European Neutrals have started to work somewhat in concert in practically all areas dealt with at the CSCE, something they were not used to doing before. They did not (and do not) constitute a group. They are bound by no institutional ties. They cannot rely on any common infrastructure, any secretariat. Multilateral consultations take place occasionally. Defence Ministers, for example, met in 1984. There used to be regular meetings of the Secretaries of State for Foreign Affairs up to 1970, meetings which have again been held twice yearly since the fall of 1984. But generally speaking, outside of the CSCE process, the Neutrals have very limited and sporadic multilateral relations among themselves. They co-operate essentially on a bilateral basis.[2]

This is understandable. The European Neutrals are heterogeneous. They present different geographical, cultural, social and economic characteristics. They have lived through various historical experiences and differ in the form of their governments and in the strength of their national defences. Their neutrality does not have identical historical roots and is not understood in practice in the same manner. The external constraints which they face, such as the one imposed by geography – in other words neighbourhood – are dissimilar. This explains why the Neutrals do not give similar content to the concept of the 'policy of neutrality' which constitutes for all of them the backbone of their foreign policy. This heterogeneity is also reflected in the divergent ways the Neutrals assess the European situation, perceive their interest and what their security needs are, approach arms control and set up priorities, to the extent that it is often difficult for them to reach agreements. Rivalry at times exists between Neutrals. They are sometimes also suspicious of each others' intentions and policies. This heterogeneity is important. It limits the magnitude of the role (already marginal) which the Neutrals can collectively play within – and to some extent, outside of – the CSCE process.

This is the background against which the possible contributions of the European Neutrals in the field of confidence- and security-building measures should be analysed. These contributions are more likely to take place within the CSCE process. The possibility of the Neutrals playing a role outside this context – probably then on an individual basis, as part of their good offices policy – should not, however, be excluded.

Three roles can be envisaged for the European Neutrals which have already partly been played in the past.

1. A role in suggesting measures and ways to implement them. So far a number of proposals have been floated, formally and informally:

- The creation of a flexible and informal mechanism, a sort of 'Salon des ambassadeurs', proposed by the government of Switzerland, which would give an opportunity to a State to present a complaint about the implementation by one party of a given CSBM to representatives of the 35 countries engaged in the CSCE process and through which the party against which a complaint has been lodged could present is own point of view. The other representatives could make suggestions. No compulsory decision would be taken. This type of meeting could be convened within hours when matters are urgent, and the mechanism would serve to obtain clarification 'when a doubt arises as to a participating State's compliance with its commitments'.[3] It would allow them to clear up misunderstandings.
- The possibility, suggested by the Swedish government, for a state which suspects a severe breach of the CSBM regime to make a request for observation at very short notice. This observation by challenge would take place, exceptionally, when vital national interests are at stake, as opposed to routine on-site inspection or observation by invitation.
- The possibility, an idea circulated by Austria, for a party faced with a request for verification through on-site inspections, or for observation by challenge, to have a say in the choice of the inspectors, or of their countries of origin. This procedure could partially ensure that the inspectors would be independent to the dispute. In this perspective, a body of potential inspectors – for example nationals of neutral countries, who could be involved in all kinds of verifications, on-site inspections, etc. – could be established.[4] Another approach would be merely to draw up a list of 'trustworthy' inspectors possessing the required technical expertise and know-how, available on request for such verifications.
- The drafting of a 'code of conduct' 'which would contain all elements where common ground exist between East and West'.[5] This code would most certainly be of a non-legally binding nature. In some ways, the Final Act of Helsinki as well as the concluding documents of Belgrade and Madrid already constitute the embryo of such a code.
- The establishment of a system of surveillance of sensitive areas

where undeclared military activities might take place and of verification through satellite in which the Neutrals could co-operate, or which they could even set up on their own. This system would most likely be limited to verification of measures related to conventional warfare. This proposal is based on the suggestion made in May 1978 at the 10th special session of the UN General Assembly by President Valéry Giscard d'Estaing who advocated the establishment of an international satellite monitoring agency. It was referred to in Switzerland in the summer of 1982, and was advanced by both Switzerland and Sweden in 1985.

One should also mention, among other suggestions, all the measures contained in the so-called SC 3 proposals submitted on 9 March 1984 by the N + N in Stockholm. The proposals do not, for example, refer to any parameters. This well reflects the difficulty the N + N have in agreeing on a delimited question (such as security) which has direct impact on their national interest, more so than on general matters.

2. A role in the negotiation process where the Neutrals can act as intermediaries trying to reconcile positions, and in searching for (and proposing) compromises, both on substance and on procedural matters. One should not understand compromises as half-way positions but more as innovative and realistic solutions to concrete problems, acceptable to all parties.
3. A role in the implementation of the CSBMs which would be agreed upon. The Neutrals could contribute to better communication between East and West. They might be involved in the verification process of some of the CSBMs. In many respects, this last role would be new – at least in the European context.

- Neutral countries could be involved in improved communications systems, especially if the system is multilateral.
- They might act as host to the 'salon des ambassadeurs' mechanism referred to above.
- Neutral countries could provide some of the inspectors mandated to carry out verifications, fact-finding and on-site inspections, for example in the field of chemical weapons. These inspectors would receive special training. The choice of the inspectors would be left to the state which agrees to be inspected, and which would choose from a list. Proposals along these lines have been made by the Austrian government.

- Neutral countries could also contribute to the verification of agreed CSBMs or to the surveillance of sensitive areas prone to becoming centres of international crisis by co-operating in (and providing some of the means to set up) a satellite monitoring system or any system using advanced technology monitoring devices. They could collaborate either in the data collection or in the interpretation, or in both. Mention should be made in this context of Sweden's co-operation with France in the launching of a surveillance satellite in 1986.
- Neutral countries could play a co-ordinating role and provide the secretariat for any inspection and verification system of any European security commission which could be set up – system which could involve NATO and Warsaw Pact individual experts. Reluctance to create any institutional machinery related to the CSCE process exists. But many co-ordinating functions – short of bringing into existence an institution – can be thought of.
- In general, many Third Party roles could be assumed by European Neutrals. They could be part of an international crisis mediation service or they could host the proposed Nuclear Crisis Control Center, to mention just two ideas.[6]

These are only some examples – some of them very 'wishful thinking', at least if one counts on their implementation in the short term. Verification certainly constitutes an area where Neutral countries might provide an original and unique contribution. It is one of the critical dimensions of the Stockholm negotiation which aimed at adopting a set of militarily significant, politically binding, interrelated CSBMs 'provided with adequate forms of verification'. Without appropriate verification it is unlikely that whatever CSBMs might be agreed upon will have practical significance. Neutral countries appear here to have an important card in their hands.

The possibility of neutral countries playing a role in the field of CSBMs raises a number of questions. It should also not be exaggerated. This role is likely to be marginal. Neutral countries are small and their means are modest. Their power and their capacity to influence are limited. Their neutrality imposes some self-restraint. It does not allow them, for example, to act as referees. Can Neutral countries' involvement contribute to raising confidence and security? Is it requested by, and acceptable to both NATO and the Warsaw Pact, and more so to both Superpowers? The USA and USSR can certainly rely on their own national technical verification means (NTM).[7] Verification by the Neutrals could cover only part of what might need to be verified. However, neutral inspections on-site might be better tolerated by the inspected party, and therefore useful. Verification and inspection by the Neutrals might also be welcomed by some segments of public opinion, and therefore raise the acceptance by the public of defence policies., There is without doubt a need for independent information gathering coupled with objective data interpretation on the level of militarisation – and on military activities, a demand for more transparency.

All these ideas are ambitious. Are they within the range of the possibilities of small neutral countries? For example, do the Neutrals possess the technical, financial and human resources to set up on their own a satellite observation system? This is doubtful. As a matter of reference, the cost of the international satellite monitoring system (ISMS) proposed by the French government was estimated in 1980 to amount to between US $1.2 and 1.7 billion, spread over 5 years for design and development, and US $125 million per annum for operating costs.[8] Moreover, the technical know-how of the Neutrals is limited, and therefore they might not be able to control the entire process of verification, meaning that they could be engaged in interpretation of data without an adequate understanding of the method through which they were collected. This situation, for the Neutrals, appears to be unacceptable.

Neutral countries could, however, concentrate on the type of verification they are technically and financially able to perform as well as to control. The verification of the wide range of CSBMs discussed – measures of notification and observation, and measures of constraints – do not always imply the most sophisticated technology and prohibitive financial means. It is finally not the technical ability to proceed to verification which matters (an ability which is also mastered by both NATO and Warsaw Pact countries) but the independence and the impartiality of the Neutrals which are at the basis of their capacity to render a service to the cause of European security.

There are thus certainly a number of responsibilities to be assumed by Neutrals in the verification of CSBMs. Should they do so collectively, meaning that they would have to co-operate closely in carrying them out? Can they do so without alienating their respective independence, and without appearing to form a group, something which is unacceptable to any of them? To what extent would a co-operation with the Non-aligned countries be feasible? What about possible involvement with NATO and Warsaw Pact states in some part of the verification process?

The capacity for Neutrals to play an effective role depends finally on a number of prerequisites. It is foremost necessary that a Neutral be perceived as really neutral and independent. Neutral countries can exert and influence only if they inspire confidence. However, the perception of what is 'neutral' is quite likely to differ. The neutrality of a country like Finland is suspicious to some western states. Switzerland's policy of neutrality might not appear to be always even-handed and endangers the credibility of its policy. This has disadvantages, but might also represent an asset. For example, when it came to look for a state which could act as a credible go-between with the United States and NATO in general, the USSR did approach Switzerland in the last phase of the Madrid Conference despite the rather critical attitude which Berne had towards the Human Rights policy followed in the Soviet Union. What mattered was finally that Switzerland enjoyed the confidence of the West, a confidence which some other neutrals had partially lost.

Any involvement of a neutral country is also subject to the condition that this involvement does not jeopardise its neutrality, which is the very status that allows it to play a role.

In conclusion, neutral countries cannot contribute to solve the nuclear dilemma as such. They may, however, help build up confidence and security, so that neither side is tempted to cross the nuclear threshold and so that, in the final analysis, at no stage does the nuclear option become irresistible.

Notes

*The author, solely responsible for the following pages, wishes to thank René Haug for his stimulating comments. These remarks were prepared at the time of the Stockholm Conference which ended in the Fall of 1986. This conference constitutes only a stage in a long process of identifying, deciding upon, and implementing measures which could significantly increase confidence and improve security within the European continent. The measures suggested in Stockholm by the Neutral countries should thus be seen from a long-term perspective and not exclusively in the context of the Conference itself (February 1987).

1. Switzerland, for example, possesses a non-professional army of 625 000 men which amounts to almost 10 per cent of the population for a mountainous territory of 41 000km^2. They are structured in 12 fields divisions, 17 independent brigades and 6 larges logistical units – all rather well equipped – which can be mobilised in less than 48 hours. The airforce has about 300 combat aircraft. Switzerland has also adopted a defence policy based on the preventive destruction of the main roads, bridges and tunnels, as well as essential elements of its industrial capacity.
2. See Daniel Frei, 'Neutrality and Non-Alignment: Convergencies and Contrasts', *Korea and World Affairs*, 3, 3, Fall 1979, pp. 279–80; and Hanspeter Neuhold, 'Die neutralen Staaten Europas und die Konferenz über Sicherheit und Zusammenarbeit in Europa', *Europa-Archiv*, 24, 1973, pp. 445–51.
3. Edouard Brunner, 'Neutral Countries and arms control: a Swiss view', summary of an address delivered at the Graduate Institute of International Studies in Geneva, 6 November 1984, p. 12 (mimeographed).
4. See *Erklärung des Politichen Direktors und Stellvertretenden Generalsekretärs für Auswärtige Angelegenheiten, Botschafter Dr Friedrich Bauer, vor der Konferenz über Vertrauens- und Sicherheitsbildende Massnahmen und Abrüstung in Europa* (Stockholm, 8 February 1985).
5. Edouard Brunner, 'Neutral Countries and arms control', p. 8.
6. See William Langer Ury and Richard Smoke, *Beyond the Hotline: Controlling a Nuclear Crisis*. A Report to the United States Arms Control and Disarmament Agency (Cambridge, Harvard Law School, 1984).
7. See David Hafemeister, Joseph J. Romm and Kosta Tsipis, 'The Verification of Compliance with Arms-Control Agreements', *Scientific American*, 252, 3, March 1985, pp. 29–35.
8. See Report from the 34th Pugwash Symposium 'An International Agency for the Use of Satellite Observation Data for Security Purposes', *Pugwash Newsletter*, 18, 2, p. 94.

14 PALs for Allies and Adversaries*

Dan Caldwell

Permissive action links (PAL) are electronic locks installed on certain nuclear weapons to preclude accidental or unauthorised use. These devices were developed and installed by the United States in some of its nuclear weapons deployed in Europe and elsewhere during the early 1960s. PALs are important means of reducing the risk of nuclear war; however, despite this importance, there is a paucity of information in the open literature about the development and current deployment of permissive action links. In this chapter I describe what permissive action links are, who has them, and present the pros and cons of sharing information about PALs, particularly in the European context.

THE DEVELOPMENT OF PERMISSIVE ACTION LINKS

In 1958 the US Congress on the recommendation of the Department of Defence amended the 1954 Atomic Energy Act to allow for dispersion of nuclear weapons to US allies in Europe. In addition, DOD proposed that military personnel from NATO countries receive training concerning the firing of nuclear weapons. Four months after Congress approved the proposed changes in the 1954 Act, Thor and Jupiter missiles were deployed in Great Britain, Italy and Turkey, and military personnel from these countries were trained in the operation of nuclear weapons.[1] To assure that the United States would retain custody and control of these nuclear weapons, the 'two-key' system was adopted. According to this plan, one key was to be in the possession of a British, Italian or Turkish officer and the other on the person of a US officer. Both keys were required to launch a nuclear weapon.

While visiting a Thor missile base at Feltwell, England, in June 1959, however, Congressman Charles O. Porter found that the RAF missile control officer had both his key and the second key that was supposed to be in the possession of an American officer. Congressman Porter noted that this lapse in regulations meant that 'the American legal reservation of control would have been effectively short-circuited so far as the use of atomic warheads were concerned on those particular missiles'.[2]

Even when regulations were observed, the two-key system did not guarantee that nuclear weapons would remain under American control. For example, following a 1961 fact-finding trip to US missile bases in Europe by members of the Joint Atomic Energy Committee, the executive director of the committee said, 'We were scared stiff by what we saw . . . we wondered what would happen if, for some reason – two NATO states falling out, perhaps – the Turk [i.e. a non-U.S. missile control officer] decided to overpower our man [the US officer] and take away his key? Why, the Turk would have himself a modern weapon, that's what.'[3]

Thus, despite the control by the US over nuclear weapons deployed in Europe that the two-key system offered in theory, it failed to assure this control in practice, and this failure highlighted the need for another more reliable control mechanism.

On January 24, 1961, a B-52 carrying two twenty-four megaton bombs crashed outside of Goldsboro, North Carolina, during a routine training mission. Fortunately, neither of the bombs exploded because each was equipped with six interlocking safety devices to prevent accidental detonation. However, technicians who examined the bombs found that five of the six safety devices on one warhead had been triggered by the crash.[4]

President Kennedy, who was inaugurated only four days before the Goldsboro crash, became deeply concerned about the possibility of nuclear war resulting from an accident. In addition, Kennedy was aware of the shortcomings of the two-key system in Europe. Stemming from these concerns, Kennedy ordered US scientists at the Los Alamos, Livermore, and Sandia labs to develop new systems for improving US control of its nuclear weapons. The work of the scientists had been preceded by a conceptual description of an improved control procedure written by a social scientist at the Rand Corporation, Fred Iklé, who had proposed that the US should place electronic locks or 'permissive action links' (PALs) on US nuclear weapons. Iklé's idea was taken up by the Kennedy Administration and translated into reality by the nuclear scientists and weapons designers in the government. In June 1962, President Kennedy issued a National Security Action Memorandum which formally established the requirement for permissive action links to be installed on US nuclear weapons in Europe.[5] In addition, this directive placed a continuing responsibility on the Atomic Energy Commission to explore improvements in the technology of PALs. Following the promulgation of this directive, PALs were installed on many US nuclear weapons in Europe and elsewhere.[6]

Permissive action links can be relatively simple; according to one nuclear physicist, 'designing a PAL is like designing a safe . . . It is essentially a digitized lock and designing it is a relatively straight forward job.'[7] In testimony before Congress, Vice Admiral Gerald Miller offered the following description:

> The Permissive Action Link (PAL) Program consists of a code system and a family of devices integral or attached to nuclear weapons which have been developed to reduce the probability of an unauthorized nuclear detonation. The devices are designed to preclude the use of a nuclear weapon without first inserting the correct numerical code. The code system is a highly secure system which permits the using unit to obtain the proper numerical code only after the PAL unlock has been authorized.[8]

PALs FOR FRIENDS AND FOES

If PALs increase the United States' control over its nuclear weapons and reduce the danger of accidental nuclear war, wouldn't the development of PALs by other countries be desirable? According to interviews conducted by the author, the US government answered this question affirmatively and provided information about US PALs to Great Britain during the 1960s.[9] There is also speculation that the US provided information about PALs to France. Even if the US has provided information about PALs to its friends, would it be desirable to provide this information to potential adversaries?

The Soviet Union's attempt to install intermediate- and medium-range ballistic missiles in Cuba in October 1962 resulted in the most serious post-Second World War crisis in Soviet–American relations. Curiously, despite the seriousness of the crisis, the Soviet Union failed to order a full alert of its missile forces.[10] The Kennedy Administration felt that one reason for the Soviets' failure to order a full alert was due to Soviet decision makers' lack of confidence in their command and control procedures. Consequently, President Kennedy and Secretary of Defence McNamara 'decided to make the

Russians aware of our permissive-action link system',[11] and on 19 December 1962, at an international arms control symposium at the University of Michigan, one of McNamara's assistants, John McNaughton, delivered a speech in which he described, in general terms, the American PAL system. According to reports, US scientists, with the blessings of the Kennedy Administration explained US PALs to Soviet scientists who attended the 1963 Pugwash meeting in Dubrovnik, Yugoslavia.[12]

The United States has considered providing information about PALs to both its friends and foes on at least two other occasions. In its final report completed in 1965, the Committee on Nuclear Proliferation, chaired by Roswell Gilpatric, concluded: 'We should consider appropriate assistance to the United Kingdom, France and the Soviet Union in connection with the development of [deleted] and safety devices for their respective weapons.'[13] In an interview with the author, a member of this committee recalled that the committee considered providing PAL technology to other nuclear weapons states, which provides some evidence that the security deletion in the above quotation referred to PALs.[14] In addition, according to former SALT negotiator Sidney Graybeal, the United States was prepared to exchange information on PALs as part of the negotiations that resulted in the 'Accidents Measures Agreement' of 1971, but the negotiations never got down to specific details; they remained at a high level of generality.[15]

The United States has given information concerning permissive action links to Great Britain and the Soviet Union in the past. Should the US exchange technology concerning PALs to these countries as well as others? Before addressing this question, it is necessary to briefly review the status of other states' nuclear weapons control procedures.

WHO HAS PALs?

Even though the technology for permissive action links need not be very complicated, there is some question concerning which nuclear weapons states have PALs on their weapons. No doubt much of this uncertainty is due to the high degree of secrecy surrounding the command, control and nuclear release procedures of these countries. Despite the paucity of information concerning PALs in the unclassified literature, there is at least a limited amount of information. I will present the information available in open sources according to three categories of states: US allies (Great Britain and France), US adversaries (the Soviet Union and the People's Republic of China), and possible proliferators (India, Israel and Pakistan).

As I have already noted, there are indications, based on the interviews that I have conducted, that the United States provided information, and possibly even the technology, for PALs to Great Britain. The case of France is less clear; however, in November 1980, President Giscard d'Estaing described French release procedures in the following terms:

> These decisions are naturally prepared with all the chain of command and responsibility, notably the Chief of Staff of the Armed Forces, who plays an essential role in managing these means. But the decision and the execution depends upon the President of the Republic alone . . . *who gives a formula transmitted by relays to the means of execution*[16]

Apparently the French have adopted a variant of the two-key system: two French officers in each IRBM command post, SLBM command centre and bomber 'must separately receive coded orders to fire and then act simultaneously for the nuclear weapons to be armed and launched.'[17] In addition, Wilfrid Kohl has pointed out that separate sets of orders must be issued to activate the Mirage IV bombers and the nuclear bombs that they carry. The planes 'are also equipped with "black boxes" that can be activated directly by remote control signals from the civilian political authority to neutralize the atomic bombs, as an added safety measure'.[18]

Because of the closed nature of the Soviet and Chinese societies, it is very difficult to obtain information about the nuclear weapons control programmes of these countries. In the Soviet Union, special units of the Committee on State Security (KGB) guard and control nuclear weapons storage facilities, some located as far as fifty miles from missile launch areas.[19] In his analysis of Soviet nuclear weapons control procedures, Professor Stephen Meyer concludes that Soviet strategic missiles were 'given electronic locks to prevent unauthorized use'.[20] In reaching this conclusion, Meyer relies on a number of pieces of evidence, including the following statement by Marshal V. F. Tolubko, the Commander-in-Chief of the Strategic Rocket Forces:

> Modern missile weapons are highly automated systems, with modern electronic-computing technology, for remote control and

> monitoring. Built-in diagnostic systems permit continuous monitoring of all essential parameters, provide for the most reliable functioning of equipment, safe utilization, and fully exclude unsanctioned operation.[21]

Not all Western analysts of the Soviet military accept Meyer's conclusion. For example, the following statement made by then Defence Minister Ustinov suggests that the Soviet Union does not have PALs on all of its nuclear weapons:

> The Soviet Union needs to set up a still more strict framework in the training of troops and staff, the determination of the composition of arms, the organization of still more strict control for the assured exclusion of the unsanctioned launch of nuclear weapons from tactical to strategic.[22]

According to Meyer, the SS-20 is the first Soviet missile with the warhead mated to it and not stored in a facility separate from the launcher. Two of the possible inferences can be drawn from this fact are: 1. that the Soviets have perfected PAL technology and now have high confidence to control their nuclear weapons using only technological and not human (i.e., KGB) means, or alternatively, 2. that the Soviets have not perfected PALs, but believe it necessary nevertheless to deploy SS-20 missiles that can be fired without the cumbersome and time-consuming KGB control mechanism.

Very little is known concerning the command, control and nuclear weapons release procedures for the People's Republic of China.[23] Several American scientists and national security experts who have visited Chinese governmental ministries and institutes have raised the topic of permissive action links with their Chinese counterparts and have elicited no response. In the words of one US scientist, the PAL issue at present is a 'total non-starter' in China.[24]

I have described much of what is publicly known about the nuclear weapons control procedures of the states that possess nuclear weapons. There is, however, another category of countries – the possible proliferators – that should be briefly considered. Since India claims that it tested only a 'peaceful nuclear device' and not a nuclear weapon in May 1974 and because Israel does not admit to having nuclear weapons, these states, as well as other possible proliferators, have not published anything about their policies on this subject. Given the development programmes of the potential proliferators, however, some conclusions are at least plausible, if not likely. For example, given the amount of nuclear information that Israel has obtained from Western sources, it is possible, if not probable, that Israel has PALs. Because of the state of nuclear development in India, it is unlikely that India has PALs. Because Pakistan has relied on China and non-nuclear weapons states (which do not have PALs) for nuclear information, it is also unlikely that Pakistan has PALs.

If the potential proliferators do not have nuclear weapons, as they contend, then there is no need to control them, just as there is no need to buy automobile insurance if one does not own a car. However, if one has an expensive, luxury car – say a Porsche – stored secretly in a garage, then it makes a great deal of sense to buy insurance, even if no one else knows you have a car. In short, PALs provide valuable insurance for potential proliferators against accidental or unauthorised use.

A PROPOSAL FOR THE SHARING OF PAL TECHNOLOGY

Permissive action links provide the leaders of states that possess nuclear weapons increased confidence that these weapons will not be used as a result of accident or unauthorised action. Although there is little in the open literature about this subject, it is clear from the brief survey presented in this chapter that the control and release procedures of the nuclear weapons states differ significantly. In some cases – particularly in the cases of China and the possible proliferators – it is not clear that the leaders of these countries have thought about, much less ordered the implementation of, a PAL programme.

Given the important role that permissive action links can play in increasing the control and safety of nuclear weapons, it would be desirable for an international conference to be convened to discuss the basic idea behind PALs, how they work and the technology associated with PALs. Such discussion and exchange of information could take place in a small group of states consisting of those mentioned in this paper or, perhaps more logically, in the Committee on Disarmament negotiations. What are the potential advantages and disadvantages of this proposal?

POTENTIAL ADVANTAGES

As mentioned previously, the chief advantage of this proposal, were it to be implemented, would be to reduce the danger of either an accidental or unauthorised detonation of nuclear weapons. To see the possible benefits of this proposal in the European context, consider the following scenario. Assume that a major NATO–Warsaw Pact confrontation, similar to the 1948 or 1961 Berlin crises, develops. The crisis escalates and NATO intelligence learns that Soviet KGB units in Eastern Europe are transporting nuclear warheads from storage depots to missile sites. This information would be a valuable indicator to NATO that the crisis was getting very serious. It would also cause Western decision makers to grow more anxious and reduce crisis stability. Assume that in response to the Warsaw Pact actions NATO began to disperse its nuclear weapons. Such dispersion would be less threatening if the Warsaw Pact decision makers knew that NATO retained positive control over all nuclear weapons. (In fact, the desire to maintain positive control over nuclear weapons appears to be one of the major reasons that the United States has removed over 2000 of the smaller, older nuclear weapons from Western Europe during the past several years.[25])

There are several reasons why the public deployment of PALs by NATO and the Warsaw Pact would be desirable. In a simulation of a European crisis catalysed by unrest in East Germany, Alexander George and his colleagues found that uneven control of nuclear weapons by the two teams representing NATO and the Warsaw Pact contributed to a destabilising action-reaction cycle of escalation.[26] If the Warsaw Pact had PALs installed on its nuclear weapons and if Warsaw Pact decision makers were confident that NATO leaders could retain positive control over their nuclear weapons even if dispersed, then fears of an accidental launch would be decreased and crisis stability increased.

Second, if PALs were installed on all nuclear weapons, the danger of terrorists or sub-national factions gaining effective control over a nuclear weapon would be reduced.

Third, by exchanging information on permissive action links and other control procedures with one another, the nuclear weapons states could possibly improve their current procedures and PALs.

Fourth, most experts on nuclear proliferation now assume that it is no longer a question of *whether* proliferation will occur; rather, the question is *when* proliferation will occur.[27] In a proliferated world, PALs become a very important confidence-building mechanism.

POTENTIAL DISADVANTAGES

Just as there are a number of potential advantages with this proposal, there are also a number of potential disadvantages. If the United States were to exchange information on PALs with other states, it is possible that hitherto secret information could be disclosed compromising the security of US nuclear weapons. There are, however, different levels and different types of PALs (see Appendix 1 for a listing of currently deployed US PALs).[28] The United States should only disclose information concerning its early PALs and no information concerning the design of its most recent ones.

Second, if multilateral discussions of PALs took place, information about permissive action links could fall into the wrong hands; for example, terrorist groups, which could conceivably use the information to make a stolen nuclear weapon operational by wiring around the PAL, just as car thieves 'hot wire' cars. Although this is a potential disadvantage to sharing PAL information, it is also an argument for increased sharing. Some US PALs are surrounded with a protective skin. If this skin is damaged, the PAL is destroyed making it impossible to wire around the PAL. It is unclear whether other nuclear weapons states have a similar safety mechanism and the US could describe this system as an international exchange of PAL information, providing, of course, that such a description would not reduce the security of US nuclear weapons.

Third, if as a result of multilateral discussions, the Soviet Union were to shift its reliance to electronic control of its nuclear weapons and reduce its reliance on the KGB for such control, a specific US intelligence indicator could be damaged. At present, the US intelligence agencies closely monitor movements of the KGB units that guard Soviet nuclear weapons storage facilities. This provides US intelligence analysts with an important indicator of Soviet military mobilisation. Given the Soviet historical reliance on the KGB for the control of nuclear weapons and the Soviet penchant for centralisation, it is unlikely that the Soviets would abandon their current control system for a purely technologically based system.

Fourth, if the multilateral group of countries proposed in this paper were to provide information on PALs to 'possible proliferators', some would undoubtedly charge that the group was providing an incentive for 'going nuclear'. While this is, in theory, true, in practice the motivations for developing nuclear weapons are most often nonrational and would probably not be affected by a factor as marginal in importance as the availability of information about PALs.

The central conclusion of this paper is that the world would be a safer place if all nuclear weapons were fitted with permissive action links. The Committee on Disarmament is a possible forum for a multilateral exchange of information concerning PALs to take place. If such an exchange occurred, it clearly would not totally remove the greatest danger of our time, the threat of nuclear war, but it would incrementally reduce this threat.

Appendix I

Permissive Action Links Currently on U.S. Nuclear Weapons[29]

Category of PAL	*Weapon deployed On*
B	B61-0: Nuclear Bomb
D	B61-2, B61-5: Nuclear Bomb
	W-70: Lance (MGM 52) short range missile
	W-79: 8 inch (203mm) artillery
	W-80: Air-launched Cruise Missile (ALCM) and Tomahawk Cruise Missile
	B-83: B1B, B-52, FB-111 (main gravity bomb for the B-1B)
	W-82: Artillery Fired Atomic Projectile for 155mm artillery
F	B61-3: Nuclear Bomb
	B61-4: Nuclear Bomb
	W84: Ground-launched Cruise Missile
	W81: Navy Standard-2 missile
	W85: Pershing II (launch requires PAL)

Notes

*For comments on an earlier draft of this chapter, the author would like to thank Richard A. Brody, Thomas H. Etzold, P. Terrence Hopmann, and Richard Smoke.

1. Joel Larus, *Nuclear Weapons Safety and the Common Defense* (Columbus: Ohio State University Press, 1967), pp. 80–81.
2. Congressman Charles O. Porter quoted in ibid., p. 82.
3. James Ramey quoted in Larus (note 1), pp. 83–84.
4. Ralph E. Lapp, *The Weapons Culture* (New York: W.W. Norton, 1968).
5. US Department of Defence and US Department of Energy, *Long Range Nuclear Weapon Planning Analysis for the Final Report of the DOD/DOE Long Range Resource Planning Group* (Washington, D.C., July 15, 1980), p. A 2–6.

6. M. Leitenberg, 'Background Information on Tactical Nuclear Weapons (Primarily in the European Context)', in Stockholm International Peace Research Institute, *Tactical Nuclear Weapons: European Perspectives* (London: Taylor and Francis, 1978), pp. 41–42, 49, 56, 129. See also Paul Buteux, *The Politics of Nuclear Consultation in NATO 1965–1980* (Cambridge University Press, 1983), pp. 210–13.
7. Author's interview.
8. 'Testimony of Vice Admiral Gerald Miller', US Congress, House, Committee on International Relations, *First Use of Nuclear Weapons: Preserving Responsible Control*, Hearings, 94th Congress, 2nd Session, March 1976, p. 93.
9. Author's interviews.
10. CIA report quoted in Edward Klein and Robert Littell, 'SHH! Let's Tell the Russians', *Newsweek*, 5 May 1969, p. 47.
11. Herman Kahn quoted in ibid. For a similar account of this incident, see Gregg Herken, *Counsels of War* (New York: Alfred A. Knopf, 1985), p. 169.
12. Klein and Littell (note 10), p. 47.
13. *A Report to the President by the Committee on Nuclear Proliferation*, Roswell L. Gilpatric, Chairman, 21 January 1965; declassified 20 October 1982. I am indebted to Richard Brody for calling this to my attention.
14. Author's interview.
15. Author's interview with Sidney Graybeal, 19 April 1985.
16. Giscard d'Estaing in *Le Monde*, 19 November 1980 (emphasis added); quoted by David S. Yost, 'French Nuclear Targeting', in Desmond Ball and Jeffrey Richelson (eds), *Strategic Nuclear Targeting* (Ithaca: Cornell University Press, 1987).
17. Général François Maurin, 'La mise en place operationnelle de la triade stratégique (Mirage IV, SSBS Albion, SNLE) et des chaines de contrôle,' Paper presented on September 28, 1984, at the colloquium on 'De Gaulle et la dissuasion nucléaire (1958–1969),' Organized by the Institut Charles-de-Gaulle and the Université de Franche-Comté, pp. 16–17; quoted by Yost (note 16).
18. Wilfrid L. Kohl, *French Nuclear Diplomacy* (Princeton: Princeton University Press, 1971), p. 182.
19. Oleg Penkovskiy, *The Penkovskiy Papers* (New York: Doubleday, 1965), p. 331; William F. Scott, 'Soviet Aerospace Forces and Doctrine', *Air Force Magazine*, March 1975, p. 33.
20. Stephen M. Meyer, 'Soviet Perspectives on the Paths to Nuclear War', in Graham T. Allison, Albert Carnesale, and Joseph S. Nye Jr. (eds), *Hawks, Doves and Owls: An Agenda for Avoiding Nuclear War* (New York: Norton, 1985), p. 192.
21. V. F. Tolubko, 'Novoye perdovoye–v uchebyy protsess', *Krasnaya Zvezda*, 26 January 1984, p. 2; quoted by Meyer, ibid.
22. D. F. Ustinov, 'Otvesti ugrozu yadernoy', *Pravda*, 12 July 1982, p. 4; quoted by Meyer (note 20), p. 189.
23. One of the few unclassified sources with information about this subject

is US Library of Congress, Congressional Research Service, *Authority to Order the Use of Nuclear Weapons (United States, United Kingdom, France, Soviet Union, People's Republic of China)*, December 1975, pp. 23–9.

24. Author's interview.
25. Alexander L. George, David M. Bernstein, Gregory S. Parnell, and J. Phillip Rogers, *Inadvertent War in Europe: Crisis Simulation* (Stanford: Centre for International Security and Arms Control, Stanford University, June 1985), p. 51.
26. Ibid.
27. This is the position, among others, of Lewis Dunn, *Controlling the Bomb; Nuclear Proliferation in the 1980s* (New Haven: Yale University Press, 1982).
28. Thomas B. Cochran, William M. Arkin, and Milton M. Hoenig, *Nuclear Weapons Databook. Volume I: U.S. Nuclear Forces and Capabilities* (Cambridge: Ballinger Publishing Company, 1984).
29. The information in this table is derived from ibid.

15 Crisis Management by Crisis Prevention: Reducing Major Power Involvement in Third World Conflicts*

Peter Wallensteen

DANGERS OF ESCALATION

Many proposals have come forth to ease the tension between East and West. Some focus on arms developments, others take up diplomatic issues. In addition, some have raised the question of crisis management and crisis prevention. Can crises be prevented even before they have taken place? The Palme Commission on Disarmament and Security suggested, in its 1982 report, ways of restraining superpower involvement in Third World conflicts. Such conflicts, it was argued, could escalate and ultimately result in nuclear confrontation between the United States and the Soviet Union. Certainly, the commission also paid attention to conflicts over issues in Europe and to problems in Eastern or in Western Europe.

However, the commission raised a question that lately has received increasing attention: the dangers of superpower confrontation over Third World issues. In his statement to the United Nations on 24 October 1985, President Reagan pointed to the need for settling regional conflicts as they play 'a large role in building suspicions and tensions'. Reagan's initiative explicitly concerned Afghanistan, Cambodia, Ethiopia, Angola and Nicaragua. It included negotiations with the Soviet Union over Afghanistan, and, at a later stage, also over other issues. The goal, he said, was not to force a settlement on the parties. The initiative concerned issues that have, for the American public, justified armaments and reduced Soviet credibility.

President Reagan's proposal could be seen as a confidence-building measure resting on the hope to reduce tensions between the two major powers through negotiations over these Third World issues. A Soviet list of threatening local conflict situations might not be identical to the American one. Soviet analyses, as seen for instance in the speech by the Soviet foreign minister Shevardnadze at the United Nations on 24 September 1985, stress *Apartheid* in South Africa and Israeli policies in the Middle East, rather than the five issues mentioned by Reagan. Often, proposals for dialogue on issues emphasised by Soviet representatives have been interpreted, in the West, as ways for the Soviet Union to get involved in matters not of their concern. However, in 1985 discussions on regional issues were initiated. The summit meeting in Geneva, 19–21 November 1985, made it evident that present priorities differed, the Soviet Union being more interested in arms control and disarmament than in the conflict settlement issues raised by the American side.

Still, this means that Third World conflicts are on the agenda of the superpower talks, although their significance may vary for the parties, depending on issues and circumstances. The importance of these questions can be understood also from a quick look at modern history. The record shows that all wars with superpower troops involved since the Second World War have been in the Third World (Korea, Vietnam, Afghanistan) and all of them have strained the relations between the two. These issues, at a minimum, might impede the development of confidence and detente, and, at a maximum, might involve the two in a dangerous direct confrontation.

Some developments in the European debate also point to the importance of Third World issues. In fact, there is a shift in perception. The emphasis in scenarios on the outbreak of war seems increasingly to be on escalation of conflicts *to* Europe rather than *from* Europe.

First, there is a widespread perception that any change in Europe can come about only at the expense of the other, and that, as a consequence, no party will attempt such a change. Thus, the relations *between* the blocs are at a stalemate. The only likely changes are those that could come *within* the existing configurations. Some such changes will affect the relations also between the blocs. Few of them might, however, lead to the outbreak of a war in Central Europe, although nobody would deny the dangers involved.

Second, during the period of detente, the competition between the United States and the Soviet Union focused on Third World issues more than First World ones (Wallensteen, 1985). The high marks of detente, as far as the USA was concerned, coincided with the Vietnam war. During the same period, the Soviet leadership was preoccupied with China. During the latter part of the 1970s the USA and the USSR came increasingly into confrontation over Third World issues: the Middle East, Southern Africa, the Horn of Africa, South West and South East Asia, Central America. It might even be argued that detente collapsed over the 'failure' of both parties to 'succeed' in this competition, returning the focus to missile questions and Central Europe.

Third, it is likely that the present pattern of armed conflicts will continue in the future. This means that most armed conflicts will take place in the Third World. Third World countries, thus, remain interesting as markets for arms export. The strategic significance of areas outside the pact arrangements might increase. 'Vertical' proliferation of nuclear weapons is in fact a horizontal geographical spreading of these weapons. This makes bases and port facilities of global significance, and a number of areas gain importance in major power military planning. To this could be added the tendency, in the USA as well as in the USSR, to depict Third World conflicts in the light of the East–West struggle. For these reasons, Third World areas gain increasing significance for the major powers and, in particular, for the United States and the Soviet Union.

This means that we can expect the presence of the two superpowers in such areas, and ultimately also increasing commitment from them to various actors. This is where the danger of escalating links resides, in the final analysis involving European territory.

In a recent publication, Miroslav Nincic illustrates such links that could result in the escalation of Third World conflicts to Europe (Nincic, 1985). He finds three forms: direct participation of European forces in a local conflict, indirect participation through the use of European facilities to support allied involvement in such a local conflict, and the use of European territory for 'counter-moves' against the adversary.

All these links primarily involve military connections: troops, use of facilities, comparative military advantages. The basic assumption is that military action of one party will trigger military counteraction from the adversary. Other actions might have less of an escalatory potential, notably diplomatic or economic measures.

However, the danger of escalation is not the only issue. From a Third World perspective, major power involvement suggests that conflicts become more difficult to handle and that their development might more be dictated by 'outside' interests than by 'local' ones. The conflicts might become prolonged, as more weapons will be available than would otherwise would have been the case. The conflicts might become more harmful, as the weapons introduced from 'outside' might be more destructive. Conflict settlements (if any) might become imposed (no matter what Reagan says) rather than mediated.

Thus, it is of great interest to investigate ways of preventing excessive major power involvement in Third World conflicts. This amounts to managing superpower conflict by preventing conflict from arising in the first place. Such measures, in other words, might be in the interest not only of Third World or European countries, but also important for the superpowers themselves.

APPROACHES TO CONFLICT PREVENTION

There are at least four ways in which superpower involvement in Third World conflicts can be prevented.

Classical balance of power thinking suggests that if power *A* has intervention capability, *A* will be deterred from intervening if power *B* also acquires such a capability. Consequently, neither *A* nor *B* will, in fact, intervene. The resulting stalemate will be to the advantage of all involved. Thus, it has been argued that the fact that the Soviet bloc now can intervene in Third World countries means that one more 'imperialist monopoly' has been broken, and that this will reduce interventions in general. Partly, the rationale for the US Central Command seems to be along this line of argument as well. The obvious drawback is that these arguments work equally well 'backwards': they become arguments for intervening as quickly as possible. The one who is first 'on the ground' will deter the other. Thus, this results in *early* intervention rather than in intervention prevention.

A second line of thought is the one of *disarming intervention forces*, e.g. if none of the parties have airlift capabilities available, there is less incentive for intervention, at least for rapid interventions. There is little prospect for an agreement eliminating such forces as they are seen as requirements for airlifts to Central Europe rather than for interventions in the Third World. Still, it might be possible to suggest some remedies along this line, for instance, prohibiting certain types of stationing in certain areas.

A third way points to the possibility of *military defence against intervention*, e.g. that Third World countries would acquire, on their own or in concert, forces which are capable of preventing superpowers from intervening. Obviously, some countries already today hope to maintain their neutrality by being able to deter major powers. However, interventions are probably more likely in times of internal or inter-state conflict when defence efficiency might by highly reduced. Finally, this approach invites an arms race between intervention and anti-intervention forces, at high costs for both sides.

A fourth way of handling the problem would then be to find ways of *restraining* the superpowers from intervening. Such restraints always exist, but mostly for internal reasons. In the American case, the War Powers Act is one such element, in the case of the Soviet Union, strategic priorities as well as economics might often speak against intervention. Also, the intervention experiences have been traumatic for both the United States and the Soviet Union, also restraining them.

The protracted war in Afghanistan makes another Soviet intervention at the same time less likely, and might reduce its interest in intervention in the period following the war. This is particularly true if the war ends in defeat, but it also applies in the case of compromise or victory. There is some parallel to the American experience. The United States was capable of launching an intervention in Santo Domingo during the escalation of the Vietnam war, but has been less intervention prone after that.

These examples point to internally motivated restraints. More interesting might be to consider restraint as part of an international arrangement. There are a number of such ideas, two drawing particular interest at this present time. One is the code of conduct proposal, associated with the detente policy of the 1970s, and the second one is the major power concordat proposed in the Palme Commission.

Thus, let us from the perspective outlined, try to evaluate these two proposals. The discussion suggests that a successful measure should (a) reduce superpower contention and improve the chances for a durable detente between the United States and the Soviet Union, (b) strengthen local actors and local initiatives for conflict resolution, (c) increase the significance of global institutions in the field of conflict resolution, and, finally, (d) be politically acceptable. Let us systematically compare the two ideas with respect to these four requirements.

TWO PROPOSALS: AN EVALUATION

Proposals

A *code of conduct* is found in the so-called Basic Principles Agreement between the United States and the Soviet Union concluded in 1972 between President Nixon and Secretary General Brezhnev. It was part of the detente policy and was signed together with the first SALT agreement in Moscow 1972. It explicitly departs from the fear of escalation. The danger of nuclear war makes it necessary for the two powers and their leaders to do 'their utmost to avoid military confrontations and to prevent the outbreak of nuclear war'. Consequently they, 'will be prepared to negotiate and settle differences by peaceful means'. The most operative part of the agreement is the following section:

> Both sides recognize that efforts to obtain unilateral advantage at the expense of the other, directly or indirectly, are inconsistent with these objectives.

The agreement also specifies that:

> The USA and the USSR have a special responsibility as do other countries which are permanent members of the United Nations Security Council to do everything in their power so that conflicts or situations will not arise which would serve to increase international tensions.

An agreement more specifically addressing the question of nuclear war was concluded in Washington in 1973. The Basic Principles Agreement remained significant throughout the 1970s.

The Basic Principles Agreement is vague, and does only partly address our present topic. Its operative section does not specifically exclude intervention, as it only specifies that certain 'gains' are *not* to be made from interventions, namely such 'gains' that are at the cost of the other signatory. In a sense, this resembles more an agreement on status quo than an anti-intervention pact: the present world situation is maintained, and, if it is to be changed, it has to be done in a way that does not change the power distribution in an unfavourable direction for the two protagonists. Thus, it would allow interventions, for instance, within informally established zones of influence. The agreement, in other words, is more one on how to deal with new issues, outside such zones. It then becomes a measure for evaluating the other party with respect to such issues.

It is, consequently, consistent that the American leadership objected to the Soviet-supported Cuban reinforcements of MPLA in Angola in 1975, on the grounds that this was a Soviet action outside the areas in which the Soviet Union was normally operating ('thousands of miles from Cuba and the Soviet Union and where neither can claim an historic national interest', President Ford wrote to the House Speaker; Matheson, p. 67). Similarily, one of President Carter's objections to the Soviet invasion of Afghanistan in 1979 was that this was the first time Soviet troops were used outside the lines drawn by the end of the Second World War (Matheson, p. 95).

The second proposal, the major power *concordat*, is distinctly linked to the United Nations and collective security thinking. It proposes a

> political agreement and partnership between the permanent members of the Security Council and Third World countries. Its scope would be limited to Third World conflicts arising out of border disputes or threats to territorial integrity caused by other factors... It would be underpinned by an understanding – concordat – among the permanent members of the Security Council to support collective security action, at least, to the extent possible, of not voting against it. (Common Security, pp. 162–3)

This proposal, unlike the previously mentioned one, is linked to border conflicts. Another feature of this proposal is its explicit concern with United Nations and the permanent members of the Security Council. It is in one sense more narrow than the previous proposal as it concerns only one category of conflict. In another sense it is wider as it involves many more of the major powers. The proposal has been presented in the Palme Commission final report, but it has received surprisingly little attention. It belongs, however, to a general discussion on how to reduce the dangers of confrontation between the two major powers.

Are all interventions prevented?

Both proposals attempt to *restrain the use of military force* by the superpowers, or the permanent members of the Security Council, that is, the major powers. There are obvious reasons for selecting this particular group, notably because of the dangers of escalation and the use of nuclear weapons. Also, the permanent members of the Security Council have among the largest forces in the world, and, have, historically, been heavily involved in interventions, confrontations and wars. There are some additional reasons for focusing this particular group, not the least that it makes an agreement largely self-monitoring. Each of these five powers constantly keeps an eye on one another. Also, their mutual relationships (whether conflict or co-operation) have been fairly stable over time (with the exception of China), meaning that there is a certain predictability. By restraining the use of military force by this particular group, if fully implemented, a drastic reduction in the use of military force would, theoretically, result.

However, the experience from the Basic Principles Agreement suggests that there are *additional ways* for major powers to involve themselves in conflicts, even for military involvement. The Basic Principles Agreement alludes to this, as it mentions 'directly and indirectly' as two separate routes. Both the Soviet Union and the United States have been able to circumvent the wordings (if not the spirit) of their own agreement by resorting to the use of surrogate troops (proxies or allies, neither concept is neutral). Examples are the interventions in Angola (on behalf of MPLA) and in Zaire (on behalf of Mobutu). In these two cases, the interventions had a dramatic impact on the outcome of the local conflict, but the superpowers did not supply their own troops. Their support in logistics was decisive, however.

Thus, it could be argued that both proposals leave considerable loop-holes: if only superpowers or major powers are restrained, these powers would certainly attempt to use others, less inhibited actors to carry out required designs. In fact, this could lead to the opposite of the suggested: the major powers gain an interest in controlling their allies more closely, in order to have them perform more consistently and more frequently, tasks of interest to the superpowers themselves. Thus, by leaving other states unrestrained, it could be argued, such actions are sanctioned. Alternatively, it could be argued, that if the major powers are not acting, others would 'fill the gap' on their own. To this could be responded that the UN Charter actually restricts all member-states from using force, and what the two agreements suggest is simply to reaffirm this, with respect to some states that are particularly prone to military action.

If military action is restrained, however, this does *not* suggest that military action is *excluded*. According to the Basic Principles Agreement the parties will do their 'utmost' to avoid military confrontation, whereas in the concordat the UN Security Council would act collectively. Thus the code does not rule out force by the majors themselves, and in the concordat, force is permitted within the United Nations framework (the UN military staff committee is revived, for instance). In practice, one could argue, both proposals aim at *gaining time* for negotiation and contemplation, or for non-military type of action (diplomacy, economic actions, etc.). Obviously, this adds realism to them. It is difficult to believe that the superpowers would restrain themselves if something highly important to them were in danger of being 'lost'. This is why the Basic Principles Agreement introduces the notion of 'advantage'. The perception of a 'disadvantage' for one simultaneously meaning an 'advantage' for the other is a situation which could become threatening and frustrating, two important triggers for action. Thus, only as long as some kind of symmetric outcome is likely and the issues at stake are less than vital for the majors are they likely to accept restraining themselves.

It might be precisely because of this that the Palme Commission proposes border conflicts as the targets. Such conflicts are more limited in scope, and, since 1947, a near-consensus seems to have developed in the global community of states that borders are not to be changed. The major changes of territory following the Second World War and the division of the Indian subcontinent appear to be the largest and most important redrawings of borders since 1945. These changes all took place in 1945–7, i.e. forty years ago. This does not suggest that there have been no border conflicts since 1947; almost the contrary is true.

It does suggest, however, that the global community of states has been very reluctant to change borders, and that there is a preference for keeping borders the way they are. This has, for instance, been illustrated by the OAU decision on borders in Africa or in the Helsinki Final Act, concerning borders in Europe. Thus, the major powers in the Security Council have somewhat of the same attitude toward these issues, and none of them, generally speaking, expect to make any 'gains' on these particular grounds. It is perhaps symptomatic that the only successful example of active Soviet mediation is in such a dispute: the 1965 conflict between Pakistan and India. With respect to, for instance, Latin American disputes, the American record is one of trying to mediate and finding solutions, rather than attempting to exploit the situations. In the remarkable *volte-face* on the Horn of Africa, the United States and the Soviet Union seems to have agreed that, despite alignments, the Ethiopian–Somalian border should not be changed by violent means.

Thus, border disputes prove to be a set of issues where status quo, or conservatism, is the preference for both major powers, and where neither will make an effort to obtain unilateral advantage. In a sense, these are issues where both might feel themselves equally vulnerable: if borders were to be redrawn, also the question of how the present American or Soviet borders were arrived at might be raised.

Neither proposal is very precise in terms of what is at heart of the agreement. The Basic Principles Agreement restrains the parties from obtaining *unilateral advantage*, but the definition of this is left wide open. Already in *Proposals*, above, some examples have been given of American interpretations, following from situations which have been seen as violations by the United States. The Soviet reactions to such allegations have not been very helpful or particularly clarifying. Some of the Soviet arguments have rested on their interpretation of peaceful coexistence as compatible with support for anti-imperialism, which then, implicitly might be a 'loss' to the US but is no particular 'gain' for the Soviet Union: it is simply the predetermined march of history (Matheson, p. 43ff).

Neither party has made much effort to define the terms more closely. It is not hard to see why this has not taken place: it might lead to a closer formalisation of the world as divided into spheres of influence, something which both, in theory, reject vehemently. It suggests, however, that attempting to restrain parties by specifying outcomes that are not to be allowed might not be a particularly promising route. Not only are the outcomes hard to predict, but they are, furthermore, not easily defined in mutually agreeable terms.

The concordat proposal rests on a definition of *border conflict*. As this issue is less conflictual, and not so much at the centre of the superpower conflict, there might be a greater chance of finding a multilaterally-agreeable definition of a border conflict. Scholarly work certainly has been operating with definitions of border conflicts for a long time. Furthermore, working with a link to the United Nations Security Council, it might be possible to apply the actors' own definition of what a border conflict is. Thus, *as part of the concordat a list could also be given, as agreed among the contesting countries, which border conflicts the concordat applies to*. Not only does this have the advantage of providing clarity but it would also suggest to the United Nations what conflicts there are to work on, in order to prevent the outbreak of violence.

By having the parties themselves define the border conflicts it also becomes less possible for the parties, at later stages, to argue that they are *not* involved in a border conflict and, thus, attempts to invite outside powers become more difficult. Furthermore, this suggests that the outside powers actually have an instrument for declining to become involved, by referring to the concordat. Principles of commitment (alliances, friendship treaties or moral imperatives) could be checked by the legal document included in the concordat. As a matter of fact, the United Nations could already initiate work on an *International Border Conflict Register* before such a concordat is established.

In sum: although the ambitions of the two proposals are similar, it appears that the concordat on border conflicts has the advantage of clarity and operationalisation. None of the proposals specify in more concrete terms what is not allowed, however. The recent historical experience suggests that this has to be developed more concretely. It appears often easier to define which *actions* are not to be taken rather than to work on motives, outcomes or other elements of a conflict.

Who are Restrained and who are Activated?

How do these proposals affect the involved parties? Do they have an impact on superpower contention? Do they encourage local and global initiatives? Let us here discuss these three issues systematically.

The Basic Principles Agreement clearly aimed at *reducing the competition between the United States and the Soviet Union*. Although the agreement is expressed in general terms, and, thus, applicable to many different situations, the agreement has largely, by both parties, been related to conflicts in the Third World. If carried out, it would mean that the parties find a new measure of success for their activities in this part of the world: the degree of restraint shown. However, the debate has turned exactly the other way. Instead the parties have accused one another of not abiding by the agreement, and thus, if one is unrestrained, the other feels free to do whatever is needed. The agreement becomes an instrument of blame.

This development was not obvious at the time and it was not inevitable. As a matter of fact, initially adherence to the agreement was pointed to by American leaders. In the October War crisis in 1973 and in the crisis in Portugal in 1974, American statements pointed out that the Soviet Union operated according to what could be expected. Thus, there was the possibility of using the agreement for praise. With increasing differences praise gave place to blame.

Furthermore, the agreement would, if taken seriously, also result in a shift in military allocations. To act in Third World conflicts requires long-range air transportation and naval forces. A successful agreement would result in an allocation away from such military expenditure. The record is clearly in the opposite direction: both these types of expenditure have increased. As a matter of fact, the Soviet support for Ethiopia in 1977 showed its remarkable capability of airlifting operations. Consequently, the invasion of Afghanistan gave impetus for the American side to embark on a programme for Rapid Deployment Forces, a long-distance intervention force.

The agreement, in other words, did not achieve its ambition to reduce superpower activities. The reasons were many, not the least the general vagueness of the agreement itself. However, it also ran counter to something which is highly valued by the major powers themselves: the freedom of movement, to act in an unrestrained manner whenever 'needed'. This makes agreements vague. It suggests that an agreement that is less vague and has more operative qualities would be a more effective restraint, but it would at the same time be more difficult for the major powers to subscribe to it.

The concordat proposal avoids some of these problems, first, by focusing on an issue where there is more consensus, and second, by linking it to an alternative procedure: the Security Council. However, border conflicts are not among the most frequent types of conflicts in the Third World. The recent instances of heavy conflicts between Third World countries are mostly related to internal developments and concern regimes more than frontiers.

The only ongoing conflicts which can clearly be labelled border conflicts are those between Iran and Iraq (again this description misses some important aspects of the conflict), Chile and Argentina, Peru and Ecuador, perhaps Chad and Libya. But some of the most significant conflicts in Africa, those around South Africa or the Horn cannot be defined simply as border conflicts, neither can the intricate conflicts in Indochina, although the border issue in this case might play some role. The concordat proposal would restrain the major powers from action, but not to such a significant degree that it would really challenge their ability to act. Thus, it becomes a proposition that has some likelihood of acceptance, but at the same time it is reforming only a very small segment of the entire problem of interventionism.

Still, neither the Basic Principles Agreement nor the concordat is very explicit about what actions major powers are restrained from carrying out. There are not only other actors that could act (independently or as surrogates, as outlined above) but also other ways of acting, ways that the major powers already might prefer: shows of force, rather than uses of force; delivery of weapons rather than own deployments, etc. Restraint in such areas would have to be incorporated.

Indirectly, both propositions could be said to *encourage local initiatives*, although none of them explicitly addresses this question. If, however, it remains clear that major powers will be reluctant to become involved, the local parties will have to find other ways of handling their dispute. In case of symmetry, the chances might be favourable for negotiations of agreement, in cases of asymmetry, as perceived by at least one party, other ways of waging the conflict might be pursued: regional alliances, clandestine support or development of new strategies.

The Iran–Iraq war illustrates this well. Neither country is waging a war on behalf of any outside power, the incompatibilities are to be found between the competing parties themselves, and given that at least one party sees an asymmetry, efforts are made to bring the war to a victorious end, rather than finding an agreement. Thus, the absence of major power influence might not necessarily mean that the war effort as such will be restrained. Still, the lack of open major power involvement (with the exception of France) in favour of either of the two parties might have slowed down military action, and made it less possible for either side to win. Furthermore, in the absence of major power influence, considerable efforts have been made by neighbours, non-aligned countries and the United Nations, to make the parties come to terms with one another. It seems that the fact that the majors have not intervened, has stimulated others to take action. The lack of success might be due to a completely different set of factors.

The number of efforts to find a solution to the Iran–Iraq war contrasts with the lack of such efforts in the Ethiopia–Somalia conflict, where the majors have been heavily involved. The local parties have been forced to return to the *status quo ante*, the old border, but this has simply not been sufficient to stop fighting. On the contrary, Somali organisations continue to carry out attacks in Ogaden. In this case, the superpowers have found a way of reducing the amount of violence, but their involvement has not brought the conflict closer to a solution. As the *status quo ante* gave rise to the war in 1977, a return to that status of course means that the frustrations have intensified, not the least in view of the tremendous sufferings.

Certainly, these two examples are not enough for a conclusion that superpower involvement in general helps or prevents local initatives. For such a conclusion we would need a closer analysis of many more situations. The more successful recent examples of conflict resolution seem, however, to be either in areas of one major power being the only one involved, but taking a role as mediator (e.g. Rhodesia/Zimbabwe; India, Pakistan) or no one involved (e.g. Zaire, Angola, Zambia). The record of 'peace-building' through one major imposing its will is not encouraging (e.g. Lebanon, Angola).

The chances for local initiatives to operate in the absence of major power involvement would of course increase, if there were institutions that could fill the gap. However, most organisations involving, for instance, neutral and non-aligned countries are, almost by definition, loose bodies. It runs counter to the idea of non-alignment to make firm commitments to non-aligned organisations, as ultimately such bodies could resemble pacts. Still, several such organisations have been able to record certain successes: the League of Arab States in the Iraq–Kuwait and Yemen conflicts, the Organisation for African States in the Morocco–Algeria conflict. At present the development and strengthening of such bodies has stagnated. There is a trade-off which is important to exploit: the more and the stronger such bodies there are, the more persuasive becomes the argument for restraining major power relations. Obviously this connection also could operate in the reverse direction, thus strengthening the tendency: restraint seems to encourage local initiative.

The concordat proposals point to the UN Security Council as the alternative. However, it could be argued that this actually means involving the major powers in the conflict. Thus, the UN Charter reference to regional organisation could more explicitly be utilised.

Finally, there is an interesting and perhaps more rapidly developing alternative: the use of *non-governmental organisations*. Frustration with the inefficiency of governmental bodies could lead to a proliferation of initiative on this basis. Thus, the World Council of Churches has been active in mediation (the war in the Sudan) as has the Vatican (Chile–Argentina). These organisations have one distinct advantage over governmental bodies: their interests are more credibly linked to non-military values than to military ones, and consequently they are less susceptible to exploitation. Furthermore, other organisations, such as political internationals or trade union internationals gain an increasing international coverage. It appears that non-governmental organisations are at the present time developing more successfully and showing more creativity than are governmental organisations.

Both the Basic Principles Agreement and the concordat proposal makes reference to *the United Nations* and to the Security Council, the former in a more customary way, the latter in an explicit ambition to improve its role. Undoubtedly, the detente policy, as pursued by the United States and the Soviet Union during the 1970s, was to a large degree a bilateral relationship. In a business-like manner, the two improved their relations. This meant that the United States recognised the Soviet Union as an almost legitimate party of the same stature as any other power, whereas the Soviet Union undertook to restrain itself and act like such a 'normal' power. Thus, neither was interested in having other countries entering their discussions.

As a consequence the United Nations Organisations was kept outside the main developments: summit meetings were held in the capitals rather than under UN auspices, arms treaties were negotiated directly between the two rather than within existing UN frameworks, etc. Both, for different reasons, preferred to have it this way. Certainly, this meant that the United States had a problem of reassuring its allies that it did not go too far, or that it went as far as the allies wanted. Either way, the USA gradually drew increasing suspicion from West European countries. As it also preferred to deal with China in this way, disenchantment was noticable in East Asia, not the least in Japan.

The increasing bilateralism gave rise to fear of a superpower condominium where the interests of the rest of the world would yield to the interests of the superpower themselves. Revolt resulted: right wing Americans who believed that the Soviet Union could not be treated as an equal and legitimate party, Western Europeans, who feared that the US was about to abandon Western Europe or turn it into the arena of a limited nuclear war (Wallensteen, 1985). It is not hard to conjecture that similar developments took place with respect to the Soviet Union, both internally and within its alliance.

The bilateralism of the Basic Principles Agreement as well as of the detente policy also draw criticism from Third World and neutral countries. Thus, the idea has again emerged to give the United Nations, as a more representative forum, a greater role. The tension between the United States and the Soviet Union might provide such an opportunity. Bilateralism is, presently, hard to restore, although this is what many critics of the present 'cold war' would prefer, and thus, there might be a possibility of using other fora, such as the UN. There is, however, no automatic connection, as is made clear by the experience of the 1970s. If one wants to strengthen the United Nations, this requires an ambition to do exactly this, rather than anything else.

The concordat would restrain the permanent members of the Security Council, and bind them to give collective security a chance. In that sense it is a more ambitious undertaking than at first glance might be apparent. Not only does it require an agreement, in writing, among five states on what is allowed and what is not allowed to be done in border conflicts. Also it requires support from Third World countries, or at least a majority. Some countries might be particularly crucial to the support of such an agreement, notably those that are involved in border disputes or are known to be interventionist. Additionally, it presupposes the establishment of a UN military command, involving intricate questions of finance and administration.

In a sense the concordat proposal ties the countries much more than their adherence to the International Court of Justice, which can operate only if the countries bring the issue to the Court, which they are likely to do only when a conflict is acute and when they expect to benefit from such a move. In the concordat proposal, however, countries involved in potential conflict would already beforehand limit their possibility to take action. The concordat in all its simplicity, is a remarkable step towards creating an international security regime. Considerable detail will have to be worked out.

In sum: measures of preventing major power intervention in Third World conflicts could have some of the desirable effects. Superpowers would find ways of not involving themselves, if there were stronger regional bodies to take up some of the tasks majors might find themselves necessary to carry out. The main problems seem, however, to reside in the fact that there are few such alternatives available, that it is difficult to reach an agreement of what is permissible in a given conflict, which conflicts the restraint should apply to, and finally, the 'climate' of the superpower relationship in general.

CONCLUSION: A FEASIBLE MERGER?

The dangers of Third World conflicts escalating to major power confrontation is of growing concern. A revival of detente and a removal of threats to international peace and security would have to come to grips also with this problem. In fact, the detente policies of the 1970s explicitly addressed the problem, and also in proposals for more constructive superpower relations in the 1980s has this problem figured. However, there are many ways in which it could be handled. Thus, there appears to have been an emphasis on classical balance of power thinking, where interventions are managed by deterring the adversary from intervening. Such policies rather reinforce the dangers of escalation, as they lead to rapid and early interventions, rather than non-intervention. Thus, the emphasis has to lie on the possibilities of developing mechanisms of restraint.

Thus, interest has been focusing on two proposals, here labelled the *code of conduct* and *concordat* proposals. The first one is associated with the detente thinking of the 1970s, the latter emerges from the Palme Commission of the early 1980s. The former is conceived of in the form of a major power agreement, the latter is seen as extension of the United Nations Security Council, inviting UN action in times of crisis.

Although both these proposals have the same ambition, to restrict superpower involvement in Third World conflicts, the approaches are highly diverging, as are their political realism. In a sense, the route taken in the code of conduct approach, as indicated by the Basic Principles Agreement of 1972, has a greater feasibility. There is already an agreement, the criticism against it is known and there might be room for improvement. For instance, the agreement could be made more precise as to what actions are prohibited. As the framework has been one of direct American–Soviet negotiations, only two parties are involved. However, an improved agreement would benefit from being more open, to allow also other major powers to enter. In fact, this would mean developing it in the direction of a concordat. The two approaches, in other words, could be developed into one.

One problem in the Basic Principles Agreement is the vagueness of its central concept of 'unilateral advantage'; it would become clearer if it *specified the type of actions that are not allowed*. This has clear advantages from the point of view of verification as well as predictability. Actions are more easily monitored, and the danger of quick preventive action can deter action in the first place. Thus, the agreement could specify several sets of actions that are to be prohibited. Such a specification could, for instance, *prohibit*:

- *the use of the signatories own armed forces* in the zone of combat (whether regular or other types of troops),
- *military aid from a signatory to a conflicting party as long as armed struggle is pursued, or as long as there is no peace agreement of sorts* (definitions of military equipment might follow the specifications in the Cocom lists of strategic materials prohibited for export from the West to the East, a list presumably well-known to both superpowers, for different reasons)
- *military export from a signatory to a conflicting party, for a period in time extending beyond the implementation of a peace agreement.*
- *the signatories from giving assistance to other countries to carry out any of these measures.*

Such an agreement certainly would be more specific and, thus, violation becomes easier to establish.

The concordat proposal requires reference to actions that are not allowed. However, the concordat proposal has been limited to border conflicts. The area of application of a code agreement has also to be raised. Neither the USA nor the USSR would accept an agreement restraining their actions in the central arena, in Europe. Thus, either an area or an issue has to be specified. Specifying areas, however, means specifying zones of influence, which neither party recognised, at least in theory. For instance, the USA might prefer to retain a military option in the Central American or Caribbean area, the Soviet Union along its borders. Thus, by stating that the area of restraint is, for instance, Africa, is at the same time implying that the rest of the world is a 'free zone'.

The issue approach then becomes more 'attractive' to the superpowers. This is one advantage of restraint in border conflicts. These are not easily defined, however. It is important that the parties agree in an early stage to which conflicts the agreement applies. A feasible solution might be to *create a register of existing border conflicts*. The hope, furthermore, would be that this register could be *gradually extended*, either by extending the definition of border conflict or by adding new categories, or by simply adding new conflicts of any type to the register. A conflict would be included in the register as part of a move *by the involved parties themselves*.

The code of conduct approach does not include a proposal for alternative action. The concordat idea suggests that the conflict shall be brought to the attention of the Security Council and that the Council shall commit itself to undertake collective action to preserve peace. With such a commitment increased possibilities are given for the Security Council to act, and, not the least, for the Secretary General. This appears as a way out of the problem of developing alternatives to major power intervention.

In summary, a combined approach amounts to adding to the UN charter a commitment, on the one hand by the major powers, to refrain from action, and on the other hand, by countries involved in conflict, to specify that they will turn to the Security Council rather than to fighting. The former agree to this through a particular document, whereas the latter do the same by having their conflict registered by the United Nations. In a sense an agreement on the Non-Use of Force has been arrived at, in ways similar to the agreement on non-proliferation of nuclear weapons. In the same way some monitoring would be required, but this time, rather than creating a separate agency, such duties could be left to the Secretary General.

Also, in this reduced format, the basics of the concordat proposal are kept intact, at the same time as some of the self-interests of the major power are considered. Thus, all the parties might have an interest in following the proposition, and in that sense, the agreement would become a self-monitoring one. As the breach by one also frees another party, all parties will constantly watch what the others are in fact doing. Together, they might become a collective watchdog for peace.

Notes

*This chapter relates to research on regional conflicts and strategic confrontations, carried out with the support of UNESCO. Also the contribution of the Swedish Department of Foreign Affairs is acknowledged. This chapter has benefited from the input of scholars from the First, Second and Third Worlds.

References

Blechman, B. M. and Kaplan, S. S., *Force without War. U.S. Armed Forces as a Political Instrument* (Washington, D.C.: The Brookings Institution, 1978).

Common Security, The Report of the Independent Commission on Disarmament and Security Issues under the Chairmanship of Olof Palme, 1982.

Donaldson, R. H. (ed.), *The Soviet Union in the Third World: Successes and Failures* (Boulder, Co.: Westview Press, 1981).

Frei, D. (ed.), *Managing International Crisis*, (Beverly Hills: Sage, 1982).

George, A. L. (ed.), *Managing U.S.–Soviet Rivalry: Problems of Crisis Prevention* (Boulder, Co.: Westview Press, 1983).

Hoffmann, S., *Primacy or World Order. American Foreign Policy since the Cold War*, (New York, N.Y.: McGraw-Hill, 1978).

Kaplan, S. S., *Diplomacy of Power. Soviet Armed Forces as a Political Instrument* (Washington, D.C.: The Brookings Institution, 1981).

Keal, P., *Unspoken Rules and Superpower Dominance* (London: Macmillan, 1983).

Kissinger, H., *For the Record. Selected Statements 1979–1980* (Boston, Little, Brown: 1981).

Matheson, N., *The 'Rules of the Game' of Superpower Military Intervention in the Third World 1975–1980* (Washington, D.C.: University Press of America, 1982).

Nincic, M., *How War might spread to Europe*, SIPRI (London: Taylor & Francis, 1985).

Wallensteen, P., American–Soviet Détente: What Went Wrong?, *Journal of Peace Research*, 1985: 1.

Part V

Conventional Arms, Arms Control, and the Nuclear Threshold

16 How Can Arms Control Raise the Nuclear Threshold in Europe?

Jonathan Dean

In discussing the potential contribution of arms control to raising the nuclear threshold in Europe, the general approach taken here is that there are already a number of good ideas on this subject, that some of them may bring some modest progress in the next several years, and that the political process in the countries of the Western coalition is likely to promote even more serious action within the decade. Despite a great deal of contrary evidence, it may be that the East–West military confrontation in Europe has already passed a watershed and, however imperceptibly and confusedly, is gradually running down. Something even more fundamental than the role of nuclear weapons in defence and deterrence may be involved.

As we look at the situation of conventional defence in Europe, we find, as with the strategic nuclear relationship, that an uneasy East–West balance has been preserved at increasingly high cost to both sides, a cost estimated at about two-thirds of world total expenditures for armed forces of over a trillion dollars annually. In Central Europe, NATO standing forces of some 22 divisions seem capable of dealing with the most plausible and most feared type of Soviet attack, an attack with minimal preparation using the bulk of the 26 Soviet divisions in Eastern Europe. A full mobilisation of Soviet and Pact forces would transcend NATO's capabilities, but also risks world-wide conventional and nuclear war which most believe the Soviet leadership is unwilling to undertake. Whatever view one takes of the programme to deploy American intermediate-range missiles in Europe, the November 1983 Bundestag vote confirming the NATO decision to deploy the missiles, a vote taken in the face of broad Eastern threats of an 'ice age' in East–West relations and of a 'pallisade of missiles' directed against West Germany and Western Europe, was an important development. It showed that the other main fear of Western leaders, that the Soviet Union could use its great military strength as an effective source of intimidation and political pressure against Western Europe, was also not materialising. That fear will not materialise as long as there is a reasonable degree of political solidarity between the United States and Western European governments – an area which causes considerably more long-term worry than the state of NATO defences.

Yet many see reasons for unhappiness about European defence. Soviet conventional forces in central Europe and the Western USSR have continued to improve qualitatively through reorganisation and better weapons, including better fighter-bombers, better armour, better artillery, better helicopters, anti-aircraft and anti-tank weapons. Their nuclear forces have increased. NATO too has improved, but, given the higher cost of NATO military manpower and equipment, there is no chance of numerically matching the Pact. There are logical answers to this problem of NATO conventional strength, among them, closer co-operation with France and greater force specialisation by NATO countries. But the plain fact of the matter is that European apprehension about the possibility of Soviet attack is not strong enough to overcome the political obstacles to these actions. The status quo of defence forces below the optimum – and of no East–West arms reduction – is essentially acceptable to all NATO governments and the political parties which form them, although it is increasingly less acceptable to European public opinion. And, as we shall comment further, that status quo seems eminently acceptable to the Soviet Union.

Western European opinion on defence issues seems more seriously fragmented now than at any time since the onset of the Cold War. As the heritage of the INF deployment controversy, the defence consensus of the past 25 years has split down the middle. The mass public demonstrations against INF are no more, but the programme of the anti-nuclear movement, as with so many movements of the past, has been institutionalised and taken over by the parties of the left as part of their own programmes. Efforts to convert anti-nuclear sentiment in the European public into support for improvements in conventional forces have not had broad success, partly because the rationale used, the concept of dealing with a reinforcing Soviet second echelon, has suggested a long conventional war which Western European opinion abhors as much as a short nuclear one. And, for years to come, the new controversy over SDI and ballistic missile defence and over the nuclear weapons reductions tentatively agreed upon at the 1986 Reykjavik Summit, will cast even more doubt on the viability of extended deterrence, complicate arms control, and catalyse anti-nuclear sentiments.

The modest improvements which are made in NATO forces are unlikely to bring significant changes in the East–West force balance. However, there is a qualitative change in European public attitudes which incremental adjustments in the rationale and nature of NATO defence programmes will not be able to meet. For some time, the NATO countries will probably continue to go the route of maintaining rough equality with the Pact at an ever increasing level of armaments, paralleled by increasing public discontent over this approach to defence. None the less, the nuclear threshold has been pushed upward, psychologically at least, through the controversy over INF deployment and the rise of anti-nuclear sentiment, culminating in the concept of 'no early use', a concept which needs to be filled out with real meaning.

The Geneva negotiations are of course important for the future of nuclear deterrence as well as for the future of other arms control efforts in Europe. If agreements in Geneva are reached, they will give impetus to arms control in Europe. Similarly, if results in Geneva are long delayed, there will be pressure for substitute actions. The course of the Geneva talks through the end of 1986 appears to confirm that the ingredients for an agreement exist, but simultaneously to raise doubts that these components will be used to reach a complete and fully articulated strategic reduction agreement during the present US administration. A high degree of mutual suspicion, weaknesses in decision making on both sides, compliance and verification problems, and the chaos-creating SDI element are the main reasons for this prediction. An INF agreement, if it comes, would increase interest in negotiated conventional reductions.

Two arms control negotiations covering European subject matter have taken place in Stockholm and Vienna. Only one of these multilateral negotiations, the CDE, has in fact resulted in a finished agreement (in September 1986). It is highly improbable that an MBFR agreement will be concluded, but it is likely to be replaced by new negotiations covering the broader area from the Atlantic to the Urals. In fact, there may be more momentum in these negotiations than in the bilateral US–Soviet nuclear talks, and it may have to do with their multilateral configuration. The CDE outcome contains a commitment on non-use of force and several useful confidence-building measures on prenotification of force movements originally proposed by NATO participants, and it is probable that it will continue in a second phase.

What is the military significance of this first CDE agreement and its connotations, however indirect, for the nuclear threshold?

This first CDE agreement contains no reductions, no limitations on the size of forces, and no restrictions on military activities, with the exception of prohibiting force activities of 40 000 men unless notified a year in advance and of over 70 000 men unless notified two years in advance. It will make no direct contribution to damping down the NATO-Pact arms race. The competition in modernised armaments will in fact remain unrestricted. Moreover, present Western proposals suspend the requirement for pre-notification and presence of observers in the initial stages of alerts, a major exception which was insisted on by commanders on both sides who wish to continue testing the state of readiness of their forces. Additional exceptions exist for troops in transit from other areas via Europe to third areas and for force movements not under unified command. These exceptions create a big loophole in the coverage of CDE measures. Moreover, it is difficult to see that even future phases of CDE would have any capacity to cope with force reductions or limitations.

On the positive side, a first CDE agreement along the lines sketched here will provide some useful information beyond that now available to both sides regarding departure from normal military activities or preparation for combat. It contains a provision for up to three inspections a year at all participating states including the USSR, a real and important innovation. It is probable that this conference will be followed by a successor within a year or two of its conclusion. In fact, given the interests involved, it probably will be followed by a series of future conferences on European security lasting over coming decades. Given this probability, interested people in and out of government should begin now to consider the possible content of CDE in the long term.

The future of the MBFR negotiations is much more problematical. For ten years, since the Warsaw Pact in 1976 presented data on its forces in Central Europe which the NATO participants consider incomplete, the MBFR talks have been held up by the dispute between NATO and the Pact over the number of Warsaw Pact forces in Central Europe. In recent years, NATO has been estimating these forces at about 180 000 more than shown in Eastern figures for ground force personnel alone. Yet over the years, a large number of points needed for a completed first accord in Vienna have been agreed in principle between East and West. They include agreement on the ultimate goal of equal levels in ground and air force manpower and a number of specific measures designed to verify compliance with residual force ceilings after reductions and to reduce the risk of surprise attack.

There are several possibilities of resolving the data dispute, among them NATO's December 1985 proposal to suspend the earlier NATO requirement for pre-reduction agreement on data for Warsaw Pact forces for the purposes of a limited first US–Soviet reduction, and then to resolve the data dispute on the ground through inspections rather than at the negotiating table. It may be that, if this proposal were ever carried out, we would discover that the total of Pact forces in the area is less than we have been calculating, placing a common ceiling within practical reach.

However, to be frank, there are few prospects for an outcome in Vienna. Indeed, its end was signalled by Soviet and Warsaw Pact proposals in the spring of 1986 to begin a new force reduction negotiation in the area from the Atlantic to the Ural Mountains, the same area covered by CDE, and it is likely that NATO, which gave an interim reply in 1986, will agree to hold the new negotiation within a year or two of the original pact invitation. When that decision is reached, the MBFR talks will probably be closed down. Yet the new negotiation, too, seems unlikely soon to bring major negotiated agreements. Instead, it will probably be dogged by the same problems as MBFR, particularly the reluctance of military commanders on both sides to reduce their forces, and the unwillingness of political leaders to overrule them.

This situation is doubly unfortunate because it will also mean failure by Western governments to recognise that, at this point in time, arms control agreements in Europe are perhaps more important for reducing US–European frictions than they are in the East–West context. The NATO structure is close to permanent, but these frictions are likely cumulatively to push Western Europe and the United States further apart and to erode the political substance of NATO without the emergence of any European substitute for it.

Despite the probability that Western public opinion will in coming years urge increasingly bold arms control approaches to the military confrontation in Europe, the prospects for organising any more comprehensive approach to arms control in Europe are also limited. On the Western side, the United States has a continuing disinclination to sharing control of its nuclear weapons and of its natural future with its European allies, while leaving it to them to set the price on force reductions in Europe. France is unlikely to find a strong alliance framework acceptable or, mainly because of worries about the future of Germany, to press for force reductions. Despite its concerns about nuclear weapons, majority political opinion in Federal Germany is unwilling either to act to obtain credible conventional defence or to provide momentum in entering the unknown territory of arms control agreements in which the Soviet Union is a major participant. Instead, it is likely that, for some time to come, political opinion in Federal Germany will be sufficiently turbulent to keep the entire West unsettled, without developing a sufficient internal consensus to make any given approach to defence improvement or arms control acceptable. This is not criticism, because it is possible to have great sympathy for the position of both sides of the issue in Germany, but a dispassionate forecast. And in a more general sense, France will not be able to leave its concept of autonomy in isolation to share sufficiently in the common fate of Europe to provide forward motive power.

These are important obstacles to any prospect of far-reaching arms control in Europe which could raise the nuclear threshold. But the main obstacle to success of any more ambitious approach to arms control is the Soviet interest in maintaining the status quo, at least as far as conventional forces are concerned. There is a near certainty that the Soviet Union will insist on keeping large forces in forward position in Eastern Europe, largely, although not exclusively, because of the failure of the Soviet Union and the communist governments of Eastern Europe to solve the problem of making these governments self-sustaining without the requirement of Soviet military forces to prop them up. Soviet leaders are unlikely to admit this to themselves or to review dispassionately how many forces are needed for population control. It is improbable that these Soviet forces will be used to attack Western Europe, but they will also not be moved back. Serious Soviet moves to negotiate over the status of East Germany or Eastern Europe generally would have to be preceded by radical change in the Soviet system of which there is no sign whatever.

Powerful institutional interests will continue to support this essentially political motivation for keeping Soviet troops in Central Europe. The main *raison d'être* of the Soviet ground forces and of their own claim on important allocation of Soviet resources is to deal with the Western military threat as they perceive and present it. This means in practical terms that the Soviet leadership will not only insist that large Soviet forces remain in Eastern Europe but that these forces will be well-equipped, creating a requirement for a balancing NATO force. For the foreseeable future, these factors appear to establish narrow limitations to the possible scope of reductions and limitations on the size and armament of Warsaw pact forces to which the Soviet Union will be prepared to agree. Gorbachev's more radical approach may also make itself felt here, but the conservatism of the Soviet military is formidable.

If the situation is as described, should we go ahead unilaterally to make changes in the NATO defence posture intended to create greater stability and raise the nuclear threshold, or should we try to bring in the Soviets in what we do? Probably, we should try to do the latter, at least initially, for unless we propose some balancing action by the Soviets, we may find it difficult to obtain majority support in Western public opinion for the actions we wish to undertake. Moreover, the constructive effect of nearly any measure will be increased if it is also carried out by the Soviets. We should therefore at least try for their agreement.

We should try to visualise a negotiating concept which will to some degree cope with the political obstacles to arms control in Europe described here and still bring some progress toward increased stabilisation of the NATO – Pact confrontation, and have some impact on raising the nuclear threshold. For example, if large-scale decreases in Soviet forces are improbable, would Soviet resistance over time to restructuring their forces be less than their resistance to large troop withdrawals? Could we bring the Soviets to restructure their forces in East Germany to be somewhat less threatening or to change their deployment pattern? On the NATO side, the declining German birthrate and the high cost of military forces both argue for some sort of belt of static defences along the Federal German border with the GDR in order to take the first impact of possible Soviet attack. German political opinion has thus far steadfastly rejected any such belt as deepening the division of Germany. But what if such a belt were part of an arms control agreement with the Warsaw Pact intended to reduce the risk of conflict, and both sides agreed that such zones would be helpful in doing so?

Perhaps, rather eclectically, elements from various already formulated approaches could be combined into a single concept. Using the MBFR reduction area – the MBFR forum or a new and expanded CDE, would also be the logical place to discuss this concept with the Pact – the first element would be a zone of restricted armaments on both sides of the Federal German border with the GDR and Czechoslovakia from which mobile heavy weapons – tanks, self-propelled artillery, helicopters, bridging equipment – and all nuclear warheads and nuclear delivery systems, as well as dual-capable systems, would be prohibited. To avoid large-scale disruptions, the zone should be no more than 50 kilometres wide on the NATO side. It should be 100 kilometres wide on the Pact side because of the greater depth of Warsaw Pact territory, the proximity of the most powerful Warsaw Pact member, the Soviet Union, to the German border, and the distance of the comparable NATO power, the United States from the border. There would be no restriction on the number of military personnel in the zone, or the construction of anti-tank obstacles, light-field fortifications or deploying fixed-position artillery, anti-aircraft, anti-tank and multiple rocket launchers of limited range. However, again borrowing from MBFR, there would be a freeze on the military personnel of both sides in the MBFR reduction area. And, also taken over from MBFR concepts, there would be on-site verification by inspectors of the other alliance, both of the manpower freeze and of the zones of limited armaments.

Under this approach, both sides could continue to use barracks and military installations now used, so its cost would not be great. But NATO and Pact commanders would be confronted by the choice between separating the personnel of armoured units from their equipment and storing the latter outside the zone or restructuring the forces deployd inside the zone to establish and operate static defences. A third possibility, withdrawing armoured units from the zone and constructing new facilities for them, leaving the zone substantially without forces, would be expensive and disadvantageous, especially if the opposition is building obstacles and barriers right at the dividing line.

If this approach were accepted, the combined effect of prohibiting heavy armoured units in the zone and of the overall personnel limit would probably oblige the Soviet Union to restructure their front line forces in the zone of limited armaments. Since most Soviet divisions in East Germany are stationed in a belt between Berlin and the Federal German border, the deeper the zone, the more restructuring would be required. These changes would not affect Soviet capacity to maintain political control which we have identified as their primary interest.

Under this approach, there would be no prohibition against personnel of armoured units moving into their emergency readiness positions on both sides and familiarising themselves with the area, but they would have to leave their heavy equipment behind. Manpower-poor NATO could emphasise high-tech defences in the restricted zones, manned by personnel of allied forces in their present sectors, maintaining the important deterrent effect of this stationing pattern. The fact that both sides were permitted obstacles and barriers as part of an arms control agreement agreed to by East Germany as well as other Pact states might overcome Federal German objections to erecting barriers and anti-tank defences, at least at the most vulnerable points, where such things as prepositioned pipe for liquid explosives like nitromethane can be placed in series to form barriers.

The existence of belts like these should increase NATO warning time by one to two days and result in a heavily defended zone to take the first impact of possible Pact conventional attack, with present NATO standing forces acting as mobile reserves. Adoption of this scheme would in effect cause the Soviets to have to modify the concept of massive counter-attack in response to any attack from the West which has made their tank-heavy forward position appear so menacing. This approach could not have decisive effect in making conflict in Europe impossible, but it would make it less likely. It would be especially useful in lowering the risk of war through crisis escalation and it would improve NATO's capability of dealing with conventional Warsaw Pact attack by conventional means.

This approach, that is, the creation of a zone of static defence and obstacles as a screen in front of NATO's mobile armoured forces to take the first impact, could also be pursued unilaterally by NATO. In this case, of course, NATO would not be required to thin out the zone of static defence. But its establishment would give some genuine content to the concept of no early use of nuclear weapons by creating one additional barrier, in this case a literal one, which would have to be broken through before resort is taken to nuclear weapons. And it would also be feasible for NATO to institute such a zone of static defences and simultaneously propose to the Warsaw Pact an agreement prohibiting heavy mobile weapons from a belt on both sides of the Federal German border.

There is only limited hope that agreement can be reached on approaches like this, though they should be tried. None the less, there are some grounds for relative optimism about the long-term prospects for a build-down of the NATO-Pact confrontation.

First, it is possible that, under the more modern leadership of Gorbachev, the Soviet Union will more successfully avoid direct confrontation with Western countries and appear less aggressive. Second, it is not improbable that, within the next ten years, one or more political parties committed to unilateral moves toward disarmament will come to power in a NATO country. If it happens, this circumstance will among other things bring about the seriousness of intent which is now lacking in the approach of the Western countries to arms control.

Third, developing inner-German relations are a forum for discussion of security issues which could become increasingly significant in coming decades. The motivation supporting this effort at the public and governmental level in the Federal Republic is very powerful – it provides an approved way of venting frustration at dependence on the great powers and a way to make a distinctively German contribution to world peace, even a way to make some moral restitution for the German past. The East German regime likes this approach because it gives it a role of its own and a little manoeuvre room from the Soviets. The Soviets approve it because it could increase East German influence over Federal German policy, without raising issues of change of status. The present format of such talks, dialogue between the Federal German Social Democratic opposition and the governing East German SED, is not optimal, while the Federal German government has been dissuaded by the United States from discussing the non-use of force with the GDR government. Yet there are strong prospects that the inner-German dialogue on this subject will continue indefinitely. These two states have the bulk of Soviet and of NATO forces stationed on their territory, and they may be able to work out some useful measures. Already this relationship has important security benefits. These efforts should be nurtured.

Taken together, such developments – more restrained Soviet behaviour, change of policy by the election process and the inner-German relationship, even if slow-working, may make progress toward defusing NATO-Pact confrontation and toward raising the nuclear threshold in Europe.

17 The M(B)FR Negotiations, the Military Balance and Détente in Europe

Hanspeter Neuhold

It is stating the obvious to point out that a more stable balance between NATO and Warsaw Pact conventional forces in Europe will in all probability raise the nuclear threshold. It is also a truism that an equilibrium at the conventional level will enhance deterrence: The use by the victim of a conventional aggression of its non-nuclear potential against the attacker appears more likely than the decision to resort to nuclear weapons first, no matter how emphatically the threat to do so is proclaimed. A would-be aggressor may in fact speculate that the other side will not cross the nuclear threshold for fear of triggering mutually destructive escalation which it will be unable to control.

It is equally evident that agreements on conventional arms control could lead to and stabilise a military balance between East and West at this level. This may be achieved by correcting force disparities and/or through a trade-off between each party's specific assets which the other side regards as most menacing. Increased security could be assured at lower cost, as neither alliance would be tempted to exploit military superiority for a (surprise) attack or for exerting political pressure. Lessening the risk of conventional conflict in Europe would also reduce the probability of a nuclear confrontation, at least as a result of escalation of a war begun with non-nuclear forces. This could in turn further improve the overall political climate between the two blocs, reinforce the process of détente in various areas, and facilitate arms control in other fields, most importantly that of nuclear weapons.

It is less certain that the M(B)FR talks in Vienna could make a major contribution to these desirable objectives – even if the negotiations were one day successfully concluded within the framework agreed upon by the participating States.[1] The history of these talks illustrates the difficulties of conventional arms control on the 'Old Continent'.

Apart from avoidable tactical blunders committed by NATO – such as calling for 'balanced' reductions, which in fact were meant to be unequal in order to redress an existing imbalance[2] – the genuine problems are due to basic disparities between the two alliances.[3] Unfortunately, these differences are not limited to manpower numbers and armaments, both quantitatively and in terms of their capabilities. They are compounded by geostrategic realities. On the one hand, the territory of the Eastern alliance is a huge, homogeneous land area with relatively short and direct transport routes. As a result, the deployment and movement of large forces does not pose any particular problems in almost all weather conditions. Moreover, Soviet troops withdrawn to the USSR could still remain within merely 360 to 420 miles of the main line of the East–West confrontation, the Eastern border of the FRG. On the other hand, the geographic configuration of the NATO countries makes their defence much more difficult. Furthermore, US forces which return to America would be separated by the Atlantic from the European 'theater', in other words by a distance of approximately 3500 miles.

In addition to the factors with a direct bearing on the military equation, other well-known discrepancies between the two camps further complicate efforts to conclude meaningful arms control agreements. Whether and to which extent the reforms announced and undertaken by Secretary-General Gorbachev will reduce these asymmetries remains to be seen. 'Closed' societies of the communist type are reluctant to divulge military information which is easily available in Western democracies. Communist governments are reluc- to admit to their territories foreign inspectors whose task would be to verify compliance with treaties on arms control. The populations of the 'socialist' countries in Eastern Europe seem to be more willing to accept high defence expenditures than their Western counterparts – or, at any rate, they hardly have the possibility of expressing their disagreement. Soviet troops stationed in other Warsaw Pact members not only serve the purpose of at least matching the forces deployed by NATO in Western Europe and coping with the threat which the Atlantic Alliance poses in Eastern eyes, but the presence of Soviet soldiers is also designed to maintain order and discipline throughout the 'socialist' camp. This additional function within the alliance provides another justification for the – increasing – costs which the Pact has to shoulder for its conventional forces. It is important not to lose sight of these structural asymmetries; they would cast a long shadow over any other forum to which the M(B)FR talks may be shifted.

The inherent logic (not only) of arms control negotiations leads participants to try to eliminate or at least to reduce the other sides' advantages while preserving their own assets. Small wonder, then, that the Western and Eastern positions were diametrically opposed on almost all major points at the beginning of the M(B)FR talks in 1973.

The West was convinced of the existence, in Europe, of a substantial imbalance at the conventional level in the Warsaw Pact's favour. It therefore demanded the establishment of parity through unequal, adequately verified reductions to a common collective ceiling of 700 000 men for each alliance in Central Europe as defined for M(B)FR purposes.

Arguing that a rough equilibrium already prevailed, the East proposed symmetrical cuts not only of troops in organic units but also of their armaments under national ceilings for all direct participants.[4] The Warsaw Pact wanted to see indigenous forces covered by a M(B)FR agreement disbanded, their equipment scrapped. A party suspecting a breach of the agreement could only have called for consultations. Against this background, it may be appropriate to summarise the state of the M(B)FR negotiations at the time of writing.

Since 1973, the gap between the two sides has been narrowed somewhat and informal agreement is said to have been reached on a number of points. Areas of agreement include acceptance by the 'socialist' participants of the concept of two common ceilings of 900 000 men for ground and air force personnel and of 700 000 men for ground forces alone.[5] However, this does not mean that the problem of attaining parity has been solved to the West's satisfaction, but merely that it has been shifted to the issue of data discrepancies. In addition, reductions are to take place in two phases, the first stage being limited to the withdrawal of US and Soviet troops within a year. This is to be followed by cuts by other direct participants, until the two common ceilings are reached. All parties to a single, comprehensive M(B)FR treaty would also undertake a non-increase commitment immediately after the two Superpowers have completed their phase one withdrawals. Warsaw Pact representatives have recognised the need for verification and confidence-building measures in principle and have also proposed some concrete measures of this type without, however, meeting the essence of Western requirements.

For a long time, the data and verification issues have remained the two principal stumbling blocks on the road to a M(B)FR agreement.

After Eastern negotiators had simply rejected Western figures, which indicated a clear-cut manpower superiority of WTO forces in Central Europe, as inaccurate for almost three years, they eventually tabled their own data in 1976. Yet, this apparent concession did by no means mark a breakthrough. According to Eastern figures, rough parity between the two alliances existed in the reduction area, as 805 000 ground troops 'admitted' by the Pact were almost completely matched by 791 000 NATO soldiers. However, the West claimed that the other side's ground forces totalled 962 000 men. A margin of superiority of well over 150 000 ground troops was and is regarded by NATO as militarily significant in any conventional armed conflict.

From the Western point of view, agreement on the force levels of each alliance in Central Europe was indispensable. It would not be possible otherwise to specify the size of the reductions necessary to reach the common ceilings. These reductions could in turn be effectively verified, whereas it was alleged that it would hardly be feasible to count the forces within the area of reductions.

The West also insists on adequate 'associated measures'. They are to enable the parties to monitor full compliance with a M(B)FR treaty. Moreover, such measures also ought to serve confidence-building purposes by helping avoid misunderstandings and miscalculations with respect to the intentions underlying the other side's military activities. They should foreclose the possibility of launching a surprise attack by providing early warning of major preparations for such a move.

As already mentioned, the East has agreed to such 'associated measures' in principle and has also proposed some specific steps in this direction. However, the West still considers even the most recent list not comprehensive enough.

NATO has made some concessions on the data dispute in exchange for even more stringent verification provisions.[5] In its proposal of 19 April 1984, the West abandoned its insistence on prior agreement on the numbers of *all* ground and air force personnel in the reduction zone. Instead, it requested a previous exchange of data only on ground combat and combat support forces. These troops, which amount to about 60 per cent of the total forces and 75 per cent of the ground forces in the area, have the strongest combat potential and also more apparent, 'solid' structures, so that agreement on their levels should be somewhat easier. The 1984 Western approach thus sets aside air force personnel as well as ground combat service support troops which in the West's opinion may have been responsible for much of the data discrepancy.

Moreover, NATO participants declared themselves ready to accept Eastern figures which fall within an (undefined)[6] 'acceptable range' of their data estimates. Previously, they had demanded formal agreement on precise data.

Furthermore, the exchange of data on part of the forces only was to be preceded by agreement on definitions of new categories under which those figures would be broken down. Such new counting rules would allow both sides to table official data in a completely new way.

To meet some of the Warsaw Pact's concerns, the West also proposed that both US and Soviet forces be withdrawn mainly in units in the initial phase, with only up to 10 per cent as individuals. In accordance with another Eastern demand, immediately after those reductions by the two Superpowers, a verifiable and collective no-increase obligation would enter into force which would cover the over-all levels of ground forces of all direct participants.

To balance what was seen as important concessions on its part, the West called for improvements of the 'associated measures' it had first proposed in 1979, for example as regards the numbers, duration, and area of on-site inspections or the size of inspection teams.

This at least partly new Western approach did not meet with the approval of the Warsaw Pact. Its spokesmen argued that the substance of the Western position had not changed and that the April 1984 proposals even marked a step backward in certain respects. What the West regarded as a face-saving device to break the log-jam caused by the data issue was criticised by the other side as a revival of the old dispute merely in a different form instead of dropping it altogether. In any event, Warsaw Pact participants had presented correct official figures and were not 'liars or cheaters'.[7] To make matters worse, the Western side had further increased its already 'inflated' package of verification measures in an attempt to gain military intelligence beyond the requirements of assuring compliance with an eventual agreement. The measures proposed by the East were fully sufficient to meet this objective. Warsaw Pact representatives also emphasised that the Western refusal to reduce armaments was a breach of the mandate of the Vienna talks as agreed upon in 1973. In sum, the West was accused of trying to obtain unilateral military advantages at the Pact's expense at the negotiating table.

Conversely, the West continued to find the Eastern position on the key issues unacceptable. On 14 February 1985, the Warsaw Pact introduced a draft agreement on 'The Basic Provisions of an Agreement on the Initial Reduction by the Soviet Union and the USA of Ground Forces and Armaments in Central Europe and the Follow-On Non-Increase of the Level of Armed Forces and Armaments of the Sides in this Area', which still followed the proposals submitted in 1983.[8] However, this subsequent Eastern initiative subscribed to the Western concept of a legally binding treaty instead of basing reductions on 'mutual example', 'mutual political commitments' to be guaranteed by the 'political will' of the parties. Furthermore, Warsaw Pact participants also accepted the already-mentioned Western compromise formula under which up to 10 per cent of the Superpower forces to be reduced during the first phase could be withdrawn as individuals.[9]

The 'political climate' at the Vienna talks appeared to be rather good at that time, although each side kept accusing the other of being responsible for the lack of progress in public. Neither alliance presented its proposals on a 'take-it-or-leave-it' basis, but as point of departure for discussions.

Nevertheless, there is no real light at the end of the tunnel which the M(B)FR talks have entered, and it is possible that the tunnel may collapse altogether in 1987, or soon thereafter as both sides seem to have lost interest in the M(B)FR process. Hence all possible solutions to the deadlock the negotiations have reached in Vienna over the data and verification problems deserve serious consideration to head off such an unsuccessful outcome. One such way out of the impasse seems a shift to another forum. Such a move might be preceded by a 'Quick Fix', that is a limited agreement on token reductions as envisaged for the forces of the two Superpowers during the initial stage in the proposals now on the conference table in the Austrian capital. In particular, the second phase of the Conference on Confidence- and Security-Building Measures and Disarmament in Europe (CDE) seems to lend itself to such a fresh start for a number of reasons.

1. As regards the quarrel over data, a new beginning within the larger CSCE framework would permit the Warsaw Pact countries to submit figures different from those presented previously without a loss of face.

2. In regard to the verification issue, the Helsinki Final Act already provides for a few confidence-building measures and has thus established a useful precedent. Moreover, the first phase of CDE in Stockholm reached an agreement on additional measures of this kind in September 1986. These measures had to meet four requirements laid down in the Concluding Document of the Madrid CSCE follow-up meeting in September 1983. It remains to be seen whether they really are militarily significant and adequately verifiable; they are indeed politically binding and, as a result of a major concession by the USSR, they extended to the entire European continent (and not just a zone of 250 kilometres from the Western Soviet border), as well as the adjoining sea area and air space. Several of these measures rather closely resemble those proposed at the M(B)FR negotiations.[10]

3. The integration of M(B)FR into the CSCE process would avoid the undesirable result of two geographically different sets of confidence- and security-building measures, one restricted to Central Europe and the other covering almost the entire continent. As stated above, the measures agreed on during the first phase of CDE are only politically binding. However, they might be transformed later on into legal obligations, as arrangements to verify the implementation of an agreement on the reduction of conventional forces would undoubtedly have to be from the outset.

4. Even more importantly, the extension of the area of reductions to the territories of all the European CSCE participants would eliminate one of the main deficiencies of the M(B)FR approach, that of its rather artificial and arbitrary geographic limits. The concept of cuts in conventional forces only in Central Europe – as defined for the purposes of M(B)FR – must appear discriminatory especially in (some) West German eyes. Furthermore, a mere shift of the military confrontation to other European regions outside the reductions zone would contribute little if anything to arms control and military détente on the continent.

5. The CSCE framework would be more representative and in a way more democratic, because it also includes European States which are not members of the two alliances opposing each other on the European continent. The countries forming the 'n + n' (neutral and non-aligned) group would be given the opportunity of voicing their concerns and interests. They could also perform mediatory functions, as they already did during the Geneva phase of CSCE proper, the Madrid follow-up meeting and the first phase of CDE in

Stockholm.[11] Moreover, an all-European conference would imply the participation of France, a major actor who is absent from the Vienna talks.

6. A 'New Look' at conventional force and arms control in Europe may also permit to extend the negotiations to the reduction of armaments as demanded by the East. It might include those weapon systems which each side considers most threatening and destabilising. Such a broader approach could thus come to grips with military capabilities and options instead of militarily rather insignificant numerical force reductions – another frequently criticised weakness of the M(B)FR framework.

However attractive and tempting such a fresh start may appear, the basic differences between East and West mentioned above must be borne in mind. They will not disappear simply by the decision to discuss the same problems in another forum. The extension of the number of participants, of the reductions area and of the scope of the reductions may very well turn out a double-edged sword by further complicating the negotiations. Valuable time and probably also experience and progress already made could be lost.

It may therefore be a sounder strategy not to wait for phase two of CDE or some other forum – after all, agreement on them or their successful conclusion is not a forgone conclusion. In any event a serious attempt should rather be made to reach as substantial an agreement at the Vienna talks as quickly as possible.

On the one hand, it can be argued that, even given the (real or alleged) military asymmetries in the East's favour, no responsible Warsaw Pact political leader should be expected to order a conventional military attack on any Western country. He ought to be well aware of the risks his bloc would be running, even if NATO did not eventually resort to nuclear weapons. On the other hand, cuts of no more than about 10–20 per cent of the conventional forces in Central Europe are envisaged within the given M(B)FR parameters. Such limited reductions would not decisively affect the over-all military balance and the nuclear threshold between East and West in Europe.[12] In addition to nuclear weapons, qualitative developments resulting in additional military capabilities at the conventional level have a much greater impact on this relationship. 'Emerging technologies', for example in the fields of electronics, software or new materials, merit special attention in this connection. They may revolutionise target acquisition and the accuracy and destructive power of modern munitions such as TGSM (terminally-guided anti-armour submunitions). However, even experts are divided over the crucial question of whether the Western edge in 'high tech' will offset Warsaw Pact superiority in other areas. Furthermore, the East will certainly do its utmost to catch up with the West in the technological arms race.

Although the military relevance of a M(B)FR agreement would thus be rather marginal, the stalemate at the Vienna negotiations is not likely to be overcome by more 'sophisticated' proposals along the lines on which the two sides have dug in their heels. A breakthrough seems to require an effort at a higher,[13] probably the highest political level. Major concessions especially on the thorny issues of data and verification will have to be made. It is difficult to speculate on the contents of an eventual agreement which somehow would have to be a package deal.

Nor is it easy to predict whether the successful conclusion of the negotiations in Vienna or at a CDE II will be part and parcel of a comprehensive arms control deal including nuclear (and non-nuclear space) weapons or not. One could of course argue that after the 'technical' aspects of M(B)FR have been dealt with since 1973, the time is more than ripe for an act of 'political will' to conclude a treaty. To make M(B)FR militarily relevant, this step would have to be followed by others which certainly cannot be taken overnight. Yet, even a limited agreement would be an important political gesture, a substantial confidence-building measure.[14] It could add momentum for the success of the bilateral arms control talks between the USSR and USA which resumed in Geneva in 1985 as well as to further talks on conventional arms control in a new and wider forum.

Other, equally important incentives for an M(B)FR treaty are the ever growing costs of maintaining large up-to-date conventional forces in a period of world-wide economic difficulties and increasing manpower shortages on both sides (above all, in the USSR and the FRG), despite the problem of unemployment in the West.[15]

Moreover, a success at the Vienna talks would help to satisfy public opinion which has become increasingly impatient with the lack of progress in recent arms control endeavours. It is an irony of the M(B)FR process that the voices led by Senator Mansfield[16] in the USA calling for a unilateral withdrawal of American troops from Europe, which were largely responsible for the original Western M(B)FR initiatives, have recently emerged again after they had been silenced for years.[17]

An M(B)FR agreement should not of course lead to euphoria

among politicians and in public opinion, especially not in the West. Its limitations ought to be clearly pointed out. Nor should it be allowed to create the illusion that governments could proceed to sizeable cuts in defence budgets if an adequate conventional balance is to be maintained.

To end on a more positive note, the M(B)FR talks have proven their worth as a communication channel and a mutual learning process appreciated by both alliances over the years. Participants have increased their knowledge and understanding of the other side's positions, concerns, and fears. It seems to be significant that, unlike the INF talks and START, the negotiations on M(B)FR were not broken off by the Soviet Union after NATO went ahead with the deployment of Pershing II and cruise missiles in Western Europe toward the end of 1983 in accordance with its 'dual track' decision of 1979.

Notes

1. An impressive bibliography on M(B)FR has been compiled by Reinhard Mutz (ed), *Die Wiener Verhandlungen ueber Truppenreduzierungen in Mitteleuropa (MBFR): Chronik, Glossar, Dokumentation, Bibliographie 1973–1983* (Nomos Verlagsgesellschaft, Baden-Baden, 1983).

   See in particular J. I. Coffey,'M(B)FR-Status and Prospects', *Oesterreichische Zeitschrift fuer Aussenpolitik*, 17 (1977), pp. 199–213; P. Terrence Hopmann, 'Bridging the Gaps: Problems and Possibilities for Agreement in the Vienna Negotiations on Force Reductions in Central Europe', in Karl E. Birnbaum (ed), *Arms Control in Europe: Problems and Prospects* (Laxenburg Paper No. 1, Austrian Institute for International Affairs, Laxenburg 1980), pp. 65–78; Lothar Ruehl, *MBFR: Lessons and Problems* (Adelphi Paper No. 176, 1982); Jonathan Dean, 'MBFR: From Apathy to Accord', *International Security*, 7, No. 4 (Spring 1983), pp. 116–39; Stanley Sloan, *East-West Troop Reductions in Europe: Is Agreement Possible?* (US Government Printing Office, Washington, 1983); Richard F. Staar, 'The MBFR Process and Its Prospects', *Orbis*, 27, no. 4, (Winter 1984), pp. 999–1009.
2. Since the Warsaw Pact took exception to the Western concept underlying MBFR, the Vienna negotiations officially deal with MURFAAMCE – Mutual Reduction of Forces and Armaments and Associated Measures in Central Europe. The acronym M(B)FR used in this paper is meant to take this disagreement into account.
3. Ruehl, op. cit., pp. 3–6.
4. Cf. O. Khlestov, 'Mutual Force Reductions in Europe', *Survival*, 16 (1974), pp. 293–8.

5. As outlined by Ambassador Thomas Hammond (Canada) at a press conference in Vienna on 19 April 1984. I am indebted to Dr John Karch from the US Delegation to the M(B)FR negotiations for his assistance in obtaining information on the most recent developments at the talks. For a critical appraisal of this proposal see P. Terrence Hopmann, 'Behind Reagan's Arms Control Rhetoric', *Christian Science Monitor*, 29 October 1984.
6. At least by Ambassador Hammond at the above-mentioned press conference.
7. Mr Jozef Sestak (Czechoslovakia) at a press conference in Vienna on 27 September 1984.
8. Soviet press statement in Vienna on 14 February 1984.
9. For technical reasons the author was unable to include later developments, in particular the NATO proposal of 5 December 1985 (in which the insistence on prior agreement on data was dropped in exchange for additional verification measures) and the Eastern draft agreement tabled on 20 February 1986. Neither move succeeded in breaking the stalemate. Nor was it possible to deal with recent Soviet and Warsaw Pact initiatives, notably the Budapest Appeal of 11 June 1986 and Western responses to them. Nonetheless, the basic conclusions drawn by the author still appear to be valid.
10. Cf. Richard E. Darilek, 'Building Confidence and Security in Europe: The Road to and from Stockholm', *Washington Quarterly*, 8, no. 1, (Winter 1985), pp. 131–40. See also Johan Jørgen Holst/Karen Alette Melander, 'European Security and Confidence-building Measures', *Survival*, 19 (1977), pp. 146–54; Jonathan Alford, *The Future of Arms Control III: Confidence-Building Measures* (Adelphi Paper No. 149, 1979); Dieter S. Lutz/Erwin Mueller (eds), *Vertrauensbildende Massnahmen: Zur Theorie und Praxis einer sicherheitspolitischen Strategie* (Nomos Verlagsgesellschaft, Baden-Baden, 1982); F. Stephen Larrabee/Dietrich Stobbe (eds), *Confidence-Building Measures in Europe* (Institute for East–West Security Studies, New York, 1983).
11. Adam Daniel Rotfeld, 'From Helsinki to Madrid: Conference on Security and Co-operation in Europe': Documents 1973–1983 (Polish Institute of International Affairs, Co-operative Publishers, Warsaw – no year of publication given).
12. Coffey, op. cit., pp. 209–10; Hopmann, op. cit. (footnote 1), p. 77; Ruehl op. cit., pp. 6, 30, 36.
13. As suggested by British Foreign Secretary David Owen who called for a conference of NATO and Warsaw Pact Foreign Ministers to provide the political impetus necessary to break the M(B)FR deadlock back in 1978. Mutz (ed.), op. cit., p. 44.
14. As stated by Chancellor Helmut Schmidt; Ruehl, op. cit., p. 26.
15. Ruehl, op. cit., pp. 35–6; Dean, op. cit., p. 118.
16. Phil Williams, 'Whatever Happened to the Mansfield Amendment?' *Survival*, 18 (1976), pp. 146–53.
17. Especially those of Senators Sam Nunn and Ted Stevens. Cf. Mutz (ed.), op. cit., pp. 55, 59.

18 CDE, MBFR, and the Arms Control Process

Stanley R. Sloan

The 'arms control process' from 1980 until 1987 produced no new arms control and has even lost many of the attributes one would normally associate with a 'process'. This was a substantial change from the 1970s, when Western arms control policies sought, with at least some success, to begin reducing by progressive increments the levels of nuclear and non-nuclear armaments while attempting to make war less likely by restructuring the East–West armed confrontation in Europe.

After the failure of the SALT II treaty to win ratification in the United States, and given the general impasse in other arms control areas, many analysts suggested that the arms control process had given rise to false expectations that a mutual interest in arms control would help regulate US–Soviet and East–West relations more generally. This charge may in fact be warranted to the extent that public expectations exceeded the realistic ability of the arms control process to change fundamentally the adversarial nature of US–Soviet relations. But the internal goals of the process were relatively modest. Policy usually focused on the 'do-able' rather than on the desirable: an approach that opened the way to possible agreements, but perhaps also invited disappointment with the results and, by implication, with the process itself.

The arms control process was initially called into question by critics of the SALT II treaty. For these critics, the arms control process had produced an agreement that granted the Soviet Union unwarranted advantages and which was even more objectionable given Soviet activities in the Third World.

Subsequently, the European anti-nuclear movement and the counterpart freeze movement in the United States also reflected impatience with the limited goals and accomplishments of the 'traditional' arms control approach. Peace activists sought more dramatic gains than the process seemed to offer. Saying 'no' to INF or 'freezing' the levels of existing nuclear systems were in part expressions of frustration with the decreasing likelihood that the traditional arms control process would produce meaningful limitations on nuclear or conventional weapons. This sentiment swelled the ranks of those who argued for unilateral steps toward disarmament by disavowing nuclear arms, declaring unilateral nuclear free zones, and so forth.

While the Reagan Administration has re-established the trappings of the arms control process, the President has set his policy sights on objectives well beyond the means of traditional arms control. The current US position on nuclear weapons and arms control is influenced primarily by a philosophy of self-reliance (unilateralism) and inspired by the idealistic objective of eliminating all nuclear weapons. The combination of unilateralism and idealism in the President's approach – an ironic mirror image of some perspectives on the left – inhibited progress along traditional arms control lines toward US–Soviet strategic or INF arms control.

Policies of the Soviet Union have in the past also undermined the traditonal arms control process. Moscow's historic reluctance to cut back in any substantial way the prolific production of its defence complex; its unwillingness to accept the legitimacy of US extended deterrence for Western Europe; its frequently propagandist approach to arms control issues; its unwillingness to negotiate nuclear arms control issues for over a year; and its unreasonable demands for bans on SDI research all appeared to reflect Moscow's greater interest in objectives other than re-invigorating the arms control process. Now, while Soviet leader Mikhail Gorbachev may be revising some of these approaches, his idealistic goal of eliminating nuclear weapons – just like that of President Reagan – falls outside the realm of the possible in an arms control framework.

Summing up, the arms control process has been battered from the left and the right; it is something of a rudderless ship on the sea of confrontation, with no wind in its sails and no compass to guide it in new directions.

In spite of these unpromising circumstances, two remnants of the arms control process of the 1970s have survived into the mid-1980s. They are the negotiations on mutual and balanced force reductions (MBFR),[1] and the Conference on Disarmament in Europe (CDE), child of the Conference on Security and Co-operation in Europe (CSCE).[2] Both sets of negotiations carry forward an essential ingredient of the 'traditional' arms control process: their purported goal is to create a more stable European security system by restraining the military confrontation through controls on and incremental reductions of military forces. Their essential premise, therefore, is that co-operation between the antagonists can enhance mutual security. An unexceptional premise, perhaps, but one which does not currently appear to dominate either the US or the Soviet approach to the nuclear arms control negotiations in Geneva.

Ironically, these two 'survivors' have developed in part as competing rather than as complementary negotiating forums. Much of the impetus for CDE was provided by France's rejection of the MBFR forum due to its 'bloc-to-bloc' nature. The original French proposal for a CDE was widely seen, among other things, as an attempt 'to drown MBFR in the pool of CDE'.[3]

Neither the flow of the MBFR talks nor the CSCE/CDE process were broken by the 1983–4 Soviet boycott of strategic and intermediate-range nuclear negotiations with the United States. The Soviet decision to continue these talks suggests that Moscow was sensitive to the importance the European countries – East and West – attach to the process of negotiations represented by these two sets of talks. In fact, the interest of the European countries in East–West dialogue has probably been the main force keeping MBFR alive in spite of the extended deadlock over data and verification issues, and was principally responsible for the advent of and progress in the CDE negotiations.

But while the CDE reached an agreement in 1986 on a package of confidence building measures accompanied a declaration on the non-use of force, the MBFR negotiations are in more perilous political shape than ever. The West Germans, who, more than any other Western participant in the negotiations have kept a fire burning under MBFR, have retrenched substantially.[4] West German Foreign Minister Genscher has in recent years given CDE precedence over MBFR in the FRG's foreign policy, apparently seeing the CDE forum as a way to re-involve the French in discussions of European arms control issues, while avoiding the 'special zones' problem that MBFR poses for Germany.[5] Now the approach of the West German defence ministry has also apparently cooled toward the Vienna negotiations, shifting the overall balance of the West German attitude distinctly toward scepticism.

Because the West Germans have joined the ranks of the sceptics there is virtually no political momentum behind MBFR. The shift in the West German position tends to reinforce the position of the Office of the Secretary of Defence (OSD) in the United States.

According to some reports, the OSD argued in the mid-1980s that the MBFR negotiations should be de-emphasised, for example by putting the United States representation in the hands of the US Ambassador to Austria, or by merging MBFR with CDE.[6]

The arcane nature of the MBFR negotiations has removed them almost entirely from the public view and even from the active agenda of most security policy analysts. Although there are a number of theoretical ways out of impasse on the 'data problem' (the longstanding East–West disagreement over how many troops the Warsaw Pact has in the potential reduction area), neither side appears to have the political will to make them work.[7] Continuing Soviet objections to the sort of intrusive verification measures that the West would require is based on fundamental perceptions of security requirements, deeply rooted in the nature of Soviet society and government. And, the CDE is slowly but surely intruding on MBFR territory. The possible expansion of confidence-building measures beyond the first CDE agreement would accomplish in at least a limited sense some of the MBFR goals of providing greater reassurance about military activities in Central Europe. Perhaps more importantly, the CDE is providing a framework for East–West discussion of European security issues. Because the CDE is providing this forum, the MBFR talks have lost at least part of their original justification.

The CDE has other advantages. From a Western point of view, the inclusion of the Western portions of the Soviet Union in the coverage of CDE measures is a very positive feature of CDE versus the more narrow MBFR area.[8] The fact that the CDE area is larger than the potential area of application for an MBFR agreement is helpful to the West Germans. France is an active participant in CDE, and the forum therefore more fully represents the main players in the European security game.

In 1986 a number of developments intensified the relationship between CDE and MBFR. First, in June 1986 the Warsaw Pact endorsed a sweeping Soviet proposal for reduction of nuclear and conventional armaments across Europe. The Pact proposed cuts in virtually all categories of military forces from the Atlantic to the Urals, including a cut in the numerical strength of NATO and Warsaw Pact forces by 110 000 to 150 000 troops within one or two years, leading to an eventual 25 per cent reduction in NATO and Warsaw Pact ground forces and their armaments by the early 1990s. The proposal appeared to bypass the stalemated MBFR negotiations. The Pact said that its ideas could be discussed either in MBFR, CDE, or some new forum. But most observers saw the initiative as a sign of Soviet disinterest in continuing the MBFR talks.

Meanwhile, the CDE was nearing a conclusion in Stockholm. In September 1986 the delegates reached agreement on a package of confidence- and security-building measures, expanding the scope of similar measures that the CSCE participants had agreed in 1975. The provisions for notification of military activities, invitation of observers to military exercises, and advance notification of large-scale military activities were all made obligatory (compliance with the 1975 measures was voluntary). Delegates agreed on provisions for on-site inspection from the air or ground to verify compliance with agreed measures. Because of the CDE's pan-European coverage, the European portion of Soviet territory is included in all aspects of the accord, even the on-site inspection requirements. Successful conclusion of this meeting left open the question of whether or not there should be a second-stage CDE and, if so, what it should cover. That issue is currently being considered at the CSCE review conference in Vienna, also the site of the MBFR talks.

Finally, following a six-month study of conventional arms control approaches, the NATO foreign ministers agreed in December 1986 to propose new conventional arms control negotiations with the Warsaw Pact focusing on all of Europe that presumably would replace the more narrowly defined MBFR negotiations. However, the agreement apparently papered over continuing differences between the United States and France. The United States prefers a bloc-to-bloc framework for such talks, while France would like the new approach to be developed within the nonbloc CDE framework between members of the two alliances but not the alliances themselves. In spite of these differences, the twenty-three NATO and Warsaw Pact countries participating in the CSCE review conference began meeting regularly in February 1987 to discuss the modalities for new conventional arms control negotiations.

East and West therefore appear to be cautiously working toward some changes in the way in which they approach conventional arms control issues. They remain divided, however, on acceptable terms for force reductions. The question is whether changes in negotiating venue and approach will stimulate resolution of problems that have stalemated the MBFR talks, or whether, alternatively, possible reductions will simply be put off into the more distant future.

Whether or not there is a first-stage' MBFR agreement to conclude those negotiations, it seems likely that the discussion of NATO and

Warsaw Pact military forces will be shifted to some new or modified forum. The probable outcome is that the force reduction discussions will be moved in some fashion associated with the broader CDE umbrella.

The CDE has already taken away some of MBFR's thunder. The Stockholm measures provide opportunities for closer monitoring of Warsaw Pact activities and represent at least an embryonic form of East–West security co-operation. The Stockholm measures provide ways for the NATO and Warsaw Pact nations to manage their confrontation to avoid conflict and to reduce the chance that hostilities could begin as the result of accidents, misunderstandings, or miscalculations. As long as the CDE provides a framework for East–West discussion of European security issues, the MBFR talks lose another part of their original justification.

From a Western perspective, the CDE has other advantages. The inclusion of the Western portions of the Soviet Union in the coverage of CDE measures is a very positive feature of CDE versus the more narrow MBFR area. The fact that the CDE area is larger than the potential area of application for an MBFR agreement is helpful to the West Germans, who never were completely comfortable with MBFR's clear focus on German territory. Furthermore, because France supports and actively participates in the CDE forum, the CDE therefore more fully represents the main players in the European security game.

From a Western alliance management perspective, the United States has less influence over the development of CDE than it does in bloc-to-bloc or superpower-to-superpower negotiations. However, it is also able to share the burden of difficult negotiations with its allies and is not as vulnerable to charges either of selling allied interests down the river or of ignoring avenues to possible accord. The allies are in a position to protect and advance their interests as they see them and can participate directly in the overall conduct of the negotiations. These factors, plus the demonstrated success of CDE, have strengthened the case for finally abandoning MBFR, leaving it to the CDE to work toward limiting armed forces in Europe and building a more stable European security system.

But what would be lost if something like MBFR were abandoned altogether? Although MBFR's bloc-to-bloc nature may be politically distasteful to the French, it is considered by many experts to be a far better framework for implementing and verifying actual reductions of forces and armaments than would the geographically wide and politically diffuse CDE framework. The fact that the CDE includes the European neutrals as well as NATO and Warsaw Pact states makes it difficult if not impossible to conceive how significant reduction approaches could be applied within this framework. Furthermore, while the CSCE/CDE framework expresses the wish to overcome the division of Europe, the MBFR framework embodies the reality of the current division of Europe between NATO and Warsaw Pact nations. Given that neither NATO nor the Warsaw Pact is likely to disband or be washed away by the tides of *détente* in the near future, it is useful, perhaps even necessary, to have at least one negotiating framework which reflects this reality and attempts to deal with its consequences.

The problem, after all, is not the military strategies and forces of neutrals, Sweden, Finland, Switzerland and Austria. The problem is the confrontation between the forces of NATO and Warsaw Pact nations deployed in central Europe. These opposing forces symbolise and reinforce the confrontation between the competing ideological and power groupings; they create the risk of escalation from an incident to conventional engagement; from conventional conflict to limited nuclear exchanges; and, ultimately, from limited nuclear exchanges to global nuclear war.

One of the greatest threats to stability in Europe is the large number of nuclear weapons of various ranges deployed in forward positions with NATO and Warsaw Pact forces. Current deployments and force relationships make it likely that nuclear weapons would come into play at a very early stage of conflict in central Europe. Although nuclear weapons are not currently on the agenda in the MBFR negotiations, a bloc-to-bloc framework will probably be required to deal with this issue at some point in the future[9]

These arguments, however, do not preclude some possibilities for constructively relating force reduction talks to the CDE framework. Under certain circumstances, allowing the CDE to embrace force reduction negotiations might provide a positive dynamic for both sets of talks. Such a merger could make possible linkages between the two negotiations that could mitigate some of the current shortcomings of each.

CDE's association with East–West force reduction efforts would allow CDE to continue to construct a more comprehensive confide-nce-building regime throughout Europe while leaving actual reductions of arms and armaments to the narrower NATO–Warsaw Pact talks. The enlargement of MBFR through association with CDE might help ease West German concerns about isolation in a narrow MBFR reduction zone. The application of more extensive confidence-building measures to forces in the Western military districts of the Soviet Union through the CDE might help compensate for the substantial geographic advantage the Soviet Union enjoys over the United States in the central European military equation.

An agreement reached in the NATO–Warsaw Pact forum could be acknowledged and 'blessed' by all CDE participants, including those who do not participate in the bloc-to-bloc negotiations. It might even prove possible for the neutral participants in CDE to provide facilitative assistance for monitoring of compliance with a troop reduction accord. For example, exit-entry monitoring posts to verify compliance could be manned by a contingent consisting of a host NATO or Warsaw Pact officer, an observer from the opposing alliance, and an observer from a neutral CDE participant.

By all appearances, conventional arms control discussions are at an important crossroads. The likely adjustments in negotiating forums and procedures will probably require some time to sort out. This suggests that there will be no negotiated troop cuts in the near future unless a breakthrough is accomplished toward a first-stage accord along the lines currently being discussed in the Vienna MBFR talks. Both sides say that they would like to make the transition to different arrangements on a positive note. Given the track record of these negotiations, and the uncertain state of US–Soviet arms control negotiations more generally, however, it would be unwise to count on substantial progress toward East–West troop cuts in the near future.

Notes

1. The chapters in this volume by Dean and Neuhold provide additional background information on the evolution of the MBFR negotiations. A variety of sources are available for more detailed information on the history of the negotiations. One valuable contemporary source is the record of the Hearing held before the Subcommittee on International Security and Scientific Affairs of the Committee on Foreign Affairs, US House of Representatives on 22 September 1983, entitled 'Status of Mutual and Balanced Force Reduction (MBFR) Negotiations'. The hearing includes testimony by then-US Ambassador to MBFR Hon. Morton Abramowitz and by one of his predecessors Hon. Jonathan Dean. The Hearing's appendixes include the text of a Congressional Research Service report prepared for the subcommittee by Stanley R. Sloan entitled 'East–West Troop Reductions in Europe: Is Agreement

Possible?' and several of Ambassador Dean's published articles on MBFR. Another excellent source of background information on MBFR is John G. Keliher's book entitled *The Negotiations on Mutual and Balanced Force Reductions, The Search for Arms Control in Central Europe*, published by Pergamon Press (New York) in 1980.

2. For background on CSCE, particularly concerning confidence building measures, see *Confidence-Building Measures in Europe*, edited by F. Stephen Larrabee and Dietrich Stobbe, published by the Institute for East–West Studies, New York, 1983. For ongoing detailed coverage of CSCE and MBFR arms control issues refer to the 'Arms Control Reporter', Institute for Defence and Disarmament Studies, Brookline, Mass.
3. US Congress. Senate. Committee on Foreign Relations, 'Prospects for the Vienna Force Reduction Talks. Report prepared by the Foreign Affairs and National Defence Division, Congressional Research Service (by Stanley R. Sloan) 95th Congress, 2nd Session, p. 18.
4. The tone was reflected in a speech by Lother Ruehl, State Secretary in the West German Ministry of Defence, to the 1985 NATO Symposium at the National Defence University. Similar concerns were also expressed by other West German defence officials in private discussions with the author.
5. The Federal Republic, virtually from the beginning of NATO discussions of troop reductions in Europe, has been concerned that an agreement might establish a special zone limiting the FRG's sovereignty more than that of other participants.
6. Such reports were prominent in the Washington MBFR rumour mill in the spring of 1985.
7. For a revealing discussion of the 'data problem' see Jonathan Dean's testimony before the House Committee on Foreign Affairs as reported in 'Status of Mutual and Balanced Force Reduction (MBFR) Negotiations', op. cit., pp. 20–23, 27–32.
8. The MBFR area for reductions includes, on the Eastern side, East Germany, Poland, and Czechoslovakia and, on the Western side, West Germany, the Netherlands, Belgium and Luxembourg.
9. Elsewhere in this volume, P. Terrence Hopmann discusses some of the linkages between the conventional confrontation in Europe and the risks of nuclear war.

19 Conventional Arms Control and the Nuclear Weapons Dilemma in Europe

P. Terrence Hopmann

INTRODUCTION: SEVEN PROPOSITIONS ABOUT CONVENTIONAL AND NUCLEAR ARMS IN EUROPE

This paper sets forth some fundamental propositions about the role of conventional arms control in connection with the nuclear weapons dilemma in Europe. A fundamental underlying premise of this analysis is that nuclear and non-nuclear issues in European security are inextricably linked with one another. Therefore, they should not be separated either conceptually or at the level of policy analysis and prescription. An additional basic assumption is that the attainment of an appropriate security regime in Europe is hindered by the 'security dilemma', in which measures that enhance the security of one side in the East–West conflict are often perceived by the other as detracting from their own security. Therefore, a regime intended to enhance 'common security' throughout the continent must be designed so as to reduce rather than exacerbate this dilemma.

The analysis of the requirements for confidence-building measures and arms control rests on several propositions that have been introduced by numerous other authors in this volume. These propositions will be summarised here briefly in order to lay the foundation for the subsequent analysis of confidence-building and arms control initiatives.

Most of the propositions that will be presented below cannot be 'tested' in any normal sense with empirical data. By their very nature, they involve events that have never occurred, and where very few if any similar events have ever taken place in the past. Therefore, analysis of strategy and arms control in the presence of nuclear weapons (even when the central focus is on conventional weapons, but in a region where nuclear weapons are also present) must necessarily be theoretical. Furthermore, some of these propositions also contain normative elements, and it is clear that analysts with different values might well arrive at different conclusions. Therefore, these propositions must be evaluated largely on the basis of their logical consistency and their plausability, given what we know about the nature of modern weapons technology and political systems. They are presented here largely to provoke discussion, by laying out some basic arguments in terms as stark as seems possible.

Proposition 1. The only role of nuclear weapons anywhere – including in Europe – is to deter their use by others against the territory of one's own state or of one's allies

This proposition reflects the fundamental belief, reaffirmed in this volume by Rear Admiral John Marshall Lee, that nuclear weapons are not useful instruments of military power or of political influence. The destructive consequences of their use are likely to be so great in proportion to any other objectives that their utilisation for any other purpose than to deter their use by others is likely neither to be credible to potential enemies nor politically tolerable in any society. Therefore, in this context, so-called tactical or battlefield nuclear weapons represent a contradiction in terms.

This proposition is especially striking in Europe. NATO's 'flexible response' strategy proposes initiating the use of nuclear weapons if NATO's forces are being overrun by a Warsaw Pact conventional attack. Since the NATO alliance is essentially defensive in its goals, if it decides to use these weapons on the battlefield, they must necessarily be used in large numbers on West European, especially West German, territory. That simple fact is likely to mean that any victim of a conventional attack will be self-deterred from launching such a nuclear response. Knowing this, a potential aggressor may not be deterred in the absence of an adequate conventional capability on the part of NATO. While nuclear weapons may add an additional element of uncertainty for an attacker, they also add a significant element of risk for the defender.

Proposition 2. Any use of nuclear weapons runs an excessively high risk of escalating to the level of all-out nuclear war

Recent discussions of limited nuclear war have suggested that it might be possible to terminate a nuclear conflict before major, civilisation-threatening damage had occurred. While this is perhaps possible, it is by no means assured. A variety of research on crisis decision-making under high stress, summarised herein by Lincoln Bloomfield, certainly suggests that calm, rational decision making is likely to be extremely difficult under such conditions. After the outbreak of a conflict in Europe, decisions will almost certainly have to be made in short time and under conditions of high threat and intense pressure, all of which militate against making a controlled response.[1] Furthermore, the possible loss of communications, command, and control could mean that it would be impossible to negotiate a termination of a war once it had become nuclear, or to order the conflict terminated even if such a decision were reached.

Therefore, it is extremely risky to plan in advance on the assumption that one can control escalation once a nuclear conflict has begun. Of course, if deterrence does break down and a conflict becomes nuclear, all efforts should be made to try to terminate it as soon as possible, and this can be aided by the creation of mechanisms for crisis control, established and in place prior to the outbreak of any incident. But it would be foolhearty to assume in advance that this objective could be accomplished.

Proposition 3. While the major objective of national security policy and military force must be to prevent the outbreak of any kind of war, if this fails and war does break out, a nuclear war is likely to be far more destructive than a conventional war

While the idea has become popular in some quarters in Europe in recent years that all wars in Europe are equally bad, and therefore must be deterred through the threat to resort to ultimate force,[2] it is highly likely that a nuclear war would escalate out of control. Therefore, a nuclear war is likely to destroy human civilisation as we know it, either directly or due to long-term effects such as the 'nuclear winter'. Without wishing to suggest that conventional wars are in any sense acceptable events, the fact remains that at least there is a reasonable likelihood that human civilisation could recover from one, just as it did from the immensely destructive two world wars of this century. While any war in Europe would have far-reaching and terrible consequences, one still ought not to lose sight of the different likely consequences for the whole of human civilisation between an all-out nuclear war and a conventional conflict.

Proposition 4. Deterrence in Europe is more likely to fail, not as a result of a deliberate breach of the peace, but through the escalation of an incident that extends beyond the initial expectations of any participants

Most military planning in Western Europe seems to be based upon the assumption that the next war is likely to break out in the same way as the last war in Europe, by a blitzkrieg attack from Warsaw Pact forces most likely directed against West Germany. Therefore, NATO's emphasis on 'forward defense' is designed to deal with this kind of assault, to prevent it from penetrating deep into West German territory. Although such a scenario is theoretically possible, it is none the less extremely unlikely. The possibility that any such major assault might escalate to nuclear war would seem to be too great for any sensible Soviet leader to even contemplate running the risk.

By contrast, a far more likely scenario for the outbreak of war would entail some political incident that turned unexpectedly to violence. This could include an incident at the inter-German border, such as unrest arising from within East Germany that spilled across the border in one way or another. The problem that this situation creates for Western security is that military preparations designed to halt the major assault may be quite inappropriate for dealing with such a situation. Indeed, measures such as the forward placement of nuclear weapons, which may maximise deterrence against the blitzkrieg, may force military commanders into a difficult choice between 'using' or 'losing' their nuclear weapons early in a conflict. Such a situation can obviously contribute to turning a serious, but potentially manageable, situation into all-out nuclear war. Indeed, the management of such incidents requires instead a military capability to hold off advancing forces with the lowest level of military force possible, while trying to buy time for negotiations and conflict resolution procedures to achieve results. Otherwise, NATO runs a serious risk of turning any conflict into the one it was prepared to fight, even if the incident that sparked the conflict would not normally seem to be a cause for which it is worth running the risk of nuclear holocaust.

Proposition 5. A mutual agreement between East and West in Europe that neither side will use nuclear weapons first, accompanied by concrete measures on both sides to reinforce such an agreement, would reinforce the firebreak between conventional and nuclear war

A mutual 'no-first-use' posture, as recently proposed by the American 'gang of four',[3] may reduce deterrence slightly in Europe, but it does carry with it the important advantage of making the firebreak between conventional and nuclear war more pronounced. While escalation is possible in any military conflict in Europe, it is still this firebreak which provides the most clearcut threshold at which escalation can be halted before reaching the ultimate calamity. Therefore, as Admiral Lee argues in his chapter, it is in everyone's interest that this firebreak be kept as clear as possible. Furthermore, this would force NATO to pay more attention to the requirements for an adequate, affordable, and non-provocative conventional defence, which in the end would provide a more credible deterrent than relying upon the suicidal threat to use nuclear weapons.

Proposition 6. Avoidance of the outbreak of conventional war, and, if it does break out, of its escalation across the nuclear threshold, depends in large measure on the perception by all parties of a stable balance of defensive conventional forces

Conventional war, as already noted, is not extremely likely to occur in Central Europe. Both members of NATO and the Warsaw Pact are aware of the fact that the stakes are so high and the forces so great that a chance of escalation to the nuclear level always exists, even in the presence of a 'no-first-use' agreement. Furthermore, even in the absence of escalation across the nuclear threshold, all parties recognise that a conventional war is likely to be extremely destructive and costly. Therefore, neither party is likely to initiate intentionally a conventional attack unless they believe that they can win quickly and decisively, with minimal costs to themselves and minimal risks of nuclear escalation. These conditions are likely to exist only if there is an extreme imbalance in both the quantity and quality of conventional forces in Central Europe, in which one side or the other perceives that it can achieve such a clearcut and rapid victory. Of course, if one side or the other perceives that such an imbalance exists, this may be sufficient to destabilise mutual deterrence in Europe, even if the objective distribution of capabilities is in fact not so one-sided.

As previously argued, conventional war could also occur in Europe, not through a deliberate surprise attack, but rather through the escalation of smaller incidents that got out of control, leading to the introduction of larger units of conventional military force. In the event of such unintentional outbreaks, the military balance in Central Europe may be of substantial significance in averting escalation across the nuclear threshold. In the event of any substantial inequality in quantity and/or quality of forces, the side that initially found itself at a disadvantage in the conflict might be tempted to initiate the use of nuclear weapons in order to try to seize a quick advantage and reverse the flow of battle. Therefore, conventional asymmetries which can produce these kinds of pressures to escalate must be avoided if at all possible. A stable conventional balance is thus essential not only to avert a surprise attack but also to bring a quick halt to an inadvertent outbreak of fighting before it crosses the nuclear threshold.

Proposition 7. Mutual perceptions of a stable conventional balance in Europe are eroded both by gross inequalities in quantity of forces on opposing sides and by a rapidly escalating conventional arms race, especially in offensive technologies

Deterrence at any level requires the ability to persuade a potential aggressor that they will stand to lose more from attacking than they expect to gain. Therefore, anything which promotes a perception that one side or the other could conceivably 'win' a conventional war obviously destabilises deterrence. It does so both by making the party having an advantage in either of these categories more likely to attack and by making the party that perceives itself inferior in conventional forces to consider rapid escalation to the nuclear level. Conventional superiority, therefore, does not necessarily offer a clearcut advantage; indeed, it may be disadvantageous even for its possessor if it prompts the opponent to contemplate a rapid crossing of the nuclear threshold.

Stability in Europe requires some significant effort to reduce the widely perceived quantitative advantages possessed by the Warsaw Pact relative to NATO in categories such as manpower, tanks, tactical aircraft, and other similar systems. To provide a stable deterrent, NATO must have sufficient conventional forces to be able to convince a potential aggressor that the defence can hold against an attack, without at the same time being provocative and thus unduly exacerbating East–West tensions.

Therefore, as Richard Smoke argues in his chapter, the solution to the problem of conventional defence does not lie in a Western response of developing and deploying a whole new generation of technically sophisticated, provocative weapons, such as those called for by the 'Air-Land Battle' concept. Because these weapons will invariably be perceived as being offensive in purpose, and because they will be perceived as threatening to overcome even significant numerical advantages, they will almost certainly set off a spiral of new conventional weapons being developed and deployed by both sides in Central Europe. Because the outcome of such an arms race cannot be known in advance, and because, even if neither party achieves a clearcut superiority in such weapons, a quantitative weapons race will lead to far greater capabilities for destruction in the event a conventional war breaks out in Europe, it will almost invariably destabilise the current condition of mutual deterrence at the conventional level in Europe. Therefore, avoiding such an offensive technological race at the conventional level is at least as important as improving the quantitative balance of forces in that region.

CONVENTIONAL ARMS CONTROL AND THE NUCLEAR THRESHOLD

Conventional arms control in Europe is a necessary complement to nuclear arms control – to prevent the outbreak of conventional war and to reduce the likelihood of its escalation to the nuclear level. It needs to include a number of different kinds of specific measures in order to achieve the major objectives of strengthening conventional deterrence and avoiding escalation.

First, negotiations can attempt to establish a greater quantitative parity in forces, especially in the Central European zone surrounding the two Germanies. This has been the primary objective of the Vienna negotiations on Mutual and Balanced Force Reductions (MBFR) in Central Europe. Here the major focus has been on establishing a common manpower ceiling in the central region, with agreement having been achieved at least in principle on a ceiling of 900 000 combined air and ground personnel and a subceiling of 700 000 ground personnel. Yet the forces and geographical territory covered in these negotiations have been very much circumscribed, and greater success might be obtained through a broadening of the agenda in either of two directions.

One possibility is to go beyond a focus on manpower parity to try to establish greater parity in overall force structures. It is certainly true that the introduction of armaments into serious consideration in Vienna offers a number of additional and undesirable complexities, especially for systems such as aircraft that can be easily moved in and out of any control zone. Yet an expansion of the scope of these negotiations would also bring into the discussions some areas of greater psychological concern, including Western preoccupation with Warsaw Pact advantages in tanks and other armoured vehicles. In addition, it would help to restrict the rapid expansion of entirely new kinds of weapons systems, which are especially dreaded by Warsaw Pact states.

A second possibility is to expand the geographic scope. Many Germans, for example, are very much concerned about the implications of reductions in and around the two Germanies, while no restrictions would apply in nearby territory such as Hungary or the Western military districts of the Soviet Union. Others in the East have expressed some concern that territories of countries such as France are not covered in the Vienna negotiations. Therefore, a forum with broader participation, such as the Conference on Disarmament in Europe (CDE), might be a more appropriate framework. On the other hand, shifting the issues from MBFR to CDE at this point would also mean that a considerable number of understandings already reached among a smaller group of states might be jeopardised by introducing them into the context of the larger conference. In addition, there are significant advantages from retaining the inter-alliance forum in Vienna, especially to deal with issues like armaments limitations, perhaps including tactical nuclear weapons, that almost certainly cannot be negotiated in an all-European forum.

Whatever the region covered or whatever the scope of an agreement, the essential point is that the goal must be a more widespread perception of parity of conventional forces in Europe. Given that an attacker generally needs to possess a substantial numerical superiority of conventional forces in order to have a satisfactory prospect of success, approximate force parity, even if restricted only to manpower (which, after all, is required to make use of armour, artillery, etc.), would substantially reduce fears of conventional aggression on the European continent.

Progress in the Vienna negotiations on Mutual and Balanced Force Reductions, which opened in 1973, has been extremely slow, and agreement has seemed to be most elusive. Indeed, since about 1980, the process of negotiation has frequently been characterised by 'one step forward, two steps backward'. The major obstacle to agreement, as noted in this volume by both Jonathan Dean and Hanspeter Neuhold, has been the disagreement about the current size of Warsaw Pact forces stationed in the reduction zone in Eastern Europe. Since agreement on these data has been impossible, the only remaining solution seems to be to agree to achieve the common ceiling, and then to seek to verify whether both sides have complied through more intensive observation on the ground. The Warsaw Pact has on several occasions indicated a tentative willingness to accept some intrusive verification measures, perhaps including fixed points where troops enter and leave the zone, manned by foreign observers, as well as a limited number of inspections of forces remaining within the zone.

In November 1985, NATO proposed an initial reduction of some 5000 US troops and 11 500 Soviet troops. Following this first stage reduction, 30 annual inspections would take place on each side's territory over the next three years to try to reduce the discrepancies between NATO's and the Warsaw Pact's data on the size of Eastern forces in the zone. However, at the same time the West rescinded an earlier commitment to continue reductions beyond initial Soviet and American withdrawals, and they apparently dropped insistence on the common ceiling as a goal to be achieved. Given the very limited nature of reductions proposed, and the extensive number of required inspections, such a position is unlikely to be acceptable to the Warsaw Pact. However, a similar arrangement that reduced the number of inspections to a reasonable quantity, while also retaining full commitments by all parties on both sides to reduce to the common ceiling, might provide a way around the remaining obstacles. If this were done, then an initial MBFR agreement might assure a quantitative parity of conventional manpower between NATO and the Warsaw Pact in the Central European area.

Second, it is necessary to do more through conventional arms control than just to achieve quantitative parity. The situation could become extremely unstable if a qualitative arms race took place, even in the context of quantitative equality. Yet this is certainly possible if NATO moves ahead with plans for a sophisticated force of new offensive conventional weapons, accompanied by revised tactical concepts such as those called for in 'Air-Land Battle' or the 'Follow-On Forces Attack'. It is far more important that any technological developments that occur be restricted to the realm of measures designed to provide for the non-provocative defence of Western Europe against attack, of the kind proposed in this volume by Frank Barnaby and Egbert Boeker, without at the same time endangering the Eastern European's perception of the requirements for their own security. Although no such measures have been discussed in any formal negotiations to date, there is no reason in principle why such measures ought not to be added to the agendas of negotiations in either MBFR or CDE, or perhaps in a new negotiating forum established for that specific purpose.

Third, it is essential also to assure both NATO and the Warsaw Pact that the other is not preparing to launch a surprise attack. No matter what geographical scope might be agreed upon for the negotiations in Vienna, inevitably large numbers of forces stationed inside the Soviet Union and in the continental United States and at American bases world-wide will be available to reinforce units already stationed in Central Europe. The rapid or secretive augmentation of forces by either side in the Central European region could be extremely destabilising, and even under present circumstances the possibility that this could be done at any time undermines mutual confidence. Therefore, the agreement reached in the initial phase of CDE in Stockholm in September 1986 may be extremely valuable. Confidence- and security-building measures were adopted requiring advance notification of all activities outside garrisons involving more than 13 000 men, with compulsory invitation of observers if more than 17 000 men are involved. These measures should help to guard against rapid and circuitous buildups of conventional forces near the European dividing line. This agreement requires reporting of any large-scale troop movements into and out of the Central European region, as well as any large-scale manoeuvres taking place in the region, with provisions for inspections to see that such activities do not go unreported.

Additional confidence-building measures may play a prominent role in any future round of CDE. These could include actual constraints on the size of manoeuvres or of the number that could be held within a year's time. Additionally, measures for crisis control and reduction might be considered that would set up a permanent mechanism to facilitate the process of negotiation in the event of a crisis or threatening incident in Europe. In addition, security zones might be created along the East–West border within which deployments would be restricted to fixed passive barriers and highly mobile units equipped primarily with short-range, precision guided weapons; such zones might also be denuclearised altogether. Finally, measures concerning land troop movements and manoeuvres might also be extended to unrelated air and naval units in the vicinity of the European continent.

In other words, these measures should all be designed to provide reassurance in practice that neither side is planning to resort to force to resolve disputes. This can best be facilitated by demonstrating the non-provocative posture of a wide range of military activities. Over the long term, these measures are intended to reinforce habits of co-operation between both sides that highlight for both the common interests in avoiding war in Europe despite remaining differences across many issues. Only in this way can a regime be established that will eventually make it possible to overcome the 'security dilemma' and to develop measures that enhance the joint security of both sides simultaneously.

If present confidence-building measures are combined with the other two broad sets of measures, then they can work in tandem to reduce tensions and instabilities in Central Europe. Approximate force parity can remove the preconditions for any immediate military offensive. Limitations of the technological, conventional arms race can prevent quantitative stabilities from being upset by qualitative breakthroughs. And confidence-building measures provide assurances that currently established balances cannot be rapidly upset without giving substantial warning to the other side, thereby allowing compensatory responses by a potential victim of a surprise attack. Of particular importance for NATO is the fact that a violation by the Warsaw Pact of an East–West agreement would represent a clear and unambiguous threat, which would make it easier for the alliance to take the difficult political decision to mobilise prior to an actual attack. As Hans Günter Brauch, among others, has pointed out in his chapter, the early mobilisation of West German reserves and territorial defence forces could make a critical difference in resisting a Warsaw Pact attack by conventional means. This might also provide additional warning necessary to bring in American and British reinforcements to Europe from their home bases.

All three measures combined thus should make it extremely unlikely that either side would initiate a conventional attack against the other, thereby enhancing mutual conventional deterrence. But if a conflict did break out, especially through the escalation of some incident that began to get out of control, the more equal balance of forces in Central Europe should make a decisive victory by either side less likely. This in turn would make it far less likely that a potential 'loser' in a conventional war might decide to escalate to the nuclear level. It should also enhance the chances for the diplomatic negotiation process to be engaged before the conventional conflict had flamed out of control, thereby also restraining the pressures towards escalation.

NUCLEAR ARMS CONTROL AND STABILITY IN EUROPE

Conventional arms control agreements should be linked to measures of nuclear arms control in Europe – both to provide incentives for the success of conventional restraints and to reduce even further pressures for escalation across the nuclear threshold. Several measures of nuclear arms control are necessary both in order to make the conventional measures proposed above more politically acceptable and to reinforce the threshold between conventional and nuclear conflict.

First, a mutual agreement against the first use of nuclear weapons will further strengthen the firebreak by making it less likely that either side will rapidly cross the nuclear threshold. While such an agreement will never guarantee that nuclear war will not occur in Europe, it at least will put the political emphasis on avoiding escalation to the nuclear level. Furthermore, because such a provision has been strongly favoured in the past by the members of the Warsaw Pact, its acceptance by NATO might provide leverage in order to encourage the East to agree to more equitable force ceilings in Central Europe and to more intrusive verification procedures than they have been willing to accept to date. Politically, such an accord will also reinforce the necessity of stabilising the conventional arms balance in order to reduce fears in many Western countries that a 'no-first-use' policy will make conventional war significantly more likely.

Second, a 'nuclear free zone' along both sides of the Central European frontier will also strengthen the nuclear firebreak. Proposals such as those introduced by the Palme Commission in Europe might thus be given more serious consideration. This would especially require the withdrawal of all tactical and intermediate-range nuclear weapons away from the front lines. Beyond the obvious psychological benefits of reducing tensions resulting from the direct confrontation of nuclear-armed troops, this will also reduce pressures on both sides for rapid escalation of any conflict to the nuclear level. It will thus avoid placing nuclear weapons in a position where they must be used or lost early even in a relatively small non-nuclear confrontation in Central Europe. Such a concrete measure could also reinforce the commitment against the first use of nuclear weapons.

Third, negotiations should attempt to establish rough parity at the lowest possible level in both tactical and intermediate-range nuclear forces stationed on the European continent, including the British isles and the European parts of the Soviet Union. Such negotiations ought not to draw arbitrary distinctions among states, and should thus include participation by all nuclear states on the continent in both the negotiations and the limitation agreement. Similarly such negotiations should not draw arbitrary distinctions among different nuclear delivery vehicles in Europe, such as by isolating out intermediate-range missiles as in the 1981–3 INF negotiations; rather all tactical, medium- and intermediate-range delivery vehicles ought to be considered. The goal of such an agreement should be to assure that neither side can achieve any significant military advantage by crossing over the nuclear threshold. These limits might then provide the first step towards a quantitative reduction of European nuclear weapons on both sides. Furthermore, qualitative restraints, such as limitations on terminal guidance systems, ought to be introduced in order to prevent the stationing of first-strike capable weapons on the continent. Admittedly, however, such restraints may be difficult to realise in the aftermath of the deployment of Pershing II and Ground-Launched Cruise Missiles by the United States in Europe, both possessing such capabilities.

Fourth, range limitations ought to be placed on nuclear delivery vehicles based in Europe in an effort to reduce the threat that these weapons provide to command, communications, and control of both the Warsaw Pact and NATO. Again, such an arrangement may be difficult to achieve after deployment of Soviet SS-20s and American Pershing IIs and GLCMs. Yet an appropriate goal of the INF component in the Geneva negotiations should be to reduce and, if possible, to eliminate such intermediate-range delivery vehicles stationed in Europe. Such an agreement appeared within reach at the Reykjavik Summit in 1986, had not the US–Soviet disagreement about SDI intervened to prevent an accord on a largely unrelated issue, that is INFs in Europe. If the Soviets ease their position on this issue, as Gorbachev has suggested in February 1987, an agreement to eliminate INFs in Europe may be within reach.

CONCLUSION: TOWARDS A NEW SECURITY REGIME IN EUROPE

All of the previous arguments boil down to the central point that nuclear and conventional arms control in Europe need to be considered under one overall framework, which may lay the foundation for a European security regime that is capable of overcoming the security dilemma and approaching common security, for both East and West. Viewing these various measures as part of an overall regime poses several significant advantages.

First, both nuclear and conventional arms control measures are designed to serve essentially the same objective, namely deterring the outbreak of war and preventing escalation across the nuclear threshold. Therefore, they need to be considered conceptually as part of the same package.

Second, the combined consideration of these issues provides for trade-offs that often cannot be achieved when these issues are treated individually. Indeed, the asymmetries between NATO and the Warsaw Pact in force structures, weapons technologies, and military doctrines are often considered to be a major obstacle to arms control. However, these same asymmetries may be exploited to facilitate critical trade-offs across issues, creating new 'packages' of agreements. For example, Soviet interests in a 'no-first-use' agreement can be traded off against NATO's interest in parity of conventional manpower, by creating a package agreement that both will consider to be desirable, whereas alone each agreement has generally been opposed by one military bloc or the other.[4] They also can be politically reinforcing, for example, if conventional manpower parity also makes a no-first-use agreement more politically acceptable in Western Europe, since under these conditions neither side could exploit a significant conventional advantage. Improved confidence building measures, such as those adopted in 1986 at Stockholm, can also be perceived as aiding verification across a wide spectrum of arms control agreements, both conventional and nuclear.

Over the past thirty years arms control has moved from an unrealistic attempt to do everything in one neat package, under the heading of general and complete disarmament, to the opposite extreme of pursuing *ad hoc* agreements, seizing upon whatever opportunities for agreement present themselves. The step-by-step approach has run out of steam, since it often seems not to have added up to anything. Particularly in regard to the European area, an overarching theory of security as a guide to arms control has been almost totally absent, in partial contrast to the era of strategic arms control in the 1970s when the theory of mutual deterrence through mutual assured retaliation provided a common framework to guide negotiations. In order to make greater progress in negotiations in Europe, such a conceptual framework for a security regime needs to be created. While the details of specific agreements on confidence building and arms control may need to be negotiated separately and one at a time, it is evident that a more comprehensive view is required. The building blocks must clearly be seen to construct a stable edifice.

Therefore, without abandoning entirely the opportunistic approach which seeks to reach agreement whenever feasible, a great deal more attention needs to be paid to designing security regimes for Europe that will do two things: 1. interlock arms control at both the conventional and nuclear level in order to enhance deterrence and to raise and reinforce the nuclear threshold, and 2. to promote defence postures on both sides in Europe that provide each side with confidence in its own security without detracting significantly from the perceptions of security by the opposing side. Only then can arms control in Europe best achieve its goals of augmenting mutual deterrence of war and seeking to provide for the earliest termination of any hostilities that do break out, especially before they cross the forbidding nuclear threshold. Only then can it contribute to the longer-run goal of creating a stable security regime which may eventually make fears and perceptions of major war in Europe a thing of the past.

Notes

1. Ole R. Holsti, 'Time, Alternatives, and Communications: The 1914 and Cuban Missile Crises', in Charles F. Hermann (ed.), *International Crises: Insights from Behavioral Research* (New York: The Free Press, 1972), pp. 58–80.

2. See Karl Kaiser, Georg Leber, Alois Mertes, and Franz-Josef Schulze, 'Nuclear Weapons and the Preservation of Peace: A German Response', *Foreign Affairs*, vol. 60, no. 5, Summer 1982, p. 1164.
3. McGeorge Bundy, George F. Kennan, Robert S. McNamara, and Gerard Smith, 'Nuclear Weapons and the Atlantic Alliance', *Foreign Affairs*, vol. 60, no. 4, Spring 1982.
4. For further development of this position see P. Terrence Hopmann, 'The Path to No-First-Use: Conventional Arms Control', *World Policy Journal*, vol. 1, no. 2, Winter 1984.

Part VI

The Domestic Political Context

20 Labour's Defence and Security Policy

Mike Gapes

> At the heart of the problem is the dilemma that, if you wish to deter war by the fear that nuclear weapons will be used, you have to appear to be prepared to use them. But if you do so, and the enemy answers back, you are very much worse off than if you had not done so, if indeed you can be said to be there at all.
>
> To pose an unacceptable risk to the enemy automatically poses the same risk to yourself; but to attempt to reduce the risk, in order to make the threat of use more credible, by some form of limiting nuclear war, begins to make the risk more acceptable and therefore less of a deterrent. The more acceptable nuclear war may appear to be, the more likely it is that it will actually come about, and, even if it is limited in some way, the effects on those who live in the countries in or over which the nuclear weapons are exploded will be catastrophic.
>
> To call the results defence or security makes a mockery of the term.
>
> Field Marshall, Lord Carver, Chief of the British Defence Staff 1973–6.[1]

Nuclear deterrence has changed a great deal since 1945. The popular perception that we still live in an age of 'Mutually Assured Destruction' is of course factually correct, even if it is no longer the official doctrine of the USA and NATO.

Any nuclear war involving even a fraction of the world's nuclear arsenals could result in catastrophe. The nuclear winter would not respect national boundaries. No country, whether nuclear or not, whether aligned or neutral, could be a sanctuary.

Neither the USA nor the USSR will give up their own nuclear weapons whilst the other superpower possesses nuclear weapons. However, both sides already possess massive overkill capacity – far more than would be required for an assured retaliatory capacity or 'minimum deterrence'. Both superpowers could drastically reduce their arsenals, either simultaneously or in a series of reciprocated steps, without in any way reducing their security. The people of Europe have a great interest in encouraging this process and removing all nuclear weapons from their continent.

Disarmament will not happen overnight; it will be a process. Removing the most dangerous land-based, short-range and intermediate-range nuclear weapons, designed for fighting a nuclear war, would greatly enhance the security of Europe and the world. The new counterforce systems and the doctrines of limited nuclear war and decapitation of the control centres of the USSR provide a threat to the future of Europe. As the threshold between nuclear and conventional weapons is lowered, as flight times on both sides are reduced, the illusion is fostered that nuclear weapons are just like any other weapons. Nuclear 'deterrence' as it has developed is a dangerous or even suicidal approach to defending our society and way of life.

A comprehensive report, 'Defence and Security for Britain', was presented to the 1984 Annual Conference of the British Labour Party in Blackpool, where it was adopted by a massive majority of four to one (5.3 million to 1.3 million on a card vote) and thus became part of the Party Programme from which the manifesto for the 1987 Election was drawn.[2] This has been followed by a further statement on 'Defence Conversion and Costs' adopted by the 1986 Annual Conference, and the launching in December 1986 of a public campaign 'A Modern Britain in a Modern World – A Power for Good'.

'Defence and Security for Britain' represented an important watershed for the Labour Party. In the past there had been serious divisions in the Labour Party on the tactics to be followed in achieving nuclear disarmament. 'Defence and Security for Britain' has united the overwhelming majority of the Party. It makes clear the firm commitment of Labour to defence and collective security within NATO. It calls for significant changes in NATO strategy and it outlines a policy for European defence and security which is in many respects very similar to the policies adopted by other European socialist parties – including those in the Netherlands, Belgium, Denmark, Norway, Greece and West Germany. Labour's policy is firmly European in its orientation and parallels similar discussions in other European socialist parties over the last seven years. Labour calls for concentration on 'Defensive Deterrence' and 'Common

Security'. One of the major sections of the Report is entitled 'Changing NATO Strategy'.

The report sets out the 'objectives of defence policy'. It makes clear that 'the most important responsibility of any government is to protect and enhance the security of its citizens'. However, in the nuclear age 'real security does not come from fighting wars but in preventing wars'. Security and freedom cannot be defended by using nuclear weapons because any use of nuclear weapons is likely to result in national suicide. 'Britain's defence policy should be based upon dissuasion rather than retaliatory national suicide, by mounting forces which are designed as unambiguously as possible, for defensive purposes only'.[3] However, 'the case for a non-nuclear defensive deterrence policy does not depend on taking a sanguine view of Soviet policy'.[4]

150 governments defend their countries without possessing nuclear weapons. Other European countries have the resources and technology to develop nuclear weapons but have chosen not to do so. For these countries national nuclear weapons are not thought necessary as a 'deterrent' to external aggression. Non-nuclear conventional weapons combined with economic, political and diplomatic means are regarded by the overwhelming majority of countries as adequate deterrents against any threat. Membership of NATO does not require members states to have nuclear weapons of their own, or to have US nuclear weapons on their territory.

Half of the Alliance countries – including Denmark, Norway and Spain in Europe, and Canada in North America – do not have nuclear weapons on their territory.

In the age of nuclear weapons, true security does not come simply from the benefit of alliance with other countries. It is also dependent upon the attitudes of the supposed adversary. Consequently countries cannot have true security alone or even by alliance. True security can come only from developing 'common security' between East and West, North and South. As the report argues, 'in a nuclear age no-one is secure unless we are all secure'.[5]

> It is the clear wish of the Labour Party and the British people that Britain should continue to participate in the collective security aspects of the North Atlantic Treaty Organisation. It is also our clear aim to secure a non-nuclear defence policy for Britain within NATO ... Such moves would inevitably result in changes in Britain's relationship with the United States. We believe such

> changes are long overdue and would be welcomed by intelligent people on both sides of the Atlantic.[6]

Labour calls for a 'new internationalist initiative' to transform relations within NATO and the Warsaw Pact. This could assist the 'phasing out of the cold war bloc politics into which Europe is currently frozen'.[7] The Report argues that

> a collective West European voice could make a strong impact on the NATO decision-making process. The growing tensions and conflicts in relationships between the USA and the European members of NATO are but symptoms of a deeper malaise. Britain could make a contribution to longer term change in Europe and within both alliances by adopting a true policy of non-nuclear 'defensive deterrence' inside NATO.[8]

However, the Labour Party is wary of creating a 'third bloc' based on British and French nuclear weapons. The growing differences and tensions between West European countries and the USA could lead to the development of an anti-American 'Euro-Gaullism' in Europe and the beginnings of a 'Third Bloc' mentality. Such ideas of a European Defence Community are not new but, in the present situation, they would not be a step forward. Indeed, they could lead to a British–French–West German military axis based on 'independent' nuclear weapons. This would seriously complicate international relations and make disarmament and arms control negotiations even more difficult. It would also entrench the bloc division in Europe.

The Report states that Labour's 'immediate goal' is an agreement by NATO to adopt a policy of 'No First Use' of nuclear weapons. This would be a first step to a change in NATO's strategy to make it consistent with such a declaration. It would also involve real initiatives for nuclear disarmament, with a goal of enhanced security for the entire European continent. Once a No First Use policy had been agreed, Labour would then press NATO to support negotiations with the Warsaw Pact for a European Nuclear Weapon-Free Zone.[9]

To achieve such a 'No First Use' strategy (as opposed to a simple policy declaration) will require fundamental military reform based on several inter-related developments. The most important and necessary reform of all must be the removal of nuclear weapons from NATO and Warsaw Pact forces on the Central Front. Removal of NATO's battlefield nuclear weapons will in itself release resources for conventional defence. It is a precondition for moving towards an effective, non-suicidal defence for NATO.

Changes of military tactics of NATO forces on the Central Front are necessary. These might include a greater dispersal of NATO forces near the East/West German border, so as to improve the defensive posture of NATO's conventional forces. Labour supports use of temporary obstacles and barriers on the East/West German border which could be deployed in times of crisis. They could greatly enhance the prospects for successful defence and decrease the relative effectiveness of a given offensive force.

There may be a case within emerging European plans for a redesigned Central Front for reorganising and enhancing NATO's reserve forces. The increasing destructiveness and accuracy of 'conventional' weaponry and the increasing vulnerability of large 'high value' military hardware including long-range aircraft, warships and main battle tanks is generally thought to have given increasing advantage to the defence. The revolution in precision guided weapons has very considerable implications for the defence of Europe. NATO already has well over 200 000 conventional anti-tank weapons with which to counter some 18 000 Warsaw Pact tanks on the Central Front. New defensive anti-tank weapons make it even less necessary to match tank for tank.

The Labour Party believes that NATO could mount a credible, effective, non-nuclear defence within the resources now available. NATO and Britain require sufficient, but not excessive, military spending. Labour is strongly critical of the Conservative Government's plans to cut spending on new non-nuclear defence equipment in order to pay for expensive nuclear weapons.

> If NATO is to move to a non-nuclear policy this will require adequate, modern, effective conventional forces. Labour will oppose cuts in NATO defensive conventional forces introduced by the Tories to enable them to persist with their Trident and Fortress Falklands programmes.[10]

A reduced emphasis on long-range high-technology weaponry, with the very sophisticated and expensive Command, Control, Communications and Intelligence (C^3I) that it requires, will also help curb the growth in costs of NATO's weapons programmes. Labour calls for increased emphasis on anti-tank weapons, coastal defence, territorial defence and barriers.

Labour's priority is a non-nuclear defence policy for Britain and

NATO. The report makes clear that long-term reductions in military spending, although desirable, are less important than halting and reversing the nuclear arms race. Although a reduction in the defence burden remains a long-term goal,

> the rate at which this will occur will depend on circumstances which cannot be predicted in advance, including the timing of savings from the adoption of a defensive deterrence policy; the level of economic growth under future Labour governments; changes in NATO strategy; and the progress towards mutual and balanced conventional force reductions.[11]

Labour will be able to spend more on Britain's conventional defence forces and Britain's contribution to NATO by allocating the savings from cancelling Trident to maintain and improve Britain's real defences.

'Defence and Security for Britain' points out how British forces in West Germany could play an important role in changing NATO strategy; Britain has 55 000 troops in the British Army of the Rhine and 10 000 men and women in the Royal Air Force in Germany:

> BAOR and RAF Germany are an important political symbol of Britain's commitment to the collective security of Western Europe. But at present they operate in a nuclear armed role to which we are opposed. The Labour Party is committed to removing all nuclear weapons – including those battlefield nuclear weapons with BAOR and RAF Germany. However, we recognise that changes in the role of British forces in Germany will require consultation with our allies.[12]

As part of the policy of 'No First Use' the Labour Party supports, as an immediate step, establishing a 300-kilometre wide battlefield nuclear weapon-free zone on both sides in Central Europe, as proposed by the Palme Commission and the Swedish government.[13] This would greatly assist confidence-building and détente. Labour will press NATO to change its strategy and then press both NATO and the Warsaw Pact to remove all their battlefield nuclear weapons and abolish or convert all 'dual capable' systems.

Labour is also opposed to the production of enhanced radiation (neutron) weapons. We will refuse to permit their deployment in Britain.

The Report explicitly rejects the so-called 'Deep Strike' strategies currently being considered within NATO. Whilst welcoming increased emphasis on some defensive new technologies, the Labour Party expresses reservations about the so-called 'emerging technology' proposals and the associated 'Deep Strike' 'Follow on Forces Attack', 'Air-Land Battle' and 'Air-Land Battle 2000' doctrines:

> Defence policy should not send the wrong political signals to a potential enemy. A policy of defensive deterrence is not compatible with an offensive military posture such as proposed in the new 'deep strike' strategies.[14]

There are other objections to an over-emphasis on emerging technologies as a 'technological fix' for the *political* problems of the North Atlantic Alliance. One of the most serious objections is cost. NATO could do much more to improve its defensive conventional deterrent by the simple expedient of better organisation, rather than by spending countless billions on the new technologies: 'Above all, military technology and strategy must be subservient to politics, just as defence policy cannot be isolated from foreign policy but must be determined by it'.[15]

Labour's Shadow Foreign Secretary, and former Defence Minister, Denis Healey, has argued forcefully for such military reforms. During the 40th Anniversary of VE Day celebrations in Moscow he took the opportunity to press this case with the new Soviet leaders.

> I made one suggestion to my Soviet hosts which clearly intrigued them. At present the structures and strategy of both the NATO and the Warsaw Pact forces, while intended for defence, pose a clear threat of attack to the other side; for they rely on early use of nuclear weapons, on aircraft suitable for deep-strike, and on highly mobile tank units. If both sides moved to a non-provocative strategy of territorial defence, with conventional forces only, their security would be enormously increased.[16]

Adoption of a 'No First Use' policy could lead on to the creation of a continent-wide European nuclear weapons-free zone between the superpowers. The concept of a European nuclear weapons-free zone is not a new one: it dates back to the Rapacki Plan of the 1950s. However, it has recently gained a new impetus. In addition, there is now a great deal of interest in the concept of a Nordic nuclear-free zone involving Norway, Denmark, Sweden and Finland, and other proposals for nuclear-free zones in the Balkans and the Iberian peninsula, and the proposal of the Palme Commission for a central European battlefield nuclear weapon-free zone, since taken up in the draft treaty for a nuclear weapons-free corridor negotiated by the West German SPD and the governing party in East Germany.

The Labour Party emphasises changing NATO strategy, particularly on the Central Front. However, there is also an important role for Britain's navy and airforce. NATO's naval role in the Eastern Atlantic is largely a British preserve. Labour 'will work with our allies to remove nuclear weapons from the Eastern Atlantic and Channel'.[17]

The report recognises how a non-nuclear defence strategy requires a strong navy and an integrated maritime policy in which the merchant navy has a vital role. Labour plans a redirection of resources towards 'a naval and air strategy designed to protect this country from invasion and to protect supplies and reinforcements for the Central Front'.[18]

The report makes it very clear that disarmament is a process:

> We are realists. The process of disarmament will not occur overnight: it will be brought about by a process of independent steps by individual countries and by international agreements following patient negotiations. We will work to build trust and detente and make strenuous efforts to improve the international climate and, step by step, contribute to greater security for Britain and the world.[19]

The document commits a Labour government to ending 'wasteful' spending on so-called 'independent' nuclear weapons and concentration on 'our legitimate defence interests and the non-nuclear defence of the United Kingdom and our allies in Europe'.[20]

The long-term policy of the Labour Party is for the removal of *all* nuclear weapons from Europe and the surrounding waters – East and West: 'We are working for a defensive conventional posture for NATO. Such a posture need not differ substantially from NATO's present conventional posture'.[21] It would be desirable to remove some obviously 'offensive' elements and to strengthen the 'defensive' emphasis. It would also be beneficial to phase out the very expensive, over-sophisticated weapons systems. There may also be advantages in greater in-depth defence in Germany.

Another priority is to work within NATO to return it to the goals set out in its Treaty and to the commitments to detente made in the now out of favour Harmel Report of 1967.[22] At present, NATO and the Warsaw Pact have virtually no formal relationship as alliances beyond the occasional exchange of observers at military exercises.

The other members leave all negotiations to the two superpowers, which dominate the respective alliances. One consequence of new relationships within the blocs could be greater contact, communication and confidence-building measures between the blocs. This might result in strengthening of detente and security in Europe as a whole and open up possibilities for further changes within the two alliances towards the long-standing goal of their mutual dissolution.

A collective European pressure and European participation in the negotiations could assist this process. In Europe our long-term goal is to replace the present division of our continent into two hostile blocs. As important immediate steps to change the international climate, Labour supports an agreement between the NATO and Warsaw Pact countries on abstention from use of force, nuclear or conventional. Confidence-building measures on an all-European level could contribute to greater security and reduce the dangers of war in Europe, even if they do not lead directly to arms reductions. Labour welcomed the successful outcome of the conference on Confidence and Security Building Measures and Disarmament in Europe (CDE) in Stockholm.

Labour will work to break the deadlock at the fourteen year-old Mutual and Balanced Force Reduction Talks (MBFR) in Vienna. It aims at a significant reduction of conventional forces, both troops and weapons, on both sides in Central Europe, and greater mutual confidence at a much lower level of armament. Development of a new forum based on the Stockholm Agreement of September 1986 could assist this process.

Labour is opposed to the development, production, stockpiling and use of chemical or biological weapons. It has called for the withdrawal of all forward stocks of chemical weapons and supports the West German SPD in its call for the removal of all stocks of poison gas from the Federal Republic of Germany and the establishment of a chemical weapon free zone in Europe.[23]

'Defence and Security for Britain' makes clear that 'Labour is committed to co-operation with our allies in the effective conventional defence of Europe'. However, it does not believe that US nuclear weapons in Britain are necessary or add to NATO's security. Labour calls for the removal of all US nuclear weapons from British soil. But it also recognises that a large proportion of the US bases and facilities in Britain have an important role in the conventional defence of Europe including the reinforcement and supply of the Central Front'.[24] A Labour Government would permit the continued use of bases and communications facilities by conventionally armed US forces. Labour will 'regularise' the presence of these US forces in Britain to ensure British control over the use of such facilities in the interests of collective security and in accordance with the NATO Treaty. In this way, it aims to enhance the real defence of Britain and Europe, contribute to changing NATO strategy, and put relations between Britain and the United States on a more equal footing appropriate to relations between two sovereign nations.

In his comprehensive speech to the Kennedy School of Government in Boston in December 1986 Labour's leader Neil Kinnock made clear that:

> we naturally remain prepared, as part of our essential contribution to the general security of NATO and also to the specific security of the United States of America, to host non-nuclear military bases and installations.
>
> This is not by any means a small contribution.
>
> There are 135 US military facilities in being or planned in Britain. That includes 25 major bases and headquarters, 35 minor and reserve bases, and 75 other facilities used by US forces.
>
> They include the early warning site at Fylingdales and a range of other major international communications and intelligence facilities such as those in Diego Garcia, Cyprus and Hong Kong.
>
> They include vital airfields such as those at Upper Heyford, Mildenhall and Lakenheath, and of course they include essential storage and other back-up facilities.
>
> Of the 135 facilities overall, just the Greenham Common Cruise Missile facility, the Molesworth Cruise Missile facility (if it ever becomes operational) and the Poseidon facilities at Holy Loch will be closed. We will also require a change to non-nuclear roles for the F-111s at Upper Heyford and Lakenheath – and the removal of nuclear weapons from elsewhere.
>
> The rest of the US facilities will remain and this contribution to Alliance and American security will be part of our continuing commitment to sustain the major obligations of membership of NATO.
>
> Our prime concern in making our contribution to the general security of NATO is the same as that which guides us in the policy for sustaining the security of Britain.
>
> At a time when, as is universally acknowledged, both NATO and the Warsaw Pact have massively more nuclear weapons than

are necessary strictly to deter a nuclear attack, it is clearly the case that any shift of weaponry from nuclear capability to conventional capability increases stability.

That is why we argue for switching weaponry and resources away from their nuclear use and towards conventional strength. That is why we make the choice in favour of qualitative and quantitative improvement in conventional forces, rather than relying upon nuclear weapons which by their very nature can never be used, because nuclear war can never be won and should therefore never be fought.

In terms of both the NATO and Warsaw Pact Alliances, there is every argument of stability in ensuring that the nuclear weapon arsenal that does exist is removed as far as possible from the immediate potential battle line.[25]

As well as supporting policies of No First Use, nuclear-free zones in Europe, a central European battlefield nuclear weapons-free zone, a nuclear weapons freeze and specific confidence-building measures, the Labour Party is also very concerned to strengthen the Nuclear Non-Proliferation Treaty and discourage the spread of nuclear weapons. The Labour Party strongly supports an early agreement on a comprehensive nuclear test ban.

Britain's own position as one of the five declared nuclear weapons states is of particular significance here.

The Conservative Government's refusal to have Polaris and Trident included in the Geneva 'INF' and 'START' nuclear negotiations was a significant factor in the breakdown of those talks in 1983. Now the new Geneva 'umbrella' negotiations could also be threatened if British and French nuclear arsenals are not taken into account. Following the visit of Neil Kinnock and Denis Healey to Moscow in November 1984, and statements made by Mikhail Gorbachev in May 1986, it is clear that action by the British Government to decommission the old Polaris system would lead to a Soviet reciprocation, and therefore the argument that this is one-sided or unilateral is no longer true.[26] An equivalent Soviet reduction in its nuclear arsenal in response would lead to a bilateral reduction in nuclear arsenals. Conversely, the unilateral 800 per cent escalation in target capacity of the Tories' Trident programme will almost certainly lead to a Soviet escalation in response. Cancelling Trident will therefore contribute to halting the growth of Soviet nuclear arsenals.

Labour is committed to the promotion of world-wide nuclear

> disarmament. We believe that Britain should take independent initiatives to promote peace and nuclear disarmament and establish an effective non-nuclear defence policy. Such a *defence* policy should make sure that any attempt at invasion or conquest is so costly to the aggressor that the latter will not think aggression worthwhile. However, the nature and deployment of such defence forces should not in themselves provoke hostility and tension. We require a true *defensive deterrence* which is capable of successful resistance; which exacts a high and unacceptable cost from any aggressor's forces; which as far as possible does not escalate the conflict; and which is consistent with a wider policy of promoting security and disarmament. A moment's thought will show that nuclear weapons, which are the most provocative and aggressive weapons ever invented by man, can have no part in such a genuine *defence* policy.[27]

Labour has made clear firstly that it has a European perspective on security, secondly that it will work within NATO for its policies, thirdly that it is resolutely committed to defending its country and its European allies, and fourthly that it will work vigorously for nuclear disarmament and a new security system in Europe and the world.

This is an ambitious agenda. No single NATO country will be able to achieve such important changes alone. Changes in strategy could take several years. However developments in other NATO countries indicate that the late 1980s and 1990s could see several European members of NATO committed to similar policies of military reform and changes in NATO strategy.

The Labour Party entered the June 1987 General Election Campaign committed to the above policies. A Labour Government would act quickly to immediately cancel the £10 billion Trident project. It would support the double zero option involving removal of all cruise missiles from Britain. But if the negotiations were to fail it would act swiftly to stop the deployment of any Ground Launched Cruise Missiles at Molesworth and send back to the USA those which had already been deployed at Greenham Common. It would also seek the removal of other US nuclear weapons – the Poseidon submarines at Holy Loch, the nuclear depth charges and the bombs for dual capable F-111 aircraft.

The process and timetable for the removal of these nuclear weapons would be a matter for consultations and discussions between Britain and the United States. As Neil Kinnock stated at the Press

Conference to launch the 'Modern Britain in a Modern World Campaign' on 10 December 1986:

> In some cases . . . the process will not be prolonged because of the ease with which weapons can be removed, and in other cases it will be longer, both for reasons of political discussion and the maintenance of the unity of NATO, and also because of the technical requirements of actual removal . . . I have continually said it could take a year, perhaps a little more, perhaps a little less, and that refers to the technical requirements . . . the process of securing the departure of those weapons is not something that can be done by a flick of a switch. It does require discussion, just as other countries in the change of nuclear and NATO roles have undertaken discussion.[28]

As to Britain's existing 'independent' nuclear weapons systems and specifically the aging Polaris submarine force, 'Defence and Security for Britain' made clear that 'Labour will on assuming office decommission Polaris from service'.[29] It would obviously take some time to dismantle the warheads and make the nuclear material in the reactor safe. Despite significantly increasing its support, and firmly re-establishing itself as the alternative Government, Labour was unable to prevent a third Conservative victory in June 1987. Some commentators and critics of Labour immediately called on the Labour Party to change its defence policy if it wanted to win in 1991 or 1992.

However there can be no doubt about the firm commitment of the Labour Party and its leader to a non-nuclear defence policy for Britain. Indeed, Neil Kinnock has frequently made clear his strong belief that nuclear weapons are unusable or suicidal.

Speaking to a rally in Plymouth in July 1985 he emphasised that there is a significant difference between nuclear weapons and every other form of weaponry known to the human race:

> [Nuclear war] involves annihilation, the genocide of the enemy, the suicide of the user, the extermination of the human habitat. That is why it is no basis for the defence of our country or of our freedom or of our values.
>
> Indeed the possession of the weapons and the need to replace them undermines our very means of effectively defending those assets.
>
> And as we and many beyond our Movement come to recognise

that about Trident so they must acknowledge the uselessness of Polaris too. Here is a weapon system whose lack of credibility is demonstrated by the need for its replacement. It is a system which does not buy us a place in any conference chamber or arms limitation talks, a system which is part of what Lord Carver calls the 'delusion of nuclear grandeur'. It does not impress potential enemies or influence established allies and it will not and cannot defend our country.

That is why we say be rid of it.

That is why we will cancel its replacement Trident.

That is why we will clear our country of all nuclear weapons.

And far from being defenceless we will be better defended for we shall sustain the strength of the forces that we can use, the forces that we can deploy, the forces that meet our needs for security and our Allies needs for dependability.

That is our commitment to the British people and to our Allies. And we shall honour it in full.[30]

Notes

1. Field Marshall Lord Carver, *The Guardian*, 14 December 1981.
2. 'Defence and Security for Britain', (London: The Labour Party).
3. 'Defence and Security', p. 5.
4. 'Defence and Security', p. 7.
5. 'Defence and Security', p. 6.
6. 'Defence and Security', p. 15.
7. 'Defence and Security', p. 15.
8. 'Defence and Security', p. 16.
9. 'Defence and Security', pp. 17–20.
10. 'Defence and Security', pp. 34–5.
11. 'Defence and Security', p. 35.
12. 'Defence and Security', p. 28.
13. 'Common Security – A Programme for Disarmament', The Report of the Independent Commission on Disarmament and Security Issues under the Chairmanship of Olof Palme (1982).
14. 'Defence and Security', p. 14.
15. 'Defence and Security', p. 14.
16. Denis Healey MP, 'A New Message from Moscow', *Observer*, 12 May 1985.
17. 'Defence and Security', p. 31.
18. 'Defence and Security', p. 31.
19. 'Defence and Security', p. 38.
20. 'Defence and Security', pp. 33–4.
21. 'Defence and Security', p. 23.
22. 'The Future Tasks of the Alliance' (Harmel Report, 1967) published in *The North Atlantic Treaty Organisation: Facts and Figures* (Brussels, 1984) pp. 289–91.
23. This was formalised in the Joint Political Initiative of the SPD with the East German Socialist Unity Party (SED) and an 'Outline of an Agreement to Establish a Zone Free of Chemical Weapons in Europe' which was published in Bonn on 19 June 1985.
24. 'Defence and Security', pp. 21–2.
25. Neil Kinnock, speech to Kennedy School of Government, Cambridge, Mass., 2 December 1986.
26. Novosti Press Agency, London Press Release, 26 November 1984. See also Neil Kinnock's speech to the Association of American Correspondents, London, 5 December 1984.
27. 'Defence and Security', pp. 22–3.
28. Neil Kinnock Press Conference to launch 'Modern Britain in a Modern World' campaign, London, 10 December 1986.
29. 'Defence and Security', pp. 27–8.
30. Neil Kinnock speech to Labour Party rally, Plymouth Guildhall, Devon, 9 July 1985.

21 Arms Control for the 'Successor Generation'

Jan H. Kalicki

Among the many problems which have bedevilled East–West relations, perhaps the most perplexing has been the failure of the two sides to engage in constructive openings with one another at the same time. The history of the past four decades is rife with examples. In the 1950s the U-2 incident dashed hopes for a new understanding between Eisenhower and Khrushchev, as did the invasion of Czechoslovakia for Brezhnev and Johnson in the 1960s. In the 1970s, the invasion of Afghanistan derailed ratification of SALT II, and East and West failed to negotiate any important agreement in the first half of the 1980s.

In each case, either Washington or Moscow was prepared to conclude important new agreements, only for the other side to engage in actions which made such agreements politically impossible. The exceptions came either when the two capitals believed their survival was at stake, or when very large public and international pressures were brought to bear. The Nazi invasion of the Soviet Union and efforts to blockade Great Britain led to the Soviet alliance with the Western powers against the Axis in the Second World War; and the two most important arms control agreements – the Limited Test Ban Treaty and the Anti-Ballistic Missile Treaty – followed widespread protests against nuclear testing in the atmosphere and against discriminating, and in the end illusory, defences against nuclear attack. In the 1980s, anti-nuclear campaigns in Europe and the nuclear freeze campaign in America were major factors leading the Reagan Administration to moderate its nuclear rhetoric and to resume arms negotiations with the Soviet Union.

Surely there must be some better way than this frustrating and sporadic process to manage East–West, and specifically nuclear, relations in the years ahead. Cannot the two systems summon the necessary leadership, and the necessary domestic and international support, to take consistent steps which will steadily lift the nuclear sword of Damocles hanging over the entire world?

With new generations of leaders emerging in both East and West, there now appears to be an opportunity to move in this direction. The last such major 'leadership convergence' came, it will be recalled, when Roosevelt and Stalin established US–Soviet relations in 1933. In 1989, new leaders in Congress and the Administration will effectively replace the Reagan era in American politics, and they will deal with a new generation of Soviet leaders under General-Secretary Gorbachev.

On both sides, there will be strong impetus to address fundamental economic problems – the mountain of debt in the United States and massive economic inertia in the Soviet Union. That impetus could readily reinforce interest in containing the arms race and limiting costly interventions in the Third World. Or it could be neutralised by contrary trends, such as renewed drives to assert military power and the escalation of Third World conflicts with superpower involvement.

Which path to follow will be one of the most important issues facing new leaders in the US and the USSR. From Moscow, Gorbachev has already underlined the priority of economic reform and concommitant reduction in international tensions. The Western response, and what the West and East do together to help modify the international environment, could have a profound impact on future Soviet behaviour and overall prospects for world order and arms control.

In this context, the 'successor' generation of American leaders will want to reject the failures of past policy and to embrace new, effective policies which accord with American values and command national support. They will want to avoid (in Harlan Cleveland's felicitous phrase) 'hardening of the categories'; to embrace that truly American mixture of pragmatism and idealism; and to begin by reducing the chances of blowing up the planet and thereby making all other problems irrelevant.

This emphatically non-ideological approach is already reflected in the pattern of votes in the US Congress on defence and arms control, including support for strategic weapons modernisation (including Midgetman and Trident as well as, regrettably, B-1 and MX) but also for continued adherence to SALT II and negotiation of a Comprehensive Test Ban Treaty.

This approach reflects the public mood as well. If there is any consistency in public opinion polls in the nuclear age, it is the overwhelming support of the American people for *both* nuclear arms control and a strong national defence. The last President to achieve that combination – and to translate it into effective policy – was John

F. Kennedy, whose greatest moments were the Limited Test Ban Treaty and the Cuban Missile Crisis. Each President since then either was enmired by Vietnam and Watergate or gave too short shrift to one or the other critical aspect of national security policy, and the result was both policy failure and public disillusionment.

In one of history's ironies, a prime example of failed arms control policy came during the Carter presidency, despite Jimmy Carter's support of arms control; and a prime example of failed defence policy came during the Reagan presidency, despite Ronald Reagan's support of military strength. From the arms control standpoint, the tragedy of the Carter Administration was its failure to build on Republican-negotiated arms limits at Vladivostok, only to see its own modest improvements wrecked three years later by a pseudo-crisis in Cuba and the brutal invasion of Afghanistan. From the military standpoint, the tragedy of the Reagan Administration was its failure to maintain Democratic-negotiated NATO commitments to the defence buildup, or to achieve anywhere near the levels of efficiency and readiness warranted by over $1.5 trillion in expenditures.

The successor generation has the opportunity to overcome this tragic legacy. To begin with, it can decisively reject the false dichotomy between defence and arms control: the greater the control of arms, the less the enemy threat to defend against. The risk of outbreak of war can be limited by reducing not only nuclear but conventional arms, particularly in their most threatening aspects, from heavy missiles to 'tactical' nuclear weapons to heavy tanks. At the same time, survivable forces can be strengthened at sea, and advanced anti-tank and other defences perfected on land.

At the political level, successors will be loathe to repeat the mistakes of either euphoric detente or unremitting confrontation with the Soviet Union. The American people neither trust the Soviet Union nor favour increasing the risk of war between our two countries. They will favour, however, assertive policies which protect US interests and narrow the range of conflict between East and West. Such a stance of 'competitive coexistence' will entail a continuation of tension by other means, but it could also lead to systematic dialogue and even US–Soviet agreement rooted in greater realism, and less subject to the damaging pendulum swings of the past. At the same time, refusal to treat all international problems as manifestations of the East–West struggle will not only put less pressure on the East–West relationship, but permit management of these problems in their local and regional terms – thereby depriving the Soviets and other antagonists of at least some of the opportunities which would otherwise develop.

In this perspective, the most important dimension of Presidential decisions and Congressional votes on foreign policy issues will be the extent to which they facilitate a new, non-ideological approach by the successor generation – or at least do not foreclose options that it may wish to exercise in the future.

Looking to the 1990s, what will be the most important policy judgements in national security and East–West relations?

The first judgement, clearly, will be whether to press ahead with defences against strategic nuclear weapons. Research and development are likely to continue if only as a hedge against breakthroughs by the other side. But testing and deployment could be brought to a halt by at least four problematic factors. The first is *viability*: no defence has been found which cannot be defeated by a more cost-effective offence, from more warheads and decoys to bombers and cruise missiles. The second is *stability*: any transition to strategic defences will be extremely unstable unless undertaken on an agreed basis, because of incentives to pre-empt such defences during a crisis. Third, and related, is *negotiability*: it would be impossible under current conditions to negotiate agreed deployments of strategic defence with the Soviets; but it would be entirely possible to negotiate major reductions of strategic offensive weapons in return for a ban on deployment and more advanced testing. The fourth is *cost*: it will be prohibitively expensive to deploy more than defences to protect ballistic missile silos and other military targets, which are hardly an antidote to nuclear attack against population centres. For these reasons strategic defence may be the subject of heated political debate, but it is likely to play a progressively smaller role in the military relationship between East and West.

The second judgement will be whether to uphold existing arms control treaties and to negotiate reductions and more comprehensive limits on nuclear and conventional weapons. Here the ABM Treaty is already under jeopardy as a result of efforts to reinterpret, amend or even abrogate it to permit deployment of strategic defences. The limits of another treaty, SALT II, have been breached by a US decision to deploy more air-launched cruise missiles on another strategic bomber; until 1986, it had been observed even though it had not been ratified. Two treaties on nuclear testing signed by President Ford, the Threshold Test Ban and PNE Treaties, may or may not be submitted for ratification with additional verification requirements.

In the political environment of the 1980s, it would be no small achievement to restore the full application of these existing treaties. And, in each case, large reductions and comprehensive limits appear negotiable in a way that has eluded the two sides in the past. In Europe, both sides are now agreed that they can and should eliminate all intermediate nuclear forces, independent of an agreement on strategic defence. An agreement on the latter would clear the way to major reductions of strategic forces. And dramatically lower quotas or thresholds on nuclear testing, or even a Comprehensive Test Ban Treaty, now appear achievable based on the status of CTBT negotiations when they were suspended in 1980.

The third judgement moves from arms control and defence to foreign policy and the very nature of East–West relations. At the final stage of the Reagan Administration, the Soviets must recognise that they will not transform its position on strategic defence or other fundamental aspects of its world view, but they can try to influence the attitudes and actions of the US successors. Americans and Europeans must also understand that basic Soviet interests remain unchanged, but the first stages of a Gorbachev Administration none the less provide an opportunity to influence its perceptions of the future Western threat – and its allocation of resources between economic and military priorities.

For each of these policy judgements, leaders on both sides must reach early conclusions if they are to affect significantly the course of future events. The first issue, the US strategic defence initiative, is politically time sensitive. Recognising the danger that future American leaders will put SDI on a back burner, the US Secretary of Defense presses for some form of deployment before 1989. Worried that SDI may develop a life of its own, the Soviets agree to US proposals for deep strategic force reductions, provided that strategic defence does not proceed beyond 'laboratory' research. In so doing, they confirm former President Nixon's view of SDI as the 'ultimate bargaining chip' – but one which may be wasted if it is not used at a time of maximum political credibility for SDI.

The second issue, adherence to existing treaties and negotiations of deeper 'cuts' and broader 'caps', lends itself particularly well to East–West agreement. In 1986, both sides agreed to unprecedented confidence-building and verification measures at the European Disarmament Conference. Followed by US–Soviet agreement to eliminate intermediate nuclear forces in Europe, the stage would be set for negotiations to reduce both short-range nuclear and conventional forces. That, in turn, would set a new political context for at least provisional adherence to ABM and SALT II limits, pending negotiation of deeper and more definitive cuts on offensive and limits on defensive forces. And it could prompt the conclusion of a comprehensive nuclear test ban treaty, which had been the goal of five presidents before the Reagan Administration refused to complete negotiations in 1981.

The third issue, East–West relations, could also develop further at both the economic and the political levels. The NATO allies could test whether limited expansion of non-strategic trade could stimulate, or reward, increases in emigration approvals for East Europeans, Soviet Jews and other groups; China and Japan could probe further with regard to long-standing territorial issues between themselves and the Soviets; and a more positive climate could develop for considering the more critical issues in the East–West relationship. Having reopened diplomatic exchanges on Afghanistan and other areas of conflict, Soviet and American leaders could expand their discussions of Third World issues. And they could pursue co-operation on issues where they and their respective allies have strong, shared interests, from nuclear safety and non-proliferation to anti-terrorism and protection of the environment. Even if these discussions do no more than to help avoid increased East–West confrontation, they will contribute to a more stable relationship and perhaps to progress in arms control.

Judgements will be reached, one way or the other, in each of these policy fields. It is entirely possible that the present stalemates will persist, fuelled by continued US–Soviet confrontations, tensions between the superpowers and their European allies, and polemics between bureaucratic and legislative factions.

But it is also possible for the successor generation to begin to restore the momentum of the arms control process; in order to do so, it must take effective steps that command the trust and backing of the public – supportive in America of strength but also of peace, distrustful of the Soviets but also opposed to continuing the arms race.

Here the first necessary step is already being taken. The USA and USSR have restored a basic minimum of mutual civility and respect in their dialogue. To expand this dialogue, both Democratic and Republican presidential candidates have proposed putting Soviet–American summits on an annual basis in order to diffuse the issue of *whether* to hold summits and focus instead on the *content* of US–

Soviet relations. In addition, the regular meetings of Secretary of State and Foreign Minister should be supplemented by regular meetings of defence ministers, military chiefs of staff and others so as to steadily build mutual understanding and confidence in the relationship at political *and* policy-making levels.

A second step could be taken independently of other arms control negotiations – but it should not be used as a pretext for avoiding progress in actually reversing the arms race. Both superpowers should strengthen and make more secure their communications and their command and control links to sharply limit the dangers of nuclear accident or miscalculation – regardless of the ups and downs of their political relationship. At the 1985 Geneva summit, both the US and the USSR expressed support for this goal, which could be implemented very rapidly.

These two steps – regular Presidential and Cabinet-level meetings and strengthened command, control and communications – could lead to a third and critical step, moving from confidence building to actually limiting the nuclear arms race. Both sides have signalled new flexibility on strategic arms – one possible trade-off would be between US superiority in bombers and Soviet superiority in missiles – but that flexibility may be designed more to trap each other on the issue of Star Wars than to make substantive progress.

If tactical postures are not to lead to a new dead-end for arms control, both Moscow and Washington must shed some illusions. Moscow must recognise that it cannot prevent all American testing of strategic defence systems. Washington must recognise that unconstrained pursuit of a strategic shield could not only profoundly unsettle the allies, but also convince the Soviets that it seeks to deny them a credible deterrent – triggering a new round in the offensive and defensive arms race, moves to doctrines of launch on warning and even pre-emptive nuclear attack, and raising the very dangers of nuclear war that must be minimised. Shedding these illusions may make possible additional steps forward with regard to both strategic defence and offensive limitations.

1. Reagan can and will proceed with SDI research and even some testing, but the critical deployment decisions will be made by his successors, not by him. In the meantime, Congress can continue to ensure that there is no funding for SDI deployment and space-based testing; the allies can continue to insist that any strategic shield must protect them just as much as the North American continent; and both can press for negotiations on all, not just some, arms control issues.

2. Since neither side wishes to upset the existing system of deterrence while a defence-based system is being pursued, both could agree to interim steps to enhance the stability of that system. With prodding from the Congress and the allies – and support from at least some of the US successors – it would not be inconceivable to achieve the dismantling or at least reconfiguring of the Soviet strategic radar at Krasnoyarsk and halting the testing of anti-satellite weapons where the US has an advantage – a package in which both sides make concessions for the sake of strategic stability.

3. Since even the Reagan Administration recognises that there will be particularly dangerous times while any defensive systems are being deployed, this provides not only the Soviets but the allies and the US Congress with an opportunity for the most extensive consultations before such a period begins. For the superpowers, these consultations will be held most probably between the new leadership around Gorbachev and the Administration succeeding Reagan, who are likely destined to learn again both the technical fallibility and the profound dangers of strategic defence – much as an earlier generation of American and Soviet leaders did between 1967 and 1972.

4. If Moscow and Washington can agree (at least tacitly) to disagree on strategic defence, they can then turn to negotiating an agreement on strategic nuclear weapons which will, in turn, make it possible for future Administrations to negotiate limits on SDI, perhaps in exchange for even greater reductions in START. Moreover, the US Congress could authorise funds for further tests of space-based or other weapons, only in the event that a mutual and verifiable moratorium has been offered by the President but not accepted by the Soviets – a logical extension of legislation sponsored by Senators Tsongas and Pressler in 1984. Such a moratorium was declared by President Kennedy over nuclear testing and helped lead to the Limited Nuclear Test Ban Treaty in 1963; a similar moratorium declared, for example, on testing and deployment of new ballistic missiles, fractionated warheads and anti-satellite weapons could also prepare the way for more enduring follow-on agreements. Unlike the past history of the arms race, where military technology always outdistanced negotiated agreements, a balanced and effective moratorium could limit its most dangerous elements and make possible the negotiation of truly meaningful agreements.

5. By circumventing or at least deferring the Star Wars impasse at Geneva, both sides could begin to build on past negotiating progress rather than repeating the previous mistakes of Presidents Carter and

Reagan, whose jettisoning of the previously negotiated Vladivostok and SALT II agreements led to months of US–Soviet recrimination and failure to make arms control progress.

6. The present political climate should not deter arms control advocates from continuing to pursue a more comprehensive approach over the longer term. No matter how successful these individual treaties will be, they will not prevent the nuclear arms race from proceeding in other ways: for example, vertically into outer space or horizontally to other nuclear weapons states. Specific arms control negotiations can and should be pursued to deal with these issues, but a more comprehensive approach will both plug more potential loopholes and attract greater domestic and international support. Despite the fragmentation of the American nuclear weapons freeze campaign as well as the European peace movements, and the continued opposition of many NATO Governments, a comprehensive and verifiable freeze over the production, testing and deployment of nuclear weapons would make an important contribution to strategic stability and to future public support for nuclear arms control. Such a freeze would encompass all the elements which have been under negotiation in START, INF and the CTB, but in addition it could lead to new limits in such areas as shorter-range nuclear systems and future nuclear weapons production – both of which could undercut the more limited agreements over time. (To the extent that weapons could not be verified, they would not be frozen, but even a partial freeze would go further than existing arms control agreements.)

By adopting two tracks in negotiations, the first linked to step-by-step agreements and the second to the more comprehensive approach, it is possible to pursue the benefits of both tracks without permitting the one to get in the way of the other.

7. Most decisively, advocates of arms control must seek ways to achieve sustained and predictable public support – and a constructive Congressional role in supporting substantive arms control progress over the long term. In the past, this progress has suffered from the absence of either serious negotiations or political support. In the 1950s and 1980s the virtual absence of negotiations fuelled widespread public pressure for nuclear disarmament in the 'ban the bomb' and nuclear freeze movements. In the 1960s and 1970s there could have been much more negotiating progress in banning nuclear tests and limiting nuclear weapons if public support had not dissipated for CTB and SALT II. Had a comprehensive instead of limited test ban

been concluded in 1963, we could have prevented the Multiple Independently Targetted Re-entry Vehicle (MIRV) and possibly the Indian nuclear explosion – arguably the most destabilising developments in the history of the vertical and the horizontal arms race.

The most important challenge today for the successors, then, is to combine serious negotiation with active public support for arms control. Negotiation must take place on both step-by-step and comprehensive levels and the strategy must involve focusing extremely high levels of political support – up to 80 per cent of Americans continue to support a mutual and verifiable nuclear weapons freeze in nationwide surveys, for example – with focused and sustained political pressure behind each forward movement in arms control. The necessary steps include the following:

Public education: The American public appears remarkably well informed on the dangers of nuclear war, with 83 per cent (according to a survey conducted by the Public Agenda Foundation, a research and education organisation) concluding that it cannot be limited or won. But 81 per cent do not know that US and NATO policy involves using nuclear weapons not only to deter nuclear attack (which they support) but to deter large non-nuclear attacks in Europe, East Asia and the Persian Gulf and to further US political and negotiating objectives (which they do not support). By becoming educated as to these other facts about nuclear strategy, the public is in a position to participate in and influence future nuclear weapons policies.

Public mobilisation: Strong public pressure was felt in both America and Europe for arms control from 1980 to 1984. However, far less public pressure has been felt since negotiations resumed in Geneva, and many public interest groups have allowed their agenda to become more diffuse just as they should have been more focused. Successors need to create opportunities, during future military debates and on other occasions, to refocus on concrete steps for arms control, such as CTB, anti-satellite weapons limitations and mutual moratoria on the testing and deployment of new weapons.

Public participation: Perhaps the most critical element is active and sustained public participation which actually helps to frame the political debate and the environment in which it takes place. The support of community leaders at the local levels – particularly religious and professional leaders including physicians, scientists, teachers and lawyers – has given nuclear arms control a grassroots and expert base which it has not had in the past. For many politicians, that translates arms control from a relatively esoteric foreign policy issue to a local constituency issue affecting their future political success. Again, this participation only becomes a positive factor for arms control progress if it is constantly activated by political leaders, public interest organisations and community leaders.

Public education, mobilisation and participation will make leaders much more aware of the political, in contrast to purely technical, nature of their decisions in this field. This process could also give the successor generation of leaders a more sustainable basis of support for policies to reduce the risk of nuclear war over the longer term.

In a 1984 briefing book, prepared by the Public Agenda Foundation and the Center for Foreign Policy Development at Brown University and entitled *Voter Options on Nuclear Arms Policy*, the process of public participation is taken one step further. Voters and other elements of informed public opinion – including press, media and public interest groups – are invited to press their political leaders to define their view of the appropriate 'mission' of nuclear weapons. (In a second phase from 1985 to 1989, these two institutions will launch broad 'campaigns' of public debate on both nuclear issues and US–Soviet relations.) By focusing the debate on the issue of *purpose* – instead of diffusing it over specific weapons and arms control measures – this project will hopefully encourage both a strategic view and analytical depth in future public discussion of this most important of issues. Four possible 'missions' are offered for nuclear weapons, which in the judgement of this co-author can lead to four different policy conclusions:

- They can serve *no* mission and should be abolished as soon as possible. Curiously, President Reagan has advocated this abolitionist view in proposing a non-nuclear strategic defence system, which will probably be impossible to achieve but likely to trigger a defensive as well as offensive arms race for reasons noted previously.

- Or they should serve the *single* mission of deterring nuclear attack against the US and its allies in NATO, Japan and South Korea. To adopt this choice could make it possible to reduce the American nuclear stockpiles by 90 per cent or more, since a few hundred survivable nuclear warheads would inflict unacceptable devastation in response to any enemy attack. But it would also require the US and its allies to make sure they can defend themselves conventionally without threatening nuclear attack and increasing the dangers of conventional conflict – a growing emphasis of discussion in allied governments and NATO councils.

- Or they can serve the *dual* mission of deterring both nuclear and large-scale non-nuclear attack against the USA and its allies – the essence of NATO strategy since that alliance was formed in 1949. To adopt this choice would require only a few thousand nuclear warheads – still far less than the more than 50 000 now in the US and Soviet arsenals – but this may be increasingly unrealistic given the Soviet ability to retaliate in kind against Western nuclear weapons. As a result, to continue this policy could require making a credible threat to commit nuclear suicide and the clear ability to take the USSR with us.

- Or they can serve *multiple* missions: deterring nuclear and non-nuclear attacks not only against America's close allies, but wherever American leaders believe their interests are at stake; maintaining parity with Soviet forces at all levels; compelling the Soviets to behave in certain ways, including more flexibility in arms negotiations; or even enabling the US to prevail militarily in a nuclear war if it should occur. Despite the increased dangers of such a choice – and the impossibility of assuring a survivable nuclear war – the US Defense Department's existing five-year defence guidance envisages multiple missions for nuclear weapons, and therefore plans the expansion of existing nuclear stockpiles to include more powerful, more usable nuclear weapons.

Once a thorough political debate is launched along these lines, within an informed electorate aware of options like those listed above, extremely important questions of nuclear policy can come to the fore, and answers to these questions can guide more specific choices facing American successors on nuclear weapons and nuclear arms control. For example, if both superpowers have more than enough nuclear warheads to serve any rational policy purpose, why continue to add more and even more dangerous nuclear weapons to already existing stockpiles? Why not proceed with a temporary, mutual and verifiable moratorium followed by a comprehensive freeze and reductions, which could be focused if possible on the most destabilising nuclear weapons systems?

Former Secretary of Defense Robert S. McNamara has raised an even more fundamental issue which could be addressed successfully by this approach. Should not the US and its allies recognise that nuclear weapons have no rational military purpose in today's world, except to deter nuclear attack? If so, the successor generation could move to reduce reliance on nuclear weapons, separate nuclear from non-nuclear weapons, make the remaining nuclear forces as survivable as possible, and pursue non-nuclear means to assure their defence. In those cases where a President does wish to use nuclear weapons to respond against a non-nuclear attack, more explicit mechanisms should be devised for both NATO and Congressional approval of such a response. This approach is made all the more desirable by effective non-nuclear technology which can neutralise the enemy's offence.

In the Public Agenda Foundation survey, an important 66 per cent of respondents said that they would be willing to pay *higher* taxes for the US defence budget if both East and West sharply reduced their nuclear weapons, but replaced these weapons with more expensive, non-nuclear forces. This policy may or may not involve a 'no-first-use' declaration for nuclear weapons: the key issue is the extent to which the West will continue to rely on them, and for which purposes, since a nuclear weapon is still possible to use as long as it exists.

The challenge is thus for the 'successor generation' to start leading with a new arms control agenda – joining the public in a debate on these issues, making informed political judgements based on this debate, and benefiting from this new popular base for implementing such an agenda propelled by a winning political coalition. Throughout this process there can be no substitute for leadership and an aroused and vigilant citizenry, but for perhaps the first time in the nuclear age the successors and the citizenry have available to them a critical combination of political power and policy impact to make an enduring difference.

Index